THE GRAMMAR OF DISCOURSE

TOPICS IN LANGUAGE AND LINGUISTICS

Series Editors
Thomas A. Sebeok and Albert Valdman
Indiana University, Bloomington, Indiana

ISSUES IN INTERNATIONAL BILINGUAL EDUCATION
The Role of the Vernacular
Edited by Beverly Hartford, Albert Valdman, and Charles R. Foster

LINGUISTICS AND LITERACY
Edited by William Frawley

THE GRAMMAR OF DISCOURSE
Robert E. Longacre

THE GRAMMAR OF DISCOURSE

Robert E. Longacre
Summer Institute of Linguistics
University of Texas at Arlington
Arlington, Texas

Plenum Press • New York and London

Library of Congress Cataloging in Publication Data

Longacre, Robert E.
The grammar of discourse.

(Topics in language and linguistics)
"Based on an earlier work, An anatomy of speech notions, 1976"—Pref.
bibliography: p.
Includes index.
1. Discourse analysis. I. Longacre, Robert E. Anatomy of speech notions. II. Title. III. Series.
P302.L59 1983 401'.41 83-3993
ISBN 0-306-41273-X

A Division of Plenum Publishing Corporation
233 Spring Street, New York, N.Y. 10013

Printed in the United States of America

To

JAMES LORIOT

pioneer in the study of discourse

PREFACE

While this volume is based on an earlier work, An Anatomy of Speech Notions (1976), the overall orientation of the present volume is distinctive enough to make it a new work. The former volume was essentially a half-way house to discourse. While including a chapter on discourse structure, it was not as a whole explicitly oriented towards considerations of context. The present volume, however, strives to achieve a more consistently contextual approach to language.

A great deal of research and theorizing concerning discourse grammar or textlinguistics has characterized the past decade of linguistic studies. This recent work has, of course, influenced the present volume. In addition, my personal research in several areas has led to increased insistence on the indispensability of discourse studies. Crucial here was my direction of field workshops involving personnel of the Summer Institute of Linguistics, first in relation to languages of Colombia, Panama, and Ecuador (1974-1975), and later in relation to languages of Mexico (1978). Of further relevance have been my own studies of narrative structure in Biblical Hebrew. Last but not least, is the stimulus and feedback which I have received from my graduate students (whose research is embodied in several theses and dissertations), especially Keith Beavon, Shin Ja Joo Huang, Larry Jones, Mildred Larson, Linda Lloyd, and Mike Walrod. Stephen Eckerd's work has been decisive in the revision of the system of cases and case frames which are found in Chapters 4 and 5. I am heavily indebted to him in these chapters.

I gratefully acknowledge here the dedicated secretarial assistance rendered by Carolyn Skinner, Eula Stephens and Anne Short, as well as the criticisms and suggestions of Harwood Hess. I also gratefully acknowledge the assistance of Kathy Niver in the final preparation and editing of the manuscript.

Robert E. Longacre
University of Texas at Arlington

ACKNOWLEDGMENT

I wish to thank the following authors, editors, and publishers for granting permission to quote from their materials in this book: R.M.W. Dixon from his 1977 article "Where Have All the Adjectives Gone?"; K.L. Pike and E. Pike for the right to reproduce their four-box diagram from Pike and Pike, 1979; to E.A. Nida and the University of Michigan Press for the right to reproduce a passage from _Morphology_ 1949; to Austin Hale for the right to reproduce a chart from his article "Towards a Systematization of Display Grammar" in the volume _Clause, Sentence, and Discourse Patterns in Selected Languages of Nepal_, which he edited, and to the publisher, the Summer Institute of Linguistics; to Harcourt, Brace, and Jovanovich for the quotation from Carl Sandburg's _Abraham Lincoln: the War Years_, Volume 1 (1939); to Father Walter Cook and the Georgetown University Press for the right to reproduce a chart from "A Case Grammar Matrix," _Georgetown University Languages and Linguistics Working Papers_ No. 6 (p. 26, fig. 3); to the University of California Press for the quotation from Stephen Pepper's _World Hypotheses_ (originally published by the University of California Press, 1942; reprinted 1970 by permission of the Regents of the University of California); to Philip Larkin for the quotation from his poem "Mr. Bleaney" from _The Whitsun Weddings_, and to the publishers, Faber and Faber; to _The Great Ideas Today_ and the _Encyclopedia Britannica_ for the quotation from Sidney Hook ("The Hero as World Figure") and Joy Bayum ("Heroes in Black and White") in the volume _The Great Ideas Today_, 1973; and to Charles Scribner's Sons for the quotation from Hemingway's "The Short Happy Life of Francis Macomber" in the third edition of _Studies in the Short Story_ (1968), edited by Adrian H. Jaffe and Virgil Scott; and to the Airmont Publishing Co. for the right to quote the passage from Mark Twain's _A Connecticut Yankee in King Arthur's Court_.

CONTENTS

INTRODUCTION

As a book on discourse, this volume is dedicated to the thesis that language is language only in context. For too long a time, linguistics has confined itself to the study of isolated sentences, either such sentences carefully selected from a corpus or, more often than not, artfully contrived so as to betray no need for further context. Thus, boards in the linguistic classroom have been filled with such sentences as 'John kissed Mary' or 'Stephen knew that Mary knew that something was wrong' to the avoidance of such sentences as 'Consequently, he kissed her' or 'Obviously he knew that Mary knew that something was wrong.' Sentences have been discussed and dissected as to possible multiple meanings and ambiguities without taking into account the natural function cf context in resolving most ambiguities. Meanwhile, many difficult problems have been restricted to partial explanations or have been totally shelved in the absence of contextual considerations. Among these problems have been deixis and the use of articles; pronominalization, and other anaphoric ways of referring to a participant; better understanding of tense, aspect, mode, and voice in verbs; use of optional temporal and spatial expressions; the function of extra-position, left dislocation, and other such features; subject selection, object selection, and other focus phenomena; the function and thrust of conjunctions and other sequence signals; and the function of mystery particles which occur in connected context in some languages, which the native speaker knows where to use and where not to use, but which defy translation. Undoubtedly, a discourse revolution (Longacre, 1979e) of some sort is shaping up in response to the demand for context and for greater explanatory power. It is hoped that this volume can be a contribution to that foment.

This volume is called _The Grammar of Discourse: Notional and Surface Structures_. As such, the goals of this volume are restricted. It is not entitled _The Semantics of Discourse_, although it contains in its title the words _Notional Structures_. The term semantics would be too broad and would indicate material of a sort especially excluded from this volume. We are not here concerned with questions concerning the referential content structure of a discourse. We are not concerned whether a text is about chickens, turkeys, or other barnyard fowl, about the love life of the ancient Greeks, about energy alternatives for America in the late 20th century, or a humorous dialogue between parents and teenagers. Rather, we are concerned in this volume with such features as plot progression in a narrative from stage to inciting incident to further build-up to a climax of confrontation to denouement and to final resolution; with dialogue relations such as question-answer, proposal-response, remark-evaluation; with ways of combining predications according to coupling, contrast, temporal succession, temporal overlap, causation, paraphrase, and the like; and with the world of role relations such as patient, experiencer, agent, goal and source. We note concerning these notions that:

1. They are not language specific but belong to the general notional structure of language as spoken by human beings anywhere.
2. They are independent of particular texts and particular referential content structure in a given language.
3. At least some of them resemble categories which we are accustomed (on lower levels) to call grammar.
4. They emerge as categories which are marked in the surface structure of at least some languages.

I believe, therefore, that all of these notional considerations belong to the form of language and to the form of discourses within it, i.e., on the formal rather than on the content side. I see, therefore, no reason why they should not be considered to be GRAMMAR as opposed to the world of referential and content structure. Admittedly, they are the deep or semantic side of grammar. But even if we admit the latter word, semantic here does not include the referential function. Rather this volume sets out to explore and catalogue notional structures which figure in the structure of discourse and to confront them with and relate them to the surface structure of discourse in various languages.

As to the grammatical surface structure of discourse, a crucial consideration is the fact that most discourses formally mark (often by a variety of devices) a discourse PEAK. In addition, often a discourse STAGE (in narrative) or INTRODUCTION (in other discourse types) is indicated as well. Further devices of aperture and finis bracket discourses in many languages. From these and other considerations we deduce a GRAMMATICAL PROFILE of a discourse in terms of Aperture, Stage/Introduction, Pre-Peak sections (Episodes in Narrative), Peak, Post-Peak sections (likewise, Episodes in Narrative), and Finis. Such a profile is a deduction from clearly marked features in the surface structure of a discourse. Furthermore, the surface structure profile is shadowed by an underlying notional structure (plot) which it exploits and marks in various ways. In similar fashion, a dialogue discourse or drama can be examined as to its overall profile.

Another grammatical consideration that is relevant to discourse is the way in which verb and noun morphosyntax are used to sort out strands of information relevance in a discourse. Thus the mainline of a discourse can be marked (in a given type of discourse) by a characteristic tense, aspect, or mood (or some combination of the three), by word order in the clause, or by a mystery particle. Various further features can also mark the more pivotal parts of the mainline from the more routine parts and can classify background, supportive and depictive material so that the more crucial bits of such information stand out.

Of considerable interest to the student of discourse is the intersection of the two sets of features briefly summarized in the preceding paragraphs. What happens to the routine marking of strands of information relevance at the peak(s) of a discourse? One thing is certain, the peak of a discourse is non-routine. It may, in fact, be thought of as a zone of turbulence in regard to the general flow of a discourse. It is, therefore, no surprise that at discourse peak markers of the mainline may be phased out, be used less frequently--or be used much more frequently than in other parts of the discourse. Granted that special peak markers can also occur, we can summarize what happens at peak by saying 'something new has been added to and something taken away.'

The above considerations (peak and discourse profile, strands of information relevance, and the intersection of these two sets of features) do not much take into account the hierarchical, constituent structure of discourse; rather they treat the structures as wholes with characteristic shapes and textures. It is important, however, that we consider in addition to these holistic concerns the constituent structure of a discourse, viz. the structuring into paragraphs, sentences, clauses, and phrases. Each of these units has also notional and surface structures. Considerable attention is given here to the notional structures of these levels. For the surface structure of the paragraph, cf. Longacre 1979c; for the surface structure of the sentence, cf. Longacre 1970c. As for the surface structure of the clause, this is obviously a somewhat well-cultivated plot of ground. My own representation of English clause structure is found in the Appendix to this volume.

One of the relatively unexplored areas of discourse structure is the relation of constituent structure to the holistic concerns already described. These are twin insights into discourse--but insights that have not yet fused into effective binocular vision. For a beginning, however, cf. Waltz 1976 (in respect to a South American language, Guanano).

This volume does not touch much on the pragmatics of discourse. Ultimately, of course, such considerations are of the greatest importance. Just as we cannot analyze isolated sentences apart from their linguistic context, so ultimately, we cannot analyze discourses aside from the behavioral context which is relevant to them (cf. Chapter 8). Nevertheless, it is not possible to do everything within the confines of a single volume. For this reason, pragmatic considerations are touched on only in a few places here. In particular, pragmatic considerations figure in the structure of Chapter 2 where dialogue is considered. Dialogue is so interwoven with practical conditions of social exchange between people that it is scarcely possible to ignore the pragmatics of dialogue. Indeed, pragmatics comes into the very matter of distinguishing and relating monologue to dialogue. As I plead in this volume, units of dialogue (to which turn-taking and repartee are relevant) are not in immediate correspondence with the size level units of monologue (morpheme, stem, phrase, clause, sentence, paragraph, discourse). Dialogue units relate rather closely to the pragmatics of the situation, while the hierarchical units within a monologue relate to the pragmatics of the situation in a more indirect way. Nevertheless, it will be necessary to insist that the form which a given text takes is responsive at multiple points to the demands of the communication situation--even though such further considerations are beyond the immediate scope of this volume. Chapter 6, however, does touch briefly on the matter of performatives assumed in monologue discourses and assumptions made relative to the whole discourse.

In brief then, this volume is almost entirely non-overlapping with such a volume as van Dijk's Text and Context (1977), whose two halves are respectively semantics and pragmatics. In the semantics of discourse, van Dijk considers mainly matters of referential content, although he gets a bit into the sort of sequential considerations which I cover in this volume as well. In the section on pragmatics he likewise touches on matters which are largely beyond the sphere of this volume.

Turning again to the notional categories which are especially featured in this volume, I suggest that the questions which are considered here are very worthwhile questions for the student of discourse. If we assemble the various notional categories which characterize human discourse in all languages, the ensemble is impressive. It amounts, in fact, to a natural metaphysic of the human mind, an anatomy of our intellects in their abstract functioning. As such, it intimately relates to our humanity and ties into certain questions discussed in the final chapter of this volume. To understand the notional structure of human discourse is to know in broad outline what to look for before we sit down to find it in discourses within a given language. Our only question will be to what degree and in what form do these various notional categories come to the surface in the surface grammar of a given language. The goal of this volume is then somewhat like the dream of the generative semanticist of the recent linguistic past. If we can describe the universal soft underbelly of language, this should greatly simplify the exploration of the upper structure. Our job will essentially be not to posit new notional categories for every language that we find, but to simply map the universal notional categories onto the grammatical structure of the surface of a language. This should considerably simplify our task.

As a whole, I avoid in this volume the term deep structure for the structures which are here assumed to underlie the surface grammar of languages. The main reason for avoiding the term deep structure is the fact that it has been used in so many different senses, from the relatively shallow deep structures of Chomsky and his immediate colleagues, to the rock bottom semantic structures of the generative semanticist. However, the term deep structure does involve a metaphor which is useful in at least one point, that is, it raises the possibility of considering that notional and surface structures are not a clear dichotomy but a polarity. If we speak of the deep and surface structure of a discourse, we can also speak of the relative depth or relative superficiality of an item of which we are speaking. We can avoid, on the one hand, frantic attempts to expunge from the surface structure grammar elements which look semantic, and on the other hand accept the fact of a formal structuring of the underlying structure as well. We can find some meaning expressed on the surface without being scandalized and we can find a formal side to the deep structure as well. These considerations are explored at the end of Chapter 7.

In the chapters which compose the body of this book: Chapter 1 relates to monologue discourse; Chapter 2 relates to dialogue discourse; Chapter 3 sketches the notional structures involved in combinations of predications; Chapters 4 and 5 deal with the internal structure of predications (the world of so-called case grammar); Chapter 6 deals with a few further problems relating to stems, words and phrases. After sketching all these notional structures in some detail, Chapter 7 suggests a framework for discourse analysis, in which all the bits and pieces can fit comfortably. If Chapter 7 is my linguistic credo, Chapter 8 is my philosophical/religious credo regarding the place of language and man in the scheme of things. Just as we need linguistic context to make isolated sentences intelligible and broad, non-linguistic pragmatic context to make discourses intelligible, so we may well raise the question as to what is necessary and sufficient to make the whole human venture something other than existential loneliness and frustration.

CHAPTER 1

MONOLOGUE DISCOURSE

The term discourse, as currently used, covers two areas of linguistic concern: the analysis of dialogue--especially of live conversation--and the analysis of monologue. In the parlance of many, discourse covers the former, and with at least some of us, discourse covers the latter. Actually, the two matters--analysis of dialogue and analysis of monologue--are separable but related concerns. Discourse analysis can properly be applied to both.

This chapter deals with broad concerns of monologue discourse and leaves the matter of the relations of monologue and dialogue to the introduction to the next chapter. One initial concern in the analysis of monologue discourse is discourse typology. Characteristics of individual discourses can be neither described, predicted, nor analyzed without resort to a classification of discourse types. It is pointless to look in a discourse for a feature which is not characteristic of the type to which that discourse belongs.

So determinative of detail is the general design of a discourse type that the linguist who ignores discourse typology can only come to grief. A case in point is that of the student of language typology or of diachronic change. For example, if in the study of word order typologies we include data from a language where different types of discourse (e.g., narrative versus expository) have differing word orders, then comparisons between two or more languages can be vitiated by the failure to control this difference. We can, if we wish, compare California oranges with Florida oranges, but it is less useful to compare California oranges with Washington apples. We may compare sentences from narrative discourse in language A with sentences from narrative discourse in language B, but it is misleading to compare sentences from narrative discourse in language A with sentences from expository discourse in language B.

After the consideration of discourse typology, some further concerns of monologue discourse are taken up here: main line versus supportive material, the role of the composer (narrator, etc.), and finally, plot and similar structures.

1. DISCOURSE TYPOLOGY IN NOTIONAL AND SURFACE STRUCTURE

It is obvious that not all monologue discourses are of the same sort. Fairy tales, novels, short stories, first person accounts, newspaper reporting of events, historiography, essays, scientific papers, sermons, pep talks, political speeches, food recipes, do-it-yourself books--all these discourses differ in ways more or less obvious. Furthermore, even some of the above are broad categories rather than specific types. Thus, within the novel itself we find contrasting types, e.g., the gothic novel with a structure about as well defined as that of Propp's fairy tales.

There are, on the other hand, similarities between certain of the types of discourses mentioned. The fairy tale, the novel, the short story, are all types of storytelling. But the fairy tale has its own peculiar structure as Propp (1928) has long since indicated. The novel and the short story, while similar, differ not only in length, but in the relative concentration of action. On the other hand, a first person novel may have much in common with a first person account of an informal sort. First person accounts, newspaper reporting, and historiography all make pretensions to factuality. Newspaper reporting imposes a certain demand that the main content be given in the first opening sentences, and that in the rest of the story the details be given in successive sentences and paragraphs. Historiography is very similar in some ways to certain varieties of the novel. Essays and scientific papers share much in common as do sermons and pep talks. Food recipes have something in common with how-to-do-it booklets, but the former are more stereotyped and restricted in content and application. Certain discourse types are then somewhat similar to others. Our classification needs, therefore, to include both broad classifications and also more narrow specification of surface types.

The classification needs, however, to allow for the difference between notional structures (deep or semantic structures) and surface structures. This is necessary in that the two do not necessarily match up well. We may have, e.g., a moral lesson given in story form, or a set of procedures given as a story of how a master craftsman implemented them, or a first person account recounted as if it were a set of procedures (see below in 1.3). In brief, notional structures of discourse relate more clearly to the overall purpose of the discourse, while surface structures have to do more with a discourse's formal characteristics.

1.1 Notional Types

To begin with, we can classify all possible discourses according to two basic parameters: CONTINGENT TEMPORAL SUCCESSION and AGENT ORIENTATION. Contingent temporal succession (henceforth contingent succession) refers to a framework of temporal succession in which some (often most) of the events or doings are contingent on previous events or doings. Agent orientation refers to orientation towards agents (cf. Chapter 5) with at least a partial identity of agent reference running through the discourse. These two parameters intersect so as to give us a four-way classification of discourse types: Narrative discourse (broadly conceived) is plus in respect to both parameters. Procedural discourse (how to do it, how it was done, how it takes place) is plus in respect to contingent succession (the steps of a procedure are ordered) but minus in respect to the agent orientation (attention is on what is done or made, not on who does it). Behavioral discourse (a broad category including exhortation, eulogy and political speeches of candidates) is minus in regard to contingent succession but plus in regard to agent orientation (it deals with how people did or should behave). Expository discourse is minus in respect to both parameters.

A certain care has been taken in positing these initial parameters, for if they are defined too broadly we get into difficulty in classifying some discourses. Thus, Hebrews chapter 11 is really an expository discourse on faith. On first inspection, however, there are difficulties in classifying this discourse. If, for example, we were to define the first parameter simply as chronological succession (as in Longacre 1976), then Hebrews 11 would be plus in respect to this parameter since it orders its examples of believing men and women according to the chronological framework of the Old Testament. It is plain, however, that the chapter does not present the actions of any person of faith as dependent on those of a person previously mentioned. There is chronological succession, but not contingent succession. The writer is exemplifying faith and simply mentions his various examples in the order in which they are mentioned in the Old Testament. Likewise, while there is a great deal of action and many agents mentioned in the chapter, the chapter is oriented towards those agents who act as examples of faith. Furthermore, there is disparity instead of identity of reference. Actually, then, if we define our two parameters carefully enough, Hebrews 11--unlike true narratives--is minus in respect to both parameters.

The first two parameters, however carefully defined, leave us with a classification much too broad for most purposes. A further parameter, PROJECTION, can be posited so as to give us eight types instead of four. Projection has to do with a situation or action which is contemplated, enjoined, or anticipated but not realized. Thus, narrative as a broad category can be subdivided into prophecy, which is plus projection, versus story, history, etc., which are minus projection, i.e., the events are represented as having already taken place. Procedural discourse likewise distinguishes varieties which are plus projection (how to do it) versus varieties that are minus projection (how it used to be done). Behavioral discourse also distinguishes plus projection (hortatory discourse or a campaign promises speech) versus minus projection (a eulogy). Finally, expository discourse which is usually minus projection can also be plus projection, e.g., a speech submitting a budget or an economic plan.

Although a scheme in three parameters captures many useful distinctions, still a fourth parameter can be posited. This fourth parameter, TENSION, has to do with whether a

	+Ag-Orientation	-Ag-Orientation	
+CONTINGENT SUCCESSION	NARRATIVE	PROCEDURAL	
	Prophecy	How-to-do-it	+Proj.
	- - - - - - - - -	- - - - - - - - -	
	Story	How-it-was-done	-Proj.
-CONTINGENT SUCCESSION	BEHAVIORAL	EXPOSITORY	
	Hortatory Promissory	Budget Proposal Futuristic Essay	+Proj.
	- - - - - - - - -	- - - - - - - - -	
	Eulogy	Scientific Paper	-Proj.

Diagram I. Notional Types (Fourth Parameter, Tension, is Not Represented) discourse reflects a struggle or polarization of some sort. This is relevant to narrative discourse of all sorts, as is seen in 4.1 of this chapter, where episodic (minus tension) narrative is distinguished from climactic narrative (plus tension). But discourses of other types can also be plus/ minus tension. A theological treatise, e.g., can present its author's views in highly argumentative fashion or in a matter-of-fact way. A treatise on the Eucharist can take the second option or it can proceed (plus tension) as follows: present three views of the Eucharist, refute each one, and then triumphantly assert the view of one's own brand of theology as the correct view at the end. The discussion in section 4.4 of this chapter is essentially a description of plus tension structures in other than narrative.

The first three parameters are exemplified in Diagram I. Tension is indicated as a fourth parameter but the further types consequent on positing this parameter are not indicated.

Notice that in the above, drama is not included as a discourse type. I feel it is preeminently a surface structure phenomenon, a way of telling a story in the most vivid possible form. I have likewise not listed the letter as a notional structure genre. I believe that the letter is preeminently a surface structure form which may partake of the characteristics of any of the four main types, i.e., we may write a letter in which we recount events to a person, in which we tell them how to do something, in which we explain a subject matter, or in which we try to influence his conduct, or maybe all by turns in the same letter.

1.2 Surface Structure Types

The scheme outlined above is also applicable to the surface structure provided that (1) we add drama as a split-off from narrative of the story variety; (2) we take account of the typical surface structure markings which encode the notional parameters; and (3) we provide for skewing of notional and surface features as discussed in 1.3.

Drama contrasts with the other discourse types in that it is essentially composed of dialogue paragraphs and these dialogue paragraphs are not composed of quotation sentences (which have formulas of quotation). This contrasts with reported dialogue in a narrative where we most commonly find that the dialogue paragraphs feature quotation sentences with quotation formulas. Only in especially lively sections of narrative do we find the dialogue paragraphs approximating the form of drama (where each character speaks out without a preceding John said . . .). Even more profound is the contrast of drama with procedural discourse which typically has a dearth of dialogue. Finally, in expository and hortatory discourses, dialogue is not so likely to occur as is pseudo-dialogue, i.e., use of apostrophe and rhetorical question. The purpose of the rhetorical question in expository discourse is to elicit attention; it is essentially a teaching device. In hortatory discourse, rhetorical questions may be used to reprimand as well as to teach.

For the purposes of surface structure classification, our two main parameters can be redefined. Thus, rather than speaking in the abstract of contingent succession, we can speak more concretely of CHRONOLOGICAL LINKAGE as characteristic of all sorts of narrative and procedural discourse, but non-characteristic of behavioral and expository discourse which have instead logical (including topical) linkage. Likewise, we can look in narrative and behavioral discourse for lines of AGENT REFERENCE (or, to speak more broadly, PARTICIPANT REFERENCE) while in procedural and expository discourse this feature is absent (procedural discourse is goal or activity focused, while expository discourse has themes rather than participants). Seen in this light, Hebrews 11 is clearly expository. It had no chronological linkage but rather links via a recurrent initial phrase "By faith (X did Y)".

The further parameter, projection, likewise has specific surface structure correlates--as has also the parameter tension. All this needs to be gone over in some detail.

As seen below (Section 2) each surface structure type has characteristic tense/aspect/voice features in the verbs that occur on its main line. Thus narrative (story) discourse has some sort of non-durative preterit, or historical present, while narrative (prophecy) has a future tense. Procedural (how to do it) has a customary present, or imperative in most languages, while procedural (how it was done) has a customary past tense. Behavioral (hortatory) has imperatives or some socially mitigated substitute for an imperative, while behavioral (eulogy) reverts to a past or customary past. Expository discourse is generally quite distinct in its preference for existential and equational clauses--often with considerable nominalization. These various tense/aspect/voice characteristics of each given type are ways of forwarding a discourse along its main line of development whether chronological or logical.

Every discourse finds a further principle of unity in terms of participants and/or themes. The surface structure correlates of participant/theme reference are largely found in the interplay of noun, pronoun, and null reference. Verb morphology with pronominal endings and/or switch reference (marking of same versus different subjects in successive clauses) is also of considerable relevance in some languages.

In languages where pronouns are frequently used the person selection of pronouns varies significantly in the various types of discourse. Thus, narrative discourse is regularly characterized by first or third person pronouns in its narrative framework. Drama--which has no narrative framework--is characterized by multiple first person and second person exchanges. In procedural discourse the non-specific, non-focused agent can emerge as first, second or third person in the surface structure, depending on the conventions of a particular language. First person may be used in the sense of first person inclusive, *This is what we all do*, or a procedural text may even be given with first plural exclusive, *This is what we do but probably you'd rather not join us in this activity*. Again, a procedural discourse may simply be second person (often stressless or reduced), *You do this, then you do that* or *Y' do this, then y' do that*. Finally a procedural discourse may be in third person whether singular or plural: *He (the competent craftsman) does this* or *They do this*. The third person references are not, however, substitutes for proper names. Proper names, were they to occur, would get us into the type of specific person which characterizes narrative as opposed to procedural discourse. In expository discourse, which is oriented to themes instead of the participants, third person pronouns and deictics are appropriate. When first person comes into an expository discourse it is the voice of the expositor himself with a performative verb. Behavioral discourse of the hortatory variety has an essential second person component. The second person reference can be softened by resort to a first person plural inclusive. Instead, therefore, of saying *You acted foolishly in this regard*, one might say *We've acted foolishly in this regard*. A further device of hortatory discourse is to use a third person to indicate a model of good behavior: *A real American does so and so*, or *A good Huichol acts as follows* (data from Joe Grimes) instead of *You should do so and so*.

In regard to the specific surface structure linkage of discourses, we find in narrative discourse very prominent use of head-head linkage (i.e., the first sentence of one paragraph cross-references to the first sentence of the following paragraph) and tail-head linkage (in which the last sentence of one paragraph cross-references to the first sentence of the following paragraph). Tail-head linkage may be varied to summary-head linkage, i.e., *having done all this, they then proceeded to* . . . . Procedural discourse has very similar linkage of the head-head, tail-head and summary-head varieties. Expository discourse tends to have linkage through sentence topics and parallelism of content. Hortatory discourse depends heavily on linkage through conditional, cause, and purpose margins or their equivalents within a given language.

We must remind ourselves that the classification into broad categories of surface structure types subsumes many specific genre within various languages. In Western European literature, the variety of genre is so great that it would require considerable time and effort to catalog them successfully. In the narrative story category we not only have the fairy tale and myth, the short story, the short short story, the novel and various varieties of novels such as historical novels, gothic novels, detective mystery stories, etc., we have, in addition, first person accounts, newspaper reporting, and historiography, which, as we have said, make pretensions to factuality. In simpler cultures with oral literatures we may find on the contrary only two or three varieties of narrative discourse, e.g., myth, first person accounts, and formal stories. In many cultures and literatures, whether complex or simple, we find a distinction in third person narrative, i.e., the variety which is neutral as to vantage point and the variety wherein the narrator identifies his vantage point with that of one character.

Procedural discourse varies from the food recipe, to the how-to-do it book, to the instruction to a particular worker for his activities on a given day. In some nonliterate communities procedural discourse is almost non-existent. In such communities, people learn by participating in activities. The verbal components are part of the whole activity complex and do not ever attain the status of a continuous monologue. Nevertheless, even in such communities the outsider does not find it too hard to elicit from people a discourse telling how to do or how to make something. In such cases the influence of the outsider results in the speedy evolution of a new discourse type.

Expository discourse can range from the familiar essay to the scientific article. It may be that descriptive discourse, in which we simply are describing something which we see, is essentially different from expository discourse.

Hortatory discourses can range from sermons, to pep-talks, to addresses of generals to the troops on the eve of an important battle. At any rate it would appear that hortatory discourse is a cultural universal. We can scarcely conceive of a culture where somebody does not give advice to somebody else orally or urge on him a change of conduct. The very idea of social control seems to imply this.

1.3 Skewing of Notional and Surface Discourse Features

It is a fact of language that whenever surface structure becomes well crystalized and marked, i.e., whenever it is opaque rather than transparent , it may be thrown out of phase with the notional structure. We must, therefore, face the fact that a given notional structure type may encode in the form of a differing surface structure type.

To begin with, note that I have not posited drama in the notional structure. I consider here that narrative and drama are two alternative ways of telling a story. Notional structure narration may be expressed as either surface type. Of the two, drama is the more vivid[1]. Having said this, we recognize the fact that discourse types differ in degree of vividness and that this difference is relevant to out-of-phase encodings of notional types into surface types. This idea must be developed briefly.

The most vivid form of discourse next to drama is narrative itself, while expository and hortatory discourse are considerably less vivid than narrative. I am uncertain just how to classify procedural discourse on the scale of vividness. Hortatory seems to be possibly the least vivid of all the discourse types. We can witness this in a Sunday morning church service. As long as the preacher is sermonizing in the narrow sense of the word, i.e., urging on people modifications of their conduct, everyone including the children gets sleepy, but when the preacher runs in a short narrative as an illustration in his sermon, it is very likely that even the children will wake up and be anxious to find out how the little storyette will work out.

Granted the preceding differences in vividness among discourse types, it is not strange that hortatory and expository materials sometimes emerge in the surface structure of narration. This is what lies behind the fable and the parable as literary forms: greater appeal to listener and reader by the adoption of a more vivid surface form. Furthermore, the fable and the parable sometimes compromise their surface structure narrative form by the occurrence of a moral slot at the end in which the thrust of the story is pointed out explicitly. With or without such an explicit surface structure slot, however, the superficially entertaining story really aims at explaining something of a rather difficult nature to us or at influencing our conduct. Thus we may have the story of the atom in which expository material concerning atomic structure is cast into narrative form. Or we may have the story of a drug addict in which the accounting of the misfortunes and sufferings of a user of heroin are held up as a bad example to frighten off other people from experimentation with that drug. Of course, whatever is presented as narrative may also be presented as surface structure drama, which is higher in the scale of vividness. This is clear in the case of medieval drama, which was not drama for its own sake, but drama for the sake of teaching the content of the Bible or inculcating certain moral values.

There may be occasions on which it is stylistically effective to present notional narration in the surface structure form of procedural discourse. An example of this occurred in a news story in the _Dallas Morning News_ (Davenport 1973). Its notional intent was to give a first person account of an apartment fire in Dallas, but it is cast in the form of procedural discourse, i.e., the pronoun _you_ is used through most of the account, _you go to bed_, _you wake up_, _you smell smoke_, etc., and cast into the present tense which is characteristic of procedural discourse in English. The thrust of it is, 'This is how you might act if you were to find yourself in the same circumstances in which I found myself'. Or, conversely, procedural discourse may be given as narrative. Thus my colleagues Jannette Forster and Myra Lou Barnard elicited Dibabawon texts relating to game procurement (Longacre 1968, Part 3). While several of their texts are clearly surface structure procedural texts, there are a few in which we are told how a certain capable hunter or trapper procured game. Here we have the story of how a master of the art behaved in implementing his art. They are surface structure narratives, which run somewhat as follows: *So and so (by name) built a fishtrap on a certain bend of a certain river a certain year. He was highly successful. He caught so and so many fish in his trap*, etc. Although this is surface structure narrative, the purpose is to inform us how to build a successful fishtrap--and of course we can learn this quite well from being told how a master trapper of fish built his trap. The possibility of encoding narrative as procedural or procedural as narrative raises the possibility that they are not too different in degrees of vividness but differ as to relative specificity (narrative) or generality (procedural).

Notice how in this discussion of the skewing of notional features of discourse types and their surface structure features we come around eventually to the discussion of intent. Intent may be expressed in terms of performative verbs which underlie the whole discourse (cf. Chapter 6) and which may or may not surface explicitly. In terms of such performative verbs, narration in its notional structure employs *I recount*; procedural discourse in its notional structure employs *I prescribe*; expository discourse, *I explain*; and hortatory discourse, *I propose*, i.e., *suggest*, *urge*, *command*. The notional structure motive may be somewhat disguised by resort to a surface structure of radically different form. Apparently the disguising of the underlying motive can make the presentation all the more effective. Thus, in that people do not like to be urged to change their conduct, presenting this hortatory material as a narrative or a drama may make it easier for them to accept it. Likewise, expository material may be livened up by being cast into a narrative or dramatic form. And, as we have seen, narrative material may achieve poignancy by being cast into procedural form and procedural material may attain a certain concreteness and authority by casting it into narrative form.

In the process, of course, new types and subtypes may emerge in the surface structure. Thus, it would appear that parable and fable are well crystalized and recognizable types in the surface structure because of the very fact that, while casting hortatory material into narrative form, they append a specific moral slot at the end (or in the case of the parable, a clue to the interpretation of the parable).

The skewing of notional and surface discourse features is according to a hierarchy of degrees of vividness, with drama as the most vivid, with narrative as the second most vivid--but with procedural perhaps not too far behind--and with expository next in the degree of vividness, and with hortatory still further on down. It appears that it is the less vivid forms of discourse which are shifted into the more vivid surface forms rather than vice versa.

1.4 Embedding Relations of the Five Surface Structure Types

A discourse of a given surface structure type may embed within a discourse of the same or different type. Certain of these embedding relations are frequent enough to merit special comment. Thus, narrative may flow into drama, so that we may have, for example, a chapter or two of a novel which is cast into dramatic form (cf. Chapter 33 in Solzhenitzyn's novel *The First Circle*). Furthermore, instances occur in a narrative discourse in which there is a projected denouement which is really an embedded procedural discourse; i.e., the story takes us up to a certain point, the events aren't over yet, but the author in effect tells us: *this is how things of this sort customarily proceed and this will be no doubt the end of the whole matter*. Thus, in a short discourse from Mexico (Chinantec, from James Rupp) about planting a chili pepper crop, a man tells how he has planted his crop, cultivated it, did the first and the second weedings, and how he can therefore look forward to reaping a harvest of a certain anticipated quality and quantity roughly within certain anticipated dates. The end of this discourse is clearly an embedded procedural discourse. Not dissimilar is a discourse in Sarangani Bilaan (McLachlin and Blackburn 1971), 'The Marriage of Nini and Ginong', in which the woman Nini tells in first person of the course of their courtship and in which the peak, i.e., the wedding itself, is an embedded procedural discourse which tells what happens at a typical Bilaan wedding.

We have already spoken of the fact that either surface structure narrative or drama may encode exposition, but it needs to be emphasized that a surface structure narrative of any length and complexity inevitably involves a quantity of EMBEDDED surface structure exposition. If such sections are very small we call them expository paragraphs (which, e.g., expound episodes of the story, or of an embedded story). On the other hand, we may have a whole embedded expository discourse at a given point within a story.

As types, expository and hortatory relate quite well also; we find that explanation of a subject can lead to a desire to urge a change of conduct on the part of those who hear what is being explained. It is interesting that the Epistle of Paul to the Ephesians consists of six chapters, the first three of which are clearly expository material, and the second three of which are just as clearly hortatory. This is a COMPOUND DISCOURSE containing two embedded discourses, one of which is hortatory.

2. MAIN LINE VERSUS SUPPORTIVE MATERIAL

The previous section has skirted the edge of a further feature of monologue discourse that requires discussion in its own right: the distinction between the main line of development in a discourse and all other material--which I here lump together under the rubric SUPPORTIVE. Actually, it is impossible to make structural distinctions among discourse types without taking this further factor into account. Thus, in regard to the distribution of tenses/aspects in various discourse types, unless we distinguish the main line versus supportive material, we can make only statistical statements. We can, e.g., say that "past tense predominates (or is very frequent) in narrative discourse; present or future, in procedural discourse; and imperatives, in hortatory discourse". If we recognize, however, the distinction between the main line and supportive material, this statement can now be made a structural statement, such as "past tense characterizes the main line of narrative discourse; present or future (depending on language and subtype), the main line of procedural discourse; and imperative, the main line of hortatory discourse". Further statements can then be made in regard to correlation of other tenses/aspects with various types of supportive material in each genre.

The easiest place to see the relevance of the distinction here suggested is narrative discourse. Gleason suggested quite some time ago that we should distinguish an event line from other material in a narrative. Grimes (1976) discusses types of information in which a fundamental distinction is between events and non-events of various sorts. Hopper (1979) has written very cogently concerning this distinction as a kind of foregrounding in discourse. Field work in many languages around the world has underscored the value of the distinction (Longacre and Woods 1976-77; Grimes 1978; Linda Jones 1979).

Consider, e.g., the following passage from Mark Twain (1964:240):

In a minute a third slave was struggling in the air. It was dreadful. I turned away my head for a moment, and when I turned back I missed the king! They were blindfolding him! I was paralyzed; I couldn't move, I was choking, my tongue was petrified. They finished blindfolding him, they led him under the rope. I couldn't shake off that clinging impotence. But when I saw them put the noose around his neck, then everything let go in me and I made a spring to the rescue--and as I made it I shot one more glance abroad--by George! here they came, a-tilting!--five hundred mailed and belted knights on bicycles!

In this paragraph some actions are reported along with a certain amount of supportive material. On first examination, the event line appears to be marked by simple past tenses: (1) turned (away my head), (2) turned back, (3) missed (the king), (4) finished (blindfolding him), (5) led (him), (6) saw (them put the noose), (7) (everything) let go (in me), (8) made (a spring), (9) made it, (10) shot (one more glance). Three of these past tenses (numbers 2, 6, 9) are, however, in adverbial clauses which serve for back-reference and cohesion. Thus, when I turned back cross-references to the previous clause I turned away my head a moment; while when I saw them put the noose around his neck reflects the next step after (4) and (5): They finished blindfolding him, they led him under the rope; and as I made it builds on I made a spring to the rescue. These three instances (2, 6, 9) are illustrative of the secondary use of past tense forms for cohesion between main events rather than reporting main events. I will, therefore, exclude them from the event line on the grounds that they are past tenses in adverbial clauses which are back-referential in function. In this fashion, in many languages it is necessary to confine the event-line to independent verbs of the requisite tense/aspect.

Other clauses in the paragraph have a supportive--often emotive and depictive--function. Here, as in most languages, clauses which are descriptive and equational are excluded from the event-line, even though their verb (here *be*) has the requisite event-line tense. This excludes in our present example *It was dreadful*, *I was paralyzed*, and *my tongue was petrified*. Some further graphic details are given in the past progressive: . . . *a third slave was struggling in the air*. *They were blindfolding him*, *and I was choking*. One clause is negative (Grimes calls this collateral): *I couldn't shake off that clinging impotence*.

One more past tense remains which I've not as yet assigned to the event-line or to supportive material: *here they came*, *a-tilting*. Note that this clause is part of the report of what the narrator saw (reported as *I shot one more glance* . . .). Furthermore, it is evident that the action reported in a past tense verb is continuative--which explains the *a-tilting* which follows. Here we again assign this clause to depictive (simultaneous) material rather than to the event-line. This is evident by what follows: *The grandest sight that ever was seen*. *Lord*, *how the plumes streamed*, *how the sun flamed and flashed from the endless procession of webby wheels*!

At this point, however, a difference in the tense/aspect system of English as opposed to Romance languages emerges. The English past tense not only characterizes the event-line but some of the supportive material as well. In Spanish and French, on the contrary, the equivalents of the verbs *came*, *streamed*, *flamed*, and *flashed* would not be past tenses but would be imperfects. In brief, the aspectual distinctions of the Romance languages (and, for that matter, Slavic and classical Greek) distinguish better the event-line versus supportive material than do the tense-forms of English.

The distinction main line versus supportive material is not the whole story, however. Some languages distinguish the more important events on the event-line from lesser, routine, and somewhat predictable events. Languages may also label some supportive material as more crucial than others (cf.

Jones and Jones 1979; Longacre 1979b). In Totonac narrative (Bishop 1979) the more important events are reported in clauses which are marked with tuncan 'and then'; while important and crucial supportive material is marked with -tza' (no simple translation equivalent) on one or more elements of the clause.

While tense/aspect can mark the routine event line, and a mystery particle or affix (Longacre 1976) can mark the more important events, word order can also play a part in such considerations. Thus Hopper (1979) describes VSO or SOV as characteristic of event line in Anglo-Saxon with SVO used for supportive material. In Biblical Hebrew VSO clauses (with a peculiar narrative tense) mark the event line while SVO clauses (not with the special narrative tense) are reserved for supportive material (Longacre 1979a).

It should be emphasized that what is on the line in one type of discourse is off the line in another type and vice versa. Thus in Anglo-Saxon, Biblical Hebrew, and Trique while VSO clauses characterize the main line of narrative and SVO clauses are off the line, in expository discourse in all three languages SVO is on the main line. With SVO on the main line of exposition, VSO clauses are found in illustrative material, e.g., narrative anecdotes.

3. THE COMPOSER

Mary Ruth Wise, in her treatment of Nomatsiguenga discourse (Wise 1968), features prominently what she calls the observer viewpoint: from what point of view is the observer conceptualizing the progress of the discourse? While I agree with Wise as to the importance of observer viewpoint, it seems to me that the observer in which we are most interested in discourse is its COMPOSER (i.e., the man who is making up the discourse and beaming it towards us). In the case of narrative discourse we call the composer the NARRATOR.

Narrator viewpoint is of great importance to narrative discourse. As we have seen, the narrator may inject himself into the story as a first person participant. On the other hand, the narrator may present in the third person a story in which either he is quite neutral as to vantage point or in which he comes down and stands beside one character and adopts the viewpoint of that character as his vantage point.

Vantage point is morphologically marked in the structure of Oksapmin (Lawrence 1972). In one sort of Oksapmin narrative, one can single out one person or one set of persons as the vantage point of a story in the third person. All verbs which refer to these people as agents must have one type of verb morphology while all verbs which refer to other people as agents must have a different type of verb morphology. The hearer is made certain by the very verb morphology at whose side he is standing in the course of the story. This device also serves for keeping participants straight in the course of the story so that fewer proper nouns or other means of explicit reference need to be used, once the reference of the morphological categories is established.

There are stories in which the hand of the narrator is very evident and there are stories in which the hand of the narrator is very covert. As an extreme, we may mention *The French Lieutenant's Woman* in which the author, John Fowles, almost spoils the story by intruding into it at several crucial points. Thus, at two important turning points of the story he pauses, thinks out loud, and says in effect: *Well, what shall I do next? Shall I give the story the usual sort of happy ending or shall I give it another sort of ending?* He says, *I'm just like God sitting up here pushing my characters around and watching how they act.* In fact at these two important points in the story he gives alternative endings, in which he brings the story to conclusion in one fashion and then switches and says in effect: *No, it probably didn't really end that way, I'd better end it in a different fashion.*

In *The House of the Seven Gables*, Hawthorne's point of view as a narrator is somewhat less intrusive, but nevertheless clearly evident. This is especially evident in Chapter 2, where Hawthorne describes to us an important day in the life of Hepzibah Pyncheon. He remarks in this chapter, *Far from us the indecorum of assisting, even in imagination, at a maiden lady's toilet. Our story must therefore await Miss Hepzibah at the threshold of her chamber.* . . Further on he refers to the house as being empty except for Hepzibah and *a disembodied listener like ourselves.* Further on Hawthorne remarks, *Let us pardon her one other pause.* . . Still a few pages further he remarks, *All this time however we are* _loitering faintheartedly on the threshold of our story. In very truth, we have an invincible reluctance to disclose what Miss Hepzibah Pyncheon was about to do._ Contrasting with novels of this sort are other novels and short stories in which the composer never surfaces overtly in his own right in the course of the entire story.

For other discourse types, we have to revert to the term COMPOSER as framer of the discourse. In procedural discourse, the hand of the composer (the giver of the procedures) is covert unless he wants to appeal to himself and his own prestige in order to give authority to the procedures. He may refer to himself by saying in effect _I did the following procedures and obtained the following results. Presumably if you follow these procedures you will also obtain the same results._ Or he may in effect say, _As a well-known practitioner of art Q, I give these procedures regarding art Q to you._ Somewhat the same situation holds regarding whether or not the composer surfaces in expository and hortatory discourse. In hortatory discourse the composer of the discourse is especially likely to get involved with his subject matter and his audience and to urge on them a certain course of conduct by virtue of the prestige invested in his person.

Actually, the role of the composer is much more pervasive than it might seem from the scattered comments of this section. I indicate the composer's role at several places in this volume. He has options on the clause level of encoding various cases as subject, or object, choice of active versus passive, and the like. He has certain options on the sentence level as to his choice of surface structure sentence pattern to encode a given notional structure. He likewise has the frequent option of whether he will encode something as a sentence or as a paragraph. All these stylistic decisions have a lot to do with the effectiveness of the overall discourse and all reflect the viewpoint of the composer. He also has the very important option of encoding something as main line or supportive--even though in approximately nine-tenths of the cases the situation is somewhat cut-and-dried and decided for him, e.g., by the situation depicted in a story.

4. PLOT AND SIMILAR STRUCTURES

I here get to the main point of this chapter, a point which it was impossible to make without first presenting a taxonomy of discourse material: distinguishing main line versus supportive material and discussing the role of the composer himself. But note what I have just said. I say that I here get to the main point of the chapter. This is an overt recognition on my part (as composer) that what I have said in previous sections is preparatory to what is in some sense a surface structure PEAK in the portion that is to follow. Furthermore, this peak occurs here in material which is expository rather than narrative, procedural, or hortatory. This is precisely why I say 'Plot and similar structures' in the head of this section. Something like plot characterizes forms of discourse other than narrative. If we grant that any discourse is going somewhere, it follows that it does not simply start and stop but that it may have some sort of culminative expression between.

Nevertheless, most of what I discuss in this section will have to do with the marking of surface structure peak in narrative discourse and how this relates to the general underlying structure of narration.

4.1 Plot as Notional Structure

I propose here that plot is the notional structure of narrative discourse in the same sense that case relations are the notional structure of the clause, and the expanded statement calculus is the notional structure of the sentence and paragraph, and repartee is the notional structure of dialogue paragraphs. To be sure, some plots may be in very low relief. Thus a first person account may be episodic, if not rambling. On the other hand, a well-written novel in third person may be episodic as well. By contrast, most types of narrative texts have a perceptible CLIMAX. What rhetoricians have since classical times identified as plot structure (originally for drama) necessarily involves such a climax. As suggested above, I would like to see plot used for the notional structure of narrative in general, even for those of episodic nature where the plot is in low relief due to absence of any perceptible climax.

The rhetorician's anatomy of plot[2] is the notional

structure of climactic narrative. Notional structure here, as everywhere, is not in necessary one-to-one correspondence with surface structure features. We should expect the surface structure to have features similar to those of the notional structure but to mark them less consistently. This is what we find. The accompanying diagram gives a suggested correlation of the notional and surface features of climactic narrative discourse. The notional structure given at the bottom of the chart is the rhetorician's scheme. The surface structure is given at the top of the chart. Arrows mark encoding of notional structure features into surface structure features. Notice that the title and formulaic aperture (<u>Once upon a time</u> . . .) are considered to be features of the surface only. The story, as regards its notional structure, gets underway with (1) Exposition, 'Lay it out'. Here crucial information of time, place, local color, and participants is given. With (2) Inciting Moment, 'Get something going', the planned and predictable is broken up in some manner. Thus a certain man has plodded faithfully to work for twenty-five years, passing certain points at hours so exact that people could have set their watches by him, but today he is one hour late--and thereby hangs a tale. With (3) Developing Conflict, 'Keep the heat on', the situation intensifies--or deteriorates--depending on one's viewpoint. (4) Climax, 'Knot it all up proper', is where everything comes to a head. Here is where the author really messes it up, brings in contradictions, and adds all sorts of tangles until confrontation is inevitable. With (5) Denouement, 'Loosen it', a crucial event happens which makes resolution possible. Things begin to loosen up. We see a way out--even if not to a happy ending. (6) Final Suspense, 'Keep untangling', works out details of the resolution. (7) Conclusion, 'Wrap it up', brings the story to some sort of decent--or indecent--end.

4.2 Correlation of Notional and Surface Features

The correlation of these notional structure features with the surface structure is our next consideration. Exposition often corresponds to a slot which we can call stage in the surface structure. Many times stage is expounded by an expository paragraph or even by a short embedded expository discourse. It may, however, be a subsidiary narrative of some length which is necessary to get the main narrative going. For Tolkien's trilogy, <u>The Lord of the Rings</u>, a

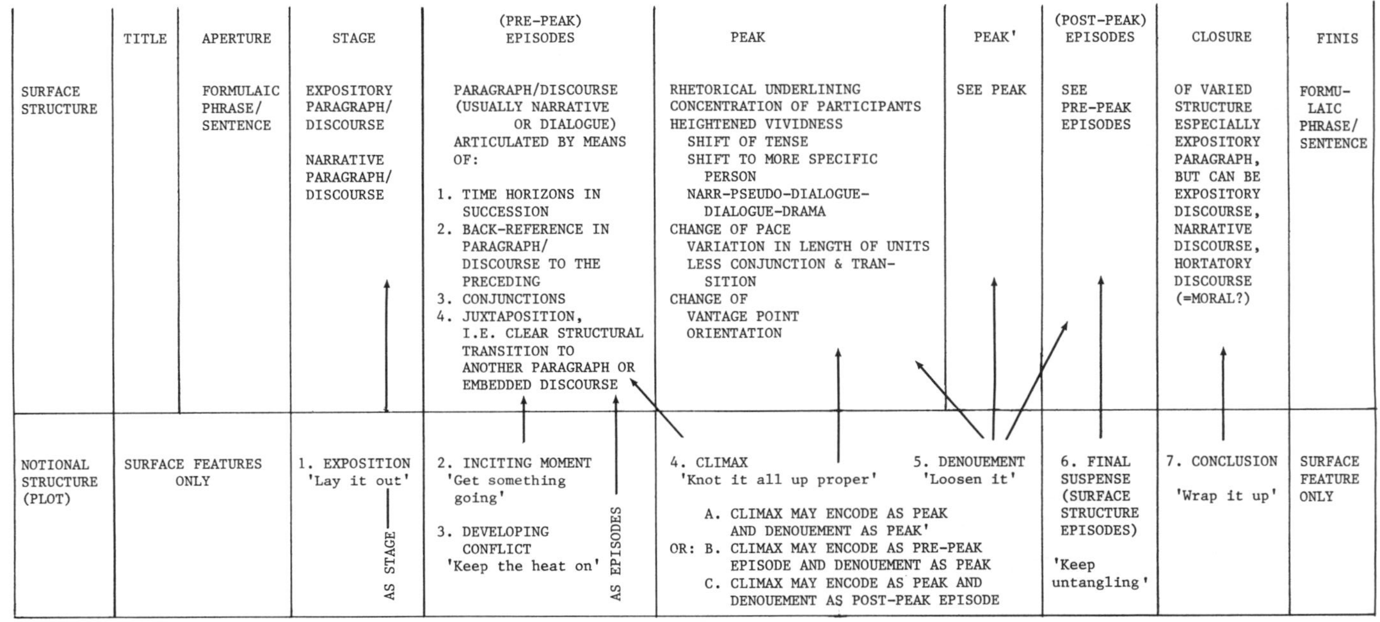

Diagram II. Narrative discourse with surface peak

complete narrative discourse of book length, _The Hobbit_, serves as stage.

Carl Sandburg's _Abraham Lincoln, the War Years_, Vol. 1 (of a four-volume work), has a chapter which begins the first volume but seems to serve as stage for the entire set. The chapter is significantly titled 'America--whither--?' and ends with a short paragraph _It was sunset and dawn, moonrise and noon, dying time and birthing hour, dry leaves of the last of autumn and springtime blossom roots. 'Nobody knows, everbody guesses.'_ Title and final sentence seem to tell us rather explicitly that this chapter is intended to be stage to the historical narrative which follows. The chapter is anecdotal throughout. This anecdotalism leads to a remarkable sentence (Sandburg 1939.1.8-12) which spans one long paragraph and mentions everything (in almost the literal sense of from soup to nuts) that might by the wildest stretch of the imagination be relevant to an understanding of America in the year 1861. The next paragraph after this long run-on one-sentence paragraph goes, _Thus might run a jagged sketch of the divided house over which Lincoln was to be chief magistrate_. The run-on sentence itself goes as follows: _Only tall stacks of documents recording the steel of fact and the fog of dream could tell the intricate tale of the shaping of a national fate, of men saying Yes when they meant No and No when they meant Perhaps; of newspapers North and South lying to their readers and pandering to the cheaper passions of party, clique, and class interest;. . . of abolitionists hanged, shot, stabbed, mutilated, disfigured facially by vitriol, their home doorways painted with human offal;. . . of automatic machinery slightly guided by human hands producing shoes, fabrics, scissors, pins, and imitation jewelries sold by a chain of Dollar Stores;. . . of women's household work lightened by labor-saving sewing machines, churns, egg beaters and like devices;. . . of lands, homesteads, fortunes and vast exploits of money and living waiting out yonder where the railroad whistle would shatter old solitudes;. . . of the clean and inexplicable mystic dream that lay in many humble hearts of an indissoluble Federal Union of States;. . . of the two hundred sixty thousand free Negroes of the South owning property valued at twenty five million dollars, one of them being the wealthiest landowner in Jefferson County, Virginia;. . . of the southern poor white often clutching as his dearest personal possession the fact that he was not born black;. . . of the Cotton States' delusion that New England and Europe were_ economic dependents of King Cotton;. . . etc. This is a truly remarkable sentence to which our sampling has not done justice. It contains many scattered observations about life in the United States at the beginning of 1861, about social issues, economic problems and storms and stresses in the body politic. This unparalled sentence--even in Sandburg--occurs here as part of the embedded discourse which expounds stage, and as a feature especially characterizing that surface structure slot.

Inciting Moment and Developing Conflict in the deep structure, i.e., the plot, usually encode as surface structure Episodes each expounded by a paragraph or an embedded discourse--although Stage may run into Inciting Moment in a very brief narrative. Inciting Moment is, however, set off from Stage by virtue of the onset of the event line with its characteristic tense. Thus, in a story in Spanish the Stage is characterized by verbs in the imperfect tense while the Inciting Moment is set off from Stage by virtue of the onset of the event line with its characteristic tense, the preterit. Keith Beavon (1979) reports that peak-like features characterize the Inciting Moment in one genre of Konzime (Cameroun) narration.

I use the term PEAK to refer to any episode-like unit set apart by special surface structure features and corresponding to the Climax or Denouement in the notional structure. Where the surface structure distinguishes two such surface units which encode both of these notional structure units, I posit Peak (Climax) versus Peak (Denouement). Climax and/or Denouement may, however, be marked in no special way in the surface structure, but may on the contrary simply encode as further surface structure episodes. When both are unmarked, the surface structure of the narrative is EPISODIC even though there are climax and denouement in the notional (plot) structure.

Apparently, some stories may have a didactic (or thematic) Peak, as well as an action Peak. Francis Woods (1980) posits this in reference to a Halbi (India) myth. Likewise, in the Genesis flood account, while there is an action Peak in Genesis 7:17-24 (where the flood waters come to crest), there is a didactic Peak in Genesis 9:1-17 (the covenant and blessing) (Longacre 1979a). A didactic Peak is a special elaboration of some episode which precedes or follows the action Peak. The action Peak is simply termed Peak in the rest of this section where it refers to a surface structure episode that correlates with either the climax or the denouement of the notional structure.

The Final Suspense encodes as one or more post-Peak Episodes while Conclusion is more likely to have special marking in the surface structure--often some non-narrative paragraph or discourse, it is typically a special moral slot in a special subtype of narrative discourse. The (formulaic) Finis is considered to be a feature only of the surface. The latter may be a formulaic sentence like _That's all_; _We're through_ or even the printed word _Finis_.

4.3 Marking of the Surface Structure Peak

It is especially crucial that we be able to recognize the peak when such a marked element occurs in the surface structure. We can then identify pre-peak Episodes and post-peak Episodes and can consequently articulate a considerable amount of the surface structure of the narrative. If, furthermore, the surface structure marks not only a Peak (corresponding to notional structure Climax) but also a Peak' (corresponding to notional structure Denouement), we are in even a better position to unravel the surface structure of the text. While the accompanying chart indicates both Peak and Peak' in the surface structure, I will describe these jointly except when it seems that there is evidence for separating them in referring to a given short story, novel, or folk tale. As we shall see, the features that mark Peak and Peak' are drawn from the same bag of tricks.

Peak (and Peak') essentially is a zone of turbulence in regard to the flow of the discourse in the preceding and following parts of the discourse. Routine features of the event-line may be distorted or phased out at Peak. Thus, the characteristic event-line tense/aspect may be substituted for by another tense/aspect. Alternatively, the characteristic tense/aspect of the main line of a discourse may be extended to unexpected uses at Peak. Particles which elsewhere mark rather faithfully the event-line of a story may suddenly be absent. Routine participant reference may be disturbed. In brief, Peak has features peculiar to itself and the marking of such features takes precedence over the marking of the main line--so that the absence of certain features or even analytical difficulties can be a clue that we are at the Peak of a discourse.

There are also, however, some peculiar features of Peak--not just minus features and distortion--which are here described in their own right.

Before discussing these features, it is important to note that we must be prepared to find in narrative structure from all over the world, well-told stories with well-defined plots which use no special device to mark a surface strucure Peak. We must be prepared to find such structures not only in folk tales from various parts of the world, but in Western European literature as well. _Great Expectations_ by Charles Dickens is probably a novel without special marking at Peak. Its style forms a clear contrast with the very different style of _A Tale of Two Cities_, which is commonly referred to as Dickens' most dramatic novel. I believe that the distinction is that _Great Expectations_ is essentially episodic in its surface structure, while _A Tale of Two Cities_ very clearly marks both the climax and the denouement as Peak and Peak' in its surface structure.

4.3.1 _Rhetorical underlining_. The narrator does not want you to miss the important point of the story so he employs extra words at that point. He may employ parallelism, paraphrase, and tautologies of various sorts to be sure that you don't miss it. A colleague of mine was taking a course in creative writing at the University of Michigan. Her professor once said, 'At this point in the story I want more words. It goes by too fast.' Let us call this device RHETORICAL UNDERLINING. It's as if you took a pencil and underlined certain lines of what you are writing.

I'm thinking of two Mixe texts (recorded by Willard Van Haitsma which he studied in a Mexican linguistic workshop). One text looked as if it had some sort of climax and/ or denouement in its plot structure. It had to do with a certain man who went through a series of vicissitudes and eventually emerged as king--whatever king means to the Mixes who have borrowed this story from Europe. But Van Haitsma as consultee and I as consultant argued repeatedly about where the surface structure peak should be in the story. There was another Mixe story which is a fairly mundane story from our point of view as aliens to that culture, but which the Mixes like quite well. This story has a point in it where the man goes out into the woods and composes a song.

We are told this several times in the same paragraph and then in the next paragraph we are told the whole thing over again once more. It appears that here is a surface structure peak which is marked very clearly. What to us is unexciting, to the Mixe is exciting. Apparently this second story has a surface structure peak while the first story is episodic in its surface structure--whatever we make of its plot structure.

A very striking example of rhetorical underlining occurs in the Hebrew text of the Genesis Flood Narrative (Gen. 7:17-24). In a very graphic passage the ever-mounting, ever-abounding flood waters are described. Finally, even the tops of high mountains are covered. A great deal of paraphrase and paraphrase within paraphrase is employed. What is striking, however, is that much of this paraphrase is presented in clauses whose verbs have the characteristic narrative tense and the word-order of event-line clauses. Elsewhere (cf. e.g. the text of Ruth) event-line verbs are not used in a paraphrase of an event. Here, however, at the Peak of the story, the characteristic event-line tense is extended to supportive materials--thus, giving the impression of amplifying and expanding the event-line. The effect is somewhat like slowing up the camera at the high point of a film (Longacre 1979a).

The importance of rhetorical underlining must not be underestimated. It is one of the simplest and most universal devices for marking the important point not only of a narration but of other sorts of discourse as well.

4.3.2 Concentration of participants. One hallmark of Peak (often encoding notional structure climax) is the crowded stage. Think of a Shakespearean play where at the dramatic height of the play everybody except very subsidiary characters are on stage; the stage is crowded, there is a lot going on. This we can see in a novel such as A Tale of Two Cities by Dickens where the Peak (deep structure Climax) is the second trial of Charles Darnay (including the reading of a long letter as evidence). Every important character is there and some lesser characters: Charles Darnay, his father-in-law, his wife, Madame Defarge, her husband, 'Vengeance', Mr. Lorry, Barsad, and Sydney Carton, who becomes the hero of the story. Only a few lesser characters, e.g., Miss Pross, are not at the trial scene. In using this device the author moves from few participants to more participants so that often the concentration of participants at Peak approximates the universal set. This would seem to be a device restricted to narrative and to drama.

4.3.3 _Heightened vividness_. Heightened vividness may be obtained in a story by a shift in the nominal/verbal balance, by a tense shift, by shift to a more specific person, or by shift along the narrative-drama parameter (see below).

(1) There may be a shift in the nominal/verbal balance. Thus for Ga'dang (Philippines) M. Walrod reports (1977) that in the narrative texts which he has analyzed, there is an over all ratio of one verb to seven non-verbs (mainly nouns). At the Peak of the Ga'dang folktales, however, there is a proportion of one verb to three non-verbs. This reflects the relatively full and fast-moving event line at the Peak.

(2) A shift in surface structure tense may occur. There is a Fore (Papua New Guinea) folk tale 'Small People can be Useful' (Scott 1973), in which a monster which was eating the sugar cane is destroyed by two small dwarfs who shoot him full of arrows. There are far past, recent past, past, present, and future tenses in the Fore language. The story starts off in the far past tense, _a long time ago_. As it proceeds and as the plot thickens, there's a shift into the recent past. Right at the notional structure Climax of the story it shifts into present tense and then at the conclusion of the story we're told _that's how it happened a long time ago_--where the far past tense is again employed.

In Kosna (also Papua New Guinea) this happens too. Here, as in Fore, the tense shift happens only in formal legend as opposed to informal first person narrative which has no such shift. In informal first person narrative there is usually recent past or remote past according to whether a person is telling a story of recent events or of something that happened in his earlier years.

A Tale of Two Cities has a tense shift at a great moment of the story. After the trial and after Sydney Carton has taken the place of Charles Darnay in jail, the drugged Darnay and his family are fleeing in the stagecoach from Paris. Suddenly we find that the story is in the present tense. This adds vividness and excitement and here marks a Peak' which encodes part of the notional structure

Denouement of the story. We can thus distinguish Peak (Climax) from Peak' (Denouement) in the surface structure of *A Tale of Two Cities*.

The House of Seven Gables uses a very similar device. As Judge Pyncheon sits dead in the parlor of the house, suddenly the story shifts into the present tense: *Judge Pyncheon . . . still sits in the old parlor . . . . The Judge has not shifted his position for a long while now. He has not stirred hand or foot . . . . He holds his watch in his left hand . . . .* Present tenses and perfectives here mark a Peak which encodes notional structure Denouement--since Climax, unmarked in the surface structure, encodes simply as a pre-Peak Episode.

Note that I have here documented a device used for marking surface structure Peak of a story both in the oral literature of Papua New Guinea and in English and American literature. This is typical of the set of devices here described. They apparently are a universal bag of tricks available to the story teller for marking peak of the story.

(3) Heightened vividness may also be obtained by a shift to a more specific person, i.e., the shift is from third person to second person to first person, or from plural to singular within a given person.[3]

This shift occurs not only in narrative but in certain procedural texts which likewise mark Peak. Some types of procedural discourses have a deep structure TARGET PROCEDURE to which the whole text is directed. The target procedure, however, may not be marked in the surface structure, just as the Climax or Denouement of a climactic narrative is not necessarily marked in its surface structure. Where the target procedure is marked as surface structure Peak we have a phenomenon not dissimilar from that found in narrative discourse. Thus, in Dibabawon (Southern Philippines) Game Procurement texts (Longacre 1978, vol. 3) we find that person shifts correlate in some texts with the onset of Peak. One such text runs: *We (inclusive), when we go to shoot fish... We do this, we do that ... and then when you see it you spear it.* Here there is a shift to second person right at the Target Procedure--where you actually spear the fish. Another such text runs: *The bird hunters among the Dibabawon, they do so and so, they make certain preparations ... . They build a bird blind ... . And then he shoots the bird.*

Again, at the point of actually obtaining the game there is a shift from third person plural to third person singular. Such shifts are not always this exact. They are somewhat approximate. They tend to occur, however, somewhere around the Peak of the procedures.

Now, to go back to *A Tale of Two Cities* by Charles Dickens, right at that crucial scene where they are fleeing from Paris, about halfway through the section suddenly we find that we (the readers) are there in the stagecoach, too: *Houses in twos and threes pass by us* .... *The hard, uneven pavement is under us* .... *Sometimes, we strike into the skirting mud* .... Here we have not only present tense (as previously noted) but first person plural inclusive as well. The whole section ends up: *The wind is rushing after us and the clouds are flying after us, and the moon is plunging after us, and the whole wild night is in pursuit of us, but so far we are pursued by nothing else.* This is the only spot in the whole novel where *we* is used to take the reader to the scene of the action itself. Here, the person shift reinforces the tense shift in marking the Peak' (Denouement).

Likewise, to refer again to *The House of Seven Gables*, at the point where we have the shift to present tense there is also a person shift, i.e., Hawthorne begins to address the dead Judge Pyncheon as he sits in his chair: *Why Judge, it is already two hours* .... *Pray, pray, Judge Pyncheon, look at your watch now* .... *Up, therefore, Judge Pyncheon, up! Canst thou not brush the fly away? Art thou too sluggish?* .... Thus, for about twelve pages, Hawthorne heckles the dead judge.

(4) The fourth device for marking vividness involves a shift along a parameter with four ordered values:

NARR → PSEUDO-DIAL → DIALOGUE → DRAMA

By pseudo-dialogue I mean resort to such devices as apostrophe (cf. the Governor Pyncheon passage above) and rhetorical question which partake of certain features of dialogue without being true dialogue. Use of such features gives us a value intermediate between narration and dialogue itself, just as dialogue itself is intermediate between pseudo-dialogue and drama.

Rhetorical question may be used with effect at the peak

of a story. For instance, the Wojokeso folk tale 'Woodchip' (West 1973) marks its Peak (deep structure Climax) by a rather long paragraph which contains a rhetorical question _Now why did he do that?_ and the answer _He did it because_ .... There is also considerable parallelism and paraphrase within this paragraph so it also has the feature of rhetorical underlining. Since these features are not found elsewhere in the story, presumably the combined resort to rhetorical question and to accompanying rhetorical underlining marks a surface structure Peak (Climax) while, as we will see later on, a further device marks surface structure Peak' (Denouement) in this same folk tale.

To refer yet again to the chapter "Governor Pyncheon" of _The House of Seven Gables_ (part of the Peak' of that novel), I have counted 53 rhetorical questions in that chapter. The next to the last paragraph of the chapter is a series of eight such rhetorical questions; only the terminal sentence of the paragraph is not a rhetorical question. So here sits Judge Pyncheon dead in the chair and Hawthorne is bombarding him with a barrage of rhetorical questions which the man isn't in any condition to answer. The intensity of this barrage of rhetorical questions is exceeded only by the book of Job--whose Peak in Chapters 38 to 41 consists largely of such questions.

The shift however may be not to pseudo-dialogue, but to dialogue. We may be in a story (characteristically a rather short discourse) in which there is no dialogue until the Peak is reached. In such stories the onset of dialogue itself signals the surface structure Peak. Such a short story is "Michael Egerton" by Reynolds Price. There is no dialogue, no direct speech at all until the Peak of the story where there is a stretch of dialogue. Some of the miracle stories of the New Testament have similar structure. This is the structure of the short embedded discourses, 'The Feeding of the Five Thousand' (Matthew 14:13-21) and 'The Feeding of the Four Thousand' (Matthew 15:29-39). In both cases the notional structure of the narrative is Episode, Climax, Denouement, while the corresponding surface structures are Episode, Peak, and Peak'. Climax is marked by the dialogue between Jesus and His disciples in which He makes the impossible suggestion to them that they feed the multitude from their own resources and in which a confrontation of sorts ensues.

A story, however, which has had previous dialogue in it can shift to drama at its Peak. Drama, as I have said, is a very vivid style of discourse in which quotation formulas drop out and people speak out in multiple I-thou relations. *The Open Boat* by Stephen Crane, close to its Climax (where the boat founders), has a stretch of drama. Here we are not told that B said so and so to A or that A said so and so to B. The various characters simply speak out one to the other. Only what they say gives clue as to who might have spoken it.

All the above instances of shifts along the narrative-drama parameter are right shifts. M. Larson (1978) has called to my attention, however, the fact that left shifts in this parameter can also occur. Thus, an Aguaruna (Peru) narrative can have dialogue right up to the peak and phase out dialogue at peak. This can be compared to a cinema story (cf., e.g. *Jaws*) where at the Peak there is no dialogue--only action.

4.3.4 *Change of pace*. The chief devices here are variation in the size of constructions and variation in the amount of connective material.

Variation in the sheer length of units (clauses, sentences, paragraphs, embedded discourse) may be important. Thus we may find at the Peak of a story a shift to short, fragmentary, crisp sentences, which emphasize the change of pace. Quite as likely, however, is the opposite development, i.e., a shift to a long run-on open type of sentence structure. Thus in Wojokeso, in the folk legend "Woodchip" which has already been referred to, the Peak' which encodes denouement (as opposed to the Peak which encodes Climax) consists of a paragraph whose second sentence is twice as long as any found previously in the entire story. It is necessary to keep in mind here that in Wojokeso (as in many Papua New Guinea languages) the sentence is unambiguously marked as to its close by the occurrence of a peculiar structure, the final verb, found nowhere else in the sentence. There is then no doubt that we have here a genuine contrast in length of sentence structure and not a mere trick of punctuation. This has a parallel in a procedural text in Wojokeso, 'Housebuilding' (West 1973), whose Peak (target procedure) consists of a single sentence which is likewise far longer than any previous sentence in the entire discourse. Normally a procedural paragraph consists of a series of steps, each of which is expounded by a sentence of no more than seven or eight lines in length at the most. Here, by contrast, all the steps are run together into the same surface structure sentence.

Hemingway's short story, "The Short Happy Life of Francis Macomber", uses the same device in English (pointed out to me by Charles Green). Run-on sentences of rollicking structure and length characterize the latter part of this story. Take the following where Macomber shoots his first buffalo: The car was going a wild forty-five miles an hour across the open and as Macomber watched, the buffalo got bigger and bigger until he could see the gray, hairless, scabby look of one huge bull and how his neck was a part of his shoulders and the shiny black of his horns as he galloped a little behind the others that were strung out in that steady plunging gait; and then, the car swaying as though it had just jumped a road, they drew up close and he could see the plunging hugeness of the bull, and the dust in his sparsely haired hide, the wild boss of horn and his outstretched wide-nostrilled muzzle, and he was raising his rifle when Wilson shouted, "Not from the car, you fool!" and he had no fear, only hatred of Wilson, while the brakes clamped on and the car skidded, plowing sideways to an almost stop and Wilson was out on one side and he on the other, stumbling as his feet hit the still speeding-by of the earth, and then he was shooting at the bull as he moved away, hearing the bullets whunk into him, emptying his rifle into him as he moved steadily away, finally remembering to get his shots forward into the shoulder, and as he fumbled to reload, he saw the bull was down (1938.126-7). A similar sentence occurs reporting the death of Macomber: Wilson, who was ahead was kneeling shooting, and Macomber, as he fired, unhearing his shot in the roar of Wilson's gun, saw fragments like slate burst from the huge boss of the horns, and the head jerked, he shot again at the wide nostrils and saw the horns jolt again and fragments fly, and he did not see Wilson now and, aiming carefully, shot again with the buffalo's huge bulk almost on him and his rifle almost level with the oncoming head, nose out, and he could see the little wicked eyes and the head started to lower and he felt a sudden white-hot, blinding flash explode inside his head and that was all he ever felt (1938.134-5).

The same device is used to mark the Peak' (Denouement) of the account of the Feeding of the Five Thousand in Matthew 14:19. It is not unusual in narrative portions of the Greek New Testament to find a participle or two at the beginning of a Greek sentence. One participle, often taking up or summarizing the content of a previous sentence, is the more usual situation. It is startling then to find in the verse just mentioned in the Gospel according to Matthew a rather long pile-up of participles at the beginning of the verse. I'll try to give somewhat the flavor of the Greek text in the over-literal and awkward translation which follows: *And ordering the multitude to recline on the grass, taking the five loaves and the two fishes, looking up toward heaven, he blessed them, and breaking them, he gave the loaves to the disciples and the disciples to the multitude.* Here the pile-up of participles *ordering*, *taking*, *looking up*, and then *breaking* before the next main verb is impressive. It results in a run-on style which creates a certain feeling of suspense as we wait for the unfolding of the main verb. It is similar in principle to the run-on sentences of Papua New Guinea and the sentences we have noted from Hemingway. Here it is interesting to see fundamentally the same device used in a Papua New Guinea culture, in the Greek New Testament of the first century A.D., and in contemporary American short story writing.

Peak may be marked not simply by a sentence or sentences of unusual length, but by paragraphs of unusual length as well. We may even find a long embedded discourse at Peak. While any string of paragraphs which belong together form by definition an embedded discourse, the surface structure peak may be marked by an explicitly quoted embedded discourse such as a letter, speech, or sermon. Thus the surface structure Peak (notional structure Climax) of *A Tale of Two Cities* is the second trial of Charles Darnay. The story of this trial is recounted in what is implicitly an embedded discourse. But the Peak of this embedded discourse is the reading of a long letter written by a former prisoner in the Bastille. This long letter occupies about sixteen pages of the novel and sheds much light on obscure corners of the previous story. As Peak of the embedded discourse (trial scene) it also marks Peak of the novel itself (just as Akron is the highest point in Summit County which in turn is the highest county in northern Ohio). This is likewise a favorite device of Ayn Rand's (cf. *Fountainhead*, *Atlas Shrugged*), i.e., the marking of a Peak (here didactic) of a novel by a rather lengthy speech by the main character.

A further device for changing the pace within a story

and thus marking transition to Peak is a stylistic change from the use of more conjunction and transition to less conjunction and transition. Thus in Ilianen Manobo oral literature (data from Hazel Wrigglesworth), a typical story such as "The Story of Ukap" (Longacre 1968, Part 3) starts out in a very deliberate way with a lot of conjunctions and long conjunctive complexes which carefully mark transitions within the story and balance the action of one character against the actions of others. About-two thirds of the way through the story this feature fades out and very few conjunctions are used for the balance of the story. Rather, simple juxtaposition of sentence with sentence and paragraph with paragraph is found. There is a perceptible change in the pace of the whole story in that where we once had deliberate and overt transition, we now have implicit and covert transition between the main parts of the story, which now rolls on swiftly toward its end.

4.3.5 *Change of vantage point and/or orientation.* I discuss here two somewhat related matters for which I have not been able to find a common taxonomic label.

There may be a change in what I call vantage point. I do not mean by this, viewpoint in the sense of sympathy with a character of a story. I mean, rather, by whom do we stand, through whose eyes do we view the story? This matter has already been mentioned in connection with discourse genre, in that we mentioned that some third person discourses have a rather neutral vantage point and others have a specific vantage point. It's time now to go into this more in detail. Let us suppose a story about Peter, Paul, and Mary. In this story we find such sentences as : *Peter and Mary come to Paul* ... . *Peter and Mary go from Paul* ... . *Peter and Mary bring things to Paul* ... . *Peter and Mary take things away from Paul* ... . *Peter and Mary become visible to Paul* ... . *Peter and Mary pass out of the sight of Paul* ... . Furthermore, we are told the inner thoughts of Paul but not the inner thoughts of Peter and Mary. In such a story you can almost draw vector lines to Paul from Peter and Mary. He is the focal person. What I'm proposing here is that while a story may consistently hold to one vantage point throughout, it is not unusual to find shifts in vantage point or even a shift from a neutral point to a specific vantage point. Such a shift most naturally occurs somewhere near Peak of the story and consequently helps mark this Peak in the surface structure.

The Open Boat by Stephen Crane, a story already referred to, has four men adrift in a small boat. A ship has sunk. At first we are not certain if any one of the four is singled out for vantage point. As the story progresses, however, we get hints that the correspondent may be more focal than the other three because we're occasionally told something of what the correspondent is thinking. By contrast, we have to infer from the actions and facial expressions of the other three what they are thinking. Finally, when we get to the point of the story where they beach the ship and make for land, where one person drowns and three get through including the correspondent, at that point we're very sure that the correspondent is focal in the story. The clue here is the use of verbs referring to motion and visibility: (1) The captain passed by him floating on a piece of wood. (2) The shore became visible to him. (3) The carpenter passed out of sight and drowned. Furthermore, now we're told extensively and in detail the thoughts which flashed through the mind of the correspondent. This overt shift to the vantage point of the correspondent partially marks the Peak of the story. Furthermore, this can be documented (not simply impressionistically asserted) by attention to specific verbs of the sort here cited. We are looking in fact all through this section for things that we can put our thumb on as overt features in the surface structure of the narrative.

A short story, "Indian Justice" by Freyre (translated from Spanish by Colford), illustrates change of vantage point. The story has to do with two travelers on the Altiplano of Bolivia who are personae non gratae with the Indians of that region because they have wrested lands from the Indians. The story starts out with the Indians coming to the two travelers or going from them. Likewise things appear to them and things disappear from them. Clearly the travelers are the vantage point of the early part of the story. Finally at the end of the story, the Indians are the vantage point and the travelers are passive as they are brought in to the waiting Indians, tortured, and killed. Here shift in vantage point marks the Peak' (Denouement); the Peak (Climax) is otherwise marked. The shift in vantage point here correlates with the phenomenon of role reversal in which the victims become the persecutors and the persecutors become the victims. But a shift in vantage point and role reversal are not to be identified as the same feature. Thus we can have role reversal in a story in which the vantage point is held constant or in which the vantage point is neutral.

Let's look now at what for want of a better name I call Orientation. By Orientation I largely mean what is encoded as surface structure subject. Most languages can encode more than one deep structure case as surface structure subject. In Narrative, very commonly the agent is encoded as subject and the patient is encoded as object. One sort of shift that can occur--the phenomenon of role reversal already referred to--simply involves switching the particular dramatis personae which occur as subject (agent) and object (patient). Thus, a story which starts out with a certain character A as subject (agent) and another character B as object (patient) can end up with B as subject (agent) and A as object (patient). As already mentioned, this results in the victim becoming the aggressor and the former aggressor becoming the victim at the Peak of the story. This is very common. There may also be other shifts, however, e.g. A as subject (agent) and B as object (patient) may be shifted so that B becomes subject (patient) and A drops into the background.

Shift of orientation frequently involves, however, not just a shifting about of participants between subject and object slots in the surface structure, but in something other than an animate participant being encoded as subject. Some very special effects can be achieved in this fashion. Thus, instrument as surface structure subject can be used effectively to picture impersonal forces closing in on the main characters of the story. In the story 'Indian Justice' by Freyre we are told that <u>the horn continues to blow</u>, although of course someone is blowing it; we're told that <u>boulders come crashing down</u>, although presumably someone is pushing the boulders down off the hilltop; and we're even told that the two men felt as if they were being carried along by forces beyond their control. There is no doubt that the encoding of instrument as subject has a lot to do with the feeling of threat and menace created in this part of the story (surface structure Peak, notional structure Climax). In 'A Field of Rice' by Pearl Buck, at the Peak (Climax) of the story there is a shift to the encoding of patient and location as surface structure subject. Consequently <u>the rice</u>, <u>the seed</u>, <u>the ricefield</u>, <u>the ground</u>, <u>the clay bottom</u> become subject. This is precisely at the point of tension in the story where the rice crop is failing because it has been planted wrongly under the influence of the

Commissar.

4.3.6 Incidence of particles and onomatopoeia. The Peak of narrative discourse may also be marked by (a) loss of characteristic particles which normally go with the event-line, and/or (b) introduction of new particles or an increase in the incidence of particles found earlier in the discourse.

Thus, in Ga'dang, Walrod reports (1977) that kanu (disclaimer of responsibility, 'so they say') regularly occurs on the event-line clauses of narratives, but drops out at Peak. Since such particles are common in most Philippine languages their possible use in a function parallel to that found in Ga'dang should be investigated.

In Guanano, jana roughly translated 'finally', occurs sporadically in routine discourse (where it has sentence-level and paragraph level functions) but is much more frequent at the Peak.

It is not uncommon to find onomatopoetic expressions restricted to or occurring with special frequency at Peak. In folktales in Indian languages of Colombia, Ecuador, and Panama, words such as Zap!, Bang!, and Wham! are especially characteristic of Peak. In quite similar fashion some popular first-person accounts , e.g., truck-driver English (data from J.M. Lewis) may have a mounting incidence of profanity and obscenity as they approach the Peak of a story.

4.4 Similar Structures

Plot in the strictest sense of the word should be reserved for the notional structure of climatic narrative, i.e., narrative where some sort of confrontation and resolution take place. But I have broadened the term plot to include low profile plots in which there is no such structure but rather a string of episodes proceeding from episode 1 to episode n. I have also referred several times to the structure of procedural discourse. There are plot-like elements in procedural discourse. We may think of the whole procedural discourse as reflecting a struggle to accomplish the goal of discourse, to carry through an activity, or to produce a product. In place of Climax and Denouement we have target procedure. Now it is time to raise the question as to whether there are plot-like elements in the structure of expository and hortatory discourse as well.

It seems evident to me that an expository discourse of the better sort reflects a certain struggle, a struggle to achieve clarity in the face of recalcitrant elements in the subject itself and possibly in the lack of background on the part of those who are to hear the discourse. Exposition of the better sort is able to clarify the main outlines of its subject in spite of these difficulties within the subject matter and within the receptors. Hortatory discourse is likewise a struggle. Here, however, the struggle is to convince the hearers of the soundness of the advice and to launch them on the course of conduct advocated or to discourage them from a course of conduct which is being proscribed. It would seem therefore that an artful expository or hortatory discourse will have a meaningful cumulative thrust. This should correlate in at least some discourses with a marked surface structure Peak. I believe that of the various devices available for marking of surface structure Peak in expository and hortatory discourse, rhetorical underlining is probably the most frequently used. I have, however, heard at least one sermon in which there was effective shift to dialogue and eventually to drama at the end of the sermon (with the preacher assuming various parts in turn).

The First Epistle of St. John has been notoriously hard to outline, yet whatever the admitted subtleties of its content structure, the surface structure of the Greek text is rather straightforward. Paragraph onset is very frequently marked with a vocative word such as _my little children_ or _beloved_. The book comes to a Peak in chapter 4 verses 7 through 21. The Peak is marked by rhetorical underlining much as in the Mixe text which was discussed earlier. Actually, the passage referred to consists of two surface structure paragraphs, the first, verses 7-10, and the second, verses 11-21. Use of the vocative _beloved_ marks the onset of each paragraph. The first short paragraph makes three essential points: _let us love_, _God is love_, and _God's love was manifested in sending His only Son into the world_. These thoughts so simply stated are elaborated in great detail in the following paragraph (verses 11-21) with addition of further material. In the second and longer paragraph, the three thoughts of the first paragraph are given in the order one, three, two, instead of in the original order. Thus we are told in verse 11 ... _we ought to love one another_. We are told in verse 14 _We have seen and bear witness that the_

Father sent His Son to be the Savior of the world, the same thought which is echoed down in verse 16 *We have known and believed the love that God has toward us*. Finally, the second main thought of the first paragraph occurs in the second half of verse 16, *God is love*. The remaining verses of the chapter reinforce the command to love and echo again the third main thought of the first short paragraph. While I have long had the intuitive feeling that this passage in the First Epistle of John was the heart of the book, we now can explain this in a formal way by resort to the notion of Peak marked with rhetorical underlining.

To go somewhat further afield we might try to look for a marked Peak in poetry rather than in prose. The poem 'Mr. Bleaney' by Philip Larkin is in some sense an expository discourse. The vantage point is that of a man who has come to take the room formerly occupied by Mr. Bleaney. He lies in the very bed where Mr. Bleaney lay and he stubs his cigarettes on the same souvenir saucer. He puts cotton wool into his ears to drown out the sound of the TV set which Mr. Bleaney had prevailed on the landlady to buy. He professes considerable knowledge of Mr. Bleaney's habits and preferences. All this is expressed in sentences of fair to middling length and rather straightforward or at least run-on structures. Then we come to the last two stanzas of the poem which run as follows:

> *But if he stood and watched the frigid wind*
> *Tousling the clouds, lay on the fusty bed*
> *Telling himself that this was home, and grinned,*
> *And shivered, without shaking off the dread*
> *That how we live measures our own nature,*
> *And at his age having no more to show*
> *Than one hired box should make him pretty sure*
> *He warranted no better, I don't know.*

To begin with, this is the longest sentence found in the poem. The eight lines compose one sentence unit. The only sentence of similar length, one of six lines, occurs at the end of the fourth stanza and runs through the fifth stanza.

> *I know his habits--what time he came down,*
> *His preference for sauce to gravy, why*
> *He kept on plugging at the four aways--*
> *Likewise their yearly frame: the Frinton folk*

Who put him up for summer holidays
And Christmas at his sister's house in Stoke.

This sentence, though long, is fairly straightforward as to its structure. I know his habits (with elision of I know before the habits are ticked off) namely what time he came down, his preference for sauce to gravy, why he kept on plugging at the four aways, and likewise their yearly frame. Yearly frame, in turn, is explained in terms of where he went for summer holidays and for Christmas. This is a run-on sentence of loose structure in which elements occurring toward the end are appositional expansions of elements which occur earlier. By contrast, the two-stanza sentence at the end of the poem is a tightly knit structure. It is really an indirect question sentence of inverted structure, i.e., something on the order of I don't know whether/if he did so and so or not. The long embedded section which expounds the quotation slot of the indirect question has the structure of a coordinate sentence in which stood and watched are grouped together along with lay and grinned and shivered. Shivered is qualified with a manner phrase without shaking off the dread and dread is in turn expanded with the words that how we live measures our own nature and at his age having no more to show than one hired box should make him pretty sure he warranted no better which is again a coordinated structure. The embedded structure from if to the word better becomes increasingly more involved and elaborated only to have us brought up short and rude with the words I don't know at the end. The whole thing has almost a Shakespearean roll. But the point I am making here is that we have a surface Peak marked not simply with a sentence slightly longer than any previous sentence of the poem, but with a sentence whose structural complexity is unparalleded by any previous sentence. Here length, reinforced with grammatical complexity (and permutation of the usual linear order) rhetorically underlines the surface structure Peak of the poem. In our examination of rhetorical underlining in prose above, we mention only paraphrase and repetition as the device used. Here it appears that sheer grammatical complexity can also function for the same purpose.

NOTES

1 While I have previously thought of vividness in terms of psychological impact, Tim Wilt has suggested to me that

it might better be understood in terms of the sheer variety of grammatical construction that is possible in a given type. By this standard, drama--which is dialogue accompanied by action--offers the greatest variety. Narrative also intrinsically offers more variety than hortatory discourse

2 I'm indebted here to Thrall, Hibbard, and Holman (1961) for the particular form of the scheme which is given, but the antecedent tradition goes back to classic times.

3 It seems plausible that the shifts here indicated proceed from low to high according to the agency hierarchy as formulated by Silverstein (1976). Clearly, any shift from third person to second person to first person is along such a hierarchy, and possibly shifts from plural to singular could also be included in the same overall arrangement. It seems that the familiar device of personifying animals and giving them human traits could be essentially the same feature, since animals rate lower than human beings on the agency hierarchy. However, personification of animals seems to run through entire stories, while here we are simply considering ways of shifting to an entity higher on the agency hierarchy as a way of marking Peak.

CHAPTER 2

REPARTEE

One of the most intricate problems in discourse analysis is that concerning the relation of dialogue to monologue. The viewpoint taken here is that the two are related but somewhat autonomous structures. The units of dialogue as described here are: utterance, exchange, dialogue paragraph, and dialogue or dramatic discourse, i.e., a conversation on a given topic. The units of monologue (as described in Chapter 7) are: morpheme, stem, word, phrase, clause, sentence, paragraph, and discourse. In relating the two types of structuring we note that: (1) The utterance is the unit bounded by what a single speaker says. As such, it is the unit which is relevant to turn-taking, repair, and other concerns of the student of live conversation (Sacks, Schegloff and Jefferson 1974; Schegloff 1979). (2) The utterance can be of any monologue size unit from morpheme to discourse. (3) An exchange--e.g., a question and answer--can involve interplay of various size units, for example, a sentence-size question can be answered by a single morpheme e.g., "No!" or by a whole discourse, e.g., by a narrative: _Well, here's what happened yesterday_.... (4) Just as a dialogue can include a monologue, so a monologue can include, i.e., report, a dialogue. (5) On the paragraph and discourse levels there are various sorts of dialogue paragraphs (as described here) and various sorts of monologue paragraphs (Longacre 1979c). There are dialogue discourses (conversation, drama) and there are monologue discourses. To repeat the viewpoint taken here: dialogue and monologue are kept as separate lines of development which intersect in many diverse ways (cf. Chapter 6).

We must not underestimate the importance of dialogue to the structure of language. How, for example, can we ever explain the so-called minor or fragmentary sentences that

Bloomfield and others have catalogued aside from recourse to dialogue? From one point of view, sentences such as the following are defective: _In the kitchen_, _Yesterday_, _Yes_; but as answers to questions in the context of dialogue, they are in no sense anomalous:

(1) _Where is the cook?_
In the kitchen.

(2) _When did you arrive?_
Yesterday.

(3) _Are you going today?_
Yes.

However, the importance of dialogue is not just that it helps us explain a few apparent anomalies. Rather we must view dialogue as a basic function of language: viz., conversational interchange between people, communication. Seen from this point of view it is monologue that is the special development. Prolonged self expression in which one person speaks to a group of people who take the passive role of hearers is clearly a secondary development.

The study of live conversation is not, however, the purpose of this chapter; rather, we content ourselves here with material that is a step or two removed from live conversation, i.e., reported or composed conversation as it occurs in oral and written texts. Such reported or composed conversation may occur in relatively small chunks. Thus, a brief exchange may be reported in a single sentence or in a dialogue paragraph. When a whole discourse is given in dialogue form, and with more or less regular use of formulas of quotation, it is a _dialogue discourse_ (Larsen 1976). When a whole discourse is given in dialogue form, but without quotation formulas, it constitutes a _drama_.

Undoubtedly we are concerned here with a different class of relations than those which are considered in other chapters of this book. Notional structures of the sort here considered may properly be termed REPARTEE. Repartee in turn encodes within the surface structure of DIALOGUE. Whichever term we use--repartee in referring to the underlying notional structure or dialogue in referring to the surface structure--the distinctive feature of the relations here considered is that they involve a SEQUENCE OF SPEAKERS.

How can repartee relations which underlie dialogue best be conceived? It is somewhat fashionable to describe the whole universe of linguistic phenomena in terms of predicate relations. From this point of view, any and every grammatical relation is a predication. How then do we describe the relation between two such sentences as the following:

(4) What did you do all morning?
Oh, I went downtown, shopped for two hours, spent an hour at the hairdresser's, and finally had lunch at Kresge's 5 & 10.

If we are to describe all linguistic relations as predications we have to assume here that there is an abstract predicate (whether D for dialogue or R for repartee) whose two arguments are the question and the answer. This is certainly one way to do it. But if we stretch the term PREDICATION to include relations as diverse as these and predications narrowly defined, will we not in turn be forced to classify our predications taxonomically as to those which involve speaker interchange and those which do not? And once we so classify predications, we recognize that the relations involved in dialogue are, as a matter of fact, unique however we may want to talk about them. As expressed elsewhere in this book, my point of view is to reserve the term predication for comparatively low-level relations of the sort most commonly encoded as clauses. As for other relations, such as combinations of predications, repartee, and plot structure, I consider them to be other sorts of calculi.

Here, as in the preceding chapter, notional or underlying structures will need to be considered in conjunction with the surface structures that encode them. It will be likewise evident, in consideration of the notional structures described in the next chapter (linguistic analogues of the propositional or statement calculus) that we cannot avoid mentioning certain sentence types and paragraph types which as surface structures encode these relations. And, of course, case relations (Chapters 4 and 5)--whether my own or anyone else's variety--have little meaning without reference to surface structures such as subject, object, indirect object and adjuncts. There is, however, even more reason for referring to the surface structure of dialogue in our discussion of repartee: viz., since there is no general agreement as to what the surface structure of dialogue is, it is therefore necessary to develop a theory of the surface structure of dialogue in conjunction with its notional structure (repartee).

To begin with, we must face the fact that reported repartee may encode on more than one level of surface structure. It is not impossible to encode a limited sort of repartee within a single sentence as in the following example:

(5) When I asked her where she had been all morning, she told me that she had gone downtown and shopped for two hours, then went to the hairdresser's for an hour, and finally had lunch at Kresge's 5 & 10.

Here the question and the answer (in indirect discourse) are given in the sentence margin and the nucleus respectively. Some languages have special nuclear surface structures to accomodate question and answer within the same sentence, as in Western Bukidnon Manobo (Elkins 1971.249). Similarly, a language (e.g., Daga of Papua New Guinea, Elizabeth Murane 1974.271-4) may have a sentence type which encodes a remark and its evaluation in the same sentence, such as He said that you were stupid--that's not true.

Probably in most parts of the world, repartee which encodes within the sentence is rather limited, as just illustrated. In the northern part of South America we find, however, languages where rather extensive repartee can be reported in a single sentence. Thus, Burns (unpublished paper, 1971) states that in Ayacucho Quechua it is possible to put virtually a whole dialogue into the same sentence by use of subordinate verbs of quotation which are marked for same or different subject. I will attempt to give some idea of the nature of such a construction in Quechua in the following example which I have composed but which is based on Burn's materials. In this example saying indicates a subordinate verb while said indicates the independent and final verb of the sentence. I will indicate after each verb of saying whether it has a subject referent which differs from that of the final verb of the sentence or whether it refers to the same subject as the final verb. This alternation of same and different subjects can thus be used to mark alternations of speakers in the dialogue. Notice the following example:

(6) "Pardon me sir, but may I stay here for the night" saying (different subject)
"Yes, I feel sorry for you, I have traveled myself and have needed hospitality" saying (same subject)
"Thank you, that is very nice of you and I appreciate your kindness" saying (different subject)
"Well, have a restful night now" saying (same subject) said the rich man

Sentences of this sort which encode a whole dialogue, have now been reported over a rather wide area (Colombia, Ecuador, Peru), e.g., in Tucanoan languages (Carolyn Waltz 1977), in Chibchan languages (Gerdel and Slocum 1976) and in Aguaruna (Larson 1978).

While such constructions as those exemplified above occur in a few areas of the world, it appears that the more usual procedure is to encode reported repartee into some sort of surface structure dialogue paragraph. Dialogue, it seems to me, constitutes as natural a paragraph unit as any other sort of paragraph which we encounter linguistically. This is true in spite of the fact that orthographic tradition in English demands an indentation with each change of speaker.

Along with the nucleus of a dialogue paragraph there may occur two sorts of peripheries, an outer periphery which consists of non-dialogue material and an inner periphery which consists of dialogue material. The non-dialogue periphery of a surface structure dialogue paragraph is setting and terminus of the sort found in the narrative paragraph plus whatever sentences occur after setting and which report events which build up to the dialogue proper--which is considered to be the nucleus of the paragraph. All this has been discussed elsewhere (Longacre 1968.1.47-48, 162-3). The dialogue periphery consists of reported comments which are preposed and postposed to the dialogue proper and which do not tie well into its central repartee but which give information as to setting, characters, circumstances, etc., in the form of additional dialogue. This is especially characteristic of dialogue paragraphs which are embedded within dramatic discourse, since in dramatic discourse of the purest variety there is no possibility for resort to nondialogue material to give background circumstances or to introduce new participants. Therefore, in place of saying,

(7a) *It was a beautiful night.*
The moon lay softly on the water.
Then John said to Mary, "I love you".
But Mary said, "At your age, John?"

we have something like the following drama:

(7b) John: *It's a beautiful night, Mary.*
Mary: *Yes, John, and how lovely the moon shines on the water.*
John: *I love you, Mary.*
Mary: *At your age, John?*

Here the real repartee is the last two sentences and the preceding sentences give background information in dialogue form.

1. SIMPLE REPARTEE

In the surface structure of a language a simple dialogue paragraph begins with an initiating utterance, IU^1. The initiating utterance encodes three notional units: question (Q), proposal (Pro), and remark (Rem). These are technical terms which label underlying units each of which has considerable variety. Question here signifies a true solicitation of information. It does not include the surface structure rhetorical question which neither expects nor asks for a reply. Nor does it include surface structure questions which are really disguised proposals. Thus a request may be made by asking concerning one of the presuppositions of request, i.e., we may say *Have you a match?* when we mean *Please give me a match.* Or we may say *Is there any more salad down there at that end of the table?* when we really mean *Pass me the salad.* All these really are notional proposals rather than notional questions. In turn, proposal as a technical term includes advice, suggestion, invitation, plan, request, threat, or command. It may be a surface structure declarative, imperative, or interrogative. The proposal does not request information but is a call to action. The third term, remark, indicates that one speaker submits to the other a declaration or commentary. Essentially it is a request for evaluation from the other party to see if they will agree or disagree with the observation of the first speaker.

A simple dialogue concludes with another unit of surface structure which I call the resolving utterance (RU). Normally the resolving utterance is produced by a second speaker rather than by the first speaker himself. It is not impossible, however, to enter into (autistic) dialogue with oneself. The resolving utterance encodes three units of notional structure repartee: answer (A)--which resolves the structure initiated as a question; response (Res)--which resolves the structure initiated as a proposal; and evaluation (Ev)--which resolves the structure initiated as a remark. As indicated, the three underlying structures which encode within the resolving utterance correspond to the three underlying structures which encode within the initiating utterance. This gives us three pairs of utterances: question-answer, proposal-response, remark-evaluation. Thus, we can have three simple dialogues such as the following:

(8) *What time is it?* (IU,Q)
It's four o'clock. (RU,A)
(9) *Come over here.* (IU, Pro)
Okay, I'm coming. (RU, Res)
(10) *The whole matter is absurd.* (IU, Rem)
Yes, indeed. (RU, Ev)

In addition, simple dialogue may have a terminating utterance (TU) which encodes two notional structures: acquiescence (Acq) and rejection (Rej), e.g., example (8) above can end with either *Good, thank you* (TU, Acq) or with *Impossible* (TU, Rej).

A dialogue which involves a riddle (called to my attention by Huttar) is a cross between autistic dialogue (where the same speaker is both questioner and answerer) and a normal question-answer exchange which involves two speakers. This results from the fact that either the addressee or the original speaker may give the content answer--depending on whether or not the addressee knows it.

Thus, we may have the following:

(11) a) How does an obligatory affix resemble a dog's tail? (IU,Q)
b) It's bound to occur. (RU,A)

in which the addressee knows the answer to the riddle. Or we may have:

(12) a) How does an obligatory affix resemble a dog's tail? (IU,Q)
b) I dunno. (RU,A)
a) It's bound to occur. (RU,A)

In the latter case, the addressee answers the question by disclaiming any knowledge of the answer. This is a rather common--and often necessary--response to a question for information:

(13) a) Which of these houses does Simon Levi live in? (IU,Q)
b) Sorry, I haven't any idea. (RU,A)

In number 12 above, however, the original speaker gives the answer to the question, much as a speaker may answer a rhetorical question in a monologue. This results in a sequence of two-RU's, both of which are consequent on the same IU. In that the structure of riddle exchange specifically allows for this possibility, we must regard the riddle exchange as a clearly marked subtype of the simple dialogue paragraph.

Simple dialogue as presented here breaks down utterance-response pairing into three more significant pairings. The situation here is taxonomically similar to that which we encounter in positing various case relations (cf. Chapters 4 and 5). We can posit relatively few cases, e.g., Austin Hale, or we can posit a rather large stock of cases (as I do). It depends on how fine grained we want to make our analysis. Likewise, in regard to repartee, it is obvious that the rather coarse grained division of notional structures into question, proposal, and remark with their paired resolving utterances is not as fine grained as some might wish. The latter will want to elaborate still further distinctions. Note, however, that the present classification does distinguish dialogues which solicit information from dialogues which call for action, from still other dialogues which simply elicit comments. This has appeared to me to be a basic division according to the notional structures here under consideration. At the same time, however, we must note the limitations of the analysis of dialogue in terms of paired utterances. There are simply many dialogues which do not structure this way and cannot be adequately explained in this fashion. This brings us on then to the next section.

2. COMPLEX REPARTEE

A complex dialogue results when the second speaker does not like to accept the dialogue on the terms suggested by the first speaker. On the contrary, the second speaker wants to evade or moderate the force of the previous speaker's utterance; he wants in some way to blunt its point. In this case the second speaker resorts to the use of a continuing utterance (CU) which appears between the initiating utterance and the resolving utterance. The continuing utterance encodes three notional structures: counter-question ($\overline{Q}$), counter-proposal ($\overline{Pro}$), and counter-remark ($\overline{Rem}$). A chain of such continuing utterances may occur between the initiating and the resolving utterances and may be of indeterminate length. In fact, a complex dialogue need not end with a resolving utterance at all. The two speakers may simply tire of sparring with each other and quit without either's ever ending the dialogue with a resolving utterance.

It is important to note that any variety of continuing utterance may follow any other variety of continuing utterance or any variety of initiating utterance. Thus, while the initiating utterances and resolving utterances are paired with each other, there is no necessary pairing of a continuing utterance with what it follows; a counter-question, a counter-proposal, or a counter-remark may all follow a question or may follow a proposal or may follow a remark. A complex dialogue is resolved when either of the two speakers concedes the game to the other by using a resolving utterance, i.e., he concedes to the point where he is willing to answer the last counter-question, respond to the last counter-proposal, or evaluate the last counter-remark.

Take for example a simple dialogue such as the following:

(14) Where are you going, Bob? (IU,Q)
Downtown (RU,A)

While many dialogues of this sort occur, it does not at all follow that the second speaker will be willing to take the dialogue on the terms suggested by the first speaker's question. He may decide to take a more active role and respond as follows:

(15) Where are you going, Bob? (IU,Q)
Why do you want to know? (CU,$\overline{Q}$)

or

Come along with me and I'll show you. (CU,$\overline{Pro}$)

or even

Oh, there are many nice places around town. (CU,$\overline{Rem}$)

When this happens, the first speaker is himself faced with a decision as to whether he will accept the dialogue on the new terms suggested by the second speaker or not. The first speaker can, if he chooses, immediately resolve the dialogue by using a resolving utterance. In this case there are three possibilities: he can answer the counter-question Why do you want to know? by saying, Oh, I just wanted to know how to contact you in case of emergency (RU,A); or he can respond to the counter-proposal Come with me and I'll show you by saying Okay, let's go (RU,Res); or he can evaluate the counter-remark There are many nice places around town with the words, Yes, that's true (RU,Ev). But it is a privilege of the first speaker, confronted with one of the above counter tokens on the part of the second speaker, to try yet again to retain control of the conversation. In this case he does not follow with a resolving utterance but with another continuing utterance. Thus, e.g., the counter-question Why do you want to know? can be followed by And why don't you want to tell me? (CU,$\overline{Q}$) or with Cool it, Bob, sit down and let's discuss this affair (CU,$\overline{Pro}$) or with You always get mad like this (CU,$\overline{Rem}$).

As we have said, a complex dialogue of this nature can either be resolved (by use of a resolving utterance with one of its three possible notional structures) or be left without a resolution. The resolution need not be pacific, e.g., the second speaker may resolve the dialogue by following the words You always get angry like this (CU, Rem) with Liar! (RU,Ev). This word expresses resolution of the dialogue. It is an evaluation of the last counter-remark. Actually of course, if the second elects to answer as above, he falls into the trap of finally accepting the dialogue on the terms prescribed by the first speaker, who thus effectively retains control of the dialogue in that he forces his opponent to resolve it on his terms. The second speaker buys the privilege of not answering the first speaker at the cost of relinquishing any hope of gaining the control and direction of the dialogue. Thus, taking the last utterance and what preceded it, we could summarize the dialogue as follows with speakers a and b.

(16) a) Where are you going Bob? (IU,Q)
b) Why do you want to know? (CU,$\bar{Q}$)
a) You always get mad like this. (CU,$\overline{Rem}$)
b) Liar! (RU,Ev)

Essentially, then dialogue of this variety is a game, the object of which is to force your opponent to resolve the dialogue on the terms which you have prescribed. In all this, note the importance of the continuing utterance. Without such a notion, we are hung up on paired utterances and find it impossible to describe dialogues of indefinite length.

3. ABEYANCE REPARTEE

Abeyance repartee encodes in a characteristic *stepped-in* dialogue paragraph. In such paragraphs a subdialogue or included exchange intervenes within a main exchange which is held in abeyance, i.e., suspended, until the included exchange is resolved.

One very frequent type of abeyance repartee is clarification repartee. This encodes in dialogue paragraphs that are similar to complex dialogue paragraphs except that (a) the continuing utterance is limited to one and only one notional structure, the counter-question, and (b) the function of the counter-question in the clarification paragraph is not to evade the force of the initiating utterance, but to clarify it. The speaker who has resort to the use of a continuing utterance in the clarification dialogue does not intend to try to wrest control of the conversation from the first speaker. On the contrary, he is only interested in clarifying the intent of the first speaker. Take the following dialogue:

(17) Mother: Anyone here want a piece of cake? (IU,Q)
One of her children: Who? (CU,$\bar{Q}$)
Mother: You. (RU,A)
The child: Yes. (RU,A)

In this example we see that the clarification repartee has a surface structure rather distinct from that of complex dialogue. To begin with, it has two resolving utterances of the answer variety. The first answer responds to the continuing utterance, counter-question; the second answer responds to the initiating utterance, question. For this reason it is *almost* possible to transform the dialogue to the following:

*(18) Mother: Anybody here want a piece of cake?
Child: Yes.
Child: Who?
Mother: You.

However, although it is almost possible to transform the dialogue as suggested above, it is really *not* possible, since it is necessary to retain in suspension the sub-dialogue Who?, You before the response Yes comes on the part of the child. It is evident that the clarification dialogue has an internal stepped structure that is distinct from that of the complex dialogue.

More complicated examples of clarification dialogue paragraph are not difficult to imagine. In the following we use progressive indentation to show the stepping-in structure of this example of clarification paragraph.

(19)

1. John: I'm inviting you to dinner with me at 2:00 p.m. Thursday. (IU,Pro)
  2. Edward: Can I bring one of my sons? (CU,$\bar{Q}$)
    3. John: Bob or Bill? (CU,$\bar{Q}$)
      4. Edward: Does it matter which? (CU,$\bar{Q}$)
      5. John: Yes, it certainly matters. (RU,A)
    6. Edward: Okay, Bob, the older one. (RU,A)
  7. John: Very well. (RU,A)
8. Edward: Okay, thanks, we'll be there. (RU,Res)

The above example begins with an initiating utterance whose notional structure is proposal. A series of see-saw counter-questions follow. Utterance 5, however, is the resolution of 4; 6 is the resolution of 3; 7 is the resolution of 2; and 8 is the resolution of the original proposal.

Other types of abeyance dialogue paragraphs undoubtedly exist but have not been well studied. Thus, while all the above examples of clarification dialogue paragraphs are limited to question-answer exchanges, consider the following in which a question-answer exchange is held in abeyance while a remark-evaluation exchange takes place:

(20) a) Are you working tonight? (IU,Q)
b) That's a timid way of asking for a date. (CU,Rem)
a) Yeah, I know. (RU,Ev)
b) No, I'm not working. (RU,A)

Likewise, in the following, a proposal-response exchange is held in abeyance while another proposal-response exchange takes place:

(21) a) Can I go fishing with you? (IU,Prop)
b) You'll bring your tent? (CU, Prop)
a) Okay. (RU, Res)
b) Fine. (RU,Res)

4. COMPOUND REPARTEE

A surface structure compound dialogue paragraph consists of two or more linked exchanges each of which is expounded by a simple, complex, or abeyance dialogue paragraph. This adds little to our knowledge of the underlying structures which are involved, except to tell us that they may link into larger and still more involved units. The seam of a compound paragraph, i.e., the joint between exchanges, is the typical spot where there may be change of speakers involved in a dialogue.

There is a certain fundamental ambiguity about whether we analyze a construction in the surface structure as a sequence of several simple paragraphs (composing say an embedded discourse within something larger) or as one long compound paragraph. This is the essential ambiguity of coordinate structure everywhere. Thus, sometimes in the structure of a paragraph in English we are uncertain whether several simple sentences are intended or one long coordinate sentence, especially if every sentence in the paragraph starts with and. Example 22 contains a comparatively unambiguous example of a compound paragraph:

(22) Ata Manobo, Philippines (Shirley Abbott)

	The other one said, "I'm really scared; it's as if there are no people here."	$EXCH_1$: COMPL DIAL P IU, Rem
	The rich man said, "Ah, let's try to call."	CU, $\overline{Pro}$
Calling,	the rich man said, "Where did you people go?"	$EXCH_2$: SIM DIAL P IU, Q
	The ghost answered, "Here I am."; but it was an evil spirit; he was lying.	RU, A

The gerundative form (in Ata Manobo) calling serves as a link between the first and the second exchanges. Notice also that there is a change of speaker. The two travelers, the rich man and his companion, are talking to each other in the first exchange, but the rich man and the ghost are talking to each other in the second exchange.

Example 23 contains a somewhat more run-of-the mill and somewhat ambiguous example from Tboli. Notice that this example starts off with a setting sentence One day we were going somewhere which seems to belong to the whole, not simply to the first exchange. Note too the marked parallelism of the three exchanges: I, he, I, he, I, he with regular alternation of speakers. Note too the general unity of subject matter. Aside from these features there is no formal indication that this is one paragraph rather than a sequence of three simple paragraphs. It seems convenient in this case in terms of the structure of the discourse as a whole to consider this unit to be one compound paragraph instead of a series of three short choppy paragraphs. Compound paragraphs can be of any theoretical length in that

(23) Tboli, Philippines (Doris Porter)

One day we were going somewhere.	SETT
I asked him about his faith and where he came from.	$EXCH_1$: SIM DIAL P IU, Q
He said, "I come from Libak, I am a Mohammedan."	RU, A
But I said, "Where did you go to school before?"	$EXCH_2$: SIM DIAL P IU, Q
And he said, "One year in Libak, one year in Cotabato and there was a school I knew about," he said, "named King's Institute and now I am studying here."	RU, A
I said, "Who is your companion?"	$EXCH_3$: SIM DIAL P IU, Q
He said, "None, I just came here alone."	RU, A

there is no limit to the number of exchanges that they may involve. For a fairly complex example of a compound paragraph, see example 159 of Longacre 1968, volume I.

5. NON-VERBAL RESOLUTION AND FURTHER PARAGRAPH TYPES

Reported repartee can involve reporting of non-verbal resolution. As we all know, in real life situations very often the response to a proposal is non-verbal, i.e., someone is told to do something and he gets up and does it and this is the answer rather than verbal activity on the part of the second person. Thus we may have such verbal-activity-plus-non-verbal-activity sequences as the following:

(24) Go down to the corner store and buy me two pounds of sugar, said John's mother.
John got up promptly and went.

or

(25) Pass me the salt, said Susan to Joan.
Joan passed her the salt.

Such structures contain initiating utterances but probably should not be considered to contain resolving utterances since the resolution is non-verbal. In some languages, such surface structure constructions have been considered to constitute a separate paragraph type (related to dialogue paragraphs) which usually has been called the EXECUTION paragraph. An execution paragraph need not involve two participants; it can report a person's own plan verbalized and then carried out, as in the following (from the parable of the prodigal son):

(26) And he said to himself, I will arise and go to my father and say unto him Father I have sinned against heaven and against you and am no more worthy to be called your son.

So he arose and went.

Here the speaker states his intention of doing something and carries it out.

Not uncommon is a structure in which both verbal and non-verbal resolution occur. This is in fact, a favored form for accounts of Christ's miracles in the New Testament. Such paragraphs often have a generalized structure which consists of IU,Prop; RU,Res; Correlate, Execution, i.e.

A man came to Jesus and asked to be cured of a sickness.
Jesus said, All right, I will cure you.
So he touched him and cured him.

Correlate, as a surface structure unit (Mansen and Mansen 1976) is whatever non-verbal activity is (here execution) reported as accompanying a verbal response.

Non-verbal resolution is not confined, however, to that modification of the simple dialogue paragraph in which there is a verbal proposal followed by a non-verbal response. There are also structures in which a question or a remark is made and in which the resolving utterance is non-verbal as in:

(27) How old are you? said the stranger to the child.
The child held up four fingers.

Here we have a question verbalized in the initiating utterance of a dialogue but the answer is non-verbal. Quite clearly, however, the gesture on the part of the child is a surrogate for saying Four years. We are tempted here to label the second half of this pair of sentences as RU,A. Consider, however, the following example:

(28) Professor Jones is really a good teacher, bubbled Sue enthusiastically.
Bill's frowning face showed that he did not share her enthusiasm.

Here we have a dialogue teed off with an initiating utterance which is a remark followed by a non-verbal evaluation. The non-verbal evaluation (facial expression) is not clearly, however, a substitute for any specific string of words. We probably here do not want to label the second sentence as RU, Ev. In this and previous examples we see paragraph types which are related to dialogue. The analysis must reflect this relationship without losing the difference between such paragraphs and dialogue proper.

In lively dialogue of the dramatic variety we may find a non-verbal activity which is not reported but is assumed by a subsequent speaker. There is one such case in the following Ata Manobo complex dialogue paragraph where the repartee assumes a non-verbal activity without which the structure of the paragraph is defective and is, in fact, unintelligible. Thus, between sentence two and sentence

(29) Ata Manobo, Philippines (Shirley Abbott)

S_1	"Halve the pig; let Lusogpit eat half."	IU, Pro: EX Paragraph Text
S_2	"He eats a lot."	Reason
Ø	[a physical prod or hit? some threatening motion?]	[CU, $\overline{\text{Rem}}$]
S_3	"Ah, Lusogpit, don't!"	CU, $\overline{\text{Pro}}$
S_4	"I'll get angry because you think I eat a lot."	CU, $\overline{\text{Rem}}$
S_5	"We're just playing," said Indong.	CU, $\overline{\text{Rem}}$

three--presumably by the same speaker--Lusogpit either pokes or threatens the speaker of sentences one and two. This is the non-verbal equivalent of a continuing utterance.

6. THE NUMBER OF SPEAKERS IN A DIALOGUE

In the above sections of this chapter we have been progressively expanding an initially simple concept of dialogue in an effort to make it adequate to explain unrestricted dialogue as we find it in the real world of reported speech. Beginning with simple repartee, I expanded this to complex repartee and abeyance structures with recognition that all these structures could combine into compound units of considerable length. This was further expanded by recognizing the occasional substitution of non-verbal activity for verbal activity in dialogue or quasi-dialogue structures (with the possibility of picking up more surface structure paragraph types in the analysis).

In all the above, little or no importance has been attached to the number of speakers involved in repartee. The assumption has been tacitly made that the essential surface structure of dialogue is not altered much by this factor. We have noticed that it is not even essential that two speakers be involved in dialogue in that one speaker can carry on a dialogue with himself and this can be reported as a dialogue paragraph differing in no essential way from the more usual sort of dialogue which involves two or more speakers (cf. the Gollum-Smeagol dialogue in Tolkien 1966. 2.303-5).

We have also to face the fact that in rapid-fire dramatic text we may not even be certain how many speakers are involved nor precisely who speaks what sentence. Indeed, in certain types of dramatic discourse, this is irrelevant. Such a discourse is the Ata Manobo dramatic text (from Shirley Abbott) called "Fencing Wild Pigs". This text takes us squarely into the milieu of an actual wild pig hunt. Many things are said by many people. The general atmosphere is created by reporting the lively repartee that characterizes the hunt. It is no great concern to know at every stage who says what or even how many speakers are involved in a given dialogue paragraph. Example (29), the one illustrating non-verbal activity, is from this text. Notice that it is clear here that somebody is baiting Lusogpit. Probably this person speaks both the preceding utterances while Lusogpit makes a non-verbal response and speaks the next utterance, but it is not clear that the first two sentences are spoken by the same person. Nor is it of great relevance. Similarly, the last sentence of the paragraph is spoken by Indong. It is probable that she also speaks the third sentence, but again, this is indeterminate and not necessary to the presentation of the activity.

On the other hand, the number of speakers involved can affect the structure of dialogue paragraphs in certain ways and may even lead to a few further surface structure types or subtypes. Thus the same initiating utterance may have several resolving utterances suggested by different people if more than two people are present. We can have a dialogue paragraph like

(30) I think that Professor Jones is a very capable teacher, said Susan. (IU,Rem)
I can't agree with you at all, said Bill. (RU,Ev)
On the contrary I certainly agree with you, said Edward. (RU,Ev)

Here there are two opposite evaluations of the same remark. Or as any parent knows, a proposal to one's children may be followed by a barrage of counter-proposals such as is contained in the none-too-hypothetical paragraph in example 31.

(31)

Children, we're going to bed right now.	IU, Pro
But I want a story first.	CU, $\overline{\text{Pro}}$
And I want to work more on my model.	CU, $\overline{\text{Pro}}$
We gotta finish this game first.	CU, $\overline{\text{Pro}}$

These are both examples of one-to-many paragraphs and may require the positing of further surface structure types, or at least of subtypes.

We may have not only one-to-many, but many-to-one dialogue paragraphs as in example 32. To summarize, one-to-many and many-to-one dialogues permit repetition of units which are not repeated in dialogues which involve only two speakers.

(32)

" Where did you go?" said his father.	IU, Q
" And why were you so long getting back?" said his mother.	IU, Q
" What I want to know is what a grandson of mine as young as you is doing on the city streets past midnight?" said his grandfather.	IU, Q
" I don't really think it's fair to be grilled like this," said Tom and ran from the room.	CU, $\overline{\text{Rem}}$

7. OUT OF PHASE RELATIONS BETWEEN NOTIONAL AND SURFACE STRUCTURES[2]

Previous sections of this chapter have assumed that notional (underlying) repartee units are in phase with surface structure dialogue units. If we are to have a theory of repartee in dialogue that is sufficient to handle all possible examples in language and literature, we must recognize that by no means are notional and surface structures in phase in all examples of dialogue. In fact, once we recognize surface units of the sort here suggested, i.e., initiating, continuing, resolving, and terminating utterances, we are in a position to recognize that some dialogues are effective precisely because they throw underlying and surface structure units out of phase. The latter sort of examples are not therefore examples of marginal grammaticality which we need to explain away, rather we must regard them, in the hands of a successful speaker or writer, as highly successful structures. In fact, we may almost say that literary style not simply tolerates but requires that notional and surface structures on many levels be thrown out of phase with each other.

While the various surface structure units posited in previous sections of this chapter typically encode the repartee units which we have suggested, when notional and surface grammar are out of phase, more than one repartee unit may encode within a given surface structure unit. Thus, if we believe that sentences as WHOLES are constituents of paragraphs and if we do not normally chop up sentences and distribute parts of sentences into paragraph level slots, we find paragraphs in which one sentence encodes too much in terms of the repartee units previously suggested. This is especially true of antithetical, coordinate, and alternative sentences (i.e., <u>but</u>, <u>and</u>, and <u>or</u> sentences) in many languages. It appears that one of the purposes of these surface structure sentence types is to permit the resolution of one exchange and the initiation of a new exchange within the domain of the same sentence. Several examples from Philippine languages follow.

The following example from Sarangani Bilaan (McLachlin and Blackburn 1971.33) illustrates use of an antithetical sentence for notional structure resolution-plus-initiation within a dialogue. Neverthless, in terms of surface structure there is apparently but one complex dialogue paragraph with four constituent utterances. The dialogue begins with an initiating utterance, which is partly accepted, partly parried by the addressee (in the second sentence). I consider that for the purposes of surface structure classification (as responding utterance versus continuing utterance) that the second and final element in a sentence outranks the first. I consider,

(33) "The Old Man and Woman", S. Bilaan, Philippines (McLachlin and Blackburn)

The bird talked, "Grandchild, wait here because I'm about to look for food for us."	IU
The little child talked, "Yes, Grandmother, but don't be long because I'm afraid."	CU
"Don't be afraid; this will be the sign when I arrive..."	CU
"Yes."	RU

therefore, that in the second sentence, the words of the little child essentially parry the thrust of the first speaker, and that the whole should be considered to be a continuing utterance in the surface structure. But this utterance is in turn parried by the utterance of the first speaker, the bird, in the third sentence, which also is classifiable as a continuing utterance. Resolution is not reached until the fourth sentence where the child simply says *Yes*.

On closer examination we note, however, that the first of the two continuing utterances of the surface structure has two underlying notional components. First of all, the child responds *Yes* to the proposal of its adopted parent. But this response figures as the first base of an antithetical sentence in the second part of which the child makes a proposal of its own: *Don't be long because I am afraid*. The first speaker in turn, in the second of the two continuing utterances, responds to the child's proposal with her own counter proposal *Don't be afraid*. But this in turn is only the first base of a sentence the second base of which involves a further proposal, i.e., *this will be the sign when I arrive* (freely interpretable as "I propose to give you an identifying sign"). It is to the last that the child responds with the word *Yes* of the last sentence. In brief, we have three exchanges in the notional structure: proposal, response; proposal, counter-proposal; and proposal, response. In the second and third sentences of the dialogue an exchange is resolved and a new exchange opened in the

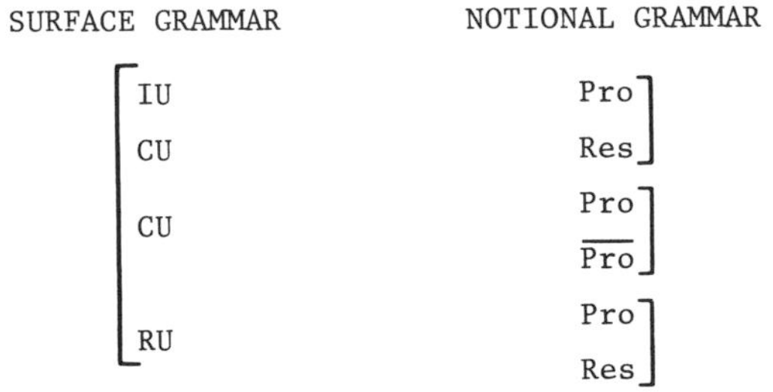

SURFACE GRAMMAR	NOTIONAL GRAMMAR
IU	Pro
CU	Res
CU	Pro
	$\overline{\text{Pro}}$
RU	Pro
	Res

Diagram I

same sentence. This is possible by use of the antithetical sentence in the first continuing utterance with the word but, and a coordinate sentence without an explicit coordinator in the second continuing utterance, i.e., omission of such a word as and or furthermore . In the accompanying Diagram I the surface structure and the notional structure are compared and contrasted.

What then? This means that here (as probably always) our surface structure units have more abstract and vague meanings than the relatively concrete and situationally oriented meanings of the underlying structure. In the above dialogue, the initiating, continuing and resolving utterances are seen as units which encode the alternating utterances of a dialogue rather than anything as specific as question, proposal, answer, etc. The notional structure units are the more semantically consistent counterparts of the surface structure units. This is not dissimilar to what we encounter on the clause level, where such surface structure functions as subject and object are more abstract and vague than the relatively concrete notional units agent, patient, experiencer, etc.

Let me emphasize again the fact that antithetical and coordinate structures in some instances are best explained by recourse to their function in dialogue. Here but almost comes to mean something on the order of "yes, I heard you and will dispose as follows of what you just said, nevertheless, I intend to open up for consideration a new angle of the situation". Similarly, and comes to mean something on the order of "I've heard you and take account of what you said and am going to add certain further considerations."

A further example from Itneg (Walton 1971.288) involves a surface structure alternative sentence. This is part of a long complex dialogue of which I give only one exchange which is relevant to my immediate purpose:

(34) "Kobonyan", Itneg, Philippines (Chas. Walton)

"Hide me or I'll be found by the soldiers."	IU, Pro + Rem
"Oh, not so, that's why you go there to hide," said the child.	RU, Ev + Res

The first structure *Hide me or I'll be found by the soldiers* conforms well to what we call the notional structure *warning* in the following chapter. In terms of dialogue, however, the two terms of the alternative sentence correspond to proposal and remark. The proposal is *Hide me now* ; the remark is in effect *I fear I'll be found by those soldiers* . The first part of the second sentence evaluates the remark at the end of the first sentence while the second half of the second sentence is really a response to the proposal found in the first half of the first sentence. The evil spirit asked the child to hide him and the child in effect said *Okay, you go there to hide* , meaning *I concur with your suggestion* . This gives us the structure seen in diagram II.

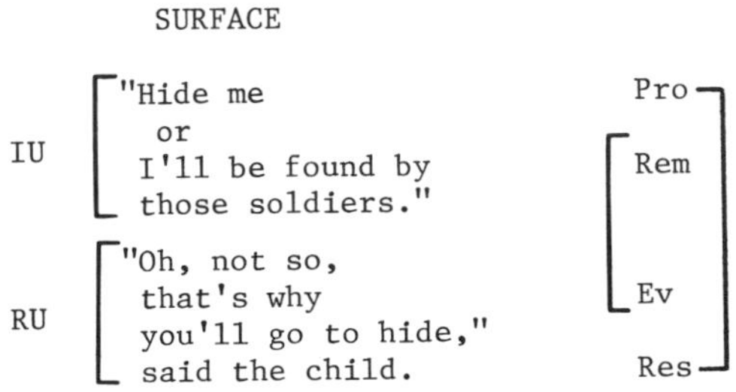

```
                SURFACE

        ┌"Hide me                       Pro ─┐
        │   or                              │
   IU   │  I'll be found by          ┌ Rem  │
        └  those soldiers."          │      │
        ┌"Oh, not so,                │      │
        │  that's why                └ Ev   │
   RU   │  you'll go to hide,"              │
        └  said the child.              Res ┘
```

Diagram II

Here an alternative sentence as exponent of the initiating utterance and a coordinate sentence as exponent of the resolving utterance make possible the presence of the one exchange intervening in the center of the other (cf. Section 3). Again, note the importance of the alternative sentence along with the coordinate and antithetical sentences in making possible out of phase relationships between notional and surface structure.

A long Maranao complex resolved dialogue paragraph (from a story "Diwata Kasarip" transcribed by Robert Ward) provides a very striking example of notional and surface structures out of phase in the dialogue paragraph. In the presentation of the English translation of this bit of Maranao text, I number the sentences consecutively in the left hand margin and give the surface structure grammatical analysis in the right hand margin. In that each quotation formula goes with a quote that is typically several sentences long, we have here a frequently encountered situation in direct quotation sentences in which a whole paragraph involving several sentences expounds quote within the quotation sentence itself. I have, however, for convenience of numbering, assigned the quotation formula to the first grammatical sentence which occurs in this quote. Thus while sentences one to three really compose one long direct quotation sentence, this more comprehensive structure is ignored in the numbering of the left-hand margin but acknowledged in the right-hand margin. Notional structures are ignored in the initial presentation of this example.

(35) "Diwata Kasarip" 5.34, Maranao, Philippines (R. Ward)

S_1	When they brought him to Inigambar and when Inigambar saw him she said, "Greetings Diwata Kasarip, son of Sultan Nabi Bakaraman and Ba'i sa Sinara'aman of Komara Mantapoli.	IU: *Dir. Q.S.* whose Q: COORD HORT PARA PRELIM
S_2	Why did you take our dresses?	SEC_1
S_3	Give them to me for I am dying of cold."	SEC_2
S_4	Diwata Kasarip replied and said. "Greetings to you Princess Inigambar a Olan, daughter of Sultan and Ba'i sa Antar a Langit.	CU: *Dir. Q.S.* whose Q: HORT PARA PRELIM
S_5	I will give you your dresses provided that you will let me accompany you to Antar a Langit.	EXHOR
S_6	Never mind if I did not get your clothes, if you will let me accompany you, I will look for them for you."	REINF
S_7	Inigambar replied and said, "I will request (plead with, bargain) you that you not accompany us because if you do not know it, there is now a big celebration in Antar a Langit because Radia Mangawarna is celebrating his coming marriage to me.	CU: *Dir. Q.S.* whose Q: HORT PARA EXHOR

S_8	The only thing that is delaying it is that the (dowry) requirement of the Sultan of Antar a Langit – a golden deer and a golden dog, have not yet been produced."	REASON
S_9	Diwata Kasarip said, "Let me accompany you Lady, so that I can see the festivities.	CU: *Dir. Q.S.* whose Q: HORT PARA $_{EXHOR}$
S_{10}	I also know one who owns a golden dog and a golden deer because they can only be found in Komara Mantapoli and I reckon that they cannot be secured because the owner is not at home."	REASON
S_{11}	After a long time of arguing between themselves, struggling to see who will give way to the plan of the other, Inigambar said, "Because I cannot dissuade you from going with us, bring out our dresses and you can go with us.	RU: *Dir. Q.S.* whose Q: ANTI HORT PARA SEC.
S_{12}	However, while we are going home to Antar a Langit, whatever you see you must not comment on because the moment you make any comment, we will come back to earth."	$\overline{\text{SEC.}}$
S_{13}	Diwata Kasarip brought out their clothes and gave them to them.	TU
S_{14}	They got their clothes and got dressed.	TERM

Ignoring the back-looping of paragraph structures into quotation sentences (direct quote sentence) and the quotation formulas that are found in those sentences, I give in Diagram III the simplified surface grammar tree of this dialogue paragraph.

The surface structure of the text--seen more fully in the presentation diagram and more sketchily in the tree

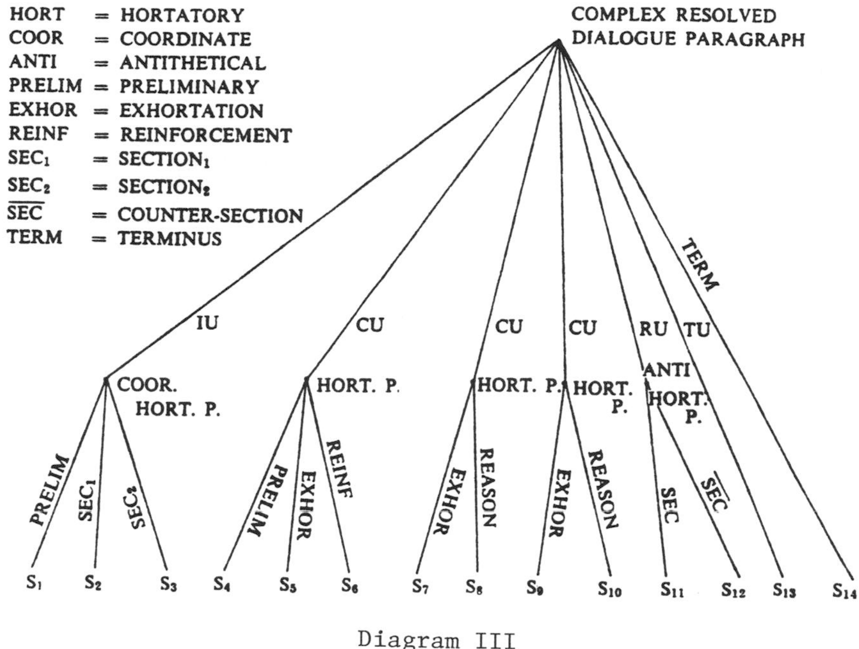

Diagram III

Surface Structure of Maranao Dialogue Paragraph
(with elimination of backlooping from sentence to paragraph)

graph of the surface structure --shows the structuring of the paragraph into direct quotation sentences with quotes expounded by hortatory paragraphs. The various sentences and paragraph structures that compose the whole are each given their proper functional place in the analysis. As constituent sentences, there can be little doubt that sentences 1-3 belong together, as well as sentences 4-6, 7-8, 9-10, and 11-12. As groups of sentences (each constituting as well one long direct quotation sentence) they are constituents of the dialogue paragraph in the same sense that sentences 13 and 14 also are constituents. Notice too that the tree graph of the surface structure of the paragraph pictures quite fairly what is really going one, i.e., there is an initiating utterance followed by a see-saw exchange between the two participants, followed by a capitulation of one participant to the demand of the other (in sentences 11 and 12), followed by the acquiescence of the other participant in sentence 13. This fits the typical surface structure of initiating utterance followed by a chain of continuing utterances followed by a resolving utterance, and a terminating utterance.

Nevertheless, there are important relations not shown in such an analysis as that just given, e.g., (1) The greeting in S_1 seems to find its counterpart in S_4. (2) Sentences 2, 3, 5, 6, 7, 9, 11, and 13 seem to form a whole which begins with a peripheral remark followed by a proposal, a chain of counter-proposals, a resolution via response, and acquiescence; the topic of this verbal hassle is Inigambar's desire to get back her clothes and Diwata Kasarip's desire to accompany her to Antar a Langit. (3) Sentences 8 and 10 correspond as remark and counter-remark. (4) Sentence 12 seems to be a minimal unresolved exchange consisting of a proposal.

These repartee relations, i.e., the notional structure, are summarized in Diagram IV which presents the notional structure of the Maranao dialogue paragraph. Notice that as a tree graph this is an unconventional graph in that lines cross each other in ways not normally permitted in such a graph. I assume, however, that the mere crossing of two lines does not constitute a node. If indeed this diagram could be given a 3-D format, it would be possible to disentangle the branches by resort to a dimension of depth.

Specifically, I assume a greeting exchange (sentences 1 and 4)--this is a phase of repartee that I have not developed but which needs to be developed. There is a further notional structure exchange in which we have a peripheral remark, sentence 2, _Why did you take our dresses?_ which really is not a question, but is a protest, _You should not have taken our dresses_. This is followed by the serious proposal that the clothes be given back to the women in sentence 3. A hassle of counter-proposals follows in sentence 5 plus 6, in 7, and in 9. We are explicitly told this in the onset of sentence 11 where it says, _after a long time of arguing between themselves, struggling to see who will give way to the plan of the other_. . . . Finally in sentence 11, Inigambar capitulates by responding to the last proposal of Diwata Kasarip, i.e., she agrees to let him go with her. This is followed by the acquiescence

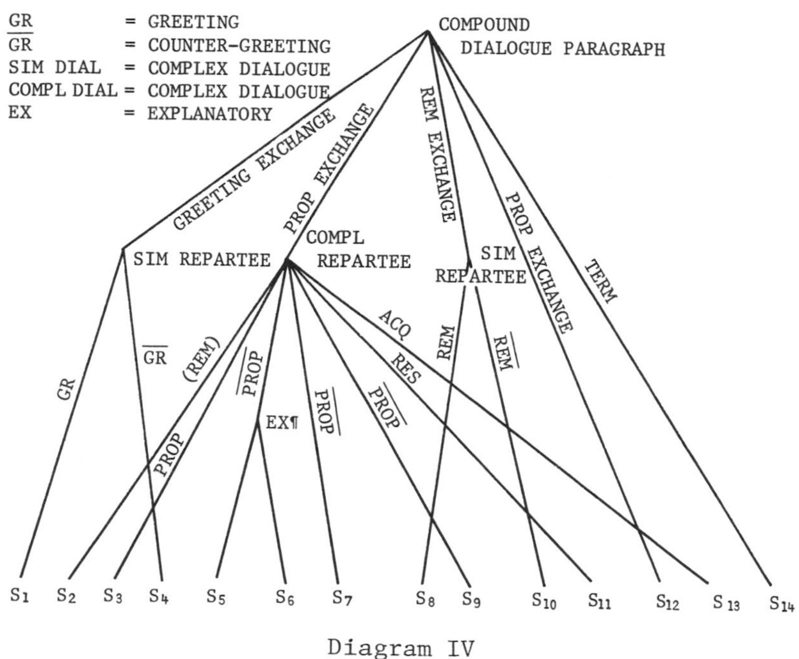

Diagram IV

Notional Structure of Maranao Dialogue Paragraph

of Diwata Kasarip himself in sentence 13. This ends the hassle over whether or not the women are to get their clothes back and as to whether or not Diwata Kasarip accompanies them back to their home. Sentences 8 and 10 are remark and counter-remark about the golden dog and golden deer which are needed for the festivities. Twelve (12) is an exchange which is initiated but is not carried through.

Notice that in this example we assume that the surface structure (normally) involves continuous units and that the notional structure may involve discontinuous units. Regardless of the discontinuities, we unravel the notional structure so as to trace the true repartee relationships which are involved within it. It must be insisted that to understand this dialogue in its breadth and complexity, we must have resort to both the surface and the notional grammar. The surface structure organization reflects better the actual interchange of the dialogue and the sequence of various utterances. The notional structure reflects better the true relations of one reported utterance in whole or part to surrounding reported utterances.

Another type of out-of-phaseness of deep and surface structures in dialogue paragraphs is reported by Fran Woods (1970) for the Halbi language of India. Here in the flow of dialogue paragraphs we frequently find two repartee relations expressed in the same sentence while the rest of the dialogue occurs normally in discrete sentences. This in itself is not unusual. We have mentioned in previous sections of this chapter the possibility that we could have, for instance, question and answer or proposal and response all in the same sentence. What is peculiar about Halbi is that the distribution of question and answer or proposal and response in the same sentence is not that which we would expect. Halbi, like English and like many languages, has a preposed temporal margin beginning with the equivalent of such English words as _when_. What is rather bizarre in Halbi is the monstrous length of the constructions which may go into the temporal margin as compared to the rather modest length of the stuff which is sometimes found in the nucleus of the sentence. Thus, we may have a sentence such as _When he had said_ . . . followed by a quote consisting of a long embedded paragraph, followed in turn by a diminutive sentence nucleus _she said "Yes"_. In such a sentence there is a minimum of dialogue material in the sentence nucleus itself and a maximum of dialogue material in the temporal margin of the sentence, i.e., the part of the sentence which is grammatically dominant carries little information and the part of the sentence which is grammatically subordinate carries a great mass of information. In this and in other respects the situation in Halbi is apparently very complex--complex to the point where Fran Woods feels that the simple distinction between underlying and surface grammar is not adequate to handle all the complexities. She posits a surface structure, a sub-surface structure, a supra-deep structure, and a deep structure, that is, she splits underlying and surface each into top and bottom levels, so that she works the same construction through a series of diagrams illustrating these various levels and feels that only down in the deepest level do we get the true repartee relations. If we consider notional and surface structure to be simply poles and not a dichotomy, then there is room for all such analyses of this sort (and others) if they lead us to a better understanding of the data.

8. REPARTEE AS A GAME

Repartee, especially in relation to simple and complex dialogue paragraphs, can be represented as a game structure. The object of the game is to get the person to whom you are talking to resolve the dialogue on your terms, and to keep him from gaining control of the dialogue and having you resolve it on his terms. I submit the following game theory diagram to summarize notional structure repartee in simple and complex repartee. Whether this is in phase or out of phase with surface structure is irrelevant to the progress of the game. These are the moves of the game regardless of the encoding surface structure. The game is open to two or more players. The order of the moves and the nature of the moves are as we have said more important than the number of players. The game opens with a choice of three moves: question (Q), proposal (Pro), or remark (Rem)--ignoring greeting and counter-greeting as well as leave taking and counter-leave taking at the end of dialogue. In the next move a further speaker can a) proceed to immediate resolution of the dialogue via the matching answer (A), response (Res), or evaluation (Ev); or b) proceed to contest the control of the conversation by introducing the (unmatched) counter-tokens: $\overline{Q}$, $\overline{Pro}$, or $\overline{Rem}$. This in turn opens up to the next speaker (who often is the initiator of the dialogue) the same set of options: a) resolution; b) effort to contest the control of the conversation. This can continue indefinitely if each speaker resorts to option (b). The two give up the game as a draw unless one succeeds in jockeying the other into a position where he resolves the dialogue by opting for (a)--which is either the next to the last move or the last move of the game. The other speaker may choose to express acquiescence or rejection as a final although optional move. In the accompanying game diagram, only the left-hand side of the diagram is worked out in detail (Diagram V).

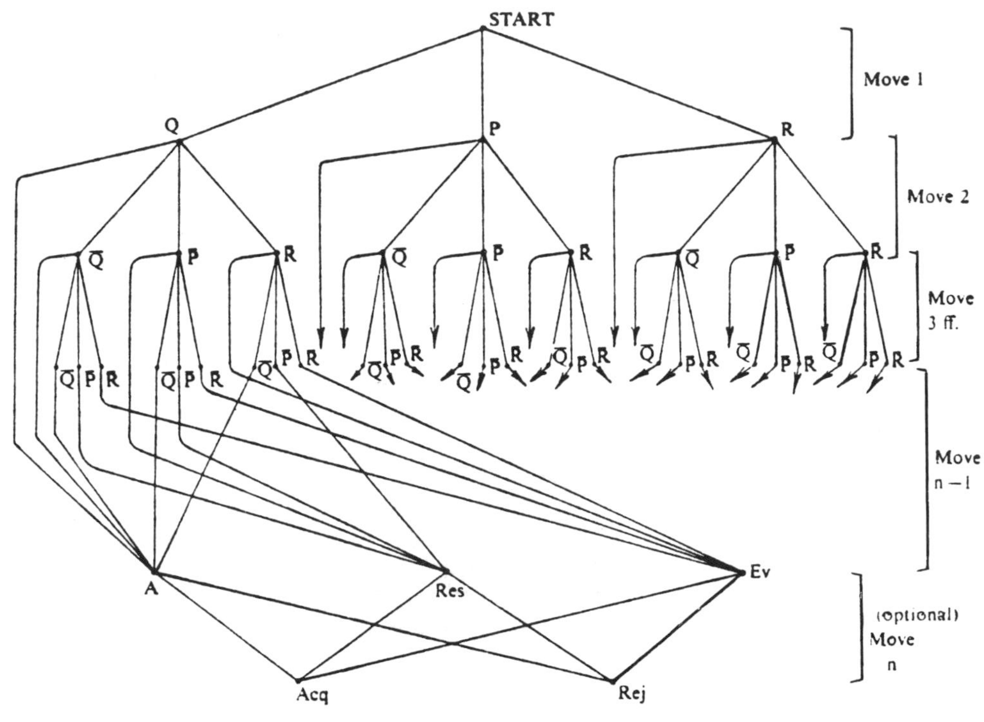

Diagram V
Repartee as a Game

9. SUMMARY

The purpose of this chapter has been to develop by successive approximations an apparatus for the description of dialogue on both notional and surface levels. Beginning with simple repartee consisting of paired utterances, we proceeded to complex repartee in which the presence of a continuing utterance made possible open dialogues of indefinite length, and then added a similar but distinct abeyance paragraph and the compound paragraph. Further flexibility was acquired by attention to non-verbal responses and modifications induced by more than two speakers. Finally, a whole new dimension of dialogue structure was attained by recognizing that the surface and notional structures may be out of phase and that the relations of the surface structure units are essentially more vague and abstract than the relatively concrete and situationally oriented relations of the notional structure, that is, of repartee. The claim is made here that the apparatus thus arrived at is applicable for the linguistic description of dialogue in any language anywhere. Tom Klammer (1971)[3] in a monograph length treatment applied essentially the same apparatus of dialogue (with a few modifications of his own) to two unrestricted corpora of data, i.e., Dickens' novel _Great Expectations_ and Shakespeare's play _Henry IV_, Part 1.

All that we have written here needs eventually to be supplemented by and compared with the current research into the nature of live conversation. Since dialogue groups utterances into exchanges which involve speaker alternation such considerations as turn-taking, bringing another person into a conversation, and repair (of a defective utterance) are current concerns. Labov and Fanshell's work (1977) has shown that conversation must essentially be studied on two levels, i.e., that of linguistic patterning and that of personal interchange.

Meanwhile, still other approaches to dialogue are afoot. Transactional analysis (Harris 1967) adds a socio-linguistic dimension of considerable importance. Taking parent, child, and adult as technical names for normal components of any personality, Harris describes dialogues as parent-parent, child-child, adult-adult, parent-child, child-parent, etc. The first three are horizontal dialogues, and of the three the adult-adult dialogue represents the desired adjustment. A parent-child dialogue is a down-striking dialogue and a child-parent dialogue is an up-striking dialogue. A further approach to dialogue is elaborated in some work of Ivan Lowe and Kenneth L. Pike (1969). In this approach certain dialogue relations are shown to have the structure of a mathematical group. The approach here given, conversational analysis, transactional analysis, and the Lowe-Pike group theory approach constitutes at present independent perspectives which need to be taken account of in a future comprehensive theory of repartee.

NOTES

1 This terminology is borrowed from Klammer. My original terminology was $speech_1$, $speech_2$, $speech_3$, $speech_4$; but on Klammer's suggestion I have replaced these with initiating utterance, continuing utterance, resolving utterance, and terminating utterance.

2 The next few pages essentially are a restatement of Longacre 1968.1.177-248. What I called lexical structure in the Philippine volumes I now call the notional structure of dialogue, or repartee. What I there called grammar, I now call the surface structure of dialogue.

3 Klammer's model differs in a few respects from mine, i.e., he treats what I term surface grammar and notional grammar as grammar versus lexical structure. He also makes more room for non-verbal behavior than I did in my earlier treatments of dialogue. He separates dialogue paragraphs into narrative dialogue paragraphs which have quotation formulas and dramatic dialogue paragraphs which do not have quotation formulas. At the time that he wrote his dissertation neither he nor I posited clarification paragraphs. I am critical of some of the examples of analyzed paragraphs which Klammer presents in that he occasionally chops up surface structure sentences in arbitrary ways in order to fit them into the constituent slots of paragraphs. But these criticisms are minor, and outweighed by my sense of gratification that Klammer has applied the apparatus of dialogue to a large and unrestricted corpus and found it adequate.

CHAPTER 3

COMBINATIONS OF PREDICATIONS

While predications (Chapters 4, 5) are like atomic particles in discourse, the combining of predications into larger units is like building molecules of (often very) complex structure from atoms. Thus, predications (usually as surface structure clauses) build into sentences, paragraphs, and ultimately discourses.

Consequently, it seems obvious that it is one thing to make a predication and another thing to combine predications into larger units. Formal logic distinguishes a predicate calculus from a statement or propositional calculus. The former involves predicates and their terms or arguments--and has had to be enlarged and enriched (case grammar) to make it adequate for the analysis of natural languages. The latter involves such notions as conjunction, alternation, and implication. This elementary apparatus is, however, too meager to describe natural languages. On the other hand more sophisticated extensions of formal logic (intensional logic, temporal logic, boulemaic logic, aletheic logic, and what-have-you), although considerably more adequate, elude and frustrate the linguist who is not a specialist in formal logic as a discipline--not to mention the plight of the linguistic technician or student.[1] It has seemed feasible, therefore, to propose in this chapter a somewhat straightforward adaptation of the basic apparatus of the statement calculus for linguistic purposes. This is in a manner parallel to that in which case grammar has adopted and expanded the predicate calculus: e.g., a three-place predicate Pabc is replaced by a notation in which the predicate P is expanded to a set of features and the arguments a, b, and c are given more explicit labels such as Agent, Patient, and Goal. In the same way we develop here various sorts of modified notation for conjunction and implication--with further attention to temporal relations and devices that embellish discourse, e.g. paraphrase and illustration.

It may be objected that the representation of the structures presented in this chapter by means of the statement calculus introduces a needless complication into linguistic description. Why, it may be argued, should not most (if not all) linguistic relations be represented in the same fashion, i.e., by means of the predicate calculus? In support of this contention certain peculiar features in the structure of Indo-European languages could be cited. Thus, looking at the structure of such a language as English, we note that such relations as the following--which I do not handle as predicates--are nevertheless paralleled by actual predicates in what may be described as a built-in metalanguage: succession, simultaneity (called overlap in succeeding sections), coupling, contrast, alternation. In English these various relations are associated with such surface structure conjunctions as *and then*, *while*, *and*, *but*, and *or* respectively. Nevertheless, corresponding with the preceding conjunctions are such expressions as *precede/follow*, *be simultaneous with*, *be coupled with*, *contrast with*, and *alternate/be mutually exclusive with*. Thus we can say not only *John went downtown and then bought a hamburger*, but we can say *John's buying a hamburger followed his going downtown*. We can say, *I spent an hour at the library while my wife shopped*, or we can say, *My spending an hour at the library was simultaneous with my wife's shopping*. We can say, *I do amateur painting and my wife collects postage stamps*, or we can say, *My doing amateur painting is coupled with my wife's collecting postage stamps*. We can say, *My horse is white but your horse is black*, or we can say, *My horse's whiteness contrasts with your horse's blackness*. We can say, *He's either dead or alive*, or we can say, *His being dead is mutually exclusive with his being alive*--or somewhat more naturally, *There are two alternatives: he is either dead or he is alive*. In all these cases, English shows a great versatility of built-in metalanguage along with a sweeping capacity for nominalizing verbs and whole clauses.

It is somewhat shocking to realize, however, that such a language as Trique and in fact the whole Otomanguean stock in Mesoamerica and many languages of surrounding stocks as well, simply have no such broad capacity for nominalization and no built-in metalanguage predicates of the sort which we have just illustrated for English. Nor is this just simply a limitation characteristic of a group of languages of Mesoamerica. In fact, on a global scale it may be the Indo-European languages which are unusual in allowing such a wealth of nominalization with built-in predicates to express relations of this sort. We could argue that a natural approach to such non-Indo-European languages as we have just cited is to set up predications versus relations involving predications and not to set up the latter as predications at all.

One thing is certain, however: there are further relations involved within language structures which are even less plausible as predications. We have already in the preceding chapter made this claim in respect to dialogue relations. Furthermore, what about plot structure? Do we set up an abstract predicate called plot whose arguments are setting, inciting moment, building tension, climax, denouement, and resolution? It is obvious that any linguistic structure may be represented as a predication if one wants to do it that way, but it seems also just as obvious that if we want to handle all linguistic structures as predications, we must immediately proceed to distinguish radically different sorts of predications--if we are to describe the full gamut of language--involving predications proper, relations between predications, dialogue relations, and plot structure. My own approach simply involves not representing all these diverse relations as predications in the first place.[2]

This chapter is essentially a reordering, revision, and expansion of the 'taxonomy of the deep structure of interclausal relations' which has already been given in a few other places, originally in two articles by Ballard, Conrad, and Longacre (1971a, 1971b) with subsequent expansion (Longacre 1972a, 1976), and in somewhat different form by John Beekman (1970; Beekman and Callow 1974), Grimes (1972, Ch. 14), and Hollenbach (1974, appendix). All the latter to varying degrees are influenced by Fuller (1959). Quite divergent from the work of all these is Halliday and Hasan (1976), which attempts to classify interclausal relations in English according to surface structure conjunctions. In this revision of the apparatus, I group the notions of the expanded statement calculus under two main heads: basic and elaborative deep structures. Conjoining, alternation, temporal, and implication are assumed to be more basic to the structure of discourse, while paraphrase, illustration, deixis (as defined here), and attribution (speech and awareness) are considered to be essentially embellishments, i.e., rhetorical devices. Notice that the basic notions of the statement calculus are essentially the logician's conjoining, alternation, and implication plus temporal--which seems to be a necessary addition. The elaborative devices are a further extension of the elementary statement calculus.

As for the symbolism employed in this chapter, P's and Q's (whether predications or complexes of predications) are indicated as combining in various ways to form larger units. The familiar symbol $\wedge$ is used for various kinds of conjoining which are not given the special symbols Δ,$\Delta_{\rightarrow}$, and $\equiv$ suggested below. The symbol $\vee$ is used for alternation not in the and/or sense but disjunctively. For degree comparison, I resort to the symbols for equality (=) and inequality (>,<). For temporal relations, I use Δ for temporal overlap and $\Delta_{\rightarrow}$ for temporal succession--plus notational devices which distinguish spans from events. For implication we have the ready-made symbol $\supset$. For paraphrase of all varieties (including gain and loss of information), I use $\equiv$. In describing the structure of deixis, while $\wedge$ continues to be used, the existential quantifier $\exists$ is used simply to indicate an existential predicate, i.e., $\exists$P is reduced to $\exists$, and E is used to symbolize an equational (a ε X) predication. Other symbols and conventions are introduced and defined in their appropriate places. A general summary and glossary of such symbols and conventions constitutes section 10 of this chapter.

In the subsections of this chapter I shall present the various deep structure notions of the enriched propositional calculus under the eight heads indicated. The presentation of these notions is followed by some further material in which an intersecting parameter, frustration, is indicated. Structures under certain of the main heads may have derived frustrated counterparts as described in Section 9 of this chapter.

1. CONJOINING

Under this heading I further distinguish coupling, contrast, and comparison.

1.1 Coupling

Coupling includes nontemporal and relations. The conjoined predicates are typically from the same semantic domain--although the exigencies of discourse structure may bring together rather unusual items in ad hoc domains relative to a given discourse. Thus we can conceive of the following brought together within a given discourse: He preaches twice a week, milks the cows twice a day, plays poker nightly, studies graph theory and topology, writes occasionally for PLAYBOY, tinkers with old cars, throws pots and pans at his wife, collects ivory elephants, and peddles heroin. All that such a sentence as the preceding does, however, is establish a novel pattern of collocation. Novel patterns of collocation certainly exist, but customary patterns of collocation exist as well. Thus in the following sentence, He's short and he's fat two descriptive predications from the semantic domain of bodily dimension are brought together. In He runs track and plays tennis two predications from the domain of sports are coupled. In He collects coins and his wife does ceramics we have predications from the domain of leisure time activities. In the three preceding examples, time considerations are irrelevant and of no concern to the speaker.

Conjoined predications may have same or different first terms. There are, however, a few possible restrictions and specializations. Thus, coupling which involves descriptives as in the first example above (He's short and he's fat) is probably limited to conjoined predications with the same first term. When such predications with differing first terms are conjoined, we may very likely find that the deep structure of contrast (see below) is involved rather than coupling. Thus, in Mary is pretty and Joan is intelligent we are likely to find that beauty and intelligence are being contrasted. At any rate such a sentence sounds smooth with a medial but. On the other hand, coupling with different first terms may imply reciprocity as in She lectures to him and he listens. Here him is second term of the first predication and (as he) first term of the second predication. She, which is first term in the first predication, is implied but not stated as second term of the second predication. Somewhat more explicit is the following: She lectured him on his personal morals and he listened meekly to her where the first and second terms of the two successive predications are clearly seen to be reversed.

Still another variety of coupling--often, but not necessarily with different first terms--turns on parallelism of predications with the varying of one term from predication to predication. In terms of surface structure this means varying the content of one noun slot from base to base as in *The men talk English, the women talk English, the children talk English* or *They talk English, they talk French, they talk Russian*. Notice that this is not the preferred surface structure pattern in English. English prefers to delete and telescope, so that the first example would emerge as *The men, women, and children all talk English* while the second would emerge as *They talk English, French, and Russian*. In some parts of the world however, fullness of structure and parallelism are preferred, so that in many parts of the Philippines and New Guinea, the surface structure is more like that which is here posited as the underlying or notional structure.

The five varieties of coupling already presented can all be symbolized as follows:

$Pa \wedge Qa$	Coupling with same first term
$Pa \wedge Qb$	Coupling with different first terms and without reciprocity
$Pab \wedge Qba$	Coupling with different first terms and with reciprocity
$Pa \wedge Qba$	Coupling with partial reciprocity
$P(a) \wedge P(b)$	... $P(n)$ Parallel Coupling

Coupling may occur on a relatively low or a relatively high level within the hierarchical structuring and layering of a discourse. Thus, within a single sentence there may occur various layers of sentence structure with coupling characteristic of the lowest level as in the comparatively simple examples already given or characteristic of a relatively high layer of structure. Frequently, the coupled elements are sentences within the same surface structure paragraph--thus giving us coordinate paragraphs as well as coordinate sentences. Note for example the following paragraph.

> (*Well, here's a bit about my family*:) *my oldest daughter married a Pole and lives in New York City. My second daughter married a Greek and lives in*

> Chicago. Jim, our oldest son, married a home town girl and lives one mile away from here. Our son Eric is unmarried and still lives at home. (That should do you until we get better acquainted.)

Aside from the introductory and concluding parts of the above paragraph--which are enclosed in parentheses--the paragraph is a coordinate structure. Each component sentence of the paragraph is a coordinate sentence involving the verb marry in its first predication, (unmarried in the final sentence) and the verb lives in the second predication. Noun phrases vary systematically from sentence to sentence: oldest daughter, second daughter, oldest son, son Eric; Pole, Greek, home town girl; New York City, Chicago, one mile away from here, at home.

When all is said and done, however, although coupling may encode in various surface structures there is one surface structure, namely the coordinate sentence, whose raison d'être seems to be encoding of coupling. Typically in many languages a coordinate sentence is a highly elastic surface structure; it encodes many things besides notional coupling. Nevertheless, encoding of coupling seems to be the primary purpose for the existence of the coordinate sentence in languages where such a sentence type is found.

1.2 Contrast

Contrast includes notional but relations. While coupling involves varying activities and varying participants, notional contrast requires paired lexical oppositions. Contrast, furthermore, must be two pronged, that is, there must be at least two opposed pairs of lexical items. Furthermore, one of these opposed pairs plays a more crucial role in establishing the contrast than does the other. The crucial lexical opposition may be expressed in two ways in the surface structure. Consequently--somewhat as a concession to the surface structure--I distinguish as notional structures the negative/positive use of the same predicate from the use of a pair of antonyms. Closely related to the former is negation of a close synonym of a predicate rather than of the predicate itself. As to the latter, languages differ considerably in the wealth of their store of antonyms. Oppositions expressed as antonyms in one language may be expressed simply as negative and positive use of the same item in another language. Furthermore, ANTONYM needs here to be broadly construed so as to include not only dictionary antonyms (*good*, *bad*; *black*, *white*; *rich*, *poor*) but also clearly opposed roles (*husband*, *wife*; *employer*, *employee*), binary spatial oppositions (*this bank*, *that bank*; *underneath*, *on top*), and binary temporal oppositions (*day*, *night*; *morning*, *afternoon/evening*). So much for the crucial lexical opposition of deep structure contrast. A second and reinforcing opposed pair must occur. The second opposed pair may be a further set of antonyms (or negative/positive use of the same item) or may simply indicate differing participants. At any rate, of the pair of antonyms (or negative/positive use of the same item) that constitute the crucial lexical opposition, one member of the pair is predicated of one participant and the other member of a differing participant.

By the above devices the notion of contrast presents to us a closed and polarized microcosm. Thus in the sentence *I don't like hamburgers, but my wife does* we are presented with a restricted universe in which there are but two protagonists, *I* and *my wife*, and two possible courses of action, *like hamburgers* or *not like hamburgers*. Antonyms can be used in place of the positive and negative use of the same predicate as in the following sentence, *I abhor hamburgers but my wife loves them*. Here we have the same two protagonists but in place of *don't like hamburgers* versus *do like them* we have *abhor hamburgers* versus *love hamburgers*. The net effect is the same in either case, i.e., a closed and polarized situation is posited.

A further variation on the above is the use of a pair of synonyms with positive and negative values rather than positive and negative values of the same predicate, as in the example *I don't like hamburgers but my wife loves them* where *like* and *love* are very close synonyms in English. Contrast involving antonyms may be symbolized as:

$$P(a) \wedge P''(b)$$
$$P(a) \wedge P''(a'')$$

where P'' is antonym of P, a'' is antonym of a, and (a), (b), and (a'') are corresponding terms with different referents.

Sub-varieties of contrast which involve negation may be symbolized:

$$\bar{P}(a) \wedge P(b) \qquad \bar{P}(a) \wedge P'(b)$$
$$\bar{P}(a) \wedge P(a'') \qquad \bar{P}(a) \wedge P'(a'')$$

where $\bar{P}$ is negation of P and P' is synonym of P.

Of a slightly different variety is contrast whose reinforcing opposed pair is an outer pair of terms referring to place, time, or oblique goals (all these are peripheral, not nuclear, in their case frames). Thus:

He's naive about some things but not naive about others
He's naive about women but not naive about business
He's naive about women but sophisticated about computers

It is characteristic of such structures that the reinforcing contrastive pair may be deleted in the surface structure. We are left with a paradox:

He's naive and he's not naive
He's naive and he's sophisticated

Symbolizing as x and y the reinforcing pair of nouns in non-nuclear roles, I formulize:

$$P(a)x \wedge \bar{P}(a)y$$
$$P(a)x \wedge P''(a)y$$

Contrast need not turn on a pair of antonyms (or negative/positive values) in the predicates themselves with the reinforcing opposition in the terms; the two-pronged opposition may occur exclusively in the terms:

Bill works outdoors during the day and indoors at night

Here the predicate with its first term (Bill works) is not repeated in the second clause. The contrast turns on further terms: outdoors versus indoors (spatial antonyms) and during the day versus at night (temporal antonyms). This further type of contrast may be symbolized:

$$P(a)xy \wedge P(a)x''y''$$

where x and y are further terms referring to space and time respectively and x'', y'' are their antonyms.

Obviously the matter of negative/positive use of the same predicate versus use of a synonym in such a negative/positive pairing versus a pair of antonyms depends somewhat on accidents of the lexical surface structure of a given language and on the inclination of the speaker at the moment. It would be possible to formulate contrast in sufficiently abstract terms to embrace all these in the same symbolism. I have, however, let our formulation of deep structure contrast be influenced by the surface structure of the lexicon. That is, we have caught our notional structures at an early stage in their derivation to surface structures.

A further variety of contrast typically requires distinct surface structure encoding in many languages. This further variety of contrast I label EXCEPTION. Exception qualifies as a sub-variety of contrast in that it has two opposed pairs. One such pair consists of negative/positive or positive/negative use of the same predicate. The second opposed pair is peculiar to the structure of exception: one term of one predicate consists of the universal set minus a given member of the set while the corresponding term of the other predicate consists of only that member. The negated predicate may go with either term, i.e., it may emerge in the surface structure of the first base of a sentence or in the second base.

Note the following example, *John spoke up but nobody else did*. Note the very similar example, *Nobody spoke up except John*. Here the same notional structure is expressed first as a surface structure antithetical sentence in English and secondly as a simple sentence with but one clause containing an *except* adjunct. The two sentences differ in the linear ordering of their constituents, i.e., in their highlighting or focus (cf. Ch. 7). Basic, however, to both sentences is the assumption that there is a universal set to which John belongs. Something can be predicated of John that cannot be predicated of the universal set. The opposite may be predicated, however, of the universal set minus John.

The second example is of greater interest in that it involves a more radical transformation and collapse in passing from the notional into the surface structure. The underlying structure (found also in the other example above) is something on the order of the following: *John spoke up; everybody--minus John--didn't speak up; John is a member of everybody*. To transform this sentence into a surface structure clause unit with an 'except' adjunct, probably the first derivational step is to permute the order of the two elements to something like everybody--minus John--didn't speak up; John spoke up; John is a member of everybody. In successive transformations (a) the negative is shifted from the first predicate to its term, and (further on down in the derivation) yields nobody. (b) The last base, the assumption John is a member of everybody is deleted. (c) The second base John spoke up is likewise deleted, leaving only: Nobody--minus John--spoke up. (d) The modification unit nobody--minus John is split and its second element is moved to a position following the verb. (e) The surface wording except John is adopted--thus giving us a simple sentence of one clause structure with subject, intransitive predicate, and adjunct: Nobody spoke up except John. The overall result is that deep structure exception encodes as a single clause which contains an except adjunct. The derivational route to John spoke up but nobody else did is not as involved as the above and is not set forth here; else in this surface structure reflects the notional structure assumption that John is a member of the universal set.

The negative may occur with the predicate which has the particular set member as its term: Everyone died except Grandfather where again we have an underlying form such as Everybody--minus Grandfather--died; Grandfather didn't die; Grandfather is a member of everybody. The Universal-set-minus-particular-member and particular-member need not be first terms of their respective clauses: He looked everywhere except his hip pocket; He fined everyone except John; He expected her anytime except today; He didn't kill anything except a field mouse.

These two sub-varieties of deep structure exception (itself a variety of contrast) may be symbolized as:

$$\bar{P}(U\text{-}a) \wedge P(a) \wedge (a \in U)$$
$$P(U\text{-}a) \wedge \bar{P}(a) \wedge (a \in U)$$

where $a \in U$ symbolizes a is a member of the universal set U, while U-a symbolizes the universal set minus that particular member. The parentheses around (U-a) and (a) serve to indicate that these terms are corresponding terms with the respective predicates but are not necessarily first terms (e.g., actors); they may, for example, be second or third terms (e.g., object, place, time).

There is a clear distinction in notional structure between coupling and contrast. Notice the role of items from the same semantic domain and the comparative unimportance of systematic negation in coupling, as opposed to the importance of negation, antonyms, and differing dramatis personae in the deep structure pattern of contrast.

Many languages have a surface structure antithetical sentence whose primary function is to encode deep structure contrast. Typically such surface structure sentences have a medial antithetical link--such as the English word *but*--as is seen in many of the above examples. A language may, additionally or alternatively, encode deep structure contrast in a paragraph or even in opposed points of a discourse. We may, therefore, have antithetical discourses as well as antithetical paragraphs. Note the following example of a brief antithetical paragraph:

> *The Browns keep their houses well-repaired, are concerned with matters of sanitation and health, and charge a moderate rent. Our landlord, however, is less scrupulous and less of a humanitarian. The roof has leaked for two years, broken windows are never repaired, and the plumbing has gone from bad to worse. On top of all this, he extorts all the rent that he can get from his tenants.*

Contrast encoding in a long sentence or paragraph may be more diffuse and harder to analyze than contrast expressed compactly within the sentence. The above paragraph has paragraph medially the strong adversative *however* which is characteristic of oppositions on the paragraph level rather than on the sentence level. The whole paragraph could be paraphrased and condensed to one sentence such as the following: *The Browns are conscientious landlords, but our landlord is not conscientious* in which *The Browns* are opposed to *our landlord* and *conscientious* is opposed to *non-conscientious*. This is worked out somewhat diffusely in that the first half of the paragraph refers to *houses well repaired* while the second half refers to *leaky roof* and *broken windows*. The first half refers to concern with *matters of sanitation* while the second half refers to *the plumbing going from bad to worse*. Again, the first half mentions *moderate rent* while the second half mentions *excessive rents*. All these are somewhat antonymical, but the clearcut use of antonyms which we often find within a single sentence gives way here to the more diffuse development which is typical of the paragraph.

1.3 Comparison

Comparison involves a type of conjoining which may be called degree conjoining. Such a sentence as *John is bigger than Bill* is superficially similar to parallel coupling, i.e. *John is big and Bill is big*. The point of the comparison is that there is a difference in the degree of bigness. It is evident that the sentence just given is only one of a set of three. I round out the set of sentences by citing the two following ones: *John is as big as Bill* and *John is smaller than Bill*. All of these involve the same predicates and differing first terms. More complex examples of comparison are seen in the following set of three sentences:

John loves Mary more than he loves Susan
John loves Mary as much as he loves Susan
John loves Mary less than he loves Susan

Within each sentence we have the same predicates and the same first terms with variation of the second term. Note again the similarity to parallel coupling. The only difference here between degree conjoining and parallel coupling is, as already stated, a difference in the relationship which associates the two predications. Consider still the following set:

John loves Mary more than Bill loves Mary
John loves Mary as much as Bill loves Mary
John loves Mary less than Bill loves Mary

Here within each sentence we have predicates which are identical and second terms which are identical, but we vary the first terms of the predicates--precisely the situation found in parallel coupling except for the very obvious difference here that we have degree conjoining.

The unique relationship of degree conjoining could be symbolized in some such way as follows:

d- $\wedge$, where d- symbolizes degree.

This is out of keeping, however, with our symbolism elsewhere for we have not used symbols to directly qualify $\wedge$, $\vee$, or $\supset$. I therefore replace this symbol with the usual mathematical symbols for equality or inequality. Thus the first set above, namely _John is bigger than Bill_, _John is as big as Bill_ and _John is smaller than Bill_ may be symbolized as follows:

$$Pa > Pb, \quad Pa = Pb, \quad Pa < Pb$$

The second set above, beginning with _John loves Mary more than he loves Susan_ may be symbolized as follows:

$$Pab > Pac, \quad Pab = Pac, \quad Pab < Pac$$

The third set, beginning with _John loves Mary more than Bill loves Mary_ may be symbolized:

$$Pab > Pcb, \quad Pab = Pcb, \quad Pab < Pcb$$

In English, comparison is expressed within the domains of a single sentence with two rather closely associated clauses and with adjectives inflected for comparison. It is not to be assumed that this is the situation the world over. In Wojokeso of Papua New Guinea (West 1973), there is a surface structure called the comparative paragraph. It has two obligatory components, each expounded by a sentence. Typical of this structure is the following:

> _That sun is good_. _The rain is bad_

which is equivalent to saying _The sun is better than the rain_; or a paragraph such as the following:

> _The black man's boats are little._ _The white man's boats are enormous_

which is equivalent to saying _The black man's boats are smaller than the white man's boats_. We could allege here that notional comparison is expressed by the Wojokeso surface structure paragraph just illustrated. On the other hand, we can just as well say that the Wojokeso surface structure encodes notional contrast, i.e., _The sun is good_ versus _the rain is bad_. Here _good_ and _bad_ are antonyms. _Sun_ and _rain_ are contrasting participants. This fits well the structure of notional contrast. Likewise, with the example involving boats.

We are forced then to the conclusion that we need not set up notional structure comparison, i.e., degree conjoining in Wojokeso at all. At this point apparently the notional structure of English and the notional structure of Wojokeso are dissimilar. It follows that comparison is not a cultural and linguistic universal, although it is a notional structure found very frequently around the world. The ideas of comparison and contrast are not too very different after all and apparently in certain portions of the world they fall together as the same deep structure. This illustrates the point that we may not expect to set up one universal catalog of notional structures applicable to all languages. Rather, we may have to settle for a catalog, i.e., a system of notional structures, that is say 90% to 95% universal.

2. ALTERNATION

Alternation includes notional *or* relations. While contrast turns on two points of difference, alternation turns on one point of difference. There are again types and subtypes of alternation, not all of which are featured within the surface structure of a given language, but which are formally distinguished in at least some languages found around the world. All varieties of alternation here considered are disjunctive, i.e., none are of the *and/or* varieties. I have yet to see a natural language with a built-in way of expressing *and/or* (not even Latin *vel* 'or' is used consistently for *and/or*).

2.1 Alternation with Only Two Possible Alternatives

This type of alternation turns on negative and positive use of the same predicate or on the use of a pair of antonyms. Again, however, antonyms must be defined not simply as dictionary antonyms, but as situational and contextual opposites, e.g., opposed roles, spatial oppositions, and temporal oppositions. This has been discussed under contrast above. Alternation which turns on use of a predicate with negative and positive values is seen in the following examples:

> _Either he did it or he didn't_
> _(I don't know whether) John came or not_
> _Is he there or isn't he?_

Alternation turning on a pair of antonyms is seen in the following:

> _Is he alive or dead?_
> _Do something good or evil (that we may know that you are gods)_

It is important to note that this sort of alternation (with but two alternatives) must be defined situationally for the purposes of speech and according to the presuppositions of a context. Thus it is pointless to challenge such an example as _Is he awake or asleep?_ on the ground that there may be a third possibility, namely _He's dead_. If in fact the hearer answers such a question with _Neither; he's dead_ then the hearer is not speaking to the question at all, rather he is challenging the presupposition of the question. The question itself presupposes that the man is alive and considers that he can be in but one of two states, _awake_ or _sleeping_. This is true in even such an example as _Either the man is working or his wife is working_. In the closed little universe of this sentence, only two dramatis personae exist, and one but not both of them is considered to be working.

An antonymic opposition may be culturally conditioned. Thus in the village of Bontoc (Philippines), there were (in 1967) two sorts of house roofs, either thatch or galvanized iron. Consequently, a question such as _Are you going to make your roof out of thatch or galvanized iron?_ implied an excluded middle in the relevant cultural situation in Bontoc, although it certianly did not imply that these are the only two possible ways of building roofs the world over.

Using symbols of the sort previously introduced, viz., bar for negation and " for antonym, I symbolize below some varieties of alternation with but two possible alternatives. The symbolization is not exhaustive. Thus, while in the last set of symbols an x is given to summarize spatial relations, various sorts of two-base alternation turning on still other terms (e.g., turning on temporal rather than on spatial oppositions) are certainly possible.

$Pa \vee \overline{P}a$
$Pa \vee P''a$
$Pa \vee Pa''$
$Pax \vee Pax''$

2.2 Alternation with More than Two Alternatives

I group here all sorts of alternation which involve more than two alternatives, e.g., _Either John or Mary or Sue will come_. This example has been given in what is probably the preferred form for English, namely, reduction of the alternation to a conjunction of nouns. In certain other parts of the world, the preference is for full structure: _Either John will come, or Mary will come, or Sue will come_. The alternation just illustrated is an alternation between the first terms of the predicates and may be symbolized as follows:

$Pa \vee Pb \ldots \vee Pn$

where n marks the last member of the series.

Such alternation may, however, turn not on a term of the predicate but on the predicate itself, as in _let's beg, borrow, or steal a new watch_, which may be symbolized as:

$Pab \vee Qab \ldots \vee Nab$

Here P, Q, and N symbolize successive predicates in a chain of such predicates. Again, the alternation may turn on some more remote term of the predicate such as space or time. In the following x, y, and n symbolize three temporal possibilities:

$Pax \vee Pay \ldots \vee Pan$

as in the example _He'll come today, tomorrow, or sometime next week_.

In many linguistic areas of the world, there are special surface structures on the sentence level to express alternation. Occasionally alternation with but two alternatives is distinguished in the surface structure from alternation with more than two alternatives. Thus in some Papua New Guinea languages, a word translatable as <u>or</u> occurs between successive sentence bases of an alternation. If the word <u>or</u> occurs also at the end of a sentence, it means an open alternation with further unstated alternatives. In effect, the final <u>or</u> says 'fill in the blank with something else, if you please'. Therefore, a sentence with but one <u>or</u> which occurs between the two sentence bases indicates alternation with only two possible alternatives. Ek-nii of New Guinea (Stucky 1970) has a structure of this sort.

Alternation may also be expressed on the paragraph level. Thus, such a sentence initial conjunction as <u>alternatively</u> or <u>on the other hand</u>, or even a phrase such as <u>another possibility is</u> may occur medially in a paragraph. In the Wojokeso language of New Guinea (West 1973), alternation is not expressed within the domains of a single sentence, but expressed only as a paragraph structure, i.e., as a sequence of two or more sentences.

3. TEMPORAL

Temporal relations are fully as important to natural languages as conjunction, alternation, and implication are to the logician's languages. The distinguishing of temporal overlap from temporal succession is a linguistic universal, i.e., all languages in some way take account of this distinction. While in some areas of the world, e.g., Papua New Guinea, this distinction is focal in the surface structure, even in areas where it is not focal it comes in for attention. Thus in English, although there are no specific sentence types built on temporal overlap versus succession, yet subordinate clauses with <u>when</u> and subordinate clauses with <u>while</u> carefully distinguish these relations. On the paragraph level in English, the use of specific conjunctions such as <u>meanwhile</u> likewise sets off overlap from chronological succession.

Four varieties of overlap and four varieties of succession are here distinguished as in previous studies. It is not claimed that the scheme is exhaustive. Thus, for example, it is possible to have a temporal relation which involves a series of events which take place within a temporal continuum. It's also possible to have overlapping series of events so that one series overlaps chronologically with another series.[3]

The various varieties of overlap are in one-to-one correspondence with the various varieties of succession which are described later in this chapter. Defining SPAN as any state or activity which is contextually presented to us as extending over a period of time and symbolizing span as $\underline{P}$ or $\underline{Q}$, we can relate spans by overlap ($\underline{P}\ \Delta\ \underline{Q}$) or by succession ($\underline{P}\ \Delta_{\rightarrow}\ \underline{Q}$). Defining EVENT as any action or happening not contextually presented to us as extending over a period of time, and symbolizing an event as $\underset{\cdot}{P}$ or $\underset{\cdot}{Q}$, we can likewise relate events by overlap (P Δ Q) or by succession ($\underset{\cdot}{P}\ \Delta_{\rightarrow}\ \underset{\cdot}{Q}$). We can similarly relate spans and events to each other. Notice here, however, that we do not preoccupy ourselves with the enormously difficult question concerning the real world classification of continuous versus punctiliar activities or happenings; we are interested rather in the relatively simpler question concerning how a given context conceptualizes and presents an activity to us. Furthermore, we do not posit temporal relations at all when the context does not seem to imply their relevance; instead we posit some sort of non-temporal relationship, e.g. coupling or contrast.

3.1 Overlap

Overlap includes notional *meanwhile* and *at the same time* relations. As already mentioned, four varieties of overlap are discussed here.

a) Span-span overlap presents two activities which are roughly conceived as starting and stopping at about the same time, i.e., with a large measure of overlap between them. In that the two activities are thus related, either may be made the initial or final base in the surface structure. Thus in the English sentences below (where *as* or *while* express coterminous overlap) either order of bases is found in the surface structure.

As/while he walked along, he prayed
As/while he prayed, he walked along

b) There may be an event which takes place during a span, e.g., *She fell asleep while nursing the baby*. Presumably the activity of nursing was going on for some time, even after the mother's falling asleep. Her event of falling asleep took place during this span of activity. Notice also the following, *He glanced back as he walked along*--where the English verb *glance* is basically punctiliar, and *there was an earthquake while I was there* where *the earthquake*, although a nominal structure, indicates a punctiliar event which took place during a span.

c) The converse of (b) is span-event overlap. Probably this should not be set up at any great depth as an underlying structure distinct from (b) above. At some level of notional structure (b) and (c) should be the same. Nevertheless, (c) emerges as distinct from (b) when through a process of ordering (linearization) a string begins to move toward encoding in a surface structure. There are surface structures in some languages where event-span overlap and span-event overlap do not have precisely the same encoding. Therefore, at some intermediate level of structure the two may profitably be distinguished. Examples:

While out walking, he stumbled
During the organ recital the page turner knocked the music off the rack

d) Event-event overlap is a notional structure which presents two punctiliar events as taking place at the same time, e.g.,

Just as he came out the car drove up
As I brought up my head, she tossed the knife

These four varieties of overlap are symbolized as:

$$\underline{P} \; \Delta \; \underline{Q}$$
$$\underset{\bullet}{P} \; \Delta \; \underline{Q}$$
$$\underline{P} \; \Delta \; \underset{\bullet}{Q}$$
$$\underset{\bullet}{P} \; \Delta \; \underset{\bullet}{Q}$$

Many languages have a surface structure simultaneous sentence whose raison d'être is the encoding of one or more varieties of overlap. In Agta this sentence type (called in Mayfield 1972 the concomitant sentence) encodes only span-span overlap. In Ibaloi (Ballard et al. 1971a), the simultaneous sentence apparently encodes all varieties of overlap. In both these Philippine languages a peculiar coordinating conjunction (meaning 'meanwhile' or 'at the same time') occurs between the sentence bases of the simultaneous sentence. Such a type, once established, is sometimes put to work to encode other relations than that for which it was originally constituted. Thus, the Ibaloi simultaneous sentence is an elastic surface structure which can on occasion encode events in close sequence (or roughly on the same chronological horizon) or simply indicate logical relation of the parts of one sentence which is embedded within another sentence. Likewise, in Fore (Scott 1973) a simultaneous sentence is found marked by the affix -*tegi* on a medial verb which is thus related to another medial verb or to a final verb; but the same structure is used, on occasion, to mark logical coupling rather than chronological relation.

Before leaving this section I would like to compare the English verbs *bring* and *take* with structures in other parts of the world--structures in which two predicates in overlap relation occur. Thus, in Trique (Longacre 1966) *bring* is *have*. . .*come* and *take* is *have*. . .*go*. Thus, *I brought the basket to you* is rendered into Trique as *I had the basket I came to you*. We find much the same situation in New Guinea languages (e.g., Telefol and many others; data from Phyllis Healey) where often the verb *pick up* is added for good measure: *pick up (something)*. . .*hold (it)*. . .*come* which I take to be equivalent to the English *pick up (something)*. . . *bring (it)*.

Confronted with this diversity of structure--with English (and Indo-European languages) on one side and certain languages of Mesoamerica and New Guinea on the other side--what underlying structures do we posit? Shall we semantically decompose the English verb *bring* into components of the sort found in these other two linguistic areas? Or shall we insist that in Mesoamerica and New Guinea one notional structure predicate is encoded as two surface structure predications? In brief, does Trique or English give us the clue to the deep structures which are encoded here, and shall we assign them following English to the predicate calculus or following Trique to the statement calculus? A third possibility is that we assume at such points slightly differing underlying structures from one linguistic area of the world to another and do not try to force the issue in either direction.

3.2 Succession

Succession includes notional _and then_ relations. As previously indicated, there are varieties of succession which are exemplified and symbolized.

a) There may be a prolonged activity followed by another prolonged activity, i.e., span-span succession. Note the following examples:

> _They played tennis for an hour, then swam for another hour_
> _She spent an hour getting supper, then half an hour eating it_
> _After his seven year reign in Hebron, he reigned thirty three years in Jerusalem_

b) There may be an event followed by a prolonged activity, i.e., event-span succession. Thus _He put wood in the stove and then sat there for an hour_. And _He started a fire and sat there for an hour enjoying its warmth_. For a more complex example, _After the death of his wife, he lived in isolation for two years_. In this example, the event which precedes the indicated span of activity is encoded not as a clause with a finite verb, but rather as a nominalized verb which is made the object of a preposition. Consequently, the whole first expression which could have been _First his wife died and then. . ._ is reduced to _After the death of his wife_, a temporal margin within the periphery of the English sentence.

c) The converse notional structure, i.e., span-event succession, is also found. Note here that span-event is not a permutation of event-span. Thus to take one of the above examples, we cannot permute the sentence _He started the fire, then sat there for an hour enjoying its warmth_ to *_He sat there for an hour enjoying the warmth of the fire and then_ *lighted it*, i.e., there is a linearity in the deep structure notion of succession. Here at least notional structures are ordered. Furthermore, in some languages span-event and event-span have rather distinctive encodings; e.g., in the Ibaloi (Northern Philippines) eventuation sentence, the commonest encoding is span-event (Ballard et al. 1971a). This sentence in fact does not encode event-span. For examples of span-event note the following:

> *It rained all morning but cleared up about noon*

(Note the irreversibility of the preceding sentence.)

> *He watched TV for two hours then got up and walked out*

d) Still another type of succession is event-event. Many languages (Papua New Guinea, Philippines) have sequence sentence types in their surface structure. A frequent encoding in such surface structure sequence sentences is event-event--in fact, an open series of such events (with an occasional span found here and there in the chain). Typically, several events are reported within a sentence, e.g.,

> *He grabbed the axe, hit the door, and broke it down*
> *He took the letter, read the return address, and tore it up*

A more restricted situation occurs when we have not an open ended sequence sentence but a binary structure with non-identical first terms (actors) within the conjoined predications. Here we may have a situation involving reciprocity as in *She gave him some water, and he drank it*, where the second term of the first predication becomes the first term of the second predication.

These four varieties (the fourth variety has two subvarieties) of succession are symbolized as:

$$\underline{P}\ \ \Delta_{\rightarrow}\ \underline{Q}$$
$$\underset{\bullet}{P}\ \ \Delta_{\rightarrow}\ \underline{Q}$$
$$\underline{P}\ \ \Delta_{\rightarrow}\ \underset{\bullet}{Q}$$
$$\underset{\bullet}{P}\ \ \Delta_{\rightarrow}\ \underset{\bullet}{Q}$$
$$\underset{\bullet}{P}ab\ \ \Delta_{\rightarrow}\ \underset{\bullet}{Q}b$$

In the last sub-variety, a common object of both clauses (such as water in the above example) is not symbolized, although when present it is a further term c in both bases. The formulation here given is sufficiently general to fit such a sentence as, She shot him and he died, where no such further term is present.

As already mentioned, open ended chains involving events and spans in various combinations underlie special surface structures (which are often called sequence sentences) in such areas of the world as New Guinea, Philippines, and portions of South America. In English by contrast, there is no special surface structure for encoding succession; instead succession encodes within the coordinate sentence. Deep structure succession also underlies narrative and procedural paragraphs. Here a special device in the surface structure, back reference, serves in many languages to expedite the flow from sentence to sentence, resulting in the 'narrative movement' of a narrative paragraph (with similar movement in procedural paragraphs). This surface structure device serves to cross reference back to a portion of a previous sentence. It encodes this reference, typically as a time margin, participial construction, or nominal phrase at the onset of the following sentence.

The following example is of a surface structure narrative paragraph. Notice how in sentence two still waiting for his order cross references back to ordered coffee and doughnuts then settled back with a sigh at the end of the previous sentence. In sentence three when they glanced back at him cross references back to he noticed the party of people two tables away. The fourth sentence is simply introduced with the word then. The fifth is simply introduced with the word again. No special sequence signal characterizes the last sentence.

> He went into the cafe, threw his books onto a table, ordered coffee and doughnuts, then settled back with a sigh. Still waiting for his order, he noticed the party of people two tables away. When they glanced back at him, he shifted his gaze quickly. Then he took out Pike's LANGUAGE and settled down to read it. Again his eyes wandered to the other party in the cafe. Only the arrival of the coffee and doughnuts saved him from further embarrassment.

4. IMPLICATION

Under this caption I discuss various devices whereby such surface structure units as sentence and paragraph (and even occasionally whole discourses) are organized logically rather than temporally--as in the previous section. While the relations described in this section are varied, all contain some sort of *if/then* sequence, i.e., an antecedent and a consequent. The simplest are those grouped under the first subhead, conditionality. Relations grouped under causation are somewhat more involved in that causation requires not simply an implication, but a given. Contrafactuality requires a given and a double implication. Warning requires a specially inflected predicate plus an undesirable implication.

4.1 Conditionality

I here subsume (1) pure conditions, (2) conditions with a universal quantifier on one term, (3) contingency, i.e., conditions which involve a temporal reference as well; and (4) proportions (correlative statements).

4.1.1 *Hypotheticality*. Hypotheticality includes certain unweighted *if* notions. This notional structure expresses a condition which implies nothing as to factuality of either member of the condition. It simply states a relation between an antecedent and a consequent, i.e., the consequent does not follow unless the condition stated in the antecedent also holds, e.g., *if she is there, I will stay*. In such a condition as this, we are not told whether she is there or not. We are only told that my staying is conditioned upon her being there. This openness as to the factuality of the condition also characterizes the following longer and more complex examples:

If large doses of vitamin C are harmful, I'll stop taking it
If the universe is fundamentally absurd, man's rationality is an anomaly
If meat is going to cost that much, let's eat beans

In general, two sorts of surface structures exist to express hypotheticality on the sentence level. In languages which have well developed systems of sentence margins, we may find a conditional margin, i.e., a preposed or postposed part of the sentence which is somewhat readily detachable and which consists of a clause or sentence subordinated by some morpheme which means _if_. There also may exist in the same languages nuclear patterns of sentence formation wherein the _if_ clause (or a sentence structure subordinated with _if_) clearly forms part of a system of mutual interdependence in a broader pattern. These are essentially _if/then_ sentences in which the parts of the sentence balance over against each other and require each other to complete their sense. I do not believe, however, that English has such a surface structure pattern in that the word _then_ in English is found in so many diverse functions, both logical and temporal, that it is hardly specific to an _if/then_ sequence. The situation, however, is somewhat different in a language such as Koronadal Bilaan (Southern Philippines). Here there is a particle _ku_ which means 'if' and a particle _na_ which means 'then'. The latter is, however, not a general ligature between any sort of margin and any sort of nucleus (it is not for example used in temporal relations at all), rather it specifically marks the apodosis of a conditional sentence, and when it occurs, the spotlight of the sentence is on the apodosis. Therefore in such a Bilaan sentence as _If you charge it, then (na) the price will be two pesos a kilo_, Norm Abrams (1968) feels that the emphasis is on the price. If, however the _na_ particle is deleted we return to a simpler structure which consists only of conditional margin and nucleus (rather than of a conditional nuclear sentence pattern). Here the highlight is not on the price, but on the charging itself: _If you charge it, the price will be two pesos a kilo_. Conditional sentences, as opposed to sequences of conditional margin plus nucleus, are derived structures in which the exponent of the margin is absorbed into the nucleus. It is not uncommon for such derived conditional sentences to have various degrees of specialized meaning (see Longacre 1968, 2.137-42).

Surface structure expressions of hypotheticality--especially those involving negation--are somewhat ambiguous with expressions of efficient cause in some languages, i.e., _if_ can be confused with _granted that. . ._ (cf. 4.2.1). In Choapam Zapotec (data from Larry Lyman) an expression _if not X then not Y_ is taken to mean _granted that not X therefore not Y_. To express hypotheticality in such a negative-negative proposition one must be very explicit: *if it is true that not X, then also we cannot say Y*.

Hypothetical conditions are symbolized as follows:

$$P \supset Q$$

4.1.2 *With universal quantifier of a term (in the antecedent)*. One frequent use of the universal quantifier is to modify a temporal term of the antecedent, as in *Whenever you come, I'll be waiting* which implies *At any and all times that you come, I'll be waiting*. Not dissimilar, however, is the use of the universal quantifier with locatives: *Wherever you go, I'll be thinking of you*. These uses of the universal quantifier with temporal or locative expressions in the antecedent of a condition are symbolized as follows:

$$P_{\forall x} \supset Q$$

where $\forall$ is universal quantifier of following element, and x is a temporal or locative. In other varieties of this notional structure the universal quantifier may be associated with still other terms, e.g., *Whomever we sent got lost*--in which the universal quantifier is associated with the second term (patient) of the first clause. This is also true in the sentence *Whatever he did, it went wrong*. The universal quantifier may, however, be associated with the first term (agent or experiencer) or the first predication:

Whoever tried to do it, never succeeded
Whoever knew it never told

The universal quantifier may also be associated with the third term (goal) as in *Whomever we gave it to, he promptly sent it back*. There is in fact no term in any case relation with which the universal quantifier cannot be associated. I symbolize these generally in the following:

$$P_{\forall (a)} \supset Qa$$

where (a) symbolizes any term in any case relationship in the antecedent while a in the consequent is first term.

While English commonly expresses the universal quantifier by compounding an interrogative pronoun with -*ever*, other languages have still other ways of encoding this relation. In Philippine languages, the typical surface structure for encoding universal quantifier on a term in the antecedent is to use an interrogative pronoun in a concessive margin. This gives us something which could be roughly translated as the following:

> *Even if* (or *although*) *when you come, I'll be waiting*
> i.e., 'whenever you come, I'll be waiting'
> *Even if we sent whom, he got lost*
> i.e., 'whomever we sent, he got lost'
> *Even if who went, he couldn't find his way back*
> i.e., 'whoever went, he couldn't find his way back'

4.1.3 *Contingency*. Here we have a type of deep structure *if* notion which involves a temporal reference, i.e., an implicational relation and a temporal relation are here brought together in spite of the fact that normally these two sorts of relations are opposed to each other. The temporal reference may be to temporal succession as in a translation from Ibaloi, *I made sure that she was well, then I let her work in the garden*. In this example, her working is contingent upon my prior ascertaining that she was well. Presumably until this was ascertained, she was not permitted to work in the garden. Here a later event is contingent on a prior event; $\underset{\cdot}{P}\ \Delta_{\rightarrow} \supset \underset{\cdot}{Q}$. Similarly a span (activity or state) may be contingent on a prior event, as in *You have to be paid before you are enthusiastic*. This may be represented $\underset{\cdot}{P}\ \Delta_{\rightarrow} \supset \underline{Q}$.

The temporal reference may, however, be to overlap. Overlap of the span-event variety is involved in the following further example translated from Ibaloi:

> *Then I will marry, when I have some money*
> *Then you should plant*, *when next April comes*

Here the events *getting married* and *planting* are to take place during the spans *when I have some money* and *when April comes* respectively. This may be represented $\underline{P}\ \Delta \supset \underset{\cdot}{Q}$. The surface structure may reverse the implicational order.

The notations which are suggested above combine Δ or $\Delta_{\rightarrow}$ for temporal relations and $\supset$ for implications.

The previous examples have been tranlations from Ibaloi. This is no accident. Ibaloi has a peculiar sentence, the contingency sentence--with surface features not found elsewhere in Ibaloi--to encode notional structure contingency (Ballard et al. 1971b.12-13). It is for this very reason that contingency has come to our attention as a distinct variety of notional structure. English has, however, no special surface structure at this point. Temporal expressions involving _when_ or _before_ serve the purpose. These are temporal margins on the sentence level--so that we can say that notional structure contingency encodes in English as time margin plus nucleus. The time margin expressing contingency need not be preposed. Preposed time margins often pick up some element of the previous sentence as background information in onset of the subsequent sentence; but time margins which encode contingency do not necessarily have this back reference function.

4.1.4 _Proportions (correlative statements)_. Here we have a type of notional structure which involves PROPORTIONALITY. It is seen in such statements as the following _The bigger they are the harder they fall_, _The harder they work the sooner they go home_. And perhaps even in the well-known adage, _As Maine goes, so goes the nation_, although the latter example is different in some ways from the former two. Each of these examples implies a set of conditional sentences, thus _The bigger they are the harder they fall_ could be broken into a set of sentences, _If they are small they don't fall very hard_; _If they are medium sized, they fall rather hard_; _If they are big they fall very hard_, where _small_, _medium sized_, and _big_ are matched with _not very hard_, _rather hard_, and _very hard_ respectively. The second example above could similarly be shown to imply a set of conditional sentences. _As Maine goes, so goes the nation_ could be said to imply both _If Maine goes Republican, the nation goes Republican_; and _If Maine goes Democrat, the nation goes Democrat_. But _Republican_ and _Democrat_ do not form an ordered set such as we find with _small_, _medium-sized_, and _big_; and _not very hard_, _rather hard_, and _very hard_.

I will symbolize these by resort to the usual notational convention of vertically ordered elements enclosed in brackets:

$$\begin{bmatrix} P1 \\ P2 \\ Pn \end{bmatrix} \supset \begin{bmatrix} Q1 \\ Q2 \\ Qn \end{bmatrix}$$

where P1...Pn and Q1...Qn are sets of matching variables. This could be alternatively formulized as $P \supset Q \; \Delta \; (dP = dQ)$ where $dP = dQ$ is shorthand for the vertically ordered elements enclosed in square brackets in the former forumlization. The d could be thought informally to mean degree but this does not square with the fact that the set of P and the set of Q are not always ordered sets, but may be unordered as in _Democrat_ versus _Republican_ implied by _As Maine goes, so goes the nation_.

We also have INVERSE PROPORTION in such sentences as _The harder I study, the less I know_ or _The harder I work, the less money I earn_. This is similar to expectancy reversal and may more properly belong under frustration as discussed below. In the surface structure of the Tausug language (Philippines) we find a sentence type especially framed to encode inverse proportion (Ashley, 1968). Perhaps this could be symbolized by resort to the same device employed in the first symbolization above, i.e.,

$$\begin{bmatrix} P1 \\ P2 \end{bmatrix} \supset \begin{bmatrix} Q2 \\ Q1 \end{bmatrix}$$

where P1, P2 and Q1, Q2 are sets of matching variables but the second set is inverted relative to the first set.

4.2 Causation

Causation, as we have said, involves not simply an implication, but a given. That is, there is not only an antecedent consequent relationship, but the antecedent is factual or is at least assumed to be so for the sake of the argument. Surface structures of languages seem to distinguish efficient cause, final cause (often called purpose), and a watered down variety of causation which I term circumstance. The distinction between efficient cause and final cause is as old as

Aristotle. While in formal logic these are not distinguished, they are quite regularly distinguished in natural languages. Presumably Aristotle's own sense of Greek structure led to his positing this distinction in the first place. The efficient cause is the cause that pushes, while final cause is the cause that pulls (teleological).

I suggest that the distinction between efficient cause and final cause is a linguistic universal. There are, to be true, languages where the surface structures of the two are very similar. In Ilianen Manobo (Philippines) the same particle su 'because' serves to indicate both. Nevertheless, even here the two are distinguished by the tense of the following verb. Thus we have a sentence in Ilianen Manobo (Jean Shand 1968) like You came because you were forced to, in which you were forced to expresses efficient cause; and a sentence such as You came because you were going to eat, which is translated 'You came in order to eat'. Here the non-past tense in the last clause indicates that final cause rather than efficient cause is encoded. Ilianen Manobo teaches us that what have often been called cause and purpose are sufficiently similar that they may rightly be grouped under causation. It teaches us at the same time that whatever may be the situation in formal logic, natural languages consistently distinguish efficient cause from final cause, even in relatively similar surface structure encodings as in Ilianen Manobo.

4.2.1 Efficient cause. This is the notional because relation. Efficient cause can be expressed in the following symbolization:

$$P \wedge P \supset Q$$

Notice that we continue to have here an antecedent consequent relationship. There is $P \supset Q$, but the P is given.

Various surface structures are found here. It is not unusual to have a cause margin in languages which have systems of sentence margins, as in the English, You didn't go because you were afraid. English also, like many languages, has both a result sentence and a reason sentence. In the result sentence efficient cause is encoded as the first base, You were afraid so you didn't go. In the reason sentence efficient cause is encoded as second base, You didn't go for you feared the outcome. Some languages do not have both a result sentence and a reason sentence but simply settle for one structure or the other. There are grounds for believing that in such circumstances it is the result sentence that is usually found. In languages such as Wojokeso (West 1973) which do not have a margin system on the sentence level, one surface structure is found, the cause and effect sentence (in effect, a result sentence), where English has three, i.e., cause margin plus nucleus, result sentence, and reason sentence.

The efficient cause can also be encoded on paragraph and discourse level. Thus the surface structure of a paragraph may have a reason slot where an efficient cause is expressed and/or a result slot in which the consequence is expressed. (See Longacre 1968, 1.115-28; 1970, 792).

Some examples of efficient cause encode as an abet verb plus a complement (analyzed as merged sentence in Longacre 1970 a. 802-13). Thus, we have surface constructions such as:

Stephen had Kathleen do it
Stephen made Kathleen do it
Stephen let Kathleen do it
Stephen caused Kathleen to do it
Stephen forced Kathleen to do it
Stephen forbade Kathleen to do it

For a fuller discussion of these, see Chapter 5, Section 3.

4.2.2 Final cause. This is the notional in order to relation. Final cause may be symbolized as follows:

$$P \wedge P \supset pQ$$

Here again the antecedent is given and there is an antecedent consequent relationship between the P and the Q which is sub-tagged as referring to purpose.

Languages with systems of sentence margins often have a purpose margin involving a morpheme which can be translated 'in order to', 'for the sake of', or something on that order. On the other hand, nuclear structures may be employed to express purpose as well. Thus in Trique there is a juxtaposed sentence structure (without medial conjunction) in which the second clause contains a verb with anticipatory mode (a sort of subjunctive and future combined) i.e., He took it, he will eat meaning 'He took it in order to eat.'

For a characteristic situation involving a variety of ways of expressing purpose, schoolbook Latin can scarcely be improved upon. Thus there not only are adverbial clauses in the subjunctive (which probably express a purpose margin), but also relative clauses with the verb in the subjunctive, whose intent seems to be to encode purpose, as in They chose a leader who would carry on the fight, where the thrust of the relative clause really is That he might carry on the fight. Latin also uses various nominalized constructions, infinitives, participles, gerundives, and the supine in various case relationships to express purpose. For example, gerendō bellō 'for the carrying on of the war' or 'in order to carry on the war' (gerundive with dative). Or infinitive of purpose (poetic) as in to snatch kisses (cf. Bennett 1945).

4.2.3 Circumstance. This is a watered down variety of causation, i.e., a notional structure which indicates In the circumstances. . . . It is similar to efficient cause, but often has a distinctive surface structure. Thus in English we use such expressions as in view of the fact that, in that and since to express something not quite as strongly put as efficient cause.

In that he can't sign his name it's going to be difficult to sell the house that he owns
In view of the fact that his health is steadily improving let's just await the outcome

This may be symbolized as follows:

$$cP \wedge cP \supset Q$$

Here again the antecedent is the given, and it is the circumstance itself which is assumed to be a given.

Many languages have special circumstantial margins with special subordinators and conjunctions to express circumstance. Furthermore, one of the functions of setting on the paragraph level (in narrative paragraphs) and stage on the discourse level (in narrative discourses) is to encode circumstances relative to the events reported in the body of the paragraph or discourse that follows.

The dual symbolizing of P and cP (in this subsection and the two preceding ones) both as given and as antecedent is notationally troublesome to some who have attempted to use this apparatus. A simpler notation--though in my opinion not as adequate as that already given--could turn on labeling the antecedent in efficient cause as eP and removing the first element in the formulizations (the part which symbolizes P as a given). By this notation, efficient cause, purpose, and circumstance could be symbolized as follows:

$$eP \supset Q$$
$$P \supset pQ$$
$$cP \supset Q$$

Notice that this notation fails to capture the general structure of causation as distinct from other varieties of implication.

4.3 Contrafactuality

Contrafactuality, as I have said above, involves both a given and a double implication. I explain the latter feature first. Such a sentence as *Had he gone, I would have gone too* involves a double implication. On some level or other, there is an implication that my going was to have been consequent upon his going. With this and nothing more we would simply have the notional structure of hypotheticality, i.e., $P \supset Q$. There is, however, a second implication indicated in the sentence quoted above; i.e., there is something on the order of *He didn't go and because he didn't go, I didn't go either*. This can be represented schematically as $P_\beta \wedge P_\beta \supset Q_\beta$, where $_\beta$ symbolizes the opposite of the positive-negative value indicated in the surface structure. We cannot use a simple bar for negation over the sign of the predicate in that we have not only positive understood as negative, but also negatives understood as positives. Note that the second implication as given above is in effect the notional structure of causation in its efficient cause variety. The P_β is given and it is considered to be an antecedent of Q_β. The total structure of contrafactuality is then a conflation of the simple structure of hypotheticality with that of causation as given above plus the tension between the unmarked and beta marked values of the antecedent and consequent. This may be symbolized as the following string:

$$P_\beta \wedge [P_\beta \supset Q_\beta] \wedge (P \supset Q)$$

(the square brackets mark here a subgrouping while the parentheses indicate a presupposition).

In English at least, such structures are not confined to examples with positive (understood as negative) in both clauses. Further examples are _If he hadn't gone, I wouldn't have complained_ (in which the surface structure is negative in both clauses, but the clauses are understood as expressing the positive, i.e., _He went so I complained_); _If he hadn't gone, I would have complained_ (in which the surface structure is negative in the first clause and positive in the second, but where in the first clause is understood as positive and the second as negative i.e., _He went so I didn't complain_); _If he had gone, I wouldn't have complained_ (where the surface structure is positive in the first clause and negative in the second, but where the sense is negative in the first clause and positive in the second, i.e., _He didn't go, so I complained_).

Contrafactual conditions are expressed in various ways in the surface structures of languages of the world. The Trique language of Mexico, for example, has no ready way to express a contrafactual condition. A contrafactual pattern exists in the grammar of the language but is of infrequent use and is not used with equal facility by all speakers. More commonly an involved paraphrase which recasts the whole paragraph is used to express contrafactuality. On the other hand, languages of the sort we find in New Guinea very typically have special verb affixation (including pronominal markers) that occur in the protasis and (sometimes) in the apodosis of contrafactual conditions, which give such conditions a strikingly unique surface structure. Intermediate between these two structural extremes are languages like English and the average run-of-the-mill Philippine language which uses some sort of past tense or non-present tense in both bases of the conditional sentence and maybe a particle or two expressing frustration in contrafactual surface structures. In the English example _Had he gone, I would have complained_ the past tense is used in both bases, and the first base of the protasis has the split verb phrase structure which is usually associated with the interrogative. Alternatively, of course, such English structures can employ if: If he had gone, I would have complained--and avoid the split verb structure in the protasis.

Languages may have structures readily recognizable as contrafactual conditions in spite of a minimum of surface structure. For an argument by Dick Elkins that all such structures should be set up as contrary to fact conditional sentences in spite of this minimum of surface structure marking, see Longacre 1968.2.144-6, and Elkins 1971. Elkin's argument in brief is that the interdependence of the two parts with their opposite positive-negative values, as well as certain tense restrictions, are quite sufficient to set up a contrafactual sentence in Western Bukidnon Manobo regardless of the dearth of further surface structure marking.

It is important to note that even where a specifically contrafactual structure has been isolated, we may not find it possible to express all positive-negative combinations of the apodosis and protasis in this type. Thus, in Ilianen Manobo (Shand 1968) there is a sentence type called negative conditional sentence which has a negative in both bases and which is clearly a contrary-to-fact condition in past time, as in the example The house would not have burned if you had not come along or I would not have believed it if I had not seen it. In this language other types of contrafactual conditions are expressed in more generalized structures.

4.4 Warning

The notional structure warning involves an inflected predicate (o-P). It expresses obligation in regard to a course of action or presents that course of action as highly desirable. A necessary characteristic of this notional structure is that the opposite course from o-P, i.e., P_β, implies an undesirable result Q of positive or negative value. Thus, expressed without ellipsis we find such a surface structure as the following We shouldn't let our torches go out because if we let our torches go out, we'll never find our way home. Here the we shouldn't let our torches go out is the o-P while If we let our torches go out is P_β and the undesirable result Q is not finding our way home. More frequently, however, this is telescoped in the surface structure to something like we shouldn't let our torches go out or/otherwise we'll never find our way home. In this surface structure only the o-P and the Q with negative value are expressed; the P_β is unexpressed. Consider also the Duidui (New Hebrides) sentence, It is good that we burn some of this paper, otherwise it would bury us--which seems to reflect the same elision as in the surface structure of English.

As to surface structure encodings of warning, English, in the full untelescoped structure referred to above, uses a cause margin which embeds a conditional margin plus nucleus, i.e., a condition of the hypothetical variety. In the telescoped English structure referred to above, the end result is an alternative sentence. In Duidui there is a specialized surface structure which I will not take time to describe here (Dewar 1970). In Ibaloi warning typically encodes in the result sentence which also encodes efficient cause (Ballard et al. 1971b.15-18).

Warning may also encode on the paragraph level. I once posited a surface structure warning tagmeme on the paragraph level for certain Philippine languages. I now posit a surface structure of slightly wider use with the label counter-consideration (Longacre 1968.1.XXVI, 123). The following paragraph translated from Sarangani Bilaan (McLachlin and Blackburn 1971.20) consists of two sentences, the second sentence of which expounds surface structure counter-consideration and encodes deep structure warning. We Bilaan when a child is born, then the placenta is born too before the cord is cut; but if...the placenta has not been born...the cord isn't cut. Because, if you don't wait until the placenta has been born, then it will be difficult at birth (passing the placenta). Notice how this could all be elided and telescoped into an English alternative sentence: We Bilaan, when a child is born then the placenta is born too before the cord is cut, otherwise it will be a difficult birth.

The notional structure warning may be symbolized:

$$(P_\beta \supset Q) \wedge \text{o-P}$$

where the implication is expressed in parentheses above is a necessary presupposition; i.e., there is an undesirable course of action, the P_β, which leads to an undesirable result either of a positive or negative nature (symbolized simply as Q). For this reason the course of action symbolized as o-P is urged upon the hearer.

5. PARAPHRASE

With this section, we leave the discussion of the basic notional structures of discourse and begin the consideration of elaborative and rhetorical devices. Paraphrase is such a device. Its status as a notional structure can be challenged. It can be argued that in the most profound structure, in the rock bottom semantics of languages, paraphrase does not exist, everything is said but once, and that saying the same thing more than once is essentially a surface structure phenomena. On the other hand, we have cases in which essentially the same paraphrase figures in several distinct surface structures. Take, for instance, the statement, _I want to take this rat poison up, I don't want to let it lie around_ (cf. Chapter 7.9). I shall call this negated antonym paraphrase. We note here, however, that it may encode at least three distinct surface structures in English. In the form just given, the sentence may be considered to be a surface structure paraphrase or juxtaposed sentence. It is a sentence type which rejects medial conjunction and has a unifying non-final intonation in English. If we permute the two members of the statement, we may say _I don't want to let this rat poison lie around, but on the contrary, I want to take it up_. Here we have a surface structure antithetical sentence. Moreover, I have heard this very same sentence encoded as a simple sentence with a cause margin: _I want to take this rat poison up because I don't want to let it lie around_. Therefore on some intermediate level, paraphrase is needed because it emerges at different places in the surface structure of languages--and even within the same language.

While I distinguish here seven varieties of paraphrase, they essentially group into three (plus summary paraphrase): (1) equivalence and negated antonym paraphrase which do not perceptibly involve addition or loss of information between two bases; (2) generic-specific paraphrase and amplification paraphrase which involve an increase in information; and

(3) specific-generic paraphrase and contraction paraphrase which involve a decrease in the amount of information. I nevertheless list these seven varieties below with the understanding that we do not press overmuch distinctions between members of the pairs just indicated, especially the distinction between generic-specific paraphrase and amplification paraphrase as well as that between specific-generic paraphrase and contraction paraphrase. We may well find that these distinctions are not at great depth but depend on somewhat accidental features of the lexical surface structure of a given language (e.g., availability of synonyms and antonyms; cf. Section 1.2 of this chapter). The distinction between certain varieties of paraphrase in terms of loss or gain of information can, however, clearly be sustained as a notional distinction. Presumably the addition of further information while continuing a sentence or paragraph and the subtraction of information while continuing such a unit reflect differing intentions on the part of the speaker. I add also summary paraphrase which seems to be a frequent device.

5.1 Equivalence Paraphrase

Sometimes a speaker feels that to say something only once is not sufficient but that he needs to say it twice or more in differing words. This is especially true in oratorical style but is by no means uncommon in daily life as well. Perhaps this is dictated by the feeling that unless a certain number of words are used in saying something, the speaker will not get through to the hearer; if we say it in two or three different ways and the hearer does not get it the first time, he may get it the second or third time. Thus we have sentences like *He capitulated immediately; he surrendered on the spot*. Here *capitulated* and *surrendered* are very close synonyms. It is hard to say that either base says more than the other base in terms of information content although we might argue that *immediately* refers more to time and *on the spot* refers more to location. Consider also the following sentence which is translated from Ibaloi: *All the soldiers left, all the Japanese left*. *Soldiers* is more specific than *Japanese* in regard to occupation. *Japanese* is more specific than *soldiers* in regard to nationality. It is at all events understood by the hearers that *soldiers* and *Japanese* are synonyms, in that the text is concerned with the Japanese army of occupation in the Philippines during World War II. Therefore, _all the soldiers left_, and _all the Japanese left_ are very close equivalents in terms of information. Or take the following sentence: _I went home, I went to the house_. Here _home_ and _house_ are in current American English close synonyms and the second base neither appreciably adds nor subtracts information relative to the first base. These deep structures may be symbolized as:

$$Pa \equiv P'a$$
$$Pa \equiv Pa'$$

where P and P′ are synonyms as are also a and a′.

In some languages (e.g., English and Ibaloi), equivalence paraphrase with more than two bases is encoded as a surface structure alternative sentence where the word _or_ simply indicates variant ways of verbalizing the same thing. Take a sentence like _Shouldn't we call in the law, or notify the police, or get some sort of protection_? Here _call in the law_, _notify the police_ and _get some sort of protection_ are all synonyms. We could say that perhaps _get some sort of protection_ is more generic than _call in the law_ or _notify the police_, but nevertheless the three expressions are very similar in content. This device (encoding of equivalence paraphrase as an alternative sentence) is especially characteristic of oratorical style in some languages. Equivalence paraphrase with multiple bases may be symbolized as:

$$Pa \equiv P'_1a \equiv P'_2a \ldots \equiv P'_na$$

where P'_1, P'_2, and P'_n indicate an open sequence of synonyms for P.

5.2 Negated Antonym Paraphrase and Similar Structures

Negated antonym is one of the closest possible varieties of paraphrase. We may argue as to whether two synonyms involve gain or loss of information content, but we are not so likely to argue that granted a pair of antonyms with the negation of one of them, the two are not close equivalents. Thus, _white_ and _not black_ are close equivalents, as are also _poor_ and _not rich_, and _short_ and _not tall_. It often makes a difference in the choice of surface structure as to where the predication with the negated antonym comes. We may consider therfore that the ordering of the unordered paraphrase is an early step in the derivation of the surface structure. In English _white_ and _not black_ are related as negated antonym paraphrase, but _white_, _not black_ versus _not black_, _white_ involve distinct linear orderings with differing implications for English surface structures. With a negated antonym in second base we derive a surface structure paraphrase sentence, i.e., _It's white, not black_. With the negated antonym in the first base of the sentence we derive a surface structure antithetical sentence, such as _It's not black, but white_ or _It's not black, but on the contrary it's white_. It is also possible to encode into a paraphrase sentence _It's not black, it's white_. For such cases with negation in the first base, the rules for English are: (1) If we repeat the first term and copula in the second base, then the simple conjunction _but_ does not appear and presumably we have still the surface structure of a paraphrase sentence. (2) We may, however, repeat the first term and copula in the second base and retain _but_ provided that it is strengthened to a conjunctive phrase (_but on the contrary_), thus casting the construction into the surface structure of the antithetical sentence. (3) If we do not repeat in the second base the first term and the copula, then the simple conjunction _but_ occurs and the construction is again cast into the surface structure antithetical sentence (Longacre 1967.18-20; 1970a.796-97).

Negated antonym paraphrase may be symbolized as:

$$Pa \equiv \bar{P}''a$$
$$\bar{P}''a \equiv Pa$$

where $\bar{P}$ stands as usual for negation and P" stands for antonym of P.

Very similar to negated antonym paraphrase is NEGATED HIGHER GRADIENT PARAPHRASE. Here we deal not with a pair of antonyms but with two lexical items which belong to a gradience scale; one of the two items is of higher rank than the other--which is characteristically near the average or median; and the higher ranking item is negated. Consider the following:

It's not hot but it's warm
It's warm but it's not hot

Although it's not hot, it's warm
It's not hot; it's just warm

Notice that while it is consistently the higher ranking item[4] that is negated, the negated item may come in either base and is not limited to the first base in order to be a grammatical antithetical sentence (the first two examples). Above, in negated antonym paraphrase, negation must come in the first base if we are to encode into a grammatical antithetical sentence. Notice also that the lower ranking item takes a word such as just when we encode within a paraphrase sentence. For further examples of this type consider:

He's a good man but he's no paragon of virtue
He's no master mechanic but he does manage to keep things repaired around here

Symbolizing the median item as P^o, I formulize (with linear ordering immaterial):

$$\bar{P}a \equiv P^o a \wedge (P > P^o)$$

where the inequality at the end $(P > P^o)$ represents the gradience scale.

Still another variety of paraphrase, similar to that just described, may be called NEGATED EXTREMES. Consider the following sentences:

It's neither hot nor cold; it's just warm
It's not black nor white; it's just grey
She's neither beautiful nor ugly; she's a plain, wholesome, ordinary kid

These sentences involve gradience scales with three values: hot, warm, cold; black, grey, white; beautiful, plain-wholesome-ordinary, ugly.

Symbolizing again the median item as P^o and arbitrarily taking P as the highest ranking item, I formulize as follows (partially suggested by Phyllis Healey):

$$[\bar{P}a \wedge \bar{P}''a] \equiv P^o a \wedge (P > P^o > P'')$$

In many English examples of the surfacing of this notional structure, we find the median term P^o implied but unstated:

He's not tall and he's not short (either)
She's neither beautiful nor ugly

I do not feel it necessary to posit here a general kind of coupling ($\bar{P}a \wedge \bar{P}''a$) which (we would have to say) frequently embeds within this type of NEGATED EXTREMES paraphrase. Rather, I feel that these surface structures are elliptical and that a median lexical item is always implied--and therefore present in the notional structure. That is, I do not believe that $\bar{P}a \wedge \bar{P}''a$ has any place in the notional structure apart from constituting a part of the structure here described, formulized, and illustrated.

5.3 Generic-specific Paraphrase

This is a very common type of paraphrase involving gain of information in the second member. In this variety, a more specific lexical item (or items) is used in the second member than in the first member. This may be represented in a Euler diagram, i.e., as two concentric circles, the first member represented by the inclusive circle, the second member by the included circle. Thus we may have a sentence such as He cooked it, he fried it in vegetable oil. In this sentence fry in vegetable oil is more specific than cook. Certainly the verb fry is more specific than the generic verb cook. We have also the added information in vegetable oil. Another example, He was executed yesterday, he was shot by the firing squad. We see that shot by the firing squad is more specific than executed. Generic-specific paraphrase may be symbolized as:

$$gPa \equiv sPa$$

where g and s symbolize generic-specific qualifications of the predicates respectively.

5.4 Amplification Paraphrase

A fourth type of paraphrase can be called amplification. This is very similar to generic-specific paraphrase, where more specific lexical items occur in the second base than in the first base. In amplification paraphrase, however, the first base is repeated in substance (often by means of a synonym), and a further phrase or two is added which gives the additional information. Thus, take the following sentence translated from Ibaloi (Ballard et al. 1971a): He was unconscious: Dabonay, a woman, had knocked him unconscious. Here the second base gives the information that the unconsciousness was due to the agency of Dabonay, a woman. In the example He sang, he sang two songs we are given in the second base the further information that it was two songs that were performed by him. He went away, he went away two weeks ago adds in the second base that it was two weeks ago that he left. Patterns may be even more varied in that we may also have a sentence such as He went away, I saw him go away where I saw him is added in the second base. Often what is added in the second base is a noun phrase which indicates a further participant or a phrase referring to place, time, or manner. In the last example, He went away of base one is incorporated as second base of an English merged sentence (Longacre 1970a.802-13) which expounds the second base of the paraphrase.

The following formulization symbolizes most varieties of amplification (noticeably not the last example, however).

$$Pa \equiv [Pba \vee Pab \vee Pax]$$

where the predication Pa of the first base may be expanded to Pba (adding a new first term b and making a the second term) or Pab (adding a new second term b) or Pax (adding an expression of time, place or manner). To formulize the last example above we would need to assume some embedding in the notional structure. I note in passing that it will scarcely be possible to avoid such embedding, but I have not thought much in this direction as yet.

5.5 Specific-generic Paraphrase

Here there is loss of information in the second base as compared to the first base. This then is the converse of generic-specific paraphrase and is not as common as the latter. An example of specific-generic paraphrase is such a sentence as They dug up Assyrian ruins, they did some excavation where dug up Assyrian ruins is more specific than did some excavation. We symbolize:

$$sPa \equiv gPa$$

5.6 Contraction Paraphrase

This form of paraphrase is very similar to specific-generic paraphrase and is the converse of amplification. There is less information in the second base than in the first base. But while in specific-generic paraphrase the loss of information in the second base is due to the use of a more generic lexical term than in the first base, in contraction paraphrase, certain lexical items (often noun phrases) which are found in first base are not found in the second base at all. Information from the first base is given either by repeating the predicate of the base or by giving it in the form of a synonym.

This sort of paraphrase was first called to my attention in the Wik-Munkan language of Queensland, Australia, by Barbara Sayers (1976.27). One of her examples may be translated as follows: _Wait, we'll bury the fish in the ashes, we'll hide (it)_, where _hide something_ is a synonym for _bury_ but where the information _fish in the ashes_ is deleted from the second base. In another example translated from Wik-Munkan, _One by one they tried to find wells, they dug_, the item _dug_ occurs in Base 2, but not the item _wells_, which is found in the Wik-Munkan Base 1. It is not hard to think of English examples somewhat parallel to these. Take the English sentence, _I won't go to see him, I just won't go_, where _to see him_ is deleted from the second base.

Most varieties of contraction can be symbolized as:

$$[Pba \vee Pab \vee Pax] \equiv Pa$$

5.7 Summary Paraphrase

This is a type of paraphrase which employs a generic lexical item in the last base after a series of more specific lexical items in the preceding bases, e.g., _John works at the sawmill; Jim at the repair shop; and Al at the print-shop--that's what they're all doing_, where _that_ and _they_ as pronouns, _all_ and _doing_ as a generic verb of activity are all used to refer back to the preceding bases of the sentence. The English sentence is characterized by gapping, i.e., _John works at the sawmill_ is given in full, but the verb _works_ is not repeated in the second or third bases.

While this is the preferred pattern in English, in many parts of the world such reduction is not looked on with favor, and it would be much more natural and stylistically pleasing to say something on the order of, _John works at the sawmill; Jim works at the repair shop; and Al works at the print-shop--that's what they're all doing._ Summary paraphrase is represented as:

$$P(a) \wedge Q(b) \wedge R(c) \ldots \equiv gN(U)$$

where P,Q, and R are successive predicates in an open sequence, gN is a generic (summary) closing predication, and U is the Universal set comprising a + b + c . . . . Usually U is expressed in a pronoun such as _they_--often with a universal quantifier, e.g., _all_. It happens that in the above example the same predicate _work_ occurs in all bases except the last, but this is not essential; at any rate _sawmill_, _repair shop_ and _printshop_ differ from base to base.

In sketching the varieties of paraphrase I have not spoken of the role of paraphrase in paragraph structure. Paragraph structure is more loose and rambling in its development than sentence structure. Our varieties of paraphrase are, however, recognizable on the paragraph as well as on the sentence level. Indeed in the various sorts of expository paragraph, paraphrase is a main device of paragraph development. Some sort of topic sentence (or TEXT as I all it) is stated early in the paragraph. Subsequent sentences develop the theme of the topic sentence by various paraphrase devices. While equivalence paraphrase is not unknown, it is more common to find generic-specific and amplification paraphrase. Negated antonym paraphrase also figures occasionally in the structure of the expository paragraph. Analyzed examples of what I call the text-expo relationship within Philippine languages are found in Longacre 1968.1.111-41. Also in hortatory paragraphs (described in the same volume) the relationship which I call exhortation-reinforcement is essentially a paraphrase relationship as well.

I cite here two examples of expository paragraph from the same page of Longacre 1968 (136, examples 109-110). The first is translated from Tboli (Porter 1968). The text (or topic sentence) is: _Before the war, there was no peace among_ the Tagabilí. This is amplified in three following sentences, the first of which is There was always fighting even over tiny matters. This sentence apparently is related to the first sentence by negated antonym paraphrase, i.e., the no peace and always fighting even over tiny matters are thus related. The third and fourth sentences seem to be related to the first sentence via generic-specific paraphrase, i.e., where the first sentence has no peace among the Tagabili the third sentence has they would put curses on people at night and the fourth sentence has they would capture children. Presumably the third and fourth sentences are simply specific lexical items expanding the no peace among the Tagabili in the text or topic sentence.

The next example is from Atta Negrito (see also Whittle 1971.216). The text or topic sentence here is School closed for the children last Thursday and Friday. The second and third sentences are in generic-specific paraphrase with this first sentence. The second sentence: For Uneng they had the last class on Thursday; that was their graduation. The third sentence is As for Antsings' class, Friday was their closing. Here the second and third sentences simply give more specific items than are found in the first sentence. Where we find children in the first sentence, we find names of particular children in the second and third sentences. Where we find a common reference to Thursday and Friday in the first sentence, we find a reference to Thursday in the second sentence and to Friday in the third sentence.

It is evident that these varieties of paraphrase are not as closely knit as those which we encountered in the examples given of paraphrase encoded as sentences. The relative openness and looseness of the last two examples are consonant with the difference between paragraph and sentence as levels of structure. Nevertheless, on the paragraph level we deal essentially with the same types of paraphrase relationships as those which we catalogued as the notional structure of sentences in the examples cited in the preceding subsections.

In closing this section on paraphrase, several comments are in order. Note that while I have spoken of equivalence as the first variety of paraphrase, pure identity is not relevant here, i.e., if we have an expression such as I won't do it, I won't do it, I won't do it!, very probably no paraphrase is intended but simply EMPHASIS. In some languages, identity recapitulation of this sort is used to express duration, i.e., *He worked for a long time* would be expressed *He worked and he worked and he worked and he worked. . ..* This is especially common in New Guinea. I believe that here we encroach on notional structures which properly do not belong to the expanded statement calculus--which is the basis of sentence and paragraph structure--but to a lower level of notional structure which we can term inflection. Here expressions of duration, inception, and termination find their place (Chapter 6, 2.1.2).

Note also the restriction which characterizes successive predications which are related by paraphrase, viz., all must have the SAME FIRST TERM. The only qualification of this statement is resort to the universal set. We have seen in summary paraphrase that we may have the last base of a paraphrase employing as its first term a summary pronoun or a noun phrase such as *they* or *all of them* or something on this order. Here set members occur with previous predications, and the term referring to the universal set occurs with the last predication. The opposite situation may occur, expecially on the paragraph level, where the first base of a paraphrase may contain a predication whose first term refers to the universal set and subsequent predications have as their first terms references to members of the universal set. This we saw in the second example of paraphrase on the paragraph level above. We also have here a further variety of paraphrase which is the converse of summary, viz., PREVIEW--with correspondingly different discourse functions.

6. ILLUSTRATION

A speaker or writer can illustrate a point, especially in expository and hortatory discourse, by using a simile or citing an example.

6.1 Simile

In this notional structure two dissimilar things are paired by virtue of their possessing one point of similarity. Differing culture areas of the world differ as to the similes that they employ.

Some languages have special structures for the simile. Such structures can be very involved and very exacting. In Trique, for example, the particle ro? 'like' occurs initially in such a construction. The verbs of both bases must be identical, for example: like does this, so does that; like goes this, so goes that; like is this, so is that; like appears this, so appears that. Here English characteristically uses like as a preposition: She is like a rose, She acts like a baby, A pretty girl is like a melody, etc. There is nevertheless a certain tendency in English to use like as a conjunction. For this and other reasons we can argue that the repeated verb is implied or understood, i.e., She is like a rose (is), She acts like a baby (acts), A pretty girl is like a melody (is). Consequently, the notional structure of English simile appears to be not dissimilar to the surface structure of simile in Trique.

In many languages similes may be shortened to metaphors by omission of the word like and by substitution of the copula verb for whatever verb originally occurred in the sentence. Thus, instead of she is like a rose, we get she is a rose and instead of she acts like a baby, she is a baby. This, of course, is a somewhat over-simplified account of the derivation of simile to metaphor. We find, for example, that apparently almost anywhere in a sentence there may be substitution of a metaphorical word for the literal word which would otherwise occur there. This is, however, essentially a sort of embedding phenomenon, with deletion of the relative and copula plus a few other adjustments. Thus, Jesus' words Go tell that fox apparently involve a substitution of fox for Herod. I assume, however, an intermediate stage which is simile: Go tell Herod who is like a fox. With deletion of the elements which intervene between Herod and fox and the addition of the demonstrative we arrive at the surface structure. It seems, therefore, safe to assume that simile is basic to the notional structure of this sort of illustration and that metaphor is a surface structure contraction of simile.

Simile may be formulized as:

$$lPa \wedge Pb$$

where l stands for likeness.

6.2 Exemplification

Exemplification is seen in such a sentence as _Choose a good name, e.g., Michael_. Here a universal set of good names is indicated, of which _Michael_ is declared to be a member. This may be formulized as:

$$P(U) \wedge P(a) \wedge (a \varepsilon U)$$

Somewhat more complex is the following example: _He has had an innovating career as seen in his introduction of the Mariachi Mass into the Sunday morning service at the Cathedral_. Here again, a universal set is indicated in _innovating career_ of which _the introduction of the Mariachi Mass_ is a member.

Exemplification, like simile, while customarily (in English) expressed within a sentence may be given more extensive development within the paragraph or the discourse. Thus a paragraph may begin: _Nations which lose the sense of self-preservation perish. Take Carthage, for example, which failed to realize in the years of the Second Punic War the seriousness of the struggle in which she found herself engaged_. . . . It is not unusual in discourse, especially of a hortatory or expository variety, to have a discourse level slot termed illustration, or something to that effect, in which either simile or exemplification figures.

7. DEIXIS

I group here a number of notions, all of which involve existential or equational predications. Originally two notional structures were set up here to accomodate two surface structure sentence types which occur within the Ibaloi language of the Philippines (Ballard et al. 1971b.9-11). I appropriate from the grammar of Ibaloi the surface structure labels, introduction and identification, as terms for the notions which are involved. Along with the description of these notional structures, I indicate the surface structures with which they are associated in Ibaloi and attempt to generalize for other languages. Finally, a few further varieties of deixis are suggested.

7.1 Introduction

Introduction is a notional structure in which existence is predicated of something or someone and then a further predication is immediately made about that existent. This may be symbolized:

$$\exists a \wedge Qa$$
$$\exists a \wedge Qba$$

where ∃ symbolizes an existential predication (cf. Chapter 5.2).

In Ibaloi there is a surface structure sentence type, a juxtaposed sentence the first base of which is expounded by an existential clause, the second of which is less restricted. Note the following two examples which are translated from Ibaloi. In the first the existent is first term in base 2 (Qa); in the second the existent is second term in base 2 (Qba):

> There was a young man named Amkidit, he lived on the mountain
>
> And there was one who went for wood, they cornered him and killed him and took his head

It is more common in languages to find this structure encoded on the paragraph level, as in the first chapter of the Gospel of St. John, There was a man sent from God whose name was John. The same came for a witness to bear witness of that light ....

It is evident that this is a structure typically used in beginning a discourse. Whether it is capable of being jammed into the same sentence as in Ibaloi or manifests itself simply as a sequence of sentences depends entirely on the structure of a given language. It may be that this is essentially the relationship involved between the stage of a discourse and its first episode.

7.2 Identification

In this notional structure a participant is introduced via a predication and then his function in the discourse is identified. The participant is other than first term of its predicate. Examples translated from Ibaloi are:

> And he bought a dog, and that was what the old men ate...
> Kimboy went back and got a hammer and that was what they used
> The Spanish picked him up on their way and he was the one who showed the way up here

This structure may be symbolized:

$$Pab \wedge Ebc$$

where E symbolizes an equational predicate, i.e., an affirmation of class membership, and where there is reciprocity of a sort--in that the second term of the first predicate becomes first term of the second predicate.

This and the preceding notional structure are very similar. The first structure is more properly used in initiating a discourse in that it essentially involves the relation of setting to the first episode. The second notional structure presented above is typically used in introducing a new participant or prop anywhere in the discourse--including, of course, its beginning. I have called both these functions deixis, using deixis as a broad term for any sort of identificational-contrastive pointing.

7.3 Some Further Varieties of Deixis

Phyllis Healey (private correspondence) suggests some further varieties of deixis which, like those already listed and illustrated, also involve existential and equational predications. The first is possibly a variety of introduction as illustrated above:

> There was a man called Peter; he was an electrician.

This can be symbolized:

$$\exists a \wedge Eab$$

A second structure is harder to classify:

> Peter was an electrician; he worked for Thomas Smothers.

This can be symbolized:

$$Eab \wedge Pa$$

Again, both these further structures seem to be concerned with introduction and identification of participants and, like those described under the sub-sections above, may serve to introduce discourses--including those embedded (as episodes) in larger discourses.

8. ATTRIBUTION

I group under this label two sorts of notional structure, specifically the attribution of an utterance or the substance of an utterance to a speaker; and the attribution of cognitive content to a conscious subject (cf. experiencer in Chapter 4). I call these relations respectively SPEECH ATTRIBUTION and AWARENESS ATTRIBUTION. I prefix w and a to the symbol P to indicate these relations respectively. Thus $wPa \wedge Qb$ symbolizes _Cyril said "Nestorius has arrived"_. Similarly $aPa \wedge Qb$ symbolizes _Cyril knew that Nestorius was coming_.

8.1 Speech Attribution

To begin with we must face the question as to whether it is legitimate to represent this notion as a structure of the propositional calculus (a combination of predications) or whether it might be better handled under the predicate calculus. Notice that in our presentation of case frames (Chapter 5) we recognize that there are SPEECH verbs which occur with surface structure complements which are prolongations of the meaning of the verb itself, i.e., range in the notional structure. Thus we have _tell a story_, _sing a song_, _preach a sermon_, _recite a poem_, _say a word_, etc. As we have said, as notional structures, these do not involve a verb and a patient but rather predicate and its range. At the deepest level of notional structure, range perhaps does not occur at all, in that it is essentially an elaboration of the verb itself. The most frequent reason for using range is to quantify or qualify in some way the product of the activity such as _the mother told her child two stories_, _she sang a touching song_, _he preached an effective sermon_ or _I wrote seven poems this morning_. Verbs of speech used in this fashion simply tell us that a certain type of verbal activity has taken place and employ range nouns to indicate roughly the nature, number and quality of the product. With most of these verbs the surface structure object (notional range) is not obligatory: _John spoke_, _Oscar preached_, _Mary recited_, _Steven sang_, etc.

But what of such a sentence as _John said, "I'm fine, but how are you?"_? Is the quotation _"I'm fine but how are you"_ related as range to the verb in the same way that _word_ is related to _say_ in _say a word_? It seems to me that the answer is negative. A range noun that further specifies verbal activity seems to me to be distinct from a quotation which is introduced by a formula of quotation. In the former we are simply told that verbal activity (or some similar activity such as singing or writing) has taken place; in the latter we are given someone's words with identification of the speaker (and possibly of the addressee). It seems to me that the latter is essentially a combination of predications in which a predication (or complex of predications) is combined with a predication which attributes the predication to someone.

An examination of the surface structure of quotations--which I believe usually constitute surface structure SENTENCES, not clauses with quotations as objects[5]--further reinforces our argument that quotations belong to the notional structure of the propositional calculus rather than to the structures of the predicate calculus. To begin with, if we consider that quotations are clauses in which the quoted words are the object, the surface structure of quotation constructions has a rather unique immediate constituent grouping, i.e., the subject and the verb group together against the so-called object. We find also that the subject and the verb move about as a block in many languages and that this block occurs either initial in the unit, final in the unit, or interrupting the unit itself, as in _John said, "I'm fine, but how are you?"_, _"I'm fine, but how are you?" said John_, and _"I'm fine," said John, "But how are you?"_. This is strange behavior for verb, subject, and object both in English and in many other languages. Verb and object are more likely to group together in most languages than are subject and verb. Furthermore, linear orders occur that do not parallel normal clause structures, and finally, the object can be of inordinate length (a paragraph or a whole discourse).

I feel then that the function of attributing the actual words or the general substance of what is said to a specific speaker is very different from simply reporting that a speech act has taken place, and I believe that the former function should be considered to be a function of the propositional calculus, i.e., a combination of predications rather than a simple predication.

Quotations emerge in the surface structures of some languages in two divergent forms: the direct quotation and the indirect quotation. The direct quotation purports to give the actual words of the speaker. In a language where the direct quotation and the indirect quotation contrast as surface structures, the use of the former is sometimes an attempt to avoid interpretation and bias (or to SEEM to avoid them). Thus a person may insist: _But I gave you his actual words_! Indirect quotation, when reporting what someone has said, involves adaptation of the words of the one quoted to the viewpoint of the reporter (i.e., the actual speaker of the sentence). This adaptation affects pronouns and expressions of time and place. Thus the direct quotation sentence _He said, 'I'll go over there tomorrow'_ can be recast as an indirect quotation sentence one day later: _He said that he would come here today_. In the indirect quotation relative to the direct quotation the lexical items _come_, _here_, and _today_ replace the items _go_, _over there_, and _tomorrow_. In addition, the modal _would_ replaces _will_ to agree with the tense of the verb _said_ in the quotation formula. But even this wholesale adaptation of viewpoint is not the end of the story. The reporter may inject his own evaluation. Thus, it is possible to place a contrastive intonation peak on the verb in the quotation formula; this plus a non-final intonation at sentence end enables the reporter to cast doubt on the intentions, veracity, or ability of the original speaker in regard to keeping his word: _He_ SAID _he would come here today_.... It is impossible to do this in the direct quotation; to attempt to do so is to confuse the hearer and cause him to believe you are actually using an indirect quotation. Thus a direct quote _He said, "I'm a fool"_ if given unifying intonation comes out as _He said I'm a fool_ which is interpreted as meaning 'He, the speaker, said that I, the reporter, am a fool'.

It is evident that the surface structure meanings of direct and indirect quotations differ considerably--as I have attempted to illustrate above. Not all languages have, however, the option of converting a direct quotation into an indirect quotation. Thus, in Agta (Mayfield 1972) while a structure loosely called indirect quotation exists it encodes awareness (cf. 8.2) not speech. There is simply no way to change He said, 'I will come' to something on the order of He said that he would come. There are, furthermore, languages which while having both direct and indirect quotations in their surface structure, greatly prefer the former to the latter. Such a language is Biblical Hebrew. Here some otherwise competent recent translations of the Old Testament Scriptures into English suffer from not translating Hebrew direct questions as English indirect quotations in places (for example multiple nesting of quotation within quotation) where the latter is more natural to English (Crim 1973).

It appears, therefore, that the surface structure direct quotation sentence is the primary device for encoding speech attribution. Where the surface structure of a given language also has an indirect quotation sentence the surface meaning of the latter must be ascertained and the constraints on its use explored.

It is important to note that the speech attribution relation characterizes not only statements but questions and commands as well: He asked, 'Are you coming or not?', He commanded, 'Don't come tomorrow'. In surface structure of a language which has free use of direct and indirect quotations this distinction intersecting with statement, question, and command gives six surface structure etic types. It is not uncommon for some of these to emerge as emically contrastive types, i.e., distinctive surface structures, in a given language. Of these one of the commonest is the indirect question.

Surface structure quotation sentences, while primarily existing to encode speech attribution, are put to other tasks in some languages. Inner speech expressed with a verb such as I think is, of course, no great departure from the function of the direct quotation nor its customary notional structure. Furthermore, as we see in the section below, the indirect quotation in many languages encodes not simply speech attribution, but awareness attribution. More radical departure from the primary encoding of quotation sentences is found in certain New Guinea languages (Deibler 1971).

8.2 Awareness Attribution

Here I have in mind such sentences as:

I know that he's coming
I saw that he was in a bad mood
I feel that things aren't working out right
I sensed that all was well

Probably the archetypal verb here is *know*. As used above, *saw* is equivalent to *come to know* (by visual inspection), while *feel* and *sensed* are equivalent to *know* with some added components of degree of probability and inference.

Again the question is bound to arise: why do we have an awareness attribution relation in the predicate calculus and also a case frame for *know* (C'1) in the statement calculus (E signifies the experience and R, range):

$$\left\{ \begin{matrix} \text{S-EXPERIENTIAL} \\ \text{COMPLETABLE} \end{matrix} \right\} \text{ER}$$

illustrated with such clauses as *Susan really knows algebra* (Chapter 5, Sec 1.4)?

Again, however, I point out that such nouns as *algebra* above are notional structure range. In the awareness attribution relation here under consideration we have, however: (a) detailed, specific cognitive content expressed in a predication; and (b) an attribution of that cognitive content to someone by means of another predication. There is, moreover, a certain general parallelism here to speech attribution where the speaker-spoken dichotomy parallels here the knower-known (cognitive content) dichotomy. If, therefore, it can be established--as I believe that it can--that the former is a relation of the enlarged propositional calculus, then this in part carries the latter.

9. FRUSTRATION

Many of the structures described in previous sections have frustrated counterparts. Frustration is, therefore, a further notional parameter which intersects the system already described.

I here use frustration as one of several possible terms to describe the relation under consideration. Expectancy reversal or even counter-expectation are further possible labels. Basic to this notional structure is an implication that there is a P which normally implies a Q, but that rather than Q the opposite positive-negative value occurs. The $P \supset Q$ implication may be so general as to be a collocational expectancy, i.e., a given lexical item normally follows another lexical item in context. On the other hand the implication $P \supset Q$ may be highly specific to a given sentence in a given discourse.

In general, the varieties of frustration are as follows: frustrated coupling (which perhaps should be viewed as frustrated efficient cause, see below); frustrated succession; frustrated overlap; frustrated hypothesis; frustrated contingency; frustrated efficient cause; frustrated final cause; and frustrated attribution. A further group of relations have to do with modality and may almost be called frustrated inertial guidance systems, in which there is frustration of intention, obligation or ability.

The following representation summarizes all varieties of frustration with the exception that the final element S of the chain does not occur in all varieties.

$$(P \supset Q) \wedge P \wedge R \wedge Q_{\beta} \wedge S$$

All structures involve some sort of implication, or collocational expectancy; there is a P which implies a Q. This is a necessary presupposition of any structure, sentence or paragraph which encodes frustration. R symbolizes blocking circumstance, event, attitude, etc. Q_{β} tells us that whether Q is basically positive or negative in value its value is reversed here from what is anticipated. S symbolizes a surrogate action which characterizes some varieties of frustration. It is rare to find all of these features of the anatomy of frustration overtly stated in the same sentence or even in the same paragraph. Customarily something is left out. More of this below in the various sections.

9.1 Frustrated Coupling

We encounter such sentences as the following: She's fat but she's not sloppy. This sentence seems to be based upon the collocational expectancy that fat and sloppy are in the same semantic domain and are likely to co-occur in the same sentence; the presupposition of this sentence is that fat implies sloppy. There is, however, some unstated blocking circumstance, e.g., the particular capacity of the woman involved to be careful about her person or dress. Thus we have in this sentence a presupposition P implies Q, a statement of P, and a Q with β value, i.e., not sloppy instead of sloppy. There is no surrogate action expressed in this sentence.

The following sentence is somewhat different.

> You're big, but you're tough (from a story of an animal which was tempted to eat a crocodile)

I have in previous work called the notional structure of such sentences as this CONFLICTING PREMISES. It is evident, however, that you're tough is simply a blocking circumstance (R) which leads to the animal's not trying to eat the crocodile. There is a presupposition in this sentence that P (big) implies some unstated Q--probably something on the order of good meal. Rather, however, than the sentence saying You're big but you're not a good meal it says You're big, but you're tough--where the toughness of the meat precludes a good meal. In this sentence, P and R are expressed, but no further elements of the anatomy of frustration.

9.2 Frustrated Succession

The concept of an EXPECTANCY CHAIN is applicable to this sub-variety of frustration. Around the world, we find expectancy chains which involve actions which customarily occur in sequence such as: leave (some place) ... go ... arrive; search ... find; waste away ... die; fall down ... smash; take out a corpse ... bury; eat a quantity of food ... be satisfied; get ... bring/take ... dispose of. Some expectancy chains are especially conditioned by the particular culture area in which they are found. Thus from Papua New Guinea, Bougainville, New Hebrides, and aboriginal Australia, we find such expectancy chains as the following: _see a pig ... catch/kill it_; _kill ... cook ... eat_; _dig ... cook ... eat_ (_referring to sweet potatoes_); _go with hooks ... tie hooks ... catch fish ... bring fish ... eat_; _cook in leaves ... put into container ... bring to the canoe ... come down_; _tie up ... put into canoe_; _climb a log ... see at a distance_. Expectancy chains may involve succession with different actors (reciprocity) as in the following: _shoot ... die_; _hit ... die_; _call ... answer_; _give_ (_to someone_) _... appreciate_; _give_ (_to someone_) _... cook_ (_it_).

Here as with other varieties of frustration we find varied fullness of expression in regard to the expression of P, R, Q_β and S. Very commonly we find sentences in which only P and Q_β are expressed: _I looked for it but couldn't find it_; _It fell down but didn't break_; _They left for Paris but didn't arrive_; _He killed and cooked his game but never ate it_; _I ate ten slices of bread but still wasn't satisfied_. Notice that these customarily encode as antithetical sentences in English where many such sentences can be explained as encodings of frustrated succession.

In other examples of frustrated succession there is a statement of the blocking circumstance (R). In English, this also encodes as an antithetical sentence but the blocking circumstance and Q_β, i.e., the frustrated action, are encoded together as a coordinate sentence embedded within the second base of the antithetical sentence. Thus we get sentences like: _I went to look for it but my glasses broke and I couldn't find it_; _He fell out of a tree but some low lying limbs broke his fall and he didn't get hurt very badly_; _He wasted away to a mere 85 pounds but the doctor arrived in time and he recovered_ (in the latter _he recovered_ is stated rather than _he didn't die_); _I called to her but she was angry and didn't answer me_; _I gave him the pig but he was lazy and didn't cook it_.

In other examples there is a statement of a surrogate action S. In English the surrogate action following on the frustrated action is customarily encoded in a result sentence with _so_, and sometimes with final _instead_. All that precedes the _so_ is the first base of the result sentence, and the surrogate action is encoded as the second base following the conjunction, e.g., _I went to look for it but my glasses broke_ *and I couldn't find it, so I went home (instead)*; *He fell out of a tree but some low lying limbs broke his fall and he didn't get hurt, so he picked himself up and went home*. Alternatively, the conjunction *so* can be moved back in the above sentences with the result that the frustrated action and the surrogate action constitute an antithetical sentence embedded as second base of a result sentence, e.g., *He fell down but some low lying limbs broke his fall, so he didn't get hurt but picked himself up and went home*. Notice that in the preceding result sentence both bases of the result sentence are embedded antithetical sentences. The two bases, each divided into two bases, encode respectively P, R, Q_β and S.

There are still other examples in which only P and R are stated without further elements. These impress me as being somewhat elliptical. While the presupposition remains that there is a P which implies a Q, the Q_β is unstated: *I searched for it but my glasses fell off and broke*; *I started out for Paris but my car broke down*.

9.3 Frustrated Overlap

Although not as frequent as frustrated succession, some sentences apparently are explicable as instances of frustrated overlap. Consider the following: *He drives down crowded streets but doesn't look out for pedestrians*. Here there is a presupposition that one who drives down crowded streets should at the same time look out for pedestrians. This is the P implies Q. The overt structure of the sentence expresses P and Q_β namely *he doesn't look out for pedestrians*. The sentence can also express a blocking circumstance: *He drives down crowded streets but is often preoccupied and doesn't look out for pedestrians*. Here the R and the Q_β are grouped together in surface structure as a coordinate sentence embedded as second base of antithetical sentence. Conceivably a surrogate action could be expressed here as well, *He drives down crowded streets but doesn't look out for pedestrians so he struck a child the other day* in which the surrogate action *struck a child* occurs rather than the anticipated action of *looking out for pedestrians*. The presupposition of this sentence involves not temporal succession as in the above subsection, but overlap, i.e., it is assumed that while one drives down a crowded street, he is looking out for pedestrians.

9.4 Frustrated Hypothesis

This variety of frustration is based on hypotheticality. Consider the following sentences: *Even if she comes, I'm not going to go with her* and *She may come for me but I'm not going to go with her*. In both these sentences the presupposition is *if she comes I will go with her*, i.e., there is a P implies Q, which is the first element in the anatomy of frustration. This is not a general collocational expectancy but a specific built-in presupposition of these sentences--signalled, in fact, by the choice of surface structure. Both sentences express in their overt structures, P and Q_β, i.e., in place of the anticipated *I will go with her* we get *I'm not going to go with her*. In surface structure the first of the above examples is a simple sentence with a concessive margin while the second is an antithetical sentence. A blocking circumstance may be expressed. Then, the second example above could be expanded to: *She may come for me but I'm not feeling well so I'm not going to go with her* in which *not feeling well* is the blocking circumstance. Blocking circumstance would more normally be expressed in the first example above as a cause margin *Even if she comes I'm not going to go with her because I'm not feeling well*. Conceivably a surrogate action could be expressed as well. *She may come for me but I'm not going to go with her; I'm going to stay home instead*.

9.5 Frustrated Contingency

The sentence below is based on a sentence which occurred under contingency above: *Even when I had made sure that she was well, I didn't let her work in the garden*. Here the presupposition of the sentence (P implies Q) seems to be that when he had made sure that she was well, he let her work in the garden; but we are told that this did not take place, rather the unanticipated result that he didn't let her work in the garden. Take also the following sentence: *Even when I have money, I'm not going to get married*. Here the presupposition is that when I have the money I will get married, but we are told in the overt structure of the sentence that P and Q_β occur, i.e., in spite of having the money, he is not going to get married. In both the above sentences the P and the Q_β are expressed. The R or blocking circumstance can also be expressed. Again, in the concessive structure it is easier to express the blocking circumstance as a cause margin at the end of the entire sentence: Even when I had made sure that she was well, I didn't let her work in the garden because I was afraid of what the neighbors might say or Even when I have money, I'm not going to get married because I'm a confirmed bachelor. The surrogate action can be expressed in regard to the first sentence: I let her work around the house instead. And, similarly for the second sentence: Rather I'm going to buy myself a new car. The two examples above can also be expressed as antithetical sentences in the surface structure but this requires some modification of the phraseology: I eventually made sure that she was well, but I still didn't let her work in the garden and I will eventually have some money, but I'm not going to get married.

9.6 Frustrated Efficient Cause

Here we find such examples as He was poisoned but didn't die. The presupposition here is that poisoning is followed by death. The P and the Q_β are stated in the overt structure of the sentence. We may also state the R or blocking circumstance: He was poisoned but they rushed him to the hospital and he didn't die. A statement of the surrogate action is not easy to imagine with such an example as the preceding. The only alternative to not dying is living, but didn't die is equivalent to live and we find ourselves with an embedded negated antonym paraphrase instead of a genuine surrogate action. The question as to the grammatical and lexical conditions under which surrogate action may occur with frustration needs further attention.

9.7 Frustrated Final Cause

Examples such as He came but didn't get a free meal are based on such sentences as He came in order to get a free meal. Here again we have the P and Q_β stated in the overt structure while the possibility of stating an R or blocking circumstance is certainly open: He came but the woman's husband was at home so he didn't get a free meal. Surrogate action is easy to imagine: He got a kick in the pants instead.

9.8 Frustrated Attribution

Frustrated attribution incorporates the structure of attribution and results, therefore, in a complex presupposition, i.e., there is a $[wP \wedge Q] \supset Q$ which is a presupposition of the entire sentence. Thus He says that she is intelligent might be considered to imply--all things else being equal--that she actually IS intelligent. In sentences of the sort under consideration here, however, the $wP \wedge Q$ is stated overtly--and often nothing more--with the implication (often dependent on intonation) that the thought or the claims thus expressed are wrong: He SAYS that she is intelligent. On the other hand, the structure of a sentence may also express the Q_β: He says that she is intelligent but she really isn't. A blocking circumstance can be stated: He says that she is intelligent but I've seen her in action, and I know that she isn't where I've seen her in action is a blocking circumstance. There is apparently no true surrogate action which can be stated here, but we may employ a paraphrase of the negated antonym variety: on the contrary she is very stupid where very stupid is a paraphrase of not intelligent.

Such structures can be termed MISTAKEN IDEA when they are in first person. Here we usually find different first terms (in the $wP \wedge Q$) as in I thought that you were quite wrong but you weren't. One may, however, have a mistaken idea in regard to oneself, I thought that I could do it, but I couldn't. In some languages (notably Ibaloi and several other Philippine languages) the verb think is used in the surface structure to express mistaken idea and the Q_β is left unexpressed. I thought he was rich (but he isn't). In many New Guinea languages the verb say is similarly used in a quotation structure which may in some languages be direct: I said (mistakenly), "He won't come".

9.9 Frustrated Modality

I'm not too happy about this subtitle. I'm tempted to entitle this section 'Frustrated Inertial Guidance Systems'. What we have here is a predicate specified as to intent, obligation, or ability but the action thus specified is not carried through. Evidently something is presupposed here like the Newtonian assumption (inertia) that a body in motion in a given direction will keep moving in that direction unless some force deflects or stops it. In parallel fashion, I assume that the intention to do an action will normally be followed by the doing of the action, that a sense of obligation regarding doing an action will similarly lead to its performance, and that the ability to do an action will also lead to its performance. In the end, however, each of these is blocked in the structures here examined, and the frustration is explicitly stated.

This notional structure has its idiosyncrasies. In the three varieties of frustrated modality we have inflected predicates. I use inflection here as a notional term (6,2.1.4), not as a surface structure label for elements which qualify a predicate in these modal ways. We have also a restriction (unlike e.g., that found in frustrated succession) that the P, the Q, the Q_β and the S if present must have the same subject referent. The R, however, the blocking circumstance, may have the same or different subject from the other predicates in the anatomy of frustration.

(1) Frustrated intent. We have here an inflected P that implies P, i.e., an intent to do P which implies a performance of P, instead of the usual P which implies Q. Again there may be a blocking circumstance R; the reversal of the intended predicate P_β; and S, the surrogate action as in frustrated succession. These may be represented formulaically as:

$$(\text{i-Pa} \supset \text{Pa}) \wedge \text{i-Pa} \wedge \text{R} \wedge \text{Pa}_\beta \wedge \text{Sa}$$

The a symbolizes the fact that this is a same-first-term string except for the blocking circumstance where the first term may be the same or different from that of the other bases.[6]

Some sentences may express only the intended action and its frustration, i.e., the i-P and the P_β as in _I intended to go but didn't_ or _I didn't intend to go but did_. The blocking circumstance may also be stated as in _I intended to go but we had visitors that night so I didn't_. Notice that this is encoded as an English antithetical sentence with its antithesis expounded by result sentence whose second base contains the P_β.

There are further refinements to be worked out here. Thus, it would appear that with a positive intention, the surrogate action can be expressed, but not with a negative intention. Accordingly, we have such sentences as *I intended to go, but visitors came so I didn't go but stayed home and entertained for the evening (instead)*. Here the *stayed home and entertained for the evening* is a surrogate for *not going* (although it approaches a negated antonym paraphrase of the other). On the other hand, in the sentence *I didn't intend to go but George urged me to go so I went*, *I didn't intend to go* is the i-P, *George urged me to go* is the blocking circumstance, and *so I went* is the P_{β}. The latter rounds out the situation. To carry out an action that one hadn't intended to carry out is at once reversal and surrogate, consequently no separate surrogate action aside from the P_{β} itself is possible.

(2) Frustrated obligation. This is very similar to frustrated intention; in fact, all we need to do is to take the formula for the previous string and substitute o-Pa for every occurrence of i-Pa. The whole structure may then be represented as:

$$(o\text{-}Pa \supset Pa) \wedge o\text{-}Pa \wedge R \wedge Pa_{\beta} \wedge Sa$$

We therefore have sentences like *I should have gone but didn't*; *I shouldn't have gone, but I went anyway*. The blocking circumstance R can of course be reported as in *I should have gone but I was tired and didn't go* or in *I shouldn't have gone, but George urged me to go and I went anyway*. Again with a positive obligation, the surrogate action S may be stated: *I should have gone, but I was tired and stayed home and had a very pleasant evening with my ten-year-old son instead*. Here *had a very pleasant evening with ten-year-old son* is a surrogate action for going.

(3) Frustrated facility (ability). This variety is not different in principle from the two preceding, but has certain peculiarities, e.g., the fact that the inflected predicate f-P is necessarily positive while i-P and o-P can be positive or negative, i.e., positive facility can figure in an expectancy chain, but hardly negative facility which would presumably lead to doing nothing. Thus P_{β} is necessarily negative and can be so symbolized with the deletion of the beta subscript. Consequently, we symbolize this notional structure as:

$$(f\text{-}Pa \supset Pa) \wedge f\text{-}Pa \wedge R \wedge \overline{P}a \wedge Sa$$

Some varying examples based on the same lexical string follow:

> I could have promoted him but I didn't
> I could have promoted him but his irresponsibility offended me and I didn't; instead I fired him
> I could have promoted him but his irresponsibility offended me

9.10 Some Restrictions

In concluding this section on frustration, I note that no one category per se, such as coupling, is transformable to a frustrative structure. Unless there is some rather close connection of expectancy between the two coupled predicates such as fat and sloppy, there is no sense of frustration at not encountering the second in its expected value, or reason for putting the word but into the surface structure, as in She is fat but not sloppy. Some varieties of coupling cannot work out in this fashion at all such as *I collect postage stamps but my wife doesn't do amateur painting (why should she?). The sina qua non of frustration is some sort of close contextual association or expectancy and the possibility of a blocking circumstance R. This is what gives this structure its peculiar texture.

10. DEFINITION OF SYMBOLS

I give here a summary definition of symbols used in the formulations of this chapter. Originally, the material below was the work of Robert Conrad in Ballard, Conrad, Longacre 1971a and 1971b. This was revised somewhat in Longacre 1972a and has since profited by the criticisms of Conrad and of P. Healey. None of my colleagues are responsible, however, for the following alternations in the original apparatus: introduction of $\exists$, collapsing of $\exists p$ into $\exists$, revision of the apparatus which expresses temporal relations.

$a \in U$	Term a is an element of set U.
a, b,..., n	Terms of predicates, always written immediately to the right of the predicate which they accompany.

x, y	Further predicate terms with spatial, temporal, or manner function.
a', x', etc.	Synonym or situational equivalent of a term a, x, etc.
a", x",etc.	Antonym or situational opposite of term a, x, etc.
Eab	Equational predication, 'term a is b'.
P, Q, R (but not U)	Predicates. If terms have been assigned to some or all of the variables to form an acceptable statement, the result is called a predication. With no terms specified, predicate symbols without temporal quantifiers refer to the entire predication. With terms specified, they refer to the predicator only.
$\overline{P}$	Negation of predicate P.
P'	Predication involving a synonym or situational equivalent of a lexical item with the same function in P.
P"	Predication involving an antonym or situational opposite of a lexical item with the same function in P.
P^0	Predication that is median in a graded scale of predications so that $P > P^0 > P''$.
$P \wedge Q$	P relates to Q by conjoining, illustration, deixis, or attribution (i.e., in some relationship other than alternation, implication, equality, inequality, temporal relations or paraphrase--all of which are indicated with special symbols).
$P \supset Q$	If P, then Q.
Pa	P with first term a.
Pab	P with first term a, and a subsequent term b.

$Pa \wedge Qb$	P with first term a, and Q with first term (actor/b, distinct from a). If no terms are specified in a predicate, it is understood that the first terms may be either the same or different.
$Pa \wedge Qa$	P with first term a, and Q with the same first term a.
$P(a) \wedge P(b) \wedge \ldots \wedge$	P(n) Conjunction of n identical predications with nonidentical terms having the same function in each predication.
P_β	Operator β changes the positive-negative value of P so that every predicate in the expression takes one of the two values. For example, $[P_\beta \supset Q_\beta]$ $\wedge$ P $\neg$ Q means any one of the four possibilities: $[\overline{P} \supset \overline{Q}] \wedge P \wedge Q$, $[\overline{P} \supset Q] \wedge P \wedge \overline{Q}$, $[P \supset \overline{Q}] \wedge \overline{P} \wedge Q$, or $[P \supset Q] \wedge \overline{P} \wedge \overline{Q}$.
$P(a)$	P involving term a which has the same function as any other term or terms enclosed in parentheses in the same expression.
$P \vee Q$	Either P or Q, but not both (exclusive disjunction).
$P_\forall a$	P with universally quantified participant term a which may not have the same function in other predications in the expression.
$P_\forall y$	P with universally quantified temporal, spatial, or manner term which may or may not have the same function in other predications in the expression.
$P(U)$	P with Universal set U as a term which has the same function as other terms in the expression which are enclosed in parentheses. For example, in $\overline{P}(U) \wedge P(a)$, U has the same function in $\overline{P}$ as term a has in P.

∃	Existential predication. 'There is ____ ______.'
U	Universal set, such as the set of all people or all places.
U-a	The set U minus the particular member a.
∀a	Universal quantifier, 'for every term a.'
Pa ≡ P'a, etc.	P'a is a paraphrase of Pa (with or without gain or loss of information).
( )	Expression enclosed in parentheses, which must be more than just a predicate term, is a presupposition with respect to the remainder of the expression not so enclosed.
[ ]	Expression so enclosed must be grouped as one unit.
$<$ $>$ $=$	In their usual mathematical significance.
{ }	Braces with matching items as in transformational-generative usage.

The following apparatus expresses temporal relations:

$\underline{P}$, $\underline{Q}$	P and/or Q denoting activities or states (spans) which are involved in temporal overlap, succession or contingency.
$\underset{\cdot}{P}$, $\underset{\cdot}{Q}$	P and/or Q denoting events which are involved in temporal overlap, succession or contingency.

Substituting $\underline{P}$, $\underline{Q}$, $\underset{\cdot}{P}$ or $\underset{\cdot}{Q}$ for any unmarked P or Q below the following additional symbols are used:

P Δ Q	P and Q are related as temporal overlap.

$P\ \Delta_{\rightarrow}\ Q$	P and Q are related as temporal succession.
$P\ \Delta \supset Q$	Q is contingent or P (as defined in 4.1.3) and temporal overlap is involved.
$P\ \Delta_{\rightarrow} \supset Q$	Q is contingent on P (as defined in 4.1.3) and temporal succession is involved.

The following nine symbols occur with subscripts preposed to predicate symbols, distinct from the terms of the respective predicates, which occur postposed. These preposed subscripts relate P to an accompanying predicate in the same expression.

aP	P which attributes an accompanying Q, cognitive content, to a given participant.
cP	P has a circumstantial relationship to the accompanying predicate.
gP	P involving a more generic predicator or term which contrasts with a corresponding and more specific predicator or term in predicate sP.
lP	P expresses a likeness or comparison with accompanying predicate.
pP	P has a purposive relationship (Final Cause) to the accompanying predicate. (Usually this is the second predicate or pQ in the formulations of this chapter.)
sP	P involving a more specific predicator or term which contrasts with a corresponding and more generic predicator or term in gP.
wP	P which attributes an accompanying Q, verbal activities, to a given speaker.

The following three symbols represent inflectional elements in the apparatus of this chapter:

f-P	P qualified so as to express ability or facility relative to the action it indi-

cates.

i-P	P qualified so as to express intent or desire relative to the action it indicates.
o-P	P qualified so as to express obligation in regard to the action indicated by P, or strong motivation for doing it.

NOTES

1 For a bibliography of advanced work in formal logic--work in which, e.g., temporal relations are taken account of, cf. van Dijk 1974.290fn, 1977:19ff.

2 Some of the thrust of this empirical argument from Mesoamerica as a linguistic area is blunted by some empirical observations from the northern part of South America. In Chibchan languages, conjunctions are essentially predicational in structure in that they consist of a verb or demonstrative stem followed by a limited set of verbal affixes. Tucanoan languages have a similar tendency to use 'do' as a conjunction.

3 For fuller discussion of temporal relations in natural languages, see Barbara Hollenbach 1973.

4 Examples have been called to my attention by Cecelia Carcelen in which the lower gradient is negated. While her examples are Spanish, I believe that translations of them make good English as well: _She's not just attractive, she's beautiful_ (Carcelen 1974.36).

5 It is unwise to be dogmatic on this score. My colleagues Alan and Phyllis Healey of the Papua New Guinea Branch of the Summer Institute of Linguistics are persuaded that for at least some of the languages of New Guinea QUOTATION CLAUSES should be posited. Phyllis Healey's treatment of Telefol quotation clauses (1964) is exhaustive and exemplary. Nevertheless, her quotation clauses are structurally quite distinct from other clause types and in fact involve embedding (quotation within quotation) that is unparalleled in other clause types. I, therefore, continue to wonder if even for Papua New Guinea languages such as Telefol the analytical option of quotation sentence against quotation clause should

not be explored.

6 Nate Waltz (1976.92) has pointed out, however, that there are pairs of reciprocal verbs 'which required change of subject between the initial predication and the expectancy reversal.' He illustrates this (p. 87) with the Guanano equivalent of 'She wanted/intended to kill him. But he didn't die. He defended himself.' Here we have $[i\text{-}Pab \wedge Qb] \wedge i\text{-}Pab \wedge Qb_{\beta} \wedge Sb$, i.e., the basic presupposition that if a intends to kill b, then b will probably die, along with a statement of the intention, a statement that b didn't die and a surrogate action of b. Waltz continues (p.92): 'This qualification presumably affects not simply Guanano but other languages (including English) as well.'

CHAPTER 4

CASES OR ROLES

A further problem for the student of discourse is the notional structure of PREDICATIONS since these are, in a sense, the atomic entities of discourse. In this chapter a set of cases or roles is posited with a view toward the case frames and classification of verbs which are presented in the next chapter. Ultimately, the relation of case grammar (so-called) to discourse is best seen in the following chapter.

It has been increasingly recognized that (a) the surface structure categories of language mark functional slots of a rather high level of abstraction; and (b) these functional slots only roughly correlate with underlying categories which are the primary linguistic encoding of the real world. Thus, in the study of Philippine languages the tradition is now old (Barnard and Forster 1954; McKaughan 1958; Miller 1964; Pike 1964; Forster and Barnard 1968; Hall 1969) that grammatical categories such as subject and object must be distinguished from situational categories, such as actor, goal, and site. Such analysis has facilitated the explanation of the peculiar surface structure patterning of focus in Philippine languages. The discussion of these matters in a comparatively little-known family of the world's languages did not, however, attract much attention on the international linguistic scene. It is Fillmore who popularized for the linguistic world the notion of CASE as underlying category. Adumbrating this in two brief articles in 1966, and then giving fuller expression in his 1968 article 'The Case for Case' (with a peculiarly apt, slogan-like title), then proceeding on to refine these notions in his summer seminar at the Linguistic Institute 1970 (Fillmore 1971), Fillmore has given us a mature discussion of the notion of case or role. Chafe's work (1970), building on

Fillmore's, and yet largely independent of it, has given us further variety of case grammar. Various elaborations of Fillmore and Chafe or conflations of the two characterize the immediate linguistic past. Thus we have Platt's elaboration of Fillmore 1968 in his 'grammatical form' versus 'grammatical meaning' for English (Platt 1971) (cf. Grimes 1972; Langendoen 1970). We have Cook's conflation of the work of Fillmore and Chafe in a continuing series of articles from 1970 to present (republished as Cook 1979). Meanwhile, John Anderson in Cambridge (1971) has proceeded to develop a localistic theory of case which in principle goes back to the writings of one Maximus Planudes who flourished around 1100 A.D. (Robins 1972). On top of all this there is a further variety of case grammar suggested by Austin Hale (1973) and followed by Pike and Pike (1977), which in its simplicity and paucity of case categories is reminiscent of the early variety of case grammar found in the Philippines in the early 1960's. Somewhat unexpectedly, Fillmore's most recent work on case relations (1977), in which the influence of relational grammar is evident, also drastically reduces the number of nuclear cases and makes them relevant to scenes in particular discourse settings.

What then? That the notion of case is very useful cannot be denied. On the other hand, the sheer confusion and variety of case schemes may well make the beginner in case grammar pause. Nevertheless, it is imperative that in such a set of sentences as the following some attempt be made to sort out the underlying role structure, regardless of the vagaries of the surface grammar of English clauses:

(1) John hit Bill
(2) John wounded Bill
(3) John broke the dish
(4) John ran a race
(5) John made a table
(6) John heard the sound
(7) John listened to the sound
(8) John loves Mary

Notice that there is a difference between the role of John in the first five examples above and in the last three. In the first five examples, John is clearly active: he hits, he wounds, he breaks, he runs, he makes something. In the last three examples John identifies the registering nervous system which picks up certain sounds, or listens to something, or experiences emotion. Example (7) is, moreover, rather peculiar in that in this example, as distinct from (6), John is both the registering nervous system and is active in the process as well. He does not simply overhear a sound, he is actively listening to it--and listening is an activity. Yet in all eight examples, John is simply surface structure subject or more properly speaking, active subject, since passive clauses also exist and present a somewhat different situation.

Turning now to the surface structure objects found in the examples above, we find some significant differences among them. Thus Bill in (1) and (2) occurs in different roles. In (2) Bill is very definitely affected by the action of John, i.e., he is wounded. In (1), Bill may suffer no great effect from being hit by John, rather he is an animate being whose nervous system registers the hit from John. In number (3), an inanimate entity, dish, is affected by the action of John. The dish passes from a state of unbroken to broken as a result of John's activity. But what is the noun race in (4)? Race appears to be a prolongation and specification of the activity of the verb run itself. It is run in a certain prescribed and specified manner. Table in (5), while in some similar way related to the activity of the verb make (as race is to run), presents the end product of the activity. What about sound in (6)? In many ways sound is to hear as race is to run. Sound is a further specification of hear. What can we hear except sound? We could, of course, have specified the source of the sound; we could have said John heard the sound of a train in the distance in which train would bring in a noun in a further role. As for the next example, sound in (7), is presumably in much the same role as sound in (6). Finally, what about Mary in John loves Mary? Notice that Mary is not necessarily affected by John's emotional feeling for her. In fact, Mary may be entirely unconscious that John loves her and therefore incapable of being affected by his emotion toward her. She neither experiences nor is affected by John's emotions. She is simply a goal towards which the emotions of John are directed.

Obviously, we have here a welter of relationships involving subject and object in the familiar surface structure pattern of English: subject, verb, object.

If we bring in the notion of instrument, we get further varieties of surface structure as in the following well-known examples:

(9) John opened the door with a key
(10) The door opened
(11) The key opened the door
(12) The door was opened

The instrument expressed as a *with* adjunct in example (9), is surface structure subject in example (11). *Door*, expressed as surface structure object in (9), is subject in (10) and (12).

From the above dozen examples we see that there are not only surface structure relationships, but there are also certain underlying relationships which move in and out of positions in the surface structure patterns. A full accounting for those patterns must describe not only the surface structures, but the underlying structures which accompany them. We will further find that certain peculiarities in surface structure are conditioned by the underlying structures which they reflect. We will further find that in crossing from one language to the other, we need not expect to find the same mapping of underlying to surface categories in one language that is found within another language. Thus in a typical Philippine language we do not find any roles expressed in the surface structure subject except the agent, experiencer, and causer (whose status as a role is doubtful). There is, to be sure, a further surface structure phenomenon called FOCUS which can single out subject, object, instrument, or associate as the topic of its clause. Whether for the understanding of a language internally, or for the exploration of new languages, we need an inventory of cases or roles to accompany our specification of surface structure.

I here define the inventory of cases which I find useful. I do not claim for this inventory any privileged status. It is built especially on the (earlier) work of Fillmore and Chafe with stimulus from other writers in case grammar. I've been impressed with Anderson's localistic theory of case to the point that I assign a greater role to source, goal, and path than is assigned by either Fillmore or Chafe in their schemes. As to terminology, in using the term PATIENT rather than OBJECT I am following Chafe. I try to define patient narrowly enough--even at the cost of positing further distinctions--to make it no longer the wastebasket case that it is in the writings of Fillmore and others. In using the term RANGE rather than COMPLEMENT I am taking a hint from Halliday's work on English clause structure (Halliday 1967 part 1). Note that my use of RANGE is distinct from that of Grimes (1976), whose use of this term indicates what I call LOCATIVE. In distinguishing MEASURE from RANGE I propose a case not suggested by previous writers on case grammar.

1. EXPERIENCER (E).

An animate entity whose registering nervous system is relevant to the predication.

The experiencer may be simply reacting to his environment as in *I'm hot*, *I'm cold*, or *I'm uncomfortable.* He may be the one to whom an emotional state is ascribed such as *nervous*, *happy*, *discouraged*, or *scared*; *brightening up*, *getting discouraged*, etc. He may be the one thus affected by someone else's activities as in *I cheered her up*, or he may be the object of an activity in which his physical state or location is not necessarily changed but in which he experiences somebody else's violence, affection, notice, etc., as in *John hit Bill*, *John kissed his wife*, etc. Similarly, the experiencer may be one who desires, wants, loves, or appreciates, who is introduced to someone or made to appreciate someone, or who suffers someone's scorn, derision, etc. Likewise, the experiencer is the subject of sensation verbs, although experiencer is coreferential with agent with a verb such as *listen* (as distinct from simply *hear*). Finally, the experiencer is the recipient of verbs of speech, i.e., the addressee, as in *The mother told her child a story*, *She sang me a song*, and with such kindred verbs as *show* in *The artist showed Tom the painting*.

2. PATIENT (P).

The entity of which a state or location is predicated or which is represented as undergoing change of state or location; the entity may be inanimate or animate (but, in the latter case, the registering nervous system or the intentionality of the animate entity is not relevant to the predication).

The patient may be simply an entity of which a state or location is predicated as in *The bolt is loose*, *The key is in the drawer*, *Joan's in Europe*. On the other hand, the patient may be that which undergoes change of state or location with or without the activity of some agent. Thus we have *The bolt came loose* and *He loosened the bolt* (where an agent is involved) and *The soap slid off the soapdish* and *He threw the soap across the room* (where again the change of location is due to the activity of an agent). Sometimes, an animate entity undergoes change of physical state or of location as in *Don fell from the chair*. We do not ask here 'What did Don do?' but 'What happened to Don?' The patient also is that which is possessed, acquired or exchanged, as in *Dick has a new book*, *Dick's acquired a new book*, or *Tom gave Dick a book*.

I also assume that certain inanimate things, especially astronomical bodies, are patients in clauses which predicate motion as a physical state or process--when such inanimate entities are not conceived of as animate in the folklore which is associated with a language and culture: *The earth rotates on its axis*. *The moon revolves around the earth*. To this we must also add examples of patients from technology.

The machine is going/running/functioning
The wheel spun around one full turn

3. AGENT (A).

The animate entity which intentionally either instigates a process or acts.

Agents either instigate a process (with action-process verbs) or perform an action (with action verbs). In either case it seems necessary to insist that intentionality is crucial to the definition of agent (cf., e.g., the definition of action in the philosophy of action and applications of that philosophy to narrative structures (van Dijk 1977: 167-187)). On the other hand, animate entities may unintentionally stimulate or condition change. In this case as seen below, the animate entity is construed as instrument (of the stimulus variety).

Thus in all the following sentences agent is instigating a process and is surface structure subject.

> Mr. Smith teaches Susan algebra
> I introduced Tom to Mary
> John smashed the dish with a hammer
> I shortened it two inches
> Harry placed the book by the phone

In a few cases, agent may be coreferential with other roles; a few such examples are shown here. In all the following examples agent is the one who acts:

> John petted the cat
> John's studying tonight (coreferential with experiencer)
> Tom listened to the owl (coreferential with experiencer)
> He's standing on the corner (where it is assumed that standing is an activity requiring expenditure of energy on the part of an animate being)
> Harriet traveled in Europe (coreferential with patient)
> George grabbed the book from John (coreferential with goal)

4. RANGE (R).

The role assigned to any surface structure nominal that completes or further specifies the predicate; the product of the activity of a predicate.

A surface structure noun such as song functions simply as a nominal prolongation of the predicate itself: Caruso sang a song. If this were all that was involved in range, then range could be treated exclusively as a surface structure phenomenon. It is evident, however, that the nominal song may be elaborated as in a beautiful song, an unusual song, an obscene song, and five songs. Furthermore, song--which is highly generic--may be replaced by more specific nouns in the same semantic domain: solo, aria, ballad, hymn, and dirge. Or song may be replaced by the name of a song: Those Were The Days; When You and I Were Young, Maggie; The Mexican National Anthem. These phrasal elaborations of song or more specific substitutions for it necessitate a deep structure representation. Clearly, what I here call range is distinct from the patient (see above) and the goal (see below).

Song has been called a cognate accusative of sing, i.e., it is a surface structure object built on the same root as its corresponding verb. But generic nouns that are associated semantically with particular verbs need not be cognate with the verb. Thus battle and fight are probably equally generic and either may go with the verb fight. Game is the generic noun that goes with play, race is the generic noun that goes with run, and food the generic noun with eat. All may be elaborated or substituted for:

battle/fight: an important battle, the Battle of Marathon, a good fight, duel
game: a dangerous game, Tiddledywinks, tennis
food: poisoned food, ambrosia, steak and eggs

The range noun may also specify the product of the activity of a predicate. With such a verb as compose, English has the nominalization composition. But this highly abstract and redundant nominal may be replaced by: five compositions, a brilliant composition, concerto, symphony, art song, rock opera. In English make has no noun of high generality associated with it; artifact is somewhat ethnological (if not archaeological). Characteristically, make is used with a variety of specific nouns: make a table, a house, wagon, etc.

What all these factitives have in common is that the entity indicated did not exist until the activity indicated in the predicate was completed. Do these factitives group naturally with such nouns as song, game, and food above in the same case? A song (unless an improvisation) exists before it is sung, although the act of singing produces a rendition of the song. Game is ambiguous. We can play the game of soccer, i.e., a specific playing of the game under given conditions (almost a RENDITION of the game). Food and drink exist before they are consumed. We might, however, suggest that they become food and drink to me only if I consume them.

I group here together these two subcases, range as specification of a predicate and range as product of a predicate. No harm comes of their being grouped together provided that we agree to recognize a certain disparity between the two.

5. MEASURE (M).

The role assigned to the surface structure nominal which completes a predication by quantifying it; the price in a transfer. While nouns expressing measure are similar to range, yet there seems to be good reason to draw this distinction; (cf. the discussion of case frames of Row F in the following chapter):

It weighs six pounds
This piece of equipment costs $500.00
He lost forty pounds
I shortened it one yard
Our team gained 10 yards
I bought it for $5.00

6. INSTRUMENT (I).

An inanimate entity or body part which an agent uses to accomplish an action or to instigate a process; any entity (unintentional with animate) which conditions an (emotional) state or which triggers a change in emotional or physical state; a potent inanimate entity which triggers such a change.

Typically an instrument is an inanimate entity which an animate agent intentionally uses to accomplish an action or instigate a process (but instruments which consist of body parts figure in here as well). The most typical occurrences of instrument are with physical action process verbs:

John cut the rope with a knife
John powdered the granules with a pestle
John covered the baby with a blanket

The instrument is not necessarily something small. We have examples such as:

The government is deepening the canal with a dredge
The construction company is widening the road with a bulldozer

Certain verbs are so specific as to instrument that instrument is not normally specified unless there is something unusual about it. Thus:

Edward speared five fish

But we may say

Edward speared five fish with a homemade speargun

With impingement verbs (see next chapter) the instrument is usually a body part although the verb hit permits a greater variety of instrument:

John kissed his wife
John petted the cat
John hit Bill with his fist
John hit Bill with a board

Normally the (body part) instrument is not specified with such verbs as kiss or pet unless there is something unusual about it such as John kissed his wife with a greasy mouth or John petted the cat with both hands. Instruments occur with other verb types besides these two.

Another sort of instrument may be called stimulus. Here either an inanimate entity or a body part conditions an emotional state or triggers a change of such state, or an animate being unintentionally accomplishes a similar end. This is discussed again in Chapter 5. Note that in such a sentence as John is discouraged at the prospect, the prospect is the emotional stimulus which causes John's discouragement. In The baby was frightened by the stranger's black moustache, black moustache is the stimulus. The stranger presumably did not intentionally frighten the child by displaying his beard. Likewise, we can have sentences such as John is scared of strangers, My Aunt is scared of cats, in which animate beings unintentionally serve as the stimulus for triggering changes of emotional states.

A third type of instrument has sometimes been called force. Here a potent inanimate entity brings about a change, as _In 64 A.D. a great fire destroyed most of Rome_, or _A tornado wrecked my house_. Possibly these could be construed as agent on the grounds that potent is superordinate to animate, so that if animate beings are agents, why should not potent--which includes animates and some inanimates--also be agent (Chafe 1970, 109-110)? If however, we make _fire_ and _tornado_ agents, we do it at the cost of compromising intention as a necessary corollary of agency. This, in turn, leads to some severe problems in separating certain process case frames from action-process frames. Note also that natural forces can be considered (in certain world views) to be instruments of deity. Conversely, however, in world views where natural forces are deity, they clearly are to be construed as agents.

7. LOCATIVE (L).

The locale of a predication. This role is more limited in distribution than source, path, and goal which replace it in many frames. The locale of a predication is the place where the predication takes place without implying motion to, from, or across the space indicated. Thus we can say _The ship sank at sea_, _The house stands in the park_, _They placed the book by the phone_, and _Harriet's traveling in Europe_.

8. SOURCE (S).

The locale which a predication assumes as place of origin; the entity from which physical sensation emanates; the animate entity who is the original owner in a transfer.

Source occurs with verbs of motion, propulsion, and locomotion as well as with verbs of acquisition, transfer, and grab. It also occurs with sensation, speech, and attention verbs. The use of source with these three types of verbs differs from type to type. With verbs of motion, propulsion, and locomotion, source indicates the locale which the predication assumes as the place of origin. With motion and locomotion verbs this is a surface structure adjunct on the clause level:

Tom fell off the chair
The boat drifted from the left to the right bank
The baby crawled from the kitchen to the front room

With propulsion verbs the source is coreferential with the agent: Tom threw the knife into the box, i.e., the trajectory begins at Tom . With sensation, speech, and attention case frames, the source specifies the entity from which a physical wave which produces a sensation emanates. Thus, Tom heard the sound of a train in the distance, where train is the source of the sound waves which Tom's ear eventually picks up, or George smelled the odor of onions, where the onions are the ultimate source of the odor. Attention verbs are not dissimilar. Again the source is the entity from which the physical wave emanates:

Tom listened to the owl/listened to the sound of the owl
The audience watched the performance of the dance troupe

where owl and dance troupe are the source from which sound waves and sight waves emanate.

With speech verbs the agent and the source are coreferential:

The mother told her child a story

Here mother is both agent and the source of the story which she tells to the child. Similarly:

Station FBRS is broadcasting right now

where Station FBRS is both agent and source.

Finally, with verbs of acquisition, transfer, and grab, the source indicates the original owner before the transfer:

Mary obtained her visa from the Australian embassy
George grabbed the book from John

With verbs of transfer the agent and the source are often coreferential:

Tom gave Bill a book
Mr. Smith sold Tom a convertible

With, however, such verbs as receive and buy, agent and goal are coreferential, while source is expressed as an adjunct on the clause level:

Bill bought a book from Tom
Bill received a book from Alice

9. GOAL (G).

The locale which is point of termination for a predication; the entity towards which a predication is directed without any necessary change of state in that entity; the animate entity who is the non-transitory or terminal owner.

With verbs of motion, propulsion, and locomotion goal specifies the locale which is point of termination for a predication:

The boat drifted from the left to the right bank
Sam swam through the water to the raft
Tom threw the knife into the box/at me

With verbs of desire, cognition, and evaluation, goal expresses the entity towards which the predication is directed without any necessary change of state in that entity. Thus Mary loves Tom (whether or not Tom even knows that she loves him) and Mary wants a Cadillac (with the Cadillac not capable of reciprocating her affection). Consider also:

Mary fell in love with Tom
I first introduced Mary to Tom

Obviously with action process verbs like introduce, Tom is conscious that he is being introduced but the dominant notion is not Tom's experiencing the introducing so much as Mary's experiencing it. With evaluation verbs the situation is somewhat tricky. In John praised Mary, presumably if Mary knows that she is being praised, she is experiencer as well as goal; but if she does not know that she is being praised, she is simply goal.

With verbs of possession, the goal encodes the owner: _Dick has a new book_. With verbs of acquisition the goal encodes the acquirer as in _Tom acquired a St. Bernard_--unless the acquisition is temporary with a view towards passing on to somebody else in which case the terminal owner is the goal. Similarly: _The department obtained a visa for Dr. Ho_. With transfer verbs the terminal owner in the confines of the clause is the goal: _Tom gave Bill a book_ where _Bill_ is goal or _Tom gave Bill a book for Sue_ where _Sue_ is goal. Agent and goal are coreferential with such verbs as _buy_ and _receive_:

> _John bought a book_
> _John received a book from Mary_

Likewise with grab verbs: _George grabbed the book from John_ where _George_ is both agent and goal. But in _George grabbed the book for me_, _me_ is the goal.

10. PATH (Path).

The locale or locales transversed in motion etc. predications; the transitory owner.

Path alone among the cases has the possibility of occurring several times in the same clause. _John traveled from Frankfurt to Naples via Geneva, Milan, and Rome_. The path may be specified all by itself with a motion verb such as _The boat drifted across the river_ or it may occur in conjunction with source and goal: _The boat drifted across the river from the left to the right bank_. Likewise with propulsion verbs we may specify either path by itself, goal by itself or path and goal (as already stated the source is coreferential with the agent in such case frames):

> _Tom threw the knife across the room_
> _Tom threw the knife into the box_
> _Tom threw the knife across the room and into the box_

With verbs of acquisition, transfer, and grab, the path indicates the transitory owner. Thus in the example already given, _The department obtained a visa for Dr. Ho_, _the department_ simply holds _the visa_ which it obtained until it can give it over to _Dr. Ho_, and is neither the original nor the terminal owner of the visa. With transfer verbs, path may pattern as indirect object in the surface structure, i.e., Tom gave Bill a book for Sue and Mr. Smith sold Tom a convertible for his wife. Or it may be coreferential with the agent as in Mr. Smith bought a book from Tom for his wife. When path occurs with a grab verb it is coreferential with the agent of that frame: Levi collected taxes for the Roman government.

11 PERIPHERAL CASES

All the cases posited above are nuclear, i.e., diagnostic of some case frames (cf. Chapter 5) as opposed to others. Furthermore, nuclear roles or cases are necessary components of the predication. By contrast, peripheral cases (Cook 1972a: modal cases) are not diagnostic of their case frames nor necessary components of them. They are, as Cook points out (1972a, 46), "independent of a particular verb." We can thus distinguish two uses of the locative as in the following pair:

I put the car in the garage
I washed the car in the garage

In the former, locative is nuclear and obligatory; it specifically occurs with put and similar verbs. In the latter, locative is peripheral, in that it is not diagnostic of the case frame, and is required neither grammatically nor semantically. Cook terms such a peripheral locative place to distinguish it from the nuclear locative.

Time and manner are peripheral cases that occur with some frequency. Time expressions, while optional in their case frames and in the surface structure clauses, are contextually specified--especially in certain discourse types which constrain their occurrence at given places.

Cook further lists as modal cases not only place, time, and manner, but accompaniment, cause, and purpose. Accompaniment is Fillmore's 1968 comitative case. Cause and purpose I believe to belong on the sentence level (cf. Chapter 3); I do not believe that they are properly part of clause structures nor of their underlying case frames. Cook also regards instrument as a modal case (but see 6. above where I demonstrate close semantic tie-in between some instruments and some verbs).

12. CASES POSITED BY HALE AND THE PIKES

Hale and the Pikes (1978) posit only actor, undergoer, and scope (also called referent). These are defined differently in different case frames so that we would not expect the actor with the verb _run_ to function like the actor with _cut_ or _love_. The Hale-Pike system--while certainly viable and useful--does not constitute as finely grained a calculus as the one here presented. For certain purposes, however, fewer distinctions (a more coarsely-grained calculus) may be preferable. To put it another way, the Hale-Pike system is not the same depth level as mine. But--and this is an important point--surface and depth are poles, not a dichotomy, and structures at varying depths correspond to varying goals and applications of theory.

These case categories, especially those described in 1-10, are the cases (roles) to which I refer in the next chapter--although a tentative addition or two is suggested there. It is imperative that the inventory of cases be kept relatively small and that the cases be defined in some systematic noncontradictory way. This has been the aim of this chapter. I do come out, however, with a larger inventory of cases than, e.g., Cook or Hale, the other two who have suggested systems of case frames. The contrast of my own set of categories with those of Hale-Pike is especially striking and invites comment.

It is instructive to map between the two systems (cf. Palmer 1978). Thus, agent and experiencer in the inventory presented here correspond to the Hale-Pike actor. Patient and range correspond to undergoer. Aside from instrument all other cases that I have suggested--Locative with its breakdown into Source, Path, and Goal, and Measure--correspond to scope. Hale has been somewhat uncertain as to the status of instrument.

Not only does my system map onto the Hale-Pike with no great difficulty, but, in effect, I have used a system similar to Hale-Pike's in Chapter 3. In Chapter 3 it is sometimes necessary to specify the terms of the predications which combine according to the enriched propositional calculus that I outline there. In specifying these terms I have not used the case categories of this chapter and the next. Rather, I indicate simply by lower case letters the first and the second terms of the component predications, thus:

$$Pab \wedge P''ba$$

where the first predicate P has two terms, a and b, while the second predicate P" has the same two referents in reverse order as its terms. This would be in a sentence such as:

<u>She</u> <u>loves</u> <u>him</u> <u>and</u> <u>he</u> <u>hates</u> <u>her</u>

Here I have settled for a shallower analysis. It seems that for the purposes of noting patterns of predicate-term relations in combinations of predications my place value representation of first term, second term, and third term (not shown here) is adequate enough. It seems, however, that for verb classification and case frame analysis relative to discourse structure--as in Chapter 5--a deeper and more detailed system is desirable. This is illustrative of the fact that analyses at varying depths serve varying purposes.

CHAPTER 5

CASE FRAMES

An understanding of the function of the cases or roles is insightful for the understanding of discourse. Even more insightful, however, is the grouping of these roles with the verb types with which they characteristically occur. To do this we must specify features which distinguish one set of verbs from another set of verbs, then we must specify the roles which occur with verbs characterized by these features. The result will be sets of verbs with characteristic constellations of accompanying substantives in given roles. The verb may of course be a verb phrase rather than a single verb and the substantives which accompany the verb may be pronouns, noun phrases, or even in some cases, substantive clauses. Such a set of verbs with characteristic accompanying nouns in particular roles is called a _case frame_.

To assemble and compare the case frames of a language is to evolve a typology or classification of its verbs. Such a classification, if well done, should serve several purposes. It is like an index of man, his interaction with his environment, his emotions, and his activities. Furthermore, a case frame can afford a substitutable module in a derivational process in which the structure of discourses and paragraphs are previous lines of derivation (cf., 3.1 of this chapter). Another consideration is that a given discourse can be shown to have related sets of verbs--not a helter-skelter ensemble--in its basic main-line structure (cf., 3.2 of this chapter). Finally, a general set of case frames has heuristic value for the elicitation of the range and variety of clause structure to be found in a language. The motivation for such classification as that here given is not that taxonomy is an end in itself, but that such a taxonomy is useful.

(A) Basic verb types	(B) + Experiencer	(C) + Benefactive	(D) + Locative
1. O_s verb broken, adj. dry, adj. dead, adj. tight, adj.	1. E_s–O verb know like want	1. B_s–O verb have have got own	1. O_s–L verb (be) in (be) on (be) under
2. O verb break, iv. die, iv. dry, iv. tighten, iv.	2. E–O verb feel hear see	2. B–O verb find lose win	2. O–L verb come go move
3. A verb dance laugh play sing	*3. A–E verb (derived) frighten please answer question	*3. A–B verb (derived) arm bribe help supply	*3. A–L verb (derived) come go run walk
4. A–O verb break, tv. dry, tv. kill, tv. tighten, tv.	4. A–E–O verb ask say speak tell	4. A–B–O verb buy give sell accept	4. A–O–L verb bring place put take

* developed as derived frames

Diagram I. Cook's Original Scheme of Case Frames (1972b) (O = Object; O_S = Object as subject; A = Agent; E, B, & L as at the head of each column)

As soon as one begins to assemble a number of case frames, similarities in sets of case frames begin to be evident. This leads to the feeling that case frames should constitute some sort of system, i.e., that they are not mere list or inventory, but a system with intersecting parameters.

As far as I know there are only two such systems which have been proposed in print up to the present time. I mention these systems summarily here; it is not my intent to describe them in detail. Cook's published system of case frames, his "Case Grammar Matrix", has two parameters (Cook, 1972b). The vertical parameter has four values (from Chafe 1970): state verbs, process verbs, action verbs, and action process. The other parameter likewise has four values: either with no further nuclear role added, or with experiencer, benefactive, or locative added (as further nuclear elements). The latter three, as defined by Cook, are found to be mutually exclusive in distribution. This gives a total of sixteen cells, all of which are filled in Cook's scheme, although some are filled by derived case frames--which as Cook observes, should be no fundamental objection to their being accounted as filled. Cook argues for such a matrix in principle--"Even if it does no more than point up the problem". See Diagram I for a presentation of Cook's system[1].

I now summarize Hale's system of case frames, without any pretense that such a summary begins to do justice to his work--which is detailed, provocative, and tested in a number of languages. His system of case frames (worked out in a Pike-directed project in Nepal) is obtained with a small set of binary features each of which has a positive and negative value (Hale 1973). He begins with the distinction stative versus non-stative. Stative case frames then divide into those that are plus actor and those that are minus actor--as do likewise the non-stative. (Hale does not feel it necessary to distinguish actor from experiencer. ACTOR with stative is obviously something different from ACTOR with non-stative.) Then the case frames that are plus actor similarly divide into those that are plus undergoer and those that are minus undergoer, while those that are minus actor likewise divide into plus undergoer and minus undergoer. UNDERGOER and ACTOR each obviously mean different things in different parametric combinations. All these finally divide into plus referent and minus referent, with REFERENT (more recently termed SITE or SCOPE) labeling a variety of relations. This

Diagram II. The Hale Chart of Clause Types

gives 8 case frames with stative verbs and 8 case frames with non-stative verbs. Curiously enough, he comes out with exactly 16 case frames, as does also Walter Cook (see Diagram II for Hale's system). In Hale's scheme as well as in Cook's, all the frames are filled in the etic categories. Hale has been demonstrating the usefulness of his frames not only in understanding individual languages, but in typological comparison of the structure of languages whether related or unrelated. The schemes of both Hale and Cook have been applied to English with considerable success.

1. A SCHEME OF CASE FRAMES

The scheme of case frames that I present here (see the accompanying summary Diagramm III and the more detailed Diagram IV-IX) is more detailed and more irregular than either of those envisioned by Cook or Hale. The scheme which I propose has two empty cells, has one cell (A3) labelled as doubtful, and has two cells for one space in row E4. Further irregularities result from taking account of reflexive case frames in charts IV-IX. It is possible, of course, that further study will eliminate some of these irregularities. Nevertheless even if the present irregularities persist they need not disturb us. I feel that nature displays a tendency to regularity along with partial irregularity. The periodic chart of the chemical elements is a case in point. The rare earth elements result in two spots of irregularity on the periodic chart. They simply do not fit in well. Does this vitiate the value of the periodic chart of the chemical elements? Quite emphatically, no! On the contrary, the periodic chart has proven its usefulness in predicting with amazing accuracy the properties of previously undiscovered chemical elements. The irregularities of the periodic chart warn us, however, that we must not always expect perfect regularity in nature. I have tried therefore to posit necessary classes of verbs and the case frames that accommodate them without undue regard for system in the early stages of discovery of such frames. After a number of frames were assembled, the attempt was then made to see if they constituted a system. The resulting system has emerged--with subsequent filling in of certain cells as suggested by the system itself.

I agree with Cook's original scheme which took as basic Chafe's proposal that we classify verbs the world over into

	STATE VERBS	PROCESS VERBS	ACTION-PROCESS VERBS	ACTION VERBS
A	{S-AMBIENT} Ø	{P-AMBIENT} Ø	{AP-AMBIENT} A Ø ?	{A-AMBIENT} Ø
A'	{S-AMBIENT EXPER} Ø E	{P-AMBIENT EXPER} Ø E		{A-AMBIENT EXPER} Ø E
B	{S-EXPER (INSTR)} E (I)	{P-EXPER (INSTR)} E (I)	{AP-EXPER (INSTR)} A E (I)	{A-EXPER (INSTR)} A E (I)
C	{S-EXPER COMPLET} E R	{P-EXPER COMPLET} E R	{AP-EXPER COMPLET} A E R	{A-EXPER COMPLET} A/E R
D	{S-EXPER DIRECTED} E G	{P-EXPER DIRECTED} E G	{AP-EXPER DIRECTED} A E G	{A-EXPER DIRECTED} A E/G A E G
D'		{P-EXPER DIRECTED COMPLET} E R S	{AP-EXPER DIRECTED COMPLET} A/S E R	{A-EXPER DIRECTED COMPLET} A/E R S
E	{S-PHYS} P	{P-PHYS (INSTR)} P (I)	{AP-PHYS (INSTR)} A P (I)	{A-PHYS COMPLET} A/P R - - - - - - - - {A-PHYS DIRECTED (INSTR)} A/P G (I)
F	{S-PHYS MEASUR} P M	{P-PHYS MEASUR} P M	{AP-PHYS MEASUR} A P M	{A-PHYS MEASUR} A/P M
G	{S-PHYS LOCATIVE (POSTURE)} P L	{P-PHYS LOCATIVE (POSTURE)} P L	{AP-PHYS LOCATIVE (POSTURE)} A P L	{A-PHYS LOCATIVE POSTURE} A/P L
G'	{S-PHYS MOTION (COMPLET)} P Path S (R)	{P-PHYS MOTION} P (L)or (S Path G)	{AP-PHYS MOTION} AP (L)or (S Path G) A/SP(L)or (Path G) A/GP(L)or (S Path)	{A-PHYS MOTION} A/P L or {S Path G}
H	{S-PHYS POSSES DIRECTED} P G	{P-PHYS POSSES DIRECTED} P G	{AP-PHYS POSSES DIRECTED (MEASUR)} A/S P G (M) A/G P S (M)	{A-PHYS POSSES DIRECTED (INSTR)} A/G P S (I)
H'	{S-PHYS POSSES MOTION} P Path G	{P-PHYS POSSES MOTION} P Path G	{AP-PHYS POSSES MOTION (MEASUR)} A/SPPathG(M) A/PathPSG(M)	{A-PHYS POSSES MOTION (INSTR)} A/Path P S G (I)

Diagram III. Features:

AMBIENT	MEASUR = MEASURABLE
EXPER = EXPERIENTIAL	LOCATIVE
INSTR = ENSTRUMENTAL	POSTURE
COMPLET = COMPLETABLE	MOTION
DIRECTED	POSSES = POSSESSION
PHYS = PHYSICAL	

state, process, action, and action process--which I here reorder as: state, process, action process, and action. In this order I note that the first three often group as against the fourth. There is considerable regularity of the patterns of derivation which carry across these three. By contrast we find a certain discontinuity in going from action process to action, so that the bulk of irregularities occur between my columns 3 and 4 in the scheme as I posit it. This consideration is partly cancelled out, however, by the observation that agent occurs only in action process and action which are thereby grouped together.

My vertical parameter is somewhat more complex than the second parameter in Cook's scheme. Furthermore, it does not show a nice ordering of its values, but approaches an unordered set. Nevertheless, as arranged on the chart, we find the greatest complexity toward the bottom of the chart and the least complexity toward the top. We find also a grand division in which rows A-D' may have experiencer but not patient, while rows E-H' can have patient but not experiencer. This plus the distribution of agent (not in the first two columns but in the last two) divides the chart into quadrants. We find, furthermore, certain natural groupings in successive rows. Thus rows A and A' both have the feature ambient. Row A is unique in not having the feature experiential; all other rows in the top half of the scheme have this feature. Row B has the feature experiential without further features except the optional instrumental. By contrast, C takes the feature completable, D takes the feature directed, while D' takes both features. In the bottom half of the scheme, E and F are primarily physical (with F adding the feature measurable), while G has also to do with location and G' with motion, H and H' have to do with possession, acquisition, transfer, and appropriation--which reflect a kind of metaphorical location and motion.

Specifically the rows run as follows. A includes ambient verbs. A' includes ambient experiential verbs. B includes verbs of emotion (psych verbs) and includes physical impingement on an animate being. C has to do with factual knowledge (<u>know</u>, <u>learn</u>, <u>teach</u>, <u>study</u>). D has to do with desire as well as acquaintance knowledge and the appreciation of persons. D' has to do with sensation and speech. E refers to physical states, processes, and actions including bodily actions. F is similarly physical and refers specifically to measure. G refers to location and kindred ideas while G' refers to motion and kindred ideas. H, as we have said, includes possession, acquisition, transfer, and appropriation, all of which somehow involve the idea of property. H' is similar but adds a semantic component of transitoriness (by having the feature MOTION instead of DIRECTION).

In addition, within certain cells I indicate reflexive case frames, with the possibility held open that such frames can be indicated for certain other cells as well. This crowding of two case frames into one cell indicates a further parameter REFLEXIVE which irregularly characterizes the scheme (cf., 2.1 below).

In the rest of this chapter, I shall first discuss the various rows of this chart along with their component cells and illustrate case frames in English. Next, I consider derived (reflexive) case frames, causatives, surface structure passive clauses, and the status of existential and equational predications. In the final section of this chapter I attempt to demonstrate the relevance of all this to the study of discourse. Of further relevance here is an appendix (in the rear of the book) which gives a summary tabulation of English surface structures with indication of the case frames that encode within them.

1.1 Ambient Case Frames (Row A)

AMBIENT verbs refer to environmental factors. In spite of the fact that English has *it* for surface structure subject in such clauses as *It's hot*, *It's warming up*, and *It's snowing*, there is no deep structure patient, or agent unless we assume some highly general noun such as *weather* or *climate*. It is also plain that the three examples above contrast as to state, process, and action. Such clauses as the following are state ambient in their underlying case frame:

It's hot

It's cold

It's sunny

The process ambient case frame is exemplified by the following:

It's warming up

It's cooling off

The action ambient case frame is exemplified in:

It's snowing

It's raining

It's hailing

In the state ambient frame we make a descriptive statement regarding the environment, in the process ambient frame we assert that there is a change of state going on in the environment, and in the action ambient frame, we assert that there is something happening in the environment. Possibly we should consider that there is an action process case frame as well, although more probably this is a causative formation (cf., 2.2) rather than an action process frame. I list it here but mark it as doubtful. Verbs in this frame have deity, nature, or something of the sort as their agent.

God caused it to warm up

Mother Nature caused it to cool off

The case frames just referred to are given below in a standard format in which all case frames will be given: (1) The derivational features which identify predicates in the various case frames and set in braces, including the abbreviatory prefixes S, P, AP, A which symbolize state, process, action process, and action respectively (as defined by Chafe and accepted here without substantial modification). These abbreviatory prefixes carry all the way down the column in which they are found and occur in no other column. (2) Following the specification of the derivational features of the set of predicates occur references to the noun roles. In the ambient case frames, there is a significant null, i.e., there is no patient or agent involved here unless we think of the weather, the environment, or something on that order as being what is talked about. In the action process frame--if this be valid--there is an agent which is deity, mother nature, or something like that. The ambient case frames are as follows:

A.	{S-AMBIENT} Ø	{P-AMBIENT} Ø	{AP-AMBIENT} AØ ?	{A-AMBIENT} Ø
	It's hot. It's cold. It's sunny.	It's warming up. It's cooling off.	God caused it to warm up. Mother Nature caused it to cool off.	It's snowing. It's raining. It's hailing.
A'	{S-AMBIENT EXPERIENTIAL} Ø E	{P-AMBIENT EXPERIENTIAL} Ø E		{A-AMBIENT EXPERIENTIAL} ØE
	The patient is hot. The patient is cold. I'm uncomfortable here (either too hot or too cold).	I'm getting too hot. John got cold (during the night).		"Oh, why doesn't it rain on me?" I got caught in the rain.

Diagram IV

{S-AMBIENT}Ø {P-AMBIENT}Ø
{AP-AMBIENT}AØ {A-AMBIENT}Ø

1.2 Ambient Experiential Case Frames (Row A')

Ambient EXPERIENTIAL case frames clearly exist for the first, second, and fourth columns, i.e., for state, process, and action predications. The state ambient experiential case frame is exemplified in the following:

The patient is hot

The patient is cold

I'm uncomfortable here (either too hot or too cold)

Here we refer to environmental factors as registering on the nervous system of an animate being. This gives us not merely a state ambient verb but a state ambient experiential verb.

The process ambient experiential case frame underlies the following clauses:

I'm getting too hot

John got cold (during the night)

Here there is a change of state in the environment and again it registers on the nervous system of an animate being.

The action ambient experiential case frame is rather marginal in English. A generation ago there was a facetious song going around The rain makes the flowers so beautiful, oh, why doesn't it rain on me? This is presumably an action ambient experiential verb. The rain is an action ambient predicate, and the reference to raining on me is experiential. Or a man might come in from a bad storm outside with his hat out of shape and complain that It hailed on me. Here, however, are we thinking of the fact that the person experienced rain or hail, or are these expressions used locatively in the underlying structure? More frequent are expressions such as I got caught in the rain--which is a surface structure encoding of this case frame plus a modal element of unexpectedness.

Action process ambient experiential is a further possibility. I'm thinking here of a frequently heard expression in Trique, Let's go outside and get warm in the sun, where get warm is a process ambient experiential verb with a suggestion of activity directed towards that end. If we are able to say I'll go outside and warm myself this would be clearly action process. Possibly, John warmed himself by the fire is also relevant here. This might pass muster as an ambient case frame, although the environment is the comparatively restricted one of closeness to the fire. The surface structures of the last two examples are, however, reflexive, and may indicate derivation from an action process verb to warm (something) of row E. Because of the doubtfulness of such examples as those cited here, cell A'3 is left blank here and in the accompanying charts.

Formulizations for these three case frames, referring to state, process, and action follow:

$$\left\{\begin{matrix}\text{S-AMBIENT}\\ \text{EXPER}\end{matrix}\right\} \text{ØE} \qquad \left\{\begin{matrix}\text{P-AMBIENT}\\ \text{EXPER}\end{matrix}\right\} \text{ØE} \qquad \left\{\begin{matrix}\text{A-AMBIENT}\\ \text{EXPER}\end{matrix}\right\} \text{ØE}$$

1.3 Experiential Case Frames (Row B)

I group here a set of case frames which I have labeled EMOTIVE, PSYCH, AFFECTIVE, and IMPINGEMENT. Emotive and psych verbs are state and process respectively. They involve an experiencer and an optional instrument (correlating with the verbal feature INSTRUMENTAL). Affective and impingement case frames are action process and action respectively. They involve an agent, an experiencer, and an optional instrument.

The emotive case frame without an instrument underlies such clauses as the following:

The cat is nervous

Mary's happy

On the other hand, an instrument (as stimulus or depressant) can be expressed as well:

John is discouraged at the prospect/about his work

Priscilla is scared of cats

Our children are scared of strangers

In the latter two examples, I assume that an unintentional animate stimulus is equal to instrument. It is not that strangers deliberately scare the children, it is rather that the strangers are the unconscious and unintentional stimulus of fright to the children. Although animates are not usually instrument, it appears that an unintentional animate may well be an instrument, i.e., stimulus, rather than an agent.

The psych case frame is process rather than state. There may be an instrument of the sort illustrated with state verbs:

Tom got scared

Mary brightened up

John is becoming discouraged at the prospect/about his work

I believe that we should also include here examples of an animate being as the unconscious stimulus. Such examples as the following suggest themselves:

John has come to be afraid of his mother-in-law

A body part of an animate being may also be instrument with the psych case frame, as in:

Our dog was frightened, i.e., *became frightened by Terry's black beard*

This may be transformed to *Terry's black beard frightened our dog*; and to *Terry frightened our dog with his black beard* which is superficially similar to the common surface structure of the affective case frame but lacks the element of intention which characterizes agents. In the latter transformation, the possessor of the noun has been elevated to subject of the sentence in the surface structure.

Affective verbs are not only action process experiential with optional instrument, they also have an agent, which as we have seen involves intention.

He amused me with his small talk

I cheered her up

He scared me with a firecracker

There are of course some ambiguous examples, such as:

John amused me yesterday

which are ambiguous as to psych versus affective underlying case frames. It could be that John happened to unintentionally amuse me yesterday, in which John was simply the animate unintentional instrument (stimulus) with a psych verb; or it could be John stayed home with me yesterday afternoon and helped me to get through a difficult day by amusing me and spending the time with me, in which case the case frame would be affective and John would be the agent.

Ambiguities of this sort and others which occasionally crop up in other examples relevant to other case frames need to be resolved in the light of discourse context. In fact, if it were possible to analyze unambiguously all examples without resort to context, then the fundamental assumptions of discourse grammar would be invalid (Longacre 1979d, 1979e).

The impingement case frame (action rather than action process) is similar to the affective case frames in the selection of noun roles. The verbs found here refer to surface contact on the experiencer. The objects are not patients (they do not necessarily undergo a change of state), but are experiencers in that their nervous systems register the act of physical impingement. With most verbs of this case frame the optional instruments are body parts.

John hit Bill with his fist

John kissed his wife with a greasy mouth

John petted the cat with both hands

John kicked the dog with his bare foot

Usually with such verbs as kiss, pet, and kick it is not necessary to specify the body part used as instrument. Only when there is something unusual as in the case of greasy mouth, with both hands, and with his bare foot do we specify. On the other hand, the verb hit is ambiguous as to whether one hits with his fist or with a stick or something else:

John hit Bill with a stick/with a crowbar/etc.

The other verbs kiss, pet, and kick do not permit a non-body-part instrument. Apparently the arm and hand may be extended by the use of some weapon but there seems no ready way to extend the body parts used in kissing and kicking.

In the Algonquian languages, which have the grammatical genders animate and inanimate, body parts are inanimate. Thus, in Cree a person (animate) kicks a ball (also animate) with his foot (inanimate). One wonders if the frequent use of body parts as instruments plus the fact that instrument is more commonly inanimate figures in this Algonquian gender classification of body parts as inanimate.

Certain putative examples of this case frame which involve verbs which are suggestive of violence are very similar to E3 examples (see below). Thus John hit Bill with a crowbar suggests more than impingement and may well belong to the physical action process case frame in which such a noun as Bill patterns as patient. Discourse context is needed to make clear the type of action which is involved, since in some contexts hit is equivalent to injure.

What about unintentional impingement such as: A stranger brushed against me in the crowd or He poked me with his elbow (in a crowded situation and unintentionally)? Here it appears that the stranger in the crowd or the one who pokes me with his elbow is not an agent who consciously uses a part of his body to accomplish something. Such examples as the latter prove simply to be psych verbs, i.e., in underlying structure they are to be grouped with

I got brushed by a stranger

I got poked with his elbow

in which the stranger and his elbow are simply instrument and I, the surface structure subject of the clause, is experiencer.

The case frames for the four cells in this row are

B.

{S-EXPERIENTIAL / (INSTRUMENTAL)} E (I)	{P-EXPERIENTIAL / (INSTRUMENTAL)} E (I)	{AP-EXPERIENTIAL / (INSTRUMENTAL)} A E (I)	{A-EXPERIENTIAL / (INSTRUMENTAL)} A E (I)
The cat is nervous. Mary's happy. John is discouraged (at the prospect/about his work). John is scared.	Tom got scared. Mary brightened up. John is becoming discouraged (at the prospect/about his work). The baby was frightened by the stranger's black moustache. The stranger (inadvertently) scared the boy with his black moustache.	He amused/annoyed me with his small talk. I cheered her up. He scared me with a fire-cracker. . . . . {AP-EXPERIENTIAL / (INSTRUMENTAL) / REFLEXIVE} A/E (I) I cheered myself up by playing the radio.	John hit Bill (with his fist). John kissed his wife (with a a greasy mouth). John petted the cat (with both hands). John kicked the dog (with his bare foot). . . . . {A-EXPERIENTIAL / (INSTRUMENTAL) / REFLEXIVE} A/E (I) John hit himself.

C.

{S-EXPERIENTIAL / COMPLETABLE} E R	{P-EXPERIENTIAL / COMPLETABLE} E R	{AP-EXPERIENTIAL / COMPLETABLE} A E R	{A-EXPERIENTIAL / COMPLETABLE} A/E R
'know'	'learn'	'teach'	'study'
Susan really knows algegra. Susan has much factual knowledge. Susan knows a lot of this world's knowledge. - understands the matter. - understands geometry quite well.	Susan has learned a lot of algebra. Susan learned her lesson! Tom forgot the matter. Tom remembered the matter.	Mr. Smith taught Susan algebra. Mr. Smith made Susan understand algebra. Mr. Smith imparted his knowledge to Susan. . . . . With suppression of E: Mr. Smith teaches algebra.	He's studying tonight. He's studying algebra. He memorized the times tables. The burglar cased the joint.

Diagram V

formulized as follows:

$$\left\{\begin{matrix}\text{S-EXPER}\\ \text{(INSTR)}\end{matrix}\right\}\ \text{E(I)} \qquad \left\{\begin{matrix}\text{P-EXPER}\\ \text{(INSTR)}\end{matrix}\right\}\ \text{E(I)}$$

$$\left\{\begin{matrix}\text{AP-EXPER}\\ \\ \text{(INSTR)}\end{matrix}\right\}\ \text{AE(I)} \qquad \left\{\begin{matrix}\text{A-EXPER}\\ \\ \text{(INSTR)}\end{matrix}\right\}\ \text{AE(I)}$$

1.4 Factual Knowledge Case Frames (Row C)

These are case frames which refer to factual knowledge. They show a progression involving the verbs _know_, _learn_, _teach_, and _study_ which are respectively state, process, action process, and action[2]. The common feature COMPLETABLE characterizes all the verbs in these case frames. This correlates with the occurrence of the role range. The first two case frames have the roles experiencer and range while the third and fourth case frames add the agent. I consider all the surface structure noun objects here to be notionally range in that in every case they specify the field of knowledge, i.e., one can say (somewhat stiffly)

Susan knows a lot of factual knowledge

or one can say (more naturally)

Susan knows algebra

where _algebra_ is simply a more specific case of factual knowledge. As is common with verbs that take range there may be resort to a substitute verb of highly generic meaning with most of the verbal content carried by the range noun. Thus _has_ replaces _know_ in some examples.

Susan has much factual knowledge

Susan knows/has a lot of this world's knowledge

Susan really knows algebra

Jim understands the matter thoroughly

Jim understands geometry quite well

The process experiential completable case frame is exemplified as follows:

Susan has learned a lot of algebra

Susan learned her lesson

(Give her time;) Susan is learning

Tom forgot the matter

Tom remembered the matter

The action process experiential completable case frame is exemplified in the following clauses:

Mr. Smith taught Susan algebra

Mr. Smith made Susan understand algebra

Mr. Smith imparted his knowledge to Susan

Mr. Smith is teaching right now

Notice the variety of surface structures above. To make understand is (roughly) equivalent to teach, but involves two verbs in the surface structure, while Mr. Smith taught Susan algebra is a surface structure transitive clause. In impart knowledge to the semantic content of the verb has been largely nominalized to a surface structure object and impart becomes the verb in the surface structure.

The action experiential completable case frame is exemplified in the following (agent and experiencer are coreferential):

He's studying tonight

He's studying algebra

He's memorizing the times tables

The burglar cased the joint

I regard most of the surface structure clauses which illustrate the verbs _know_, _learn_, and _teach_ as surface structure transitive clauses. This is because these verbs characteristically take an object. Examples occur, however, in all four case frames in which objects are deleted.

Susan knows

Susan is learning

Mr. Smith is teaching right now

He's studying tonight

These are surface structure intransitive clauses in which (by suppressing the original object) we focus on the predicate itself.

The case frames for experiential completable verbs are here formulized:

$$\left\{\begin{array}{l}\text{S-EXPER}\\ \text{COMPLETABLE}\end{array}\right\}\text{ER} \qquad \left\{\begin{array}{l}\text{P-EXPER}\\ \text{COMPLETABLE}\end{array}\right\}\text{ER}$$

$$\left\{\begin{array}{l}\text{AP-EXPER}\\ \text{COMPLETABLE}\end{array}\right\}\text{AER} \qquad \left\{\begin{array}{l}\text{A-EXPER}\\ \text{COMPLETABLE}\end{array}\right\}\text{A/ER}$$

It is possible that instrument can also occur in this row of case frames. Thus we have such sentences as _I'm learning modern Israeli Hebrew from phonograph records_ in which presumably _from phonograph records_ is instrument role with process experiential completable case frame. What about such sentences as _I learned Trique from the children at the door_ where the children, although not intentionally my teachers, became, while visiting me, the unconscious instruments of my learning a language? Here we may also have an instance of an animate being as the (unintentional) instrument. This would be very different from such a sentence as _I learned Hebrew from a rabbi_ where presumably the rabbi was the teacher. This is really equivalent to _The rabbi taught me Hebrew_ and is probably action process experiential completable, i.e., the third case frame above.

1.5 Case Frames of Desire/Cognition (Row D)

Cognition here refers to the knowledge of persons, not to factual knowledge. This distinction is of course made in the lexical structure of many languages including French and Spanish. It is, furthermore, implied even in languages where there is no lexical distinction. Thus, in the Greek and common English translations of 1 John 2:3, the question is in effect raised, _How can we know that we know God_? Here the second verb _know_ refers to acquaintance knowledge of the sort encoded in the frames of this section, while the first _know_ refers to factual or discursive knowledge of the sort discussed above.

The case frames of this row include both experiencer and goal. The case frames of the following row include experiencer and source. I posit therefore a feature, DIRECTED, in reference to the verbs of both of these rows of case frames, i.e., there is a flow here not unlike that which we find in motion verbs or verbs of transfer.

The state experiential directed case frame involves not only the verb _know_ and similar verbs _love_ and _appreciate_, but the verbs _want_ and _desire_ which may be directed towards animate or inanimate goals. Notice that in the first example below, _Mary wants a Cadillac_, Mary's wanting of the Cadillac in no way affects the state of the Cadillac itself. _Cadillac_ is not notional structure patient, it is rather the goal towards which Mary's desire is directed. Examples follow:

Mary wants a Cadillac

Tom desires her

Mary loves Tom

Mary knows Tom

Mary appreciates Tom

The process experiential directed case frame similarly includes an experiencer and a goal. Examples follow:

Mary fell in love with Tom

Mary has come to appreciate Tom

Mary has gotten acquainted with Tom

Clearly the expressions *fall in love*, *come to appreciate*, and *get acquainted with* refer to changes of state and therefore are process verbs. They are not simple verbs in the surface structure but verbal expressions involving idiom formation and paraphrasis.

The action process experiential directed case frame adds to the roles experiencer and goal a further role of agent. Here the experience is mediated by this further participant as in the following examples:

I introduced Mary to Tom

I first made Mary appreciate Tom

Through me Mary came to love Tom

The action experiential directed case frame expresses evaluation. The experiencer may occur as separate from the goal or as coreferential with it. Presumably, one evaluates someone or something to someone else: *John praised Mary to Tom*. *John is openly scornful of VW's with everyone he meets*. The experiencer, however, may also be the goal: *John makes fun of Pete* (*whenever he sees him*). If the object of an evaluation does not know that he is being evaluated, he is simply goal and whoever hears the evaluation is experiencer. If, however, the object of the evaluation knows that he is being evaluated he is both experiencer and goal. Verbs in this case frame can express a positive evaluation (*praise*), a neutral evaluation (*describe*), or a negative one (*disdain*, *scorn*). Probably judicial verbs such as *condemn*, *judge*, *accuse*, *pardon*, *exonerate* go here as well. Examples:

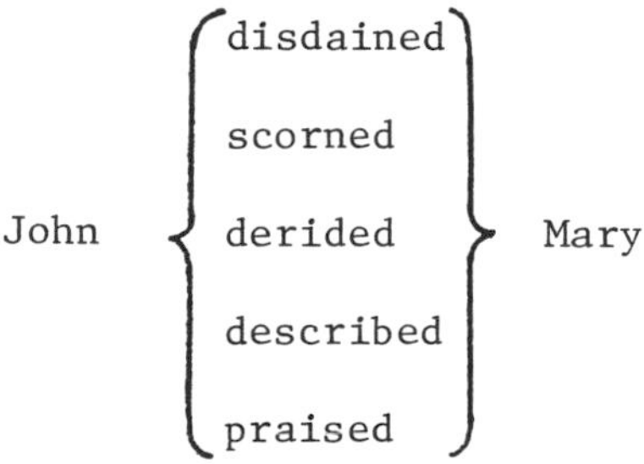

The witness accused the defendant

D.	{S-EXPERIENTIAL, DIRECTED} E G	{P-EXPERIENTIAL, DIRECTED} E G	{AP-EXPERIENTIAL, DIRECTED} A E G	{A-EXPERIENTIAL, DIRECTED} A E/G, A E G
	Mary wants a Cadillac. Tom desires her. - - - - - - - - - - - - - - - Mary loves Tom. Mary knows Tom. Mary appreciates Tom.	Mary fell in love with Tom. Mary has come to appreciate Tom. Mary has got acquainted with Tom.	I introduced Mary to Tom. I first made Mary appreciate Tom. Through me Mary came to love Tom.	John {disdained / scorned / praised / condemned / judged / flattered / accused / exonerated / derided / pardoned} Mary John described Mary to Tom. John gossiped about Mary. . . . . {A-EXPERIENTIAL, DIRECTED, REFLEXIVE} A/E/G John praised himself. John despised himself.
D'		{P-EXPERIENTIAL, DIRECTED, COMPLETABLE} E R S	{AP-EXPERIENTIAL, DIRECTED, COMPLETABLE} A/S E R	{A-EXPERIENTIAL, DIRECTED, COMPLETABLE} A/E R S
		Tom heard (the sound of) an owl. George smelled (the odor of) onions. David saw/caught sight of Bathsheba. I saw a strange sight (on Boston Common this morning). . . . . {P-EXPERIENTIAL, DIRECTED, COMPLETABLE, REFLEXIVE} E/S R Tom heard himself. Tom heard his own voice. Tom caught sight of himself (in the mirror).	The mother told her child a story. She sang me a song. The artist showed Tom the painting. Preach a sermon. Recite a poem. Say a word. Tell me. Speak, Rover, Speak! . . . . {AP-EXPERIENTIAL, DIRECTED, COMPLETABLE, REFLEXIVE} A/E/S Go preach yourself a sermon.	Tom listened to (the sound of) the owl. The audience watched the performance. The cook tasted the soup. The cook took a taste of the soup. . . . . {A-EXPERIENTIAL, DIRECTED, COMPLETABLE, REFLEXIVE} A/E/S John kept watching himself in the mirror.

Diagram VI

The jury condemned the criminal

The governor pardoned the convicted man

These case frames are formulized as follows:

$$\left\{\begin{array}{l}\text{S-EXPER}\\ \text{DIRECTED}\end{array}\right\}\text{EG} \qquad \left\{\begin{array}{l}\text{P-EXPER}\\ \text{DIRECTED}\end{array}\right\}\text{EG}$$

$$\left\{\begin{array}{l}\text{AP-EXPER}\\ \text{DIRECTED}\end{array}\right\}\text{AEG} \qquad \left\{\begin{array}{l}\text{A-EXPER}\\ \text{DIRECTED}\end{array}\right\}\text{AE/G or AEG}$$

1.6 Case Frames of Sensation, etc. (Row D')

Case frames of this row refer to sensation, speech, and attention. Apparently the first cell in this row, that of state, is not filled--but more about that later. These verbs apparently refer to a source rather than to a goal and are completable.

The process experiential directed completable case frame involves verbs which refer to the exercise of the physical senses. I cite here first some examples:

Tom heard (the sound of) an owl

George smelled (the odor of) onions

David saw/caught sight of Bathsheba

I saw a strange sight (on Boston Common this morning)

In English we may say *Tom heard an owl*. It is understood that what Tom hears is the sound of the owl. Similarly we can say *George smelled onions* and what we refer to is the odor of the onions. In Korean it is necessary to specify nouns such as *sound* and *odor* before words such as *owl* and *onion* (Hwang 1975:70). The nouns that are optional in English but obligatory in Korean are presumably RANGE. In Trique where no abstract nouns such as *sound* and *odor* exist there is still some restriction in that one cannot *hear a person* but only *what the person says*, or *words*. Possibly then there is a notional structure range noun present whatever freedom or restriction of surface structure is found in various languages. But what is the function of nouns such as owl and onion in the above example? Clearly they are the source from which the physical waves emanate which finally register on the nervous system of the experiencer, i.e., in effect, Tom receives sound waves emanating from an owl.

The verb see is slightly more problematic. The basis of this difficulty is the physical fact that light waves travel much faster than sound waves or than smell and therefore the experience of sight is a much more immediate experience. We usually do not specify such a noun as sight (notional structure range) unless we have some special reason for doing so as in the fourth sentence above, I saw a strange sight or in such paraphrases as David caught sight of Bathsheba where the lexical weight is shifted to the range and a comparatively colorless verb, primarily a carrier of tense, occurs.

The action process experiential directed completable case frame involves verbs which refer to speech and kindred functions. Again I start off with a group of examples:

The mother told her child a story

The artist showed Tom the painting

The pastor preached a sermon

The teacher recited a poem

Say a word, please

Tell me

Speak, Rover, speak

A characteristic of most range nouns is that they need not be specified. Notice that in the above, we can reduce most of these sentences to constructions without a range noun:

Harriet sang in church this morning

Mr. Evans preached

Judy recited

Mother told me

and of course the last two examples:

Tell me

Speak, Rover, speak

Notice that we have here not simply a source such as owl or onions or even Bathsheba in the previous case frame, but we have a person consciously engaged in an activity, i.e., the agent is coreferential with the source.

The action experiential directed completable case frame is here labeled attention. Verbs of this frame involve the exercise of the senses consciously on the part of the experiencer so that the agent and the experiencer are coreferential. A range noun is possible with all of these and the source is usually specified. Examples follow:

Tom listened to the owl

The audience watched the performance

The cook tasted the soup

There is occasional ambiguity of the attention case frame with the sensation case frame. Thus, we may say John smelled the roses, i.e., he happened to catch the odor of the roses as he walked in the front door of the house, versus John smelled the roses and pricked his nose in the process. In most instances, discourse context resolves such ambiguities.

We can specify range nouns in such sentences as:

Tom listened to the hooting of the owl

Here hooting is the range noun and owl is the source. In The audience watched the performance, performance is itself a range noun. We can specify also source if we say The audience watched the performance of the dramatic society.

It has been suggested that there may be state verbs in Row D' as well, and that this would fill in the empty cell on the left. If deaf and blind and mute are states, why should not such clauses as he hears, he sees, he talks be also stative? Obviously, however, these words imply a modal such as able to in the deep structure, i.e., 'he is able to hear', 'able to see', and 'able to talk', while deaf, blind, and mute imply 'not able to hear', 'not able to see', and 'not able to talk'. In this usage such nouns do not customarily specify either range or source. They are, therefore, neither directed nor completable and I regard their classification in the empty cell of D', as somewhat improbable. They are in some ways more similar to the emotive verbs of C.

Formulizations of the three case frames, sensation, speech, and attention follow:

$$\left\{\begin{array}{l}\text{P-EXPER}\\ \text{DIRECTED}\\ \text{COMPLETABLE}\end{array}\right\}\ \text{ERS} \qquad \left\{\begin{array}{l}\text{AP-EXPER}\\ \text{DIRECTED}\\ \text{COMPLETABLE}\end{array}\right\}\ \text{A/SER}$$

$$\left\{\begin{array}{l}\text{A-EXPER}\\ \text{DIRECTED}\\ \text{COMPLETABLE}\end{array}\right\}\ \text{A/ERS}$$

1.7 Physical Case Frames (Row E)

The case frames of this row refer to physical states, processes, action processes, and bodily activities. The first three columns here, state, process, and action process, form a derivational progression. Predications in these three columns are characterized by the feature PHYSICAL--which correlates with the occurrence of a noun in the role of patient. An optional feature, relative (Chafe), could be considered to characterize these three case frames--but see my discussion below. There is some discontinuity between these three and the two case frames in the action column, which are not derivationally related to the preceding three. While patient occurs in these further case frames, it is coreferential with agent.

The state physical case frame takes only a verb and a patient noun, as in the following:

The dish is broken

The blanket is wet

The bolt is loose

The pig is dead

The road is wide

With the suggested optional feature, relative, we get such clauses as:

The road is wider

The valley is deeper

Probably all such clauses imply however, an implicit comparison of some sort as in The road is wider here than back there and The valley is deeper here than back there--in which one part of the road or valley is compared to another part--or a comparison of two valleys: This road is wider and That valley is deeper. Here we have the deep structure of comparison which is properly speaking a relationship of the enlarged statement calculus and is considered in chapter 3. I, therefore, do not posit the feature relative as a characteristic of predications themselves.

The process physical case frame includes a patient noun with an optional instrument. The instrument is accidental, never something used intentionally by someone. Illustrative clauses follow:

The dish broke

The blanket has dried out

The bolt came loose

The pig died

With the optional feature instrument, we get such clauses as:

My foot got cut on a sharp rock

The bolt came loose from the vibration of the motor

It is noteworthy that in English we have to resort to something that is passive or quasi-passive to express the surface structure instrument in the fashion shown in the last two sentences.

Again, with the suggested optional feature, relative, we could get:

The road widens here

The valley deepens at this point

It is, however, an accident of English surface structure that we have state and process verbs apparently characterized by the feature, relative, in English. I think that The road widens here or The road is wider at this point are essentially the same deep structure which is--as has been stated--very probably the deep structure of comparison and not properly speaking a feature of the predicates.

The action process physical case frame has predicates with the optional feature instrumental. Here, as throughout the entire column marked action process, we find that an agent is present. The following examples are action process without the optional instrument:

John broke the dish

He cut the rope

Susan dried the blanket

Tom killed the pig

Edward speared the five fish

We trapped a bear

Bill beat up on John

It is noteworthy that most of the verbs which can be classified in this case frame delineate pretty well the sort of instrument which may be used with them. Thus, a verb like cut implies some sort of sharp instrument with a blade. Smash implies something heavy and blunt. Spear implies a spear and trap implies some kind of trap. Cover implies some kind of flexible extended surface. A few ambiguities between process and action process obscure the picture here. When we say John broke the dish, we probably mean that John dropped the dish by accident and it broke (process, with John as stimulus, i.e., unintentional instigator). We could, of course, mean 'John took a rock and deliberately smashed the dish with a rock' (action-process, with John as agent). When we say Tom killed the pig we could mean 'Tom took a knife and stabbed the pig to death' or we could mean that 'Tom happened to hit the pig with his car and killed it'. It is clear, therefore, that whenever a verb implies a specific kind of instrument, it means the instrument as used intentionally; all such uses are action process verbs with agent and instrument. Accidental or unintentional instruments are also possible with most of these verbs; in these uses, INSTRUMENTAL characterizes the verb but the case frame in process. In Mandarin Chinese the accidental instrument and the intentional instrument are distinguished in the surface structure of the language (Baron 1971).

English has some special surface structure constructions in which either patient or instrument is brought into focus as surface structure subject with suppression of the agent. While something on this order is also possible with the use of a passive clause, the structures here considered and exemplified are not passive. Consider the following set of sentences:

This fabric washes easily with Tide

This article reads smoothly

My new car drives nicely

The clothes washed for half an hour

The door opens with this key

Notice that in several of these sentences we are apparently interested in the efficiency of the process relative to the focussed patient, but in the example The clothes washed for half an hour we simply put the patient into focus in order to tell how long the process of washing took. Furthermore, in the example referring to clothes washing, no instrument is specified. We can also omit the instrument in such examples as the first: This fabric washes easily.

We also have a surface structure in English which might be called instrument focus:

This key opens that door

The stronger trap finally caught the bear

This pair of scissors cuts cardboard

There is also a further surface structure construction in English which seems to be predicate focus rather than focus on any noun in any role. In fact, the meaning of this construction seems to be to express procedure/practice. Thus we have sentences like Mother washes on Monday and irons on Tuesday. Presumably she washes clothes, but the patient is not expressed. Again, She washes with a washboard and castile soap. Again, They open at nine o'clock, but close early where a store or office of some sort is understood. In this surface structure variation of the underlying case frame, the reference to the patient is suppressed, thereby achieving focus on the process itself.

In the above, I have avoided positing further case frames in the notional structure, but have handled the constructions involved as resultant on focus in the surface structure. Considering surface and notional (deep) structure to be poles (not a dichotomy), I believe that focus is a relatively superficial phenomenon--or, in terms of constructional derivation, a relatively late rule in progressing from the semantic depth towards the surface. This, of course, means that I allow for meaning in the surface structure. I am convinced that we'll have to do this anyway. Nevertheless, even if we should put a variable called focus into the underlying (shallow) structure, we still do not, I believe, want to multiply case frames at this point. The action process case frame with instrument is especially susceptible to encoding in alternate case frames in the surface structure and the feature which determines one surface structure against another is focus--whether we choose to make focus an element of the notional, sub-surface, or surface structure. Focus, in turn, is a function of the thematicity requirements of the context.

I give here formulizations of the three case frames--state, process, and action process--before going on to present the two case frames which are found in the action column:

$$\{\text{S-PHYSICAL}\}\text{P} \left\{\begin{matrix}\text{P-PHYSICAL}\\ \text{(INSTR)}\end{matrix}\right\} \text{P(1)} \quad \left\{\begin{matrix}\text{AP-PHYSICAL}\\ \text{(INSTR)}\end{matrix}\right\} \text{AP(1)}$$

In the action column under row E we have two case frames instead of only one. The two case frames found here have the feature COMPLETABLE and the feature DIRECTED respectively; both also have the feature physical. The former characterizes the following examples:

Stephen ran a race/100 yard dash

They fought a good fight/a hard battle

The children played a game/kick-the-can

They ate too much food/sauerkraut

In these examples, agent and patient are coreferential; the agent moves himself in *running*, *fighting*, *playing*, *eating*, etc. With all these the purpose of the final noun phrase is to specify better the activity already stated in the verb itself. (See the discussion of RANGE in Chapter 4.) Range nouns are typically optional within this case frame, i.e., we can say: *Stephen ran this morning* or *Stephen ran the hundred yard dash*. Similarly we can say *The children played all morning* or *The children played kick-the-can*.

As stated in Chapter 4, I take account here of factitive verbs, i.e., those verbs which refer to the making or creation of something. Take such clauses as the following:

The carpenter made a table

The Indians make many beautiful artifacts

Beethoven composed nine symphonies

These, I suspect, are basically the same case frame as above, but in the surface structure *table*, *many beautiful artifacts*, and *nine symphonies* are surface structure objects which are obligatory to the clauses in which they occur. In notional structure these nouns are range. This is clearly seen in a language such as Greek, where the verb *poieō* 'make' has a cognate poiēma which means 'thing made' (from which our English word poem is derived). Thus, in Greek there is a clear cognate accusative with the verb make. Artifact in the second example above is broadly generic--reminiscent of poiēma in Greek. Table is, on the contrary, a quite specific noun which can be regarded as a more specific instance of artifact (or some such abstract noun). In the third example nine symphonies is a more specific instance of such a highly generic noun as composition. With the verb compose we can thus use a cognate accusative: Beethoven composed many compositions.

The second case frame found in the action column under row E is action physical directed. Here the agent exerts himself in action which is directed toward a goal.

John kicked the chair

John tapped on the glass

John knocked on the door

John stroked his chin

We can scarcely consider that chair, glass, door, and chin are patients here. They are not affected. Their physical state is not changed by the actions performed on them. Consequently, I believe that it is better to regard those inanimate objects of the surface structure as encodings of deep structure goal than of deep structure patient. The two case frames found in row E, the fourth column, are here formulized:

$$\left\{\begin{matrix}\text{A-PHYSICAL}\\ \text{COMPLETABLE}\end{matrix}\right\}\ \text{A/PR} \qquad \left\{\begin{matrix}\text{A-PHYSICAL}\\ \text{DIRECTED}\end{matrix}\right\}\ \text{A/PG(I)}$$

1.8 Case Frames of Measure (Row F)

Here we have four case frames which have a peculiar nuclear feature MEASURABLE and a corresponding role MEASURE in their case frames.

The state physical measurable case frame involves a state physical measurable predicate, and nouns in the roles

E. {S-PHYSICAL} P

The dish is broken.
The blanket is wet.
The bolt is loose.
The pig is dead.
The road is wide.

{P-PHYSICAL (INSTRUMENTAL)} P (I)

The dish broke.
The blanket has dried out.
The bolt came loose.
The pig died.
My foot got injured on a piece of glass.
The bolt came loose from the vibration of the motor.

{AP-PHYSICAL (INSTRUMENTAL)} A P (I)

John broke the dish.
He cut the rope (with a knife).
Susan dried the blanket (in the dryer).
Tom killed the pig.
The construction company is widening the road (with a bulldozer).
The govt. is deepening the canal (with a dredge).
Edward speared five fish.
We trapped a bear.
Bill beat-up on John.

Instrument focus:
This key opens that door.

Patient focus:
The door opened.

. . . .

{AP-PHYSICAL (INSTRUMENTAL) REFLEXIVE} A/P (I)

John washed and shaved.
John shaves with an electric razor.
John cut himself with a pair of scissors.

{A-PHYSICAL COMPLETABLE} A/P R

Stephen ran a race/100 yd dash.
They fought a good fight/ a battle.
The children played a game/ Ring-around-the-Rosie.
John ate (a full meal).
John drinks (too much liquor).
John is reading a book.

. . . .

The carpenter made a table.
The Indians make many artifacts.
Beethoven composed nine symphonies.
She bore a child.

- - - - - - - - - - - - - - - - -

{A-PHYSICAL DIRECTED (INSTRUMENTAL)} A/P G (I)

John kicked the chair (with his foot).
John tapped (on) the glass (with his fingers).
John knocked on the door.
John stroked his chin.

F. {S-PHYSICAL MEASURABLE} P M

The statue weighs one ton.
It costs $1.98.

{P-PHYSICAL MEASURABLE} P M

He grew an inch.
I've gained five lbs/ weight.
My bonds went down 10% / lost value.
Its cost has gone up considerably.

{AP-PHYSICAL MEASURABLE} A F M

I shortened it two inches.
I reduced the cost 10%.
I've made the cargo 35 lbs lighter.

{A-PHYSICAL MEASURABLE} A/P M

The squadron advanced a mile.
The Cowboys gained five yards.
The Army retreated 100 miles.

Diagram VII

of patient and measure:

The statue weighs one ton

This hat costs $1.98

That the expressions of measure are extrapolations from the verbs weigh and cost is evident. One ton is a further specification of the idea inherent in the verb weigh, while $1.98 is a further specification of the word cost. In this respect MEASURE resembles RANGE. But measure, unlike range, can never be a surface structure object and cannot be passivized: *One ton is weighed by the statue. Below, under measurable action, we will have a clear instance or two of minimal contrast between range and measure roles.

The process physical measurable case frame has process, physical, and measurable as the features of its predicate and, again, nouns in patient and measure roles.

He grew an inch

I've gained a lot of weight/30 lbs.

My bonds have lost value

My bonds went down 10%

The action process physical measurable case frame has action process, physical, and measurable as features of its predicate and nouns in the roles of agent, patient, and measure.

I shortened it two inches

I cut it off two inches (where 'cut off' is not equal to 'cut')

My sister lengthened her hemline two inches

They've widened the road ten feet

The action measurable case frame has action physical measurable as its predicate features and nouns in agent/patient and measure roles. The agent and the patient are coreferential.

The army advanced/retreated a mile

Our team gained/lost five yards

In addition to these examples just given, one verb cited under action physical completable above (in row E) and most of the verbs given under Locomotion (in row G') also figure in this case frame. Notice the following contrast involving the verb run (or a pair of close homophones):

a) John ran the 100 yard dash

b) John ran 100 yards

In example (a), the noun phrase 100 yard dash is simply a more specific substitute for race which is in turn range noun with run. But in example (b) the phrase 100 yards specifies how far John ran. Furthermore, running a measurable distance implies a beginning and ending point--thus making this verb run not merely an activity but locomotion (G'4), as in John ran from the school to the post office. Most verbs of G'4 may also be used here in measurable action. Thus, rather than say Mr. Ogelthrope traveled from Paris to Moscow via Warsaw or Mr. Ogelthorpe traveled in Europe this summer (both regular configurations under G'4) we could say Mr. Ogelthorpe traveled 2000 miles this summer. Similarly with verbs such as swim or crawl we can specify the measure of distance rather than the location or source, path, and goal.

I posit the following formulizations of these frames:

$$\left\{\begin{matrix}\text{S-PHYSICAL}\\ \text{MEASURABLE}\end{matrix}\right\}\text{PM} \qquad \left\{\begin{matrix}\text{P-PHYSICAL}\\ \text{MEASURABLE}\end{matrix}\right\}\text{PM}$$

$$\left\{\begin{matrix}\text{AP-PHYSICAL}\\ \text{MEASURABLE}\end{matrix}\right\}\text{APM} \qquad \left\{\begin{matrix}\text{A-PHYSICAL}\\ \text{MEASURABLE}\end{matrix}\right\}\text{A/PM}$$

1.9 Locative Case Frames (Row G)

We find here four case frames which can be characterized as location (state), allocation (process), placement (action process), and stance (action). These four case frames involve the further features LOCATIVE and POSTURE, which is optional in the first three case frames but obligatory in stance verbs.

In the locative state case frame the verb is characterized as state physical locative with the optional feature posture. The associated noun roles are patient and locative as seen below:

The knife is in the box

The key is under the rug

The house is on the corner

The statue is in the park

By substituting for the verb is a more specific verb in the surface structure, an indication of the shape, size, or posture of the patient is included. This is what I refer to as the feature POSTURE. Note the following examples which correspond roughly to the second, third, and fourth sentences above.

The key is lying on the rug

The old house is still standing on the corner

The cottage sits on the corner

The statue stands in the park

Pharoah's statue sits in the temple

Notice that the use of these more specific verbs lie, sit, and stand tells us something about the shape and posture of the patient. Presumably the key is a long flat object which can lie on the rug. The house which stands on the corner is probably a house of two or three stories. The bungalow which sits on the corner is presumably a squat one story building. The statue which stands in the park refers to the statue of a standing man, while Pharaoh's statue sitting in the temple refers to a statue of a man sitting down.

Notice that these necessarily refer to inanimate objects if they are to be classified as patient. Otherwise, if an animate object is standing, lying or sitting somewhere this is an activity which involves expenditure of energy and which requires our positing an agent in the case frame--as we will do further on in the last case frame of this row. What about, however, such sentences as the following:

The cat is on the roof

He's in Europe

Apparently these clauses also encode the locative state case frame. They simply affirm of something animate the location in which it is found. But with animate patients of this sort, we may not use the optional feature POSTURE. As we have already explained, to use posture of animate patients is to land us in the locative action case frame (stance).

The allocation case frame involves process physical locative predicates with the optional feature posture, and with nouns in the roles of patient and locative. The patient is described as coming to be in a certain location, as in The pepper got in her eye (Eckerd 1979). When the resultant position is also described, the optional feature posture is present:

The plate ended up upside down on the floor

(It fell down inside and) wedged sideways out of reach

The placement case frame involves an action process physical locative predicate with the optional feature posture and nouns in the roles of agent, patient, and locative. Notice here, as with the two preceding case frames, the noun in the locative role is obligatory and nuclear. To place a car in the garage is very different from washing a car in the garage. If we say He washed the car in the garage, in the garage simply specifies the locale of the entire activity and is a peripheral locative. But if we say He put the car in the garage the phrase in the garage is essential to the completion of the sense of the verb. Such verbs are properly classified in this case frame. Examples follow:

They placed a book by the phone

Mary put the salad in the icebox for an hour

The mother laid the baby down in the crib

He planted rice in the field

A few comments on the above examples. Notice that the second example, Mary put the salad in the icebox for an hour, doesn't mean that she stood in front of the icebox and was occupied for an hour in putting the salad into it. It rather means that she put the salad in and it was in there for the time of an hour. We see here that the emphasis is not on the activity of putting something somewhere, but on the fact that we have here action process verbs in which the patient changes location.

Such sentences as He planted rice in the field have surface structure variants, He planted the field with rice in which the locative encodes as surface structure object and the patient encodes as surface structure instrument. It is interesting to note that the same variation in surface structure encoding of patient and location as either surface structure object plus surface structure locative or surface structure object plus surface structure instrument is found in many Philippine languages (e.g., Dibabawon, Foster 1964).

Consider the next two examples which involve the optional feature POSTURE:

He laid the book by the telephone

He stood the book against the telephone

Here the use of the verb laid versus the verb stand tells us whether the book is placed in a horizontal or in a vertical position.

The stance case frame, which involves action physical locative predicates with the obligatory feature posture, makes the roles agent and patient coreferential, i.e., an animate being sustains itself in a given location with a given posture:

He's standing on the corner

The returning POW stood by his wife

The king was sitting on his throne

Phyllis is lying on the bench

For animate beings, *standing* and *sitting* presumably involve expenditure of energy--although the energy expended in *lying down* is presumably less than that expended in standing or sitting. I, therefore, posit for all these verbs an agent as well as a patient.

The case frames of this row may be formulized:

$$\left\{\begin{array}{l}\text{S-PHYSICAL}\\ \text{LOCATIVE}\\ \text{(POSTURE)}\end{array}\right\}\text{PL} \qquad \left\{\begin{array}{l}\text{P-PHYSICAL}\\ \text{LOCATIVE}\\ \text{(POSTURE)}\end{array}\right\}\text{PL}$$

$$\left\{\begin{array}{l}\text{AP-PHYSICAL}\\ \text{LOCATIVE}\\ \text{(POSTURE)}\end{array}\right\}\text{APL} \qquad \left\{\begin{array}{l}\text{A-PHYSICAL}\\ \text{LOCATIVE}\\ \text{POSTURE}\end{array}\right\}\text{A/PL}$$

1.10 Case Frames of Motion, Propulsion, Locomotion (Row G')

This row contains case frames which have feature MOTION rather than LOCATIVE, and have the noun role path. While the feature DIRECTED correlates with the occurrence of source and/or goal, path is crucial to a case frame whose verbs have the feature motion. Of the four case frames in this row, the first two are state motion and process motion, respectively, while the latter two express propulsion and locomotion. The feature physical and the role patient continue to occur here. Agent occurs in the last two case frames and is coreferential with patient in the last case frame.

The state physical motion case frame is characterized by verbs which predicate motion (as a physical state) to certain patients. The nouns in the role of patient are either astronomical bodies or products of technology (cf. Eckerd 1979). A second noun phrase, which can be considered to be path, frequently occurs in examples of this frame;

The earth rotates on its axis once every twenty-four hours

The moon revolves (makes one revolution) around the

G. {S-PHYSICAL / LOCATIVE / (POSTURE)} P L

The knife is in the box.
The key is under the rug.
The house stands on the corner.
The statue stands in the park.
Pharaoh's statue sits in the temple.
The key is lying on the rug.
The cat is on the roof.
He's in Europe.

{P-PHYSICAL / LOCATIVE / (POSTURE)} P L

The pepper got in her eyes.
The plate ended up upside down on the floor.
It (fell down inside and) wedged sideways out of reach.

{AP-PHYSICAL / LOCATIVE / (POSTURE)} A P L

They placed a book by the phone.
Chuck put the beer in the icebox for an hour.
The mother laid the baby down in the crib.
He planted rice in the field.
He planted the field with rice.
He lay the book by the phone.
He stood the book against the phone.

. . . .

{AP-PHYSICAL / LOCATIVE / POSTURE / REFLEXIVE} A/P L

Tom sat down in the chair.
Tom laid down in the bed.
The monk knelt at the altar.
Mary took her stand on the corner.

{A-PHYSICAL / LOCATIVE / POSTURE} A/P L

He's standing on the corner.
The returning POW stood by his wife.
He's sitting on the chair.
Phyllis is lying on the bench.

G'.

{S-PHYSICAL MOTION (COMPLETABLE)} P Path (R)	(P-PHYSICAL MOTION) P (L) or (S / Path / G)	(AP-PHYSICAL MOTION) A P (L) or (S / Path / G); A/S P (L) or (Path / G); A/G P (L) or (S / Path)	(A-PHYSICAL MOTION) A/P L or {S / Path / G}
The machine is going/running/functioning. The wheel spun around (one full turn). The earth rotates on its axis. The earth rotates one full rotation (every 24 hours). The moon revolves around the earth (once each month).	The ship sank at sea. The ship drifted idly in the calm sea. The ship sank into the depths. Don fell from the chair/down. The boat drifted across the river. The boat drifted from the left to the right bank. The machine is slowing down/speeding up accelerating.	Don't carry a burden through the temple enclosure! Tom carried the basket from the kitchen through the dining room into the living room. Bill drives his car to work. We pushed the boat out into the current. Tom pulled the book {over. / towards himself. / away from Susan.} Don't throw a ball in the house! Tom threw the knife {into the box. / at me. / across the room.}	Harriet traveled in Europe. He traveled from Frankfurt to Rome via Milan. The baby crawled from the kitchen to the front room. We returned from PNG via Europe. Sam swam through the water to the raft. The car crossed over the bridge from Minneapolis to St. Paul.

Diagram VIII

earth once each month

The earth orbits around the sun

The wheel spun around several turns

I also list here examples of machinery in operation--even in the absence of nouns as path:

The press is going

The machinery is running

In addition, some verbs (revolve, spin) are characterized by the optional feature completable and the occurrence of a noun as range. Temporal expressions frequently occur here as well (see examples above).

The process physical motion case frame has the features process physical and motion in its predicate; the latter correlates again with the possible occurrence of a noun in the role path. Often, however, this frame has simply a patient noun and an optional location noun. The optional location which specifies the motion as occurring at a certain place may be alternatively replaced by the cases, source, path, goal, or some combination of them. The commonly occurring combinations seem to be either source by itself, goal by itself, or source plus goal or path; but all three may be encoded within the same clause.

Particular verbs of this frame differ slightly in their precise case lineup. In the following example we have the verb sink with a patient noun without a locative of any sort.

The ship sank

This may of course be expanded to The ship sank at sea where a locative specifying location occurs. With the verb fall it is more usual to specify source. Thus we get Don fell from the chair or from a second story window. If we have no noun of this sort, we usually at least get an adverb of direction as in John fell down. Returning to the verb sink we note that we are more likely to get a specification of goal than of source: The ship sank into the depths, hardly The ship sank from the surface. With either fall or sink we may on occasion, however, get full specification of source, path, and goal. Thus, we may have The soap fell from the washbasin across the commode and onto the floor or The ship sank (more likely we would find here a more picturesque verb such as settled) from the litter-strewn surface, down through the first hundred well-lit feet and into the murky depths below. With the verb drift we may likewise get no more than specification of location: The ship drifted idly in the straits. On the other hand we may get specification of path, The boat drifted across the river, or specification of both source and goal, The boat drifted from the left to the right bank. Of the verbs which we have considered, fall and sink are verbs of vertical motion and drift is a verb of transverse motion; this does not in itself appear to be a crucial distinction. All these predications simply report what happened to someone or something rather than any action taken by someone.

Propulsion verbs are action process physical motion. In addition to the patient they have either a location noun or some combination of source, path, and goal. With a verb such as carry, patient and location can occur, or patient, source, path, and goal:

Don't carry a burden inside the temple enclosure

Tom carried the basket from the kitchen through the dining room into the living room

With most verbs in this frame, either agent and source are coreferential or agent and goal:

We pushed the boat out into the current

Tom pulled the book away from Susan

Locomotion verbs have action physical motion predicates, a coreferent noun which indicates agent and patient and a noun in the optional location role. The optional location may be replaced by some or all of the set, source, path, and goal, as in the previous case frames of this row. In the following sentence we have simply specification of location: Harriet traveled to Europe. We may, however, have specification of both source and goal: Harriet traveled from Frankfurt to Rome. We may have source, path, and goal all specified: Harriet traveled from Frankfurt to Rome via Milan or we may have simply a specification of path and nothing more: *Harriet traveled via Milan*. Further examples follow:

The baby crawled from the kitchen to the front room

We returned from New Guinea via Europe

The car crossed over the bridge from Nuevo Laredo to Laredo

Sam swam through the water to the raft

In the latter example there is specification of path and goal. I have considered that all locomotion predications have coreferentiality of agent and patient, since in every case the agent moves himself from one place to another.

These four case frames are formulized as follows:

$$\left\{\begin{array}{l}\text{S-PHYSICAL}\\ \text{MOTION}\\ \text{(COMPLETABLE)}\end{array}\right\} \quad \text{P(PATH)} \quad \text{(R)}$$

$$\left\{\begin{array}{l}\text{P-PHYSICAL}\\ \text{MOTION}\end{array}\right\} \quad \text{P(L) or} \left(\begin{array}{l}\text{S}\\ \text{Path}\\ \text{G}\end{array}\right)$$

$$\left\{\begin{array}{l}\text{AP-PHYSICAL}\\ \\ \text{MOTION}\end{array}\right\} \quad \begin{array}{l}\text{AP(L) or} \left(\begin{array}{l}\text{S}\\ \text{Path}\\ \text{G}\end{array}\right)\\ \text{A/SP(L) or} \left(\begin{array}{l}\text{Path}\\ \text{G}\end{array}\right)\\ \text{A/GP(L) or} \left(\begin{array}{l}\text{S}\\ \text{Path}\end{array}\right)\end{array}$$

$$\left\{\begin{matrix}\text{A-PHYSICAL} \\ \\ \text{MOTION}\end{matrix}\right\} \text{ A/PL or } \begin{pmatrix}\text{S} \\ \text{Path} \\ \text{G}\end{pmatrix}$$

Before passing on to the discussion of the last two rows of case frames, it is necessary to pause here and comment on the Indo-European bias which characterizes the discussion at this point. Actually, Indo-European languages (and probably a few other language stocks) represent an extreme of structural complexity in permitting the expression of source, path, and goal all in one clause and dependent on one verb. By contrast, in many other linguistic areas, all these relations are not expressed in the same clause. Thus, in Trique and other Otomanguean languages and in a typical language of Papua New Guinea three clauses are required to express source, path, and goal. "I left Oaxaca City, I passed along the highway, I arrived at Mexico City". In such languages each motion verb has associated with it two nouns one in the agent role and the other locative. The latter means source, path, and goal depending on its concurrence with a given motion verb.

1.11 Case Frames Referring to Property (Rows H and H')

In these case frames a further feature POSSESSION occurs with the predicates. Possession does not add any new cases to our case inventory but it specifies that nouns in the roles source, path, and goal must be animate. Predicates with the feature DIRECTED (Row H) occur in case frames with goal, or both source and goal. In these frames source is the original owner and goal the non-transitory or terminal owner. Predicates with the feature MOTION (Row H') specify path, and may also specify source and/or goal in their case frames. In such predicates source and goal are defined as with directed, and path indicates the transitory owner or agent in the transfer. In that the predicates in these various case frames co-occur with patients, the feature PHYSICAL is posited for their predicates as well.

The case frames of these two rows can be labeled possession, acquisition, transfer, and appropriation respectively. Verbs of acquisition do not involve expenditure of effort (no agent is present with them) but indicate <u>come</u>

into possession of. Verbs of transfer and appropriation involve the activity of an agent. Transfer verbs are transactional, and thus indicate _come into possession_ (or _forfeit possession_) _of by one's own activity_ (e.g., _buy_ or _sell_). Appropriation verbs are not transactional but indicate a physical action such as _grab_, _snatch_, _take_, _collect_. Occasionally, acquisition versus transfer or transfer versus appropriation is contextually dependent, i.e., surrounding discourse context dictates which sort of verb is intended.

The possession case frame has predicates with the features state physical, possession, and directed. It takes goal (owner) and patient (thing possessed). Examples follow:

Dick has a new book

Tom owns a lot of real estate

He has possession of the car now

The transitory possession case frame (in H') has the predicate features state physical and possession (as in H) but substitutes the feature MOTION for DIRECTED. It has nouns in the roles patient, path, and goal. In the surface structure of English, the order goal patient (of H) is permuted to patient goal after statement of path as subject in transitory possession:

Dick has a book for you

Here _Dick_ is the path over which the patient _the book_ will travel to _you_, the goal. The next example is similar:

Tom has some tickets for all of us

The acquisition case frame (H) has the features process physical, possession and directed in its predicates and has the same set of accompanying noun roles as in the preceding frame, with much the same sort of surface structure actualizations:

Tom has acquired a St. Bernard

Mary obtained her visa (here we mean simply Mary came to have her visa, not she actively got it by expenditure of effort)

The transitory acquisition case frame is like acquisition but substitutes motion for directed and adds path.

Tom got/found the tickets for you

The department obtained a visa for Dr. Ho

What I here label transfer and assisted transfer are the most complicated case frames. They compare in many ways to propulsion and locomotion in their use of source, path, and goal. Like propulsion, we find that the agent is coreferential with the source--and in one variety of transfer, with the goal. Unlike propulsion, there is one variety of assisted transfer in which the agent is coreferential with the path. Measure, i.e., price may also be specified. The features which characterize transfer predicates are action process, physical, and (optional) measureable, plus directed (in transfer) and motion (in assisted transfer).

The first examples below exemplify the sub-frames (of H and H') in which agent is coreferential with source. With agent and source coreferential we have verbs such as give, sell, and supply. Supply requires a slightly different surface structure from the other verbs.

Tom gave Bill a book (H)

In which Tom is agent and source, Bill is goal, and book is patient.

Tom gave Bill a book for Susan (H')

In which Tom is agent and source, Bill is path, book is patient, and Susan is goal. We similarly analyze the following two sentences:

Mr. Smith sold Tom a convertible (H)

Mr. Smith sold Tom a convertible for his wife (H')

The following example involving the verb supply requires a surface structure in which goal encodes as object and patient encodes as surface structure instrumental adjunct.

The U.S. supplies Israel with arms

The verb *bribe* is very similar:

The prisoner bribed the guard with a candy bar

Examples now follow of the subframes in which agent is coreferential with goal. This involves such verbs as *receive* and *buy*:

Bill received a book from Tom (H)

where *Bill* is agent and goal, *book* is patient, and *Tom* is source.

Bill bought a book (H)

where *Bill* is agent and goal, and *book* is patient.

Bill bought a book from Tom (H)

where *from Tom* further specifies source. Still other examples may be found in which agent is coreferential with path:

Bill bought a book for his wife (H')

where *Bill* is agent and path, *book* is patient, and *wife* is goal.

In that *sell* and *buy* are typical of the main two sets of words above, it is interesting to note what happens to these case frames when measure, namely price, is added. We have examples such as:

Bill sold the book for $5.00

in which *Bill* is agent and source, *book* is patient, and *for $5.00* is measure. We can further specify:

Bill sold the book to George for $5.00

where *to George* specifies goal. It appears to be somewhat awkward to try to put source, path, and goal all into the same surface structure clause in which price is also expressed:

(?) *Bill sold the book to George for his wife for $5.00*

This sentence is not so much ungrammatical as implausible and heavy.

In this respect, the verb *buy* is much the same as the verb *sell*. We can say *Bill bought a book for $5.00* in which *Bill* is mentioned as agent and goal, *book* is patient, and *for $5.00* is measure. We can likewise say *Bill bought a book for his wife for $5.00* in which *Bill* is coreferential agent and path, *book* is patient, *wife* is goal, and *for $5.00* is measure. We can also say *Bill bought a book from Tom for $5.00* where *Bill* is agent and goal, *book* is patient, *from Tom* is source, and *for $5.00* is measure. But again it would prove awkward to try to pack more into the same sentence, i.e., (?) *Bill bought a book from Tom for his wife for $5.00* gets a bit heavy.

Appropriation verbs have predicate features like those of the preceding case frames (in H and H') but are action verbs. Such verbs as *catch*--the inverse of *throw*--(G' 3) are also found here. In the frame H', the predicate features are: action physical, possession, motion, and instrumental (rather than measurable). Accompanying nouns are agent and goal (coreferential), patient, and optional source and instrument. In the frame H', the predicate features are action physical, possession, motion, and instrumental while nouns occur in the roles agent and path (coreferential), patient, goal, and source. Again, it is awkward to specify too many of these in the same surface structure clause. In *George grabbed the book from John* (H), *George* is path, *book* is patient, and *John* is source. It is possible to say *George grabbed the book from John for me*--although this is a bit heavy. Instrument may be specified in such examples as:

He picked the coal up with the tongs

A body part instrument is possible:

He snatched it with his left hand

It is definitely awkward to try to combine all these in such a clause as: (?) *George grabbed the book with his left hand from John for me*.

Some simpler examples of appropriation (H):

John caught the ball

Henry collects stamps

And a few simple examples of appropriation (H'):

Levi collected taxes for Rome

John picked it up for me

It is evident that these verbs do not portray simple acquisition (H 2 and H' 2) but an activity. It is one thing to happen to acquire something and quite a different thing to deliberately snatch or grab it. Notice also that a transaction (transfer) can specify measure (H 3 and H' 3), while appropriation specifies instrument (H 4 and H' 4).

A few residual problems remain. What of the ambiguity in such clauses as John picked it up for me meaning 'so that I could have it' versus meaning 'to save may bending over', i.e., 'doing it for me'? Similar to the latter are examples such as Tim washed the dishes for me meaning 'he did the work so that I wouldn't have to do it'. Here we have rather the idea of a substitute or proxy rather than goal. This may be a further unanalyzed case such as SUBSTITUTE. If so, it probably occurs with several case frames--especially those in the lower two quadrants of the chart.

A further problem is specification of source with appropriation verbs. It seems to me slightly forced here to specify the source, John caught the ball from Mary but I do not believe this is an ungrammatical sentence. We might ask the question as to how we classify the somewhat similar sentence John caught the measles from Mary. Here it seems to me that we have a metaphorical extension of appropriation verbs to include non-physical situations involving contagion. The question in analyzing metaphor always is: do we take the metaphor at face value and specify its case structure, or do we analyze the metaphor into its literal constituents and then analyze its case structure? The former is the more superficial, the latter the deeper analysis, and they probably serve different purposes.

As already stated, case frames of row H are considered to have predicates characterized by the feature directed, as in the following formulizations:

H.	{S-PHYSICAL, POSSESSION, DIRECTED} P G	{P-PHYSICAL, POSSESSION, DIRECTED} P G	{AP-PHYSICAL, POSSESSION, DIRECTED, (MEASURABLE)} A/S P G (M); A/G P S (M)	{A-PHYSICAL, POSSESSION, DIRECTED, (INSTRUMENTAL)} A/G P S (I)
	Dick has a new book. Tom owns a lot of real estate. He has possession of the car now.	Tom's acquired a St. Bernard. Mary obtained her visa (= came to have, not actively got).	T. gave B. a book. Mr. Smith sold T. a convertible. The U.S. supplies Israel with arms. B. received a book from T. B. bought a book from T. B. sold/bought the book for $5.00.	George grabbed the book from John. Henry collects stamps. He picked the coal up with the tongs. John caught the ball.
H'	{S-PHYSICAL, POSSESSION, MOTION} P Path G	{P-PHYSICAL, POSSESSION, MOTION} P Path G	{AP-PHYSICAL, POSSESSION, MOTION, (MEASURABLE)} A/S P Path G (M); A/Path P S G (M)	{A-PHYSICAL, POSSESSION, MOTION, (INSTRUMENTAL)} A/Path P S G (I)
	Dick has a book for you. Tom has tickets for all of us.	Tom got/found the tickets for you. The department obtained a visa for Dr. Ho.	T. gave B. a book for Sue. Mr. Smith sold T. a convertible for his wife. B. bought a book for his wife.	George grabbed the book for me from John. John picked it up for me. Levi collected taxes for Rome.

Diagram IX

$$\left\{\begin{matrix} \text{S-PHYSICAL} \\ \text{POSSESSION} \\ \text{DIRECTED} \end{matrix}\right\} \text{PG} \qquad \left\{\begin{matrix} \text{P-PHYSICAL} \\ \text{POSSESSION} \\ \text{DIRECTED} \end{matrix}\right\} \text{PG}$$

$$\left\{\begin{matrix} \text{AP-PHYSICAL} \\ \text{POSSESSION} \\ \text{DIRECTED} \\ \text{(MEASURABLE)} \end{matrix}\right\} \begin{matrix} \text{A/SPG(M)} \\ \\ \text{A/GPS(M)} \end{matrix} \qquad \left\{\begin{matrix} \text{A-PHYSICAL} \\ \text{POSSESSION} \\ \text{DIRECTED} \\ \text{(INSTRUMENTAL)} \end{matrix}\right\} \text{A/GPS(I)}$$

Case frames of row H' have instead of directed the feature motion:

$$\left\{\begin{matrix} \text{S-PHYSICAL} \\ \text{POSSESSION} \\ \text{MOTION} \end{matrix}\right\} \text{P Path G} \qquad \left\{\begin{matrix} \text{P-PHYSICAL} \\ \text{POSSESSION} \\ \text{MOTION} \end{matrix}\right\} \text{P Path G}$$

$$\left\{\begin{matrix} \text{AP-PHYSICAL} \\ \text{POSSESSION} \\ \text{MOTION} \\ \text{(MEASURABLE)} \end{matrix}\right\} \begin{matrix} \text{A/SP Path G(M)} \\ \\ \text{A/Path PSG(M)} \end{matrix}$$

$$\left\{\begin{matrix} \text{A-PHYSICAL} \\ \text{POSSESSION} \\ \text{MOTION} \\ \text{(INSTRUMENTAL)} \end{matrix}\right\} \text{A/Path PSG(I)}$$

Again, before passing onto the next main section, the Indo-European bias here evident needs to be admitted and taken into account. Just as many languages in linguistic areas other than Indo-European have nothing corresponding to row G' above, so many have also nothing corresponding to H'. This is not strange in that while row G' involves a literal and physical path, row H' involves path used in a metaphorical sense. Thus, for example Korean has no verbs and case frames of the H' variety--neither do (at least) most languages of Mesoamerica and Papua New Guinea.

2. FURTHER SYSTEMATIC CONCERNS

2.1 Reflexives

Within certain of the cells of the scheme there occur derived case frames whose predicates have the further feature REFLEXIVE. Apparently reflexivization correlates with the occurrence of a surface structure object or indirect object under semantic conditions which permit the surface structure subject and object (or indirect object) to have the same referent. Under these conditions commonly some sort of surface structure reflexive pronoun marks the object (or indirect object)--but with certain case frames somewhat more specialized structures occur. Without pretending to be exhaustive I note the occurrence of derived reflexive case frames as follows in this section.

In row B, columns 3 and 4, reflexive case frames occur without surface structure specialization (beyond the use of a reflexive pronoun):

I cheered myself up by playing the radio

I amused myself by playing solitaire

This derived case frame (B3) may be formulized as follows:

where A/E represent a conflate role.

Likewise for B4:

John hit himself with a stick

John (jumped up in the air and) kicked himself

This derived case frame may be similarly formulized:

$$\left\{\begin{array}{l}\text{A-EXPERIENTIAL}\\ \text{(INSTR)}\\ \text{REFLEXIVE}\end{array}\right\}\quad \text{A/E (I)}$$

In row D, the evaluation-judicatory case frame in column 4 likewise has a regular reflexive:

John praised himself

John condemned himself

This, in turn is formulized:

$$\left\{\begin{array}{l}\text{A-EXPERIENTIAL}\\ \text{DIRECTED}\\ \text{REFLEXIVE}\end{array}\right\}\quad \text{A/E/G}$$

where the same referent is at once agent, experiencer, and goal.

In row D', regular reflexives occur but they are infrequent (and semantically unusual) in column 3. Examples of D'2 are not so difficult to turn up:

Tom heard himself

Tom heard his own voice

Tom caught sight of himself (in the mirror)

These may be formulized:

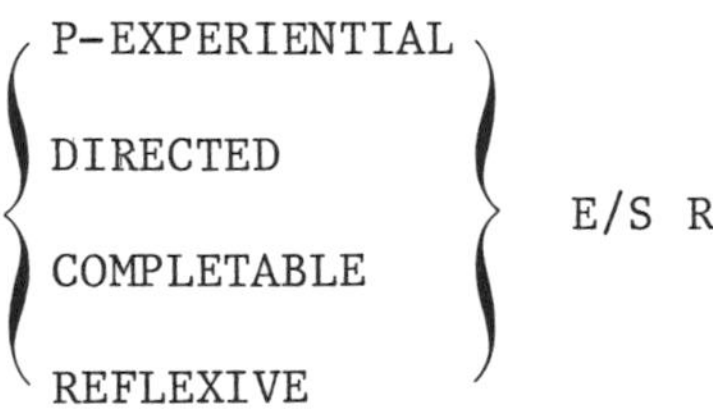

where experiencer and source have the same referent and where range nouns continue to be possible (cf. voice and sight above).

As already indicated, in D'3, reflexives are possible only sporadically and under obscure semantic conditions:

Go preach yourself a sermon

The derived case frame is:

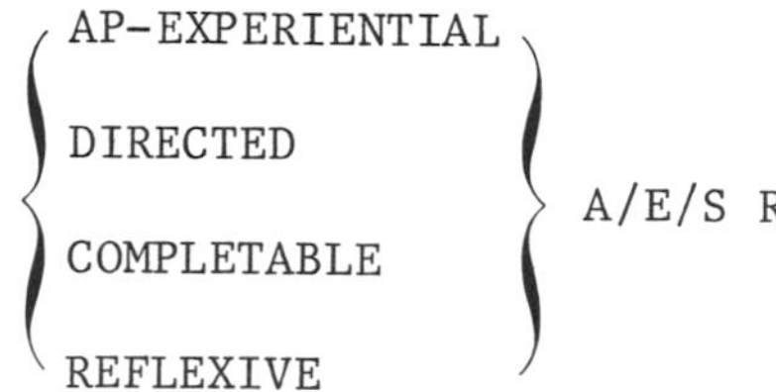

where agent, experiencer, and source have the same referent.

Likewise for D'4:

John kept watching himself in the mirror

with the formulization:

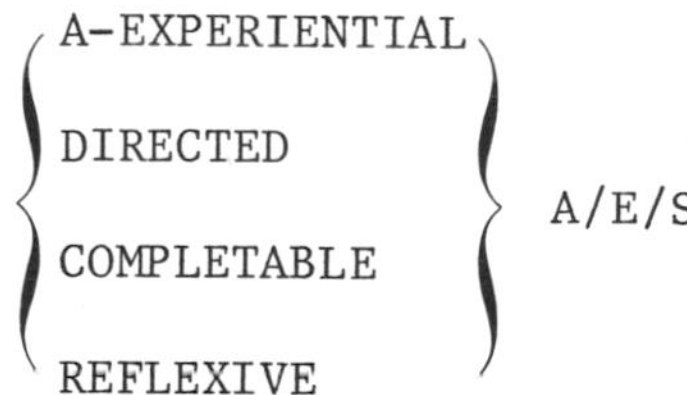

While all the preceding derived reflexive case frames issue in regular reflexive surface structures, the action process physical case frame (E3) has two surface structures for reflexives. With some verbs such as cut or trap we get the regular surface structure with the reflexive pronoun:

John cut himself with a pair of scissors

John trapped himself in his own pit-fall

With verbs such as wash and shave the reflexive pronoun may

be omitted:

John washed and shaved

John shaves with a straight razor

Whatever the surface structure, the derived case frame is:

$$\left\{\begin{array}{l}\text{AP-PHYSICAL}\\ \text{(INSTR)}\\ \text{REFLEXIVE}\end{array}\right\}\quad \text{A/P I}$$

With the action process physical locative case frame (G 3) we likewise find a surface structure which does not use the reflexive pronouns:

Tom sat down in the chair

Tom laid down on the bed

The monk knelt at the altar

Mary took her stand on the corner

The derived reflexive case frame has the obligatory feature posture whereas in the frame from which it is derived this feature is optional:

$$\left\{\begin{array}{l}\text{AP-PHYSICAL}\\ \text{LOCATIVE}\\ \text{POSTURE}\\ \text{REFLEXIVE}\end{array}\right\}\quad \text{A/P L}$$

2.2 Causatives

The term *causative* is used here to cover several problems which relate to case or role and case frame analysis. For one thing, we need to consider the suggestion persistently raised by some (cf. Anderson 1971.178ff) that case frames of the sort that I posit in column 3 should be semantically decomposed into frames of the sort found in column 2 plus a superordinate causative predication. Secondly, we need to consider the best way to conceive of the notional structure of such sentences as the following (in English): X had/made Y Vb Z or X caused Y to Vb Z (when both X and Y are _agents_). Closely related to the latter consideration is the question of whether such predications are: (1) a further column of case frames, or (2) a regular causative structure (efficient cause) as in Chapter 3, 4.2.1.

Turning to the first problem, we note the initial plausibility of considering _John cheered Mary up_ (B3) to consist notionally of 'John did so-and-so; Mary cheered up' (B2). This could be represented graphically as:

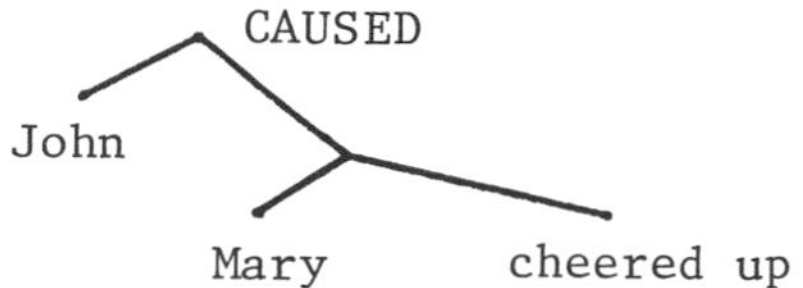

where CAUSED is an abstract predicate and _Mary cheered up_ is a complement. We might similarly posit that _Mr. Smith teaches Susan algebra_ (C3) is equivalent to 'Mr. Smith CAUSES Susan learns algebra' (C2) and in similar fashion:

John introduced Tom to Mary (D3) =

John CAUSED
Tom came to know Mary (D2)

Tom told the story to Mary (D'3) =

Tom CAUSED
Mary heard the story (D'2)

Rachel killed her husband (E3) =

Rachel CAUSED
Her husband died (E2)

-- and others.

To begin with it is important to recollect that the graphic and notional conventions which are illustrated above are inherently no better than a simple juxtaposition of two

Process	Action Process
{P-Experiential} E	{AP-Experiential} AE
Mary cheered up	John cheered Mary up

columns with derivation between them. There is no notional or theoretical superiority of the treatment of John cheered Mary up on the previous page to the above, provided that derivation is posited between the columns. The crucial question is, however: Can the Action-Process category really be subsumed under Process + a further feature CAUSATIVE? If so, then the Action Process category can be eliminated from our scheme. If not, it is necessary to retain the scheme much in its present form and the representational conventions here implied are probably better than others which might suggest some false semantic relationships.

Examining, then, the above suggested formalism which involves an abstract predicate CAUSE, we note that the plausibility varies from example to example. Probably the derivational plausibility is greatest for John cheered Mary up. The plausibility is less for the other suggested derivations. Thus, for example, John introduced Tom to Mary is not a simple equivalent of John CAUSED + Tom came to know Mary. Rather, an introduction is a social act which may or may not be effective. It is an action whose ostensible purpose may be to cause Tom to know Mary--or it may be quite perfunctory. Similarly, for Mr. Smith teaches Susan algebra. Here Mr. Smith engages in an overt activity whose ostensible purpose is to get Susan to learn algebra. Somewhat different is the by now well-discussed matter of the possible equivalence of kill with cause to die. Clearly, kill implies direct and (usually) violent action, more than bringing about death by irresponsibility and lack of attention--although extended uses of kill are found in English. In brief, we find that there is considerable semantic specialization between similar items in the Process column of my scheme and in the Action-Process column.

Even in a language with causitive derivation in its verb

morphology, we find this same picture of semantic specialization. In Trique (Mexico) verbs may be derived to causatives by the addition of a *dV-* element. But the semantic derivation is somewhat specialized. Thus, while *(g)a^{3}maʔ^{35}* means 'rain', *da^{3}ga^{3}mąʔ^{35}* means 'sprinkle'; while *(g)a^{3}če^{21}* means 'walk, move go (on wheels)', *du^{3}gwa^{3}če^{21}* means 'to push a wheeled object'; and while *(g)a^{3}ča^{21}* means 'sing, play (an instrument)', *du^{3}gwa^{3}ča^{21}* means 'to play (the radio)'. The verb 'kill', *da^{3}ga^{3}wiʔ^{35}* is clearly restricted to direct activity which results in death. A king or magistrate does not 'kill' someone in prison unless he directly does the deed. Otherwise, Trique must say 'prisoner died, caused the King'. Here the explicit surfacing of a verb 'cause/do' (cf. the abstract predicate CAUSE) is semantically contrastive with 'kill'.

It seems best, then, to retain the Process and Action-Process distinction. Similar verbs in similar case frames across columns are semantically related more or less according to the particular lexemes which are involved. A systematic notional similarity (and contrast) is seen in that Process verbs do not have an Agent, while Action Process verbs do. The over-all notional relationship is seen whatever the vagaries of particular lexical sets.

We now consider Action Process and Action case frames which enter into construction which involve an extra agent or a causer. Most of these are, as stated above, of the following structure in English: X had/made Y Vb Z or X caused Y to Vb Z., i.e., *The coach had/made John run the 100 yard dash* or *The coach caused John to run the hundred yard dash*. The corresponding Trique constructions involve postpositions of a second verb *(g)i^{3ʔ}yah^{3}* ('do, make, cause'), as in *gu^{3}nah^{2} Jua^{12} ngo^{4} ca^{3}rre^{2}ra^{3} gi^{3ʔ}ya^{3}h mai^{2}stru^{3}* ('ran John a race made the teacher') i.e., 'The teacher (coach) had John run a race'. What is common to all such examples--in English or Trique--is the bringing in of a new agent.

What shall we do with such constructions? One course would be to posit two more columns of case frames, i.e., Caused Action Process and Caused Action. Thus the case frames for Action and Caused Action would look as follows:

$$\left\{\begin{matrix}\text{A-PHYSICAL}\\ \text{COMPLETABLE}\end{matrix}\right\}\ \text{A/PR} \qquad\qquad \left\{\begin{matrix}\text{CA-PHYSICAL}\\ \text{COMPLETABLE}\end{matrix}\right\}\ \text{C A/PR}$$

There are, however, several clear reasons for not setting up such further columns of causative case frames. For one thing, more frequently than not the actual surface structure of a language (cf. English and Trique, which although widely divergent structurally agree in this respect) involves two clauses with two separate verbs here. Furthermore, while between our present columns two and three we can give many examples of lexical specialization in three as opposed to two only infrequently is this true of these further causatives which involve an additional agent.

To be true, some languages employ affixes to indicate an extra agent (causer), but this is a fairly uniform and semantically predictable sort of derivation--as in the Hebrew equivalent of 'drank Father wine' versus (Genesis 19:33), 'caused-drink daughters father wine', i.e., 'the daughters had/made their father drink wine' (where the non-causative stem of drink regularly derives to the Hiphil, a causative stem). In brief, between these further causatives and the forms which underlie them the relationship is rather straightforward and uncomplicated while this is not so of the relation of Process and Action Process in our present scheme.

Finally, the causatives which add a further agent are not really limited to <u>had/made</u> or <u>caused</u> plus a complement. While these have been chosen, as semantically the most neutral, to facilitate comparison, other 'abet' verbs may be used here, e.g., <u>permit</u>, <u>want</u>, <u>help</u>, <u>force</u>, <u>forbid</u>.

Apropos to both of the above is a comment (private communication) from P. Healey:

> The real world involves two actions and two people as agents, one for each action. Various languages encode this situation in various ways. Some, like the Philippine languages, have a single causative clause with both agent (causer) and subject (agent) tagmemes. (Actually, the agent usually ends up marked as grammatical Subject, and the subject as grammatical Object-Accessory or Referent or whatever.) Others, like English, have a merged sentence of two clauses with one Subject and one Object-cum-Subject in double function. Others, like Telefol, have a chained (merged) sentence of two clauses with one subject each (minimally marked as subject person in the verb morphology). Because there has to be specific real-world kick/push/word/look/

nod/eyebrow-wiggle from the first agent to set the second agent off, my feeling is that all clauses and merged sentences that have two distinct agents should be in the statement calculus, not the predicate calculus, even in Philippine languages. This would include sentences where the English translation has for the causer such actions as: force, send, make, allow, prevent, stop, get, have, etc.

Consequently, it seems plausible that constructions of the sort which have been discussed here properly belong under the notional structure of Efficient Cause (See 4.2.1 of Chapter 3).

2.3 Surface-Structure Passives

I now turn to the discussion of surface-structure passives and their relation to the case frames described in this chapter. As a surface structure feature the passive is not universal but it is frequent enough among the world's languages to merit extended comment.

To begin with, we must take account of the fact that almost any case frame may become an English surface structure passive if that case frame also encodes into very elastic English surface structure, subject, predicate, object. In spite of previous work to the contrary (from Chomsky 1965 on), I feel that it is easier to explain English passives this way than to try to derive them de novo from the underlying structures, i.e., from the case frames themselves. Nevertheless, we have to take account of the equally stubborn fact that not all passivizations are equally successful. Some passives, while apparently grammatically possible, sound stylistically implausible and stilted.

Some considerations which emerge from inspecting a representative number of typical passive formations are the following:

(a) Passives often are not successful if they specify the agent (with a by phrase).

(b) Passives are more successful if the passive subject is in some evident way affected by the action of the passive verb (Bolinger 1973).

(c) Passives are more successful with a general referent, i.e., when the agent, stated, or unstated, is a group, or when the entire clause is gnomic, i.e., general or proverbial in its thrust.

Consideration (a) has to be discussed in the light of thematicity requirements in connected discourse. When the object of a sentence is thematic within a paragraph (or a whole discourse) it may weaken the thematic structure of a paragraph to preserve the active form of the transitive clause. This follows from the fact that English (and many other languages) uses the subject (in most types other than procedural discourse) to express the theme in the sense of what we are talking about. If, therefore, a given noun is to be thematic, putting it in object position may not give it sufficient prominence in the clauses of a paragraph while the introduction of a further noun as subject might imply the thematicity of the latter. It is strategic in such circumstances to shift to a passive construction--which makes the thematic noun the subject and eliminates the need for mentioning any further noun. If the latter is mentioned in a *by* phrase, he is understood to be in a secondary role. This is seen, for example in the following notice regarding a popular concert on a university campus (all proper nouns are fictitious):

> *Tickets for the Mandy Moyer concert February 23 are selling fast, says John Habner (activities and organizations). More than 60 percent of the tickets have already been sold for the performance of the prize-winning vocalist, who will appear at 8:00 p.m. in Hoover Hall. Tickets for the general public are $8.00 at the E. I. Langford University Center Information Desk.*

In the above example, *tickets* is thematic. While where they are sold, their cost, and the fact they are going fast are all relevant, the persons who sell the tickets are irrelevant to the point where mentioning them at all would detract from the thematic unity of the paragraph. *John Habner* and his office (*activities and organizations*) are mentioned only as the source of information.

In brief, since the passive is often used to avoid mentioning an agent anywhere in the clause, passives that do not specify an agent often impress us as more successful.

Passive subjects, however, are not only thematic or FOCUSED, but are meant to be UNDERGOER (to use a Pikean phrase) as well. This ties into consideration (b) above. In discussing this, I use undergoer as a broader term than patient. In fact, we can contend that the surface meaning of passive construction is FOCUSED UNDERGOER. In reinforcing this, I take account of some observations by Bolinger (1973) and Wallace (1979).

Bolinger suggests that there is really a notional structure component of transitivity involved whenever a passive is successful. I have taken account of this in my restriction (b) early in this section and in my statement that the meaning of the surface structure passive construction is 'focused undergoer'. Bolinger gives two especially interesting examples which are worthy of comment. He points out that This bridge has been passed under by a dog is an unsuccessful passive, but This bridge has been passed under by countless generations of lovers is a successful passive, i.e., he feels that this implies that countless generations of lovers passing under the bridge have in some sense affected or consecrated the bridge and that therefore, a passive is proper under these conditions. He cites also a further constrastive pair of sentences: The army was deserted by the private and The army was deserted by Simon Bolivar. Presumably, the army's being deserted by its general is a much more serious matter which affects vitally its well-being. Correlating with this is the fact that the second sentence is a successful passive while the former is not.

In this regard, it is interesting to note some recent work in Asian languages considering passive and passive-like construction. Thus, Wallace observes "Numerous languages of eastern and southeastern Asia, for example, have passive or passive-like constructions which portray the subject of the clause as the victim of some unfortunate event" (Wallace 1978:1). Thus, in Japanese we might expect the equivalent of "Taroo was scolded by the teacher" but not (presumably) "Taroo was praised by the teacher". Wallace points out that Chinese, Cambodian, Thai and Lao make a similar use of the passive, while other languages (e.g., Vietnamese) have contrasting adversatives and beneficials (both passive-like) and still other languages (some Austronesian languages of Indonesia and the Philippines) have adversative passives versus neutral passives. At any rate, the 'something happened to' meaning of the passive in all these languages is not dissimilar to the English requirement that a successful passive have a notional structure transitivity requirement.

Consideration (c) is initially difficult to explain, but (a) plus (c) together amount to a generality requirement that is perhaps best understood if we note the appropriateness of the passive to expository rather than to narrative discourse. While narrative discourse is agent-oriented and treats, furthermore of the actions of particular agents, expository discourse lacks this agent-orientation and deals more with generalities.

To illustrate the interplay of these three restrictions, it is instructive to examine possible passive transformations of some particular rows in our scheme of case frames (no attempt is made here to be exhaustive).

Passives of row C (factual knowledge) apparently exist, but we must pick and choose stylistically. Apparent passives of the state experiential completable case frame emerge rather as surface structure copula plus past participle than as true passives. But here again the restrictions concerning specification of agent and generality hold. Thus while _A lot of algebra is known by Susan_ isn't overly successful, _Mathematics is better known to this present generation than to any past generation_ is more successful. Notice, however, that we have, in keeping with the adjectival character of the word _known_, changed the _by_ expression to a _to_ expression in the surface structure. Better still is all omission of the agent reference and conformity to the generality requirements suggested above as in the following: _The answer was known back then (but is forgotten now)_. In regard to the process case frame of this same row, we can of course mechanically match _Susan has learned a lot of algebra_ with the grammatically possible passive _A lot of algebra has been learned by Susan_--but this is not a particularly successful passive. With sufficient generalization, we are able to maintain even the reference to the agent as in the following: _The lessons of history are not learned by the next generation_. With the action process case frame of the same column we can mechanically match _Mr. Smith taught Susan algebra_ with _Susan was taught algebra by Mr. Smith_ and obtain a fairly successful passive. A corresponding generalized statement would be _Youngsters are not taught so much these days by the older generation as by their peer generation_.

For row D, desire/cognition, we find a similar situation. Thus, A drink was wanted by Tom is not a very successful passive, but Drinks may be wanted when food isn't is successful, as is also, Asparagus is liked by most people--which is sufficiently general to be almost gnomic (even if not true). Process verbs of row D', sensation, also have their passives. Again, however, highly specific statements involving particular agents are not as successful as less specific and more generalized statements. Thus, we can say, A snake was seen by Tom or An owl was heard by Tom. But these are not as successful as A snake was seen down by the milkhouse this morning, An owl was heard up in the pasture last night, or Snakes are often seen in the warm weather during the first days of spring. With action process verbs of the same row we have an additional complication arising from the possible presence in at least some of these lexical strings of the dative passive versus the accusative passive. Thus, The child was told a story by his mother and A story was told to the child by his mother. But with the word sing while we can say A song was sung to me by Mary, we find it less natural to say *I was sung a song by Mary. Again we can say Tom was shown the painting by the artist or The painting was shown to Tom by the artist. Here even passives referring to highly specific situations seem to be successful. We also have the verb exhibit of this case frame used with high success in such general statements as the following, An unwrapped Egyptian mummy will be exhibited all this month in the art museum.

Action process verbs of the E column also have their passives. Here again, however, the passives which refer to more specific situations are not as successful as those which refer to more general situations and omit the agent entirely. The dish was broken by Harriet is not as successful as All the dishes were broken at the same time. Action verbs in the E column, especially bodily activities, show a similar pattern of restriction. Thus, we can say The battle was fought by the soldiers, but somewhat more successfully: Battles are fought by men, not by boys. In regard to factitives, while we can say, The table was made by the carpenter, somewhat more successful is such a statement as The bridge must be built by a capable, competent engineer. The action directed verbs of this same column with various sorts of imanimate goals, show a similar pattern of restriction. Thus The door was knocked on by John or The glass was tapped on by John impress us as being rather artificial, but

The Blarney stone has been kissed by seekers of good fortune longer than we can remember is quite successful.

Placement verbs in row G take passives somewhat freely. Again, however, those which omit the agent and present themselves to us as generalized statements are more successful. Thus we can say, *The book was placed near the telephone by Tom* but somewhat more successful and pleasing is *The phonebook usually is placed near the telephone*. In regard to the contrasting surface structure encoding of *He planted rice in the field* and *He planted the field with rice* we find the corresponding pair of passives, i.e., *Rice was planted in the field* or *The field was planted with rice*. Again, we note the closeness with which the passive corresponds to the surface structure of the active. In row G' propulsion verbs act very similar. Thus we can say, *The knife was thrown into the box by Tom* and we can perhaps with a bit more success omit *by Tom* and say *The knife was thrown into the box from some distance*.

The bottom two rows, case frames which refer to possession, also permit passive formation with the same restrictions already noted. The verb *has* in the stative case frame (possession) does not permit a passive formation. With the verb *own* passives are apparently possible, although they may prove to be copula plus adjective. Thus we can say, *A convertible is owned by John*. This, however, is not as successful as the more general statement *Convertibles are owned by affluent young people*. Action process verbs of this row, i.e., transfer case frames, have, again, the distinction between dative passive and accusative passive. Thus, *Tom gave Bill a book* can have the corresponding passive *Bill was given a book by Tom* or *A book was given Bill by Tom*. These passives are apparently quite successful. We also have passives of this sort which omit entirely the specification of the agent such as *In this world workers are paid, not drones* or even *Their help is well paid*. The now familiar general-preferred-to-specific restriction holds for the action frame of this row (appropriation). Thus, while we can say *Stamps are collected by Mary*, this is not so successful as *Stamps are collected in many parts of the world*. While we can say *A fortune was amassed by John*, the indication of the size of the fortune makes possible a more successful passive such as *A great fortune was amassed by John D. Rockefeller*. We also have highly successful passives of this sort omitting entirely the mention of the agent: *Many fortunes were amassed in that era*.

2.4 Existentials and Equations

It may be doubted whether existence is a predicate in the sense that the other predicates are. In such a sentence as God exists, is exists a predicate in the same sense as read or travel or hear? Is not existence rather a condition of predication? i.e., to have a predicate we have to assume--at least for the sake of the argument--the existence of the entities which are involved in the predication. I propose that in existential clauses, a noun of which existence is affirmed or denied be called the existent. This role is exemplified in the following:

God really exists

There are no such things as unicorns

Sea serpents are real

There is no such thing as an ugly woman

Notice the great variety of surface structure in these above encodings of existential statements.

Equational statements are affirmations of set membership:

John is a soldier

Teaching is a lucrative profession

Clergymen arc parasites

Here we see that in every case there is a set, i.e., soldiers, lucrative profession, parasites, and that the clauses which we have just cited affirm that certain individuals are members of these respective sets. What, however, of such a statement as Hepzibah is my wife? Here we have to affirm that, given the structure of marriage in our present society, wife in referring to a man is a unit set. This need not distract, however, from the fact that we have here essentially an affirmation of set membership.

In brief, what I suggest is that existence and set membership be handled not as part of the scheme of cases and case frames which have been sketched above, but as something outside that scheme. We have dealt with predication divided into state, process, action process, action. Opposed to predication as a whole are existential statements and set membership statements. I believe that these compose three varieties of notional structure, and that attempts to interpret existential statements and set membership statements as predicates within a scheme of case frames such as we have elaborated here have not been successful[3]. Special relationships are involved in existence and class membership. As already suggested, let the noun of which existence is affirmed or denied be called the EXISTENT. For equational statements, let us call the two poles something on the order of CLASSIFIED and CLASSIFIER (or maybe simply MEMBER and SET).

The peculiar position of existential and equational sentences is also seen in their contextual (discourse) function. As noticed under section 7 of chapter 3, these two sorts of statements are of special relevance in the introduction of participants into narrative and their initial identification. Thus, they are especially relevant to the stage of a narrative discourse (whether independent or embedded) and the setting of a narrative paragraph. In these functions existential and equational sentences are off the main-line of development of narrative discourse.

In expository and descriptive discourse, however, existential and equational sentences are on the main-line of discourse development. Thus, in English the verb 'be' and similar verbs have special relevance in expository and descriptive prose. In Aguaruna (a language of Peru, Larson 1978) these discourse types imploy existential and equational statements that are characterized by heavy use of nominalization. Something similar is reported in Pacoh (Vietnam, data from Richard Watson), Tarahumara (Mexico, data from Don Burgess), Trique (Mexico, author's own data), and Konzime (Cameroon, data from K. Beavon). A moment's reflection on the intrinsic positing-and-classifying nature of exposition would lead us to believe that the predominance of existential and equational clauses in exposition and description is a linguistic universal.

3. RELEVANCE OF CASE FRAMES TO DISCOURSE

The final concern of this chapter is to illustrate and

support the claim that a system of case frames and verb classification--such as is here presented--is relevant to the study of discourse. As stated above, the relevance of case frames to discourse can be seen from two view points: (1) as a derivational module in the generation of a discourse from its abstract; and (2) as a way of demonstrating the semantic unity of mainline material in the analysis of a discourse. Before arguing these two points in detail, I want to point out that only a rather detailed classification of verbs can be useful to either of the above goals. Categories that are overly diffuse and inclusive are of little help either generatively or analytically.

3.1 Generatively

By generating a discourse from its abstract I mean a presentational format which relates the overall content structure of a discourse to its germinal idea by means of derivational rules. A beginning at elaborating such rules is made by van Dijk (1972), only to be later (1977) abandoned in favor of reduction rules, whereby a discourse is reduced to its abstract. Reduction rules are, however, simply the converse of derivational rules. Both are a means of relating a text as we find it to a more basic and abstract structure.

In Longacre (1977), I make some suggestions regarding the nature and content of the rules needed to generate a discourse from its abstract. The first cycle of rules, which is comparatively brief, takes us from an extremely abstract formula of given genre of discourse of a given type (e.g., a folk tale with stage, episodes, conclusion and a moral) to an abstract overall representation of the particular content of a particular discourse. The second cycle, which is much longer than the first, develops the symbols of the first cycle into much longer and more complex strings, and fills in the major conjunctions and sequence signals from abstract symbols of the first cycle. The third cycle lexicalizes verbs from abstract indicators in the former cycles. Thus, if a text is about negative evaluations (e.g., criticism, malice, hate) versus positive evaluations (praise, goodwill, love) the overall lexical tone of the discourse is set in the previous cycles. Furthermore, major participants are also indicated in the previous cycles, but whether Tom Jones will surface as Tom, Tom Jones, my neighbor's son, or a pronoun remains to be specified.

It is precisely at this crucial point in the derivation when we are about to lexicalize in rather sweeping fashion (and thus move closer to the surface structure of a text) that a type of rule, which I here term case frame substitution, becomes very useful. Previous rules of cycles one and two have built strings of logical symbols in which predications are represented as Pa, Pab, Pabc, etc., according to the notations developed in Chapter 3 (except for the fact that symbols which are more indicative of lexical content have already been chosen for text generation (e.g., $\overline{E}$ph for 'parrots negatively evaluate hippopotami'). Now, via case frame substitution this approximate notation can be replaced by something more useful, viz., the apparatus for the case frame to which the verb and accompanying nouns of the surface structure belong.

The following partial derivation illustrates the working of a case-frame substitution rule. In cross-reference to Chapter 3, I have left Paxy below--although by this stage in the derivation of the text to which this sentence belongs, such a string as Obxy (O for verbs indicative of occupational activities, b for Bill, x for place, and y for time) would be more probable. Note here that in the first rule below, P stands for the same predicate in two successive predications, a stands for the same first term with both occurrences of the predicate; x and x" are spatial antonyms, and y and y" are temporal antonyms. In brief, this is the abstract formulation of contrast (Chapter 3, section 1.2). (Rules are here numbered consecutively from one--even though they would be consequent on other rules in their derivational context.)

1. Paxy $\wedge$ Pax"y"

2. $\left\{\begin{matrix}\text{A-PHYSICAL}\\ \text{COMPLETABLE}\end{matrix}\right\}$ A/P_i RLT $\wedge$ $\left\{\begin{matrix}\text{A-PHYSICAL}\\ \text{COMPLETABLE}\end{matrix}\right\}$ A/P_i RL"T"

   (substitution of case frames for abstract formulations of (1) with addition of the peripheral cases L, T; A/P_i . . . A/P_i = identical referents of A/P) →

3. {work} A/P_i RLT $\wedge$ {work} A/P_i RL"T" (lexicalization of predicate) →

4. {work} A/P_i LT ∧ {work} A/P_i L"T" (deletion of R as undeveloped symbols; could have said 'does work' instead of 'work') →

5. {work} Bill LT ∧ {work} Bill L'T" (lexicalization of A/P_i) →

6. {work} Bill outdoors T ∧ {work} Bill indoors T" (lexicalization of L, L") →

7. {work} Bill outdoors day ∧ {work} Bill indoors night (lexicalization of T, T") →

8. Bill {work} outdoors day ∧ Bill {work} indoors night (linearization) →
   ETC.

Further transformations (9, 10, 11) give the proper surface structure to the verb and noun phrases, choose the coordinate sentence with <u>and</u> as surface structure, and delete repeated elements.

In concluding this subsection, note again the usefulness of a case frame notation and a verb classification of considerably high lexical specificity. Such a verb classification can be employed in a substitution rule of considerable power, i.e., (1) the whole Paxy symbol is <u>simultaneously replaced</u> by another string without going through a long sequence of derivational rules in which each symbol is replaced in a separate rule; and (2) the overall lexical specification--including supplying a verb with related nouns is a giant step forward towards the surface structure. Systems of case and case frames which employ broader categories would not advance us much, if at all, beyond the Pa, Pab, and Pabc notation of the former two cycles.

3.2 Analytically

From a different viewpoint, we can examine a text analytically to see what are the semantic characteristics of its main line of development. Certain assumptions are relevant here: (1) that a discourse is by definition semantically coherent; (2) that the semantic characteristics of the predicates of a discourse (whether verbs, adjectives, or nominalizations) are crucial to the semantic characterization of the whole discourse; (3) predicates on the main line of development form a coherent set; and (4) predicates which are off the line are less restricted and present a more diffuse semantic picture.

Granted the above assumptions, we may then utilize a system of case frames (equivalent to a classification of verbs) somewhat as a neighborhood graph. A well constructed scheme should bring together in at least approximate contiguity the verbs which characterize the main line of a discourse. In fact, a scheme of case frames could be tested in this fashion (if we had enough semantic analyses of the main lines of various discourses) to see if the scheme is constructed along useful lines.

While the present state of discourse analysis does not give us the data that we need to test the set of case frames which are found above in this chapter, a beginning can be made in this regard. Take, e.g., Thurber's much analyzed discourse A Lover and His Lass (van Dijk and Petöfi 1977). This text pictures, with Thurber's inimitable irony, a pair of parrots criticizing the lovemaking of a pair of hippopotami. In turn, later in that same day, the hippopotami criticize the lovemaking of the parrots. The (twisted) moral of the pseudo-fable is: "Laugh and the world laughs with you, love and you love alone."

Clearly, the text turns on verbs (often nominalized) of negative evaluation as contrasted with verbs of positive evaluation (the lovemaking). All these verbs are D4 verbs--verbs of evaluation. The negative evaluation verbs surface as disdain, derision, scornful (comments), describe (in mocking and monstrous metaphors), gossip, criticizing, and maligning. The verbs of positive evaluation surface as make love (verbal), court, exchange words of endearment. The verbs of negative evaluation are contextually associated with D'2 and D'4 verbs; i.e., the pair which criticizes the other either hears (D'2) or listens (D'4) to the other pair's courtship. Also, the negative evaluation is expressed in verbs of speech (D'3), e.g., say and exclaim. Here we have a basic constellation of D4, D'2, D'3, and D'4 verbs.

The further case frames which are associated with verbs of positive evaluation show less clustering within our scheme of case frames. Thus, with D4 positive evaluation there occur: (1) D1 verbs: love (from lover), an underlying 'he loves her' which nominalizes to her inamoratus, and entertain affection for. (2) B2 'psych' verbs, all of which are apparently paraphrases of 'to attract': have charm, have appeal, have sex appeal. (3) There are also B4 verbs of propulsion: bump around, push, pull. (4) Finally there are E4 verbs of physical activity: snort, snuffle, bumble, romp, squawk (but laugh in this context is probably a negative D4).

In summary, the main-line verbs show a tendency to cluster around rows D, D' and E--all of which are represented by action verbs, with D4 having a position of privilege in the content structure of the discourse. But B2 verbs and B4 verbs are also of importance to the content structure. It is, nevertheless, interesting that the verbs which are the most crucial to the content structure cluster rather clearly, while those that are mainline but perhaps not so crucial show some scatter. Considerably more scatter is introduced if we take account of the verbs which are in the incidental and metaphorical material.

NOTES

1 Cook has subsequently (1979) scaled his system down to include only twelve case frames. I prefer the older system (1972b) as one that gives a more detailed and useful classification. Cook's collapse of what I call range and patient into his object abolishes the distinction between action and action process in his system.

2 It is interesting that at an earlier stage of English, learn was used as a transitive verb to encode an action process predication. Thus in the Book of Common Prayer, Psalm 25, we find lead me forth in Thy truth and learn me... and in verse 8, and such as are gentle, them shall He learn His way. But even in the archaic diction of the Book of Common Prayer, by far the more frequent usage is to use the verb teach to encode this case frame. The verb learn survives in its transitive use to encode action process in substandard speech and teachers work hard in school to eliminate this substandard form from children's usage.

3 Cf. e.g., an ESSIVE case set up to handle membership statements in Langendoen 1970 and Grimes 1976.

CHAPTER 6

SOME FURTHER LEVELS OF NOTIONAL STRUCTURE

Previous chapters of this book have presented the notional structure of monologue and dialogue along with the surface structures which encode them, sketched the notional structures of combinations of predications--with a few side-glances at some of the sentence and paragraph structures which encode them, and explored the notional structure of predications. The combinations of predications are like molecules which can range from relatively simple structures to the complexities of polymers and DNA. In turn, predications are like the atoms of discourse--ranging again from very simple to very complex units. But just as atoms have sub-atomic particles, so in discourse there are units, both notional and surface, that range below the predication. Such further units of structure are explored here along with a discussion of performatives.

On going over all this ground carefully, two conclusions emerge: (1) three further lower levels of notional structure need to be posited for the hierarchical structure of monologue discourse; and (2) some performatives should be associated with the utterance--which is a level of dialogue discourse (cf. Chapter 2). I use the word <u>levels</u> here with some specialization. I do not mean by it relative degrees of depth. Rather, I mean something like hierarchical organization (morpheme, stem, word, phrase, clause, etc.) in the surface structure. The precise way in which the notional structure levels relate to surface structure levels in the grammatical hierarchy is a question to be discussed in the next chapter.

I suggest here the following additional levels for the notional structure of monologue discourse: derivation, inflection, and concretion. Derivation and inflection in the notional structure roughly correspond to stem and word in the surface. I use concretion for a notional level which corresponds very roughly to the surface structure phrase level. The correspondence with the surface structures is so approximate that resort to a neologism, CONCRETION, is justified in speaking of the notional unit.

Performatives are discussed relative both to the structure of dialogue and of monologue (cf. Chapter 4). An utterance, as previously defined in Chapter 2, consists of all a speaker says from the time he starts talking until he finishes. An utterance may be a whole monologue discourse (spoken or written) on any size level on down to a clause, or phrase, or a word. Every utterance either states or implies a performative. Some performatives have to do with dialogue (speaker exchange), while others have to do more with monologue.

1. DERIVATION

In an earlier publication (Longacre 1972) I used the term INCREMENT CALGULUS to describe a variety of relations below the predication level in the notional structure of monologue discourse. Subsequent study has shown, however, that there are two levels of notional structure here which can conveniently be described by the well-known rubrics, derivation and inflection.

In surface structure, derivation and inflection were nicely distinguished by Nida some time ago in respect to the following criteria (Nida 1949.99):

> DERIVATIONAL FORMATIONS: (1) Belong to the same general external distribution class as the simplest member of the class. (2) Tend to be 'inner formations'. (3) Tend to be statistically more numerous. (4) Have derivational morphemes with more restricted distribution. (5) May exhibit changes in major distribution class membership. INFLECTIONAL FORMATIONS: (1) Do not belong to the same general external distribution class as the simplest member of the class. (2) Tend to be 'outer formations'. (3) Tend to be statistically less numerous. (4) Have inflectional morphemes with more extensive distribution. (5) Exhibit no changes in major distribution class membership.

Under derivation Nida is talking here about the way in which we form STEMS in the surface structure, e.g., a noun from a verb stem or a noun from an adjective plus a noun. A derived noun stem which consists of two compounded roots or of a root plus a derivative affix still belongs, as Nida points out, to the same distribution class as the simplest underived member of its class. Thus, grandfather belongs to the same general distribution class as man. He also points out that derivative formations are inner (in respect to linear ordering) while inflectional formations, i.e., the surface structure WORD units are outer. The inner formation grandfather takes pluralization which is an outer layer. He has, however, qualified this both in the context of the quoted passage and in oral teaching with the admission that we sometimes find an inflectional element which is inner as compared with certain outer derivational elements. Here, again, we find ourselves involved with typical notional and surface structure differences. Nida also points out that there tend to be few inflectional affixes (e.g., noun pluralization, verb tense) which run across their entire major distribution class (e.g., noun or verb) while derivative formations are more restricted and more numerous statistically. He concludes with the well-known fact that a derivational formation may change major distribution class membership, i.e., a noun stem may be derived to a verb stem, or a verb stem to a noun stem, or an adjective stem to a noun stem, etc. This is a fair and concise summary of surface structure derivation (STEM) versus inflection (WORD).

Chafe's handling (1970) of what I consider to be notional derivation and notional inflection is not, in effect, different from Nida's surface structure distinctions. He posits such notional units as inchoative, resultative, verbalizer, feminizer, etc., all of which derive one category of surface structure grammar into another category of surface structure grammar. Thus, to add the inchoative to state, changes wide to widen (notional structure process). On the other hand, to add resultative to process changes break to broken (notional structure state). Similarly, to add the notional unit feminizer to a masculine noun such as actor, is to change it to the feminine noun actress in both notional and the surface structure.

What has troubled me about Chafe's presentation of derivation comes to a head right here. He posits certain notional structure units which are added to roots in order to specify certain surface structure switches of grammatical class in English--switches marked in a very inconsistent and haphazard way. Thus, while wide is derived to widen (state to process) by the addition of an -en we find a very similar suffix used to derive process to state in break to broken. We find also a term such as open has zero derivation between state and process. It seems to me that class switching mechanisms of this sort are essentially surface structure phenomena and not notional primitives.

All we need really to assume is that the notional structure of predicates such as wide, broken, and open has a feature called state, while the notional structure of widen, break, and open does not have this feature but rather the feature process. If there is any class switching in the notional structure it probably faces in but one direction, i.e., state is derived to process which is in turn derived to action process, and sometimes to action. This overall relation can be shown as well by juxtaposed columns on a chart as by use of the arrow of TG grammar. What I want, therefore, to posit as derivation in the notional structure is simply the features which are relevant to the definition of grammatical classes and subclasses of verbs and nouns in reference to contextual combination, e.g., case selection. The surface structure derivational mechanisms are the means whereby similar lexical stuff gets distributed into different columns.

The features which I will therefore posit as notional structure derivation are those of the sort set up as features of classes of predicates in the preceding chapter of this volume. The starting point is Chafe's set of features, but I have rejected a few of his features, added a few of my own, and made a few further changes in terminology. Thus to refer again to the large main chart (Diagram III) in Chapter 5, we find the following derivational features characterizing columns on that chart: state, process, action process, action. We also considered (and rejected) the possibility of enlarging the system of case frames there envisaged by the addition of a further column in which the feature causative is added. Reflexive is certainly a further feature which determines subframes in certain cells. Derivational features which carry across at least one whole row in the chart are the following: ambient, experiential, instrumental, completable, directed, physical, measure, locative, posture, motion, and possession. Undoubtedly, further derivational features could be suggested for verbs but they are beyond the scope of this present volume.

In reference to nouns, Chafe makes a beginning at sketching the following derivational features: count, mass, potent, animate, unique, and feminine. The count/mass distinction is well known and needs no comment here. The feature potent was an innovation on his part (Chafe 1970.109): "There seem to be some nouns however which are not animate, but which nevertheless occur as agents." He refers to such nouns as *heat* and *wind* in: *The heat melted the butter* and *The wind opened the door*. Again the feature animate scarcely needs elaboration here. Unique refers to such proper names as *Mary*, *John*, *Bill*, etc. Clearly the brief list here taken from Chafe is simply suggestive. Anyone who has worked with folk taxonomies knows the systematic way in which various features enable one to classify plants, animals, and certain other things within the context of a given language. We are also familiar with the use of componential features in analyzing kinship systems. A crucial problem here is the separation of universal notions from language-specific and area-specific classifications.

I assume here that verb vs. noun is a valid surface structure distinction which is ultimately based on the notional distinction of event versus thing. This is very evident in a language like Trique where notional and surface structure are very much in phase at this point. In Trique, nouns are very thingish. There are only two abstract nouns in the entire language, a word zo^{343} which means 'work' and a word zu^{3}nduhu^{43} which means 'favor'. Both of these terms, however, are interpreted in very concrete situational ways. For example, 'work' is something which can be recognized as a laborious bodily activity. When I was sitting at my desk and received a Trique visitor, he did not consider that I was working, nor that he was interrupting my work. Similarly, 'favor' is considered to be something very concrete like lending money or dispensing medicine. By contrast, verbs are words that refer to activities, events, and states. There is no outright way to nominalize verbs as such, although it is possible to nominalize an entire clause, i.e., the verb with all nouns related to it. The marked in-phaseness of the notional and surface structure of nouns and verbs in Trique contrasts with English, where we have many abstract nouns and nominalized verbs, and where, consequently, the notional and surface structures are very much out of phase.

Is there a notional structure category which corresponds to the adjective or qualifier? In the preceding chapter I handled all adjectives and qualifiers as varieties of predicates, namely state. It is interesting that years ago Wilbur Marshall Urban (1939.150-158) insisted that nouns, verbs, and adjectives were linguistic universals. More recently Nida (1964.57-69) in his work on semantics (especially slanted for Bible translators) has insisted on the usefulness of OEAR, i.e., Objects, Events, Abstracts, and Relationals. This has been modified by Beekman (1974, Chapter 4) to TEAR in that he prefers the term Thing to the term Object (which can be confused as the surface structure grammatical object). Setting aside relationals (which are largely functional morphemes), I note that both these men, with wide experience in handling of translation problems, feel that the notional or semantic structure requires a division into not simply nouns and verbs, but nouns, verbs, and attributes or adjectives of some kind.

Adjectives have the peculiarity that they fit into surface structure noun phrases as well as into surface structure predicates (as predicate adjectives) in most languages. At this point, Lockwood (within the context of stratificational grammar) sets up a sememe ATTRIBUTION which can emerge in the lexicotactics either as an adjective modifying a noun or as a predicate in a clause. Here, in effect, Lockwood (1972. 159-60) is not merging adjectives indiscriminately into the general classification of predicates but retains them as something apart.

Dixon (1977) has also given considerable attention to adjectives and pleads for their retention as a primitive. He says that there are the following adjective types in English: dimension, position, physical property, color, human propensity, age, value, and speed. I interpret these as derivational features of the adjective class in the notional structure of English. Dixon further points out types of semantic opposition (following Lyon's antonymy, complementarity, and converseness) that are also of use as features which characterize the various types of adjectives. Thus, with dimension, position, and physical property, antonymy is a relevant feaure, i.e., we have _big_ versus _small_, _high_ versus _low_, _hard_ versus _soft_, etc. He says, however, that we lack real antonyms in the human propensity type, i.e., we not only have _happy_ and _sad_, we have _happy_, _unhappy_, and _sad_. We not only have _cruel_ and _kind_, but we have _kind_, _unkind_, and _cruel_. We not only have _rude_ and _polite_, we have _rude_, _impolite_, and _polite_, etc. He points out that comparative color terms carry no converse meaning so that _x is redder than y_ is not equal to _y is greener or yellower than x_, etc. Toward the end of the article he makes a very significant comment: "However small an adjective class it is likely to include age, value, color, and basic dimension terms, i.e., terms such as _new_, _young_, _old_; _good_, _bad_; _black_, _white_, _red_; and _big_, _small_, _long_, _short_, _wide_, _narrow_, etc."

2. INFLECTION

2.1 Verb Inflection

I group here a number of notional features which frequently surface as verbal affixes or as elements of the verb phrase (e.g., auxiliary verbs), but which may on occasion surface as full verbs or as whole clauses in some languages.

2.1.1 _Space Time Coordinates_ (_directionals and time_). Verbs may be inflected so as to indicate direction in a system of spatial coordinates. Such inflection may indicate whether the action which is encoded in a verb entails approaching or receding movement. The point of reference is the speaker himself, the speaker/addressee, the participant spoken about in the clause as distinguished from the speaker of the clause, or a locality established by previous context. Thus, affixes indicating _come_ versus _go_ are not unusual in South American Indian languages, while in Mesoamerica auxiliary verbs meaning _come_ or _go_ are very frequent. Another type of directional found in New Guinea and Aboriginal Australian languages indicates whether an action involves upward motion, downward motion, or motion on a more or less horizontal plane. In speakers of language groups located on important river systems we sometimes find features which indicate _upriver_ versus _downriver_ or even _across the river_. Or a group which lives on the sea coast may have directionals which indicate _toward the coast_ or _away from the coast_.

A notional feature, time, may be considered to underlie surface structure features of tense--although surface structure tense systems are rarely purely temporal in significance but involve other categories such as aspect, modality, and inference. While the basic classification of time is past, present, and future, the scale may be further subdivided into, e.g., remote past versus recent past, and immediate future versus far future. The Fore language of New Guinea has an especially rich tense system which marks morphologically the following: remote past, recent past, (immediate) past, present, and future. English and Turkish, at the other extreme mark morphologically only a past tense (with the present left unmarked). Other time distinctions are handled via categories of aspect and modality. Thus, the future is marked essentially via anticipation or volition in both languages. English, which has no special way of marking the immediate future, indicates it by using a present tense: *She's coming right now*. *She's coming tomorrow*.

2.1.2 *Phasals*. Phasals indicate whether an action is beginning, continuing, or ending. Continuation here as a notion is opposed to either inception or termination: it is not simply ongoing action. We call these features respectively, inceptive, continuative, and terminative. Terminative is very close to an aspectual feature which I term completive and discuss below. A phasal feature may be marked by a verbal affix, by an auxiliary verb or particle, or by a full verb, often in a clause in especially close construction with another clause. English has a special merged sentence type, the aspectual merged sentence, for expression of phasals. In this sentence the first verb is a verb such as *begin*, *start*, *continue*, *cease*, *keep*, *stop*. The second verb is either a minimal active or passive infinitive phrase or a minimal active or passive participle phrase. Thus we have sentences like: *He began to talk/talking*, *He started to talk/talking*, *He continued to talk/talking*, *He ceased to talk/talking*, *He began to be considered persona non grata*, *He continued being talked about*, *He ceased being considered for the job*, *He continued to be considered undesirable*. Continuation is expressed in many languages by repeating either the verb or the whole clause. This is very common in New Guinea languages: *He hit it, he hit it, he hit it, he hit it, he hit it* meaning 'He kept on hitting it'.

2.1.3. *Aspect*. This rubric indicates aspect proper, i.e., features which have to do with the quality of the action indicated in the verb and, more likely than not, have discourse-level functions as well. There are at least five terms: Progressive, punctiliar, completive, repetitive, and gnomic. Progressive is marked in English with the *-ing* suffix. Notice that progressive as a notional feature is opposed not to inception and termination (as in the phasals), but is opposed to other elements in its own system, especially punctiliar. The opposition progressive versus punctiliar is important to the tense system of several European languages, e.g., there are two past tenses in both Spanish and classical Greek, an imperfect past (progressive) and a past called the preterit in Spanish and the aorist in Greek. Without claiming identity of function between the Spanish preterit and the Greek aorist, I note that both may encode punctiliar actions and may be used simply as general past tenses. Furthermore, in both languages, while the preterit/aorist marks the event-line of narrative discourse, the imperfect is found in supportive and depictive material. In Trique of Mesoamerica verb stems are inherently progressive. They are made punctiliar by the prefixation of g- or gV- prefix.

The opposition progressive versus completive is really one of incompletive versus completive. Note here that we are not emphasizing the termination itself but rather the fact that an action is either terminated or unterminated. This was an important distinction in classical Hebrew and is important to the structure of many Mesoamerican Indian languages. Thus in Zoque the suffix -u marks completive while the suffix -pa marks incompletive. Choice of -u or -pa is obligatory to the structure of the Zoque verb (Wonderly 1951). It is -u, the completive, which occurs on verbs which mark the event-line of narrative discourse.

Repetitive may be expressed in various ways; often by reduplication of a part or the whole of the verb stem. Thus, the surface structure marking of repetition may be identical with or similar to that of continuation (see above). In Trique repetition is shown by the addition of a particle in the verb phrase.

Opposed to all of the above whether progressive, punctiliar, completive or repetitive, is the gnomic aspect. Gnomic is defined here as in Chapter 5 Section 2.3 as "general or proverbial in thrust". Gnomic is not often marked by a special tense form. Rather, an already existing surface structure tense is employed in further function to express the gnomic. Thus, a frequent construction in Greek is the gnomic aorist. Here the aorist tense is used not as a past tense, but as a tense for expressing a general truth. In English, gnomic expressions are present tense: Man proposes; God disposes. As we observed in Chapter 5 regarding the surface structure of English passives, passives with a gnomic component are often more plausible than passives whose verbs are not characterized by this component. Thus, as we pointed out, while A Cadillac is owned by John is a rather unusual and forced sentence, a sentence such as Cadillacs are owned only by rich people is quite plausible. Similarly, while The glass was tapped on by John is somewhat forced, we are not at all uncomfortable with such a passive as The Blarney stone has been kissed by countless generations of tourists visiting Ireland.

Before leaving this discussion of aspect, let us note that the observer viewpoint is of considerable importance here (as everywhere). Thus, once we have characteristic inflections which serve to express such distinctions as progressive versus punctiliar, or progressive (imcompletive) versus completive, the stage is set for the usual game of playing musical chairs with notional and surface structure. In a language like classical Greek where the aorist tense is used to express punctiliar past and the imperfect to express progressive past, the viewpoint of the observer enables him to speak of a relatively prolonged activity as simply having taken place, while on the other hand, he can with equal facility focus on an activity of very short duration and emphasize that it went on for a while. Consequently, an imperfect tense may be used to speak of a relatively brief event while an aorist tense may be used to speak of a relatively prolonged event. All this is equivalent to saying that the observer has the freedom at certain points to report an event on the event line (as an aorist) or off the line (as an imperfect). At any rate the observer viewpoint--whether thought of as classifying an event qualitatively or shunting it on or off the main line--is crucial.

2.1.4 Modalities. I have in mind here the expression of desire/intent, obligation/necessity, and ability. Special desiderative or intentive verb forms are not unusual, e.g., Candoshi has a special desiderative verb form with desiderative affixes (Cox 1957). Obligation/necessity may likewise be expressed within the verb itself by means of verb affixes. In English, obligation and necessity are expressed within the verb phrase by a closed set of modal words. Obligation/necessity is, in fact, one of the main categories expressed by

English modals. Thus, according to Calbert (1971), obligation and inference are the two main parameters to the system of English modals as well as to the modals of German. Ability may likewise be expressed by an affix, by an auxiliary, or by a modal. English modals express all three modalities. Thus we find _shall_ and _will_ used to express desire or intent, _must_ to express necessity, and _can_ to express ability. I leave out of the consideration for the moment _may_ in the sense of 'be permitted to do' in that this really implies another participant, the one who permits. More about that later in a different context.

2.1.5 _Inferentials_. Here we find a scale of inference from impossible to possible to probable to factual/certain. Negative versus positive correlates with the extremes of the scale. We can equate negative with the impossible, positive with the factual/certain, and posit various intermediate degrees of qualified negative or qualified positive, which correspond roughly to the possible and to the probable.

It is a well-known fact that the English modals may express modality as defined above or, alternatively, may express inference. In accordance with the latter we can say _He must be going by now_ in the sense of 'It is very probable that he is going by now' or _He could be going by now_, in which I affirm that it is possible that he went. While there is reference in an inferential modal to some performative and its subject, I do not believe that the performative is more necessary here than at any other place in discourse. I assume that in back of ANY utterance there is a performative such as _I declare_, _I assert_, etc. I think what is in focus here is rather the scale of probability as sketched above. This is marked morphologically in some languages by resort to special moods such as subjunctive, optative, or other UNREAL moods.

2.2. Noun Inflection

I begin here with a set of categories described by Chafe (on whom I am especially dependent here), then proceed to add further categories from other sources.

2.2.1 _Some Categories Proposed by Chafe_. Chafe, for the notional structure of English, posits the categories definite, generic, aggregate, and plural. Definite and plural probably need no explanation. Definite implies prior identification on the part of the hearer in terms of previous context or situation. Plural simply means more than one individual. Generic is in some ways like the aspectual feature gnomic which we posit in verbs. Chafe feels that the feature generic in nouns is simply an extrapolation from a verb with the feature generic (in the same case frame). My gnomic aspect of verbs is not, however, precisely the same as Chafe's feature generic and I prefer at all events to make generic a feature of noun inflection--keeping in mind that the features which the noun may have and the verb may have are interrelated. Aggregate is defined by Chafe as 'a class regarded as an undifferentiated whole' (Chafe 1970.191).

Taking water as a mass noun and elephant as a count noun, Chafe on two pages (193-4) gives a paradigm of the notional structure involved at this point and their corresponding surface encodings in English. Thus the generic mass noun water encodes simply as a noun in such a sentence as Water flows downhill. The count noun elephant, when generic, encodes as the indefinite article plus the nouns in such a sentence as An elephant likes peanuts. The count noun elephant when both generic and plural encodes as a surface structure pluralized noun in such a sentence as Elephants like peanuts. The count noun elephant when both generic and aggregate encodes as a noun preceded by the definite article in such a sentence as The elephant likes peanuts. The mass noun water minus generic encodes as a noun preceded by some in such a sentence as Some water dripped on the floor. The count noun elephant when no longer generic encodes as a noun preceded by the indefinite article in An elephant stepped on my car. The count noun elephant when pluralized but marked by no further notional structure feature encodes as a pluralized noun preceded by some in such a sentence as Some elephants stepped on my car. The mass noun water when definite encodes as a noun preceded by the definite article in such a phrase as The water dripped onto the floor. Similarly, the count noun elephant when definite encodes as a noun preceded by the definite article in such a sentence as The elephant stepped on my car. And, finally, the count noun elephant when both definite and plural encodes as a pluralized noun preceded by the direct article in such a sentence as The elephants stepped on my car. In the above examples some is deletable from most of the surface structures indicated.

If we look at the above examples involving the mass noun water we note that the notional structures (a) water without any further inflectional category, (b) water plus generic, and (c) water plus definite, encode in the surface structure as (a) a noun preceded by optional some, (b) a noun, and (c) a noun preceded by the definite article respectively, i.e., there is here a one-to-one correspondence of the notional structures and the surface structures.[1]

The picture is not quite so simple if we consider the count noun elephant. Here we find that both elephant and elephant inflected as generic encode as a noun preceded by the indefinite article; while elephant definite and elephant generic aggregate both encode as a noun preceded by the definite article. The other three inflections of English nouns as indicated by Chafe have one-to-one correspondence with distinct surface forms. Thus elephant generic plural encodes as pluralized noun; while elephant definite plural encodes as pluralized noun preceded by the difinite article; and elephant plural encodes as pluralized noun preceded by some. This is summarized in Diagram 1. Note that the distribution of the English surface structure definite article does not entirely overlap with the notional structure category definite; the definite article marks generic aggregate as well as definite in the deep structure. Likewise, the English indefinite article has more than one function. Ultimately the articles of English must be described in relation to discourse structure.

The occurrence of articles as well as their usage differs, of course, from language to language. In Greek there is a definite article but no indefinite. In English there are both definite and indefinite articles. In Trique there is a definite article used only of plural nouns, i.e., the categories of definite and plural may be expressed together, but definite and singular are not expressed together in this fashion in the surface structure (rather deictics are used with the singular).

Chafe also posits two more noun inflections, unique and random: unique for use of proper names and other ways of uniquely specifying individuals; and random for such sentences as I want to find an elephant quick in which any old elephant will do provided we can find one.

2.2.2 Some Further Categories. Other languages indicate further noun inflection categories not suggested by Chafe.

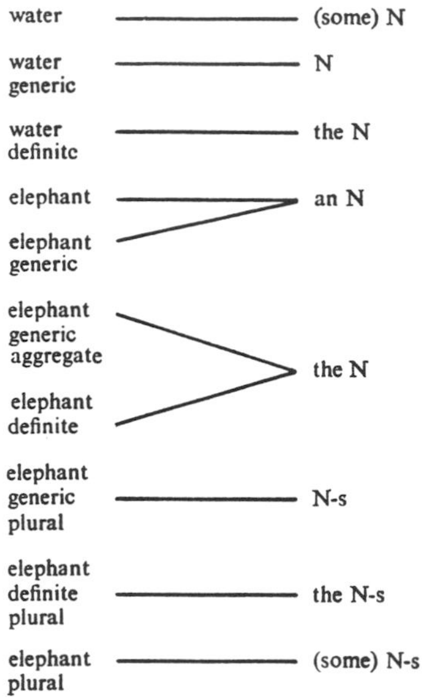

Diagram I. Some notional and surface relations in English noun inflection (cf. Chafe)

Thus, while not as frequent as the plural, dual is frequently marked as an inflectional category and sometimes trial (Australian languages). Dual is probably based on the fact that many body parts come in pairs, e.g., eyes, ears, nostrils, lips, arms, hands, legs, and feet. Thus there was a dual in classical Greek and in Hebrew. Trique expresses the dual by combining the definite article with a modified form of the numeral for two. Another quantifier-like element found in noun inflection is the allotive in which a noun or noun phrase is marked in the surface structure as referring to another member or other members of the same set. In the Jacaltec noun phrase we have a specifier slot early in the noun phrase, one of whose fillers is the item xa 'other' as in 'one other village'. Trique has complicated tonal inflections of the numerals one to six to indicate the allotive relation. Thus, while wa^5 $?nih^5$ cuh^3 means 'three eggs', wa^3 $?nih^4$ cuh^3 means 'three more eggs'.

Chafe also suggests a partitive construction which he says is essentially a noun noun relation in the notional structure so that one of the elephants would always be interpreted as 'one elephant of the elephants' with the word elephant occurring twice in the phrase. This seems to me unnecessary even in the notional structure in that all we have indicated is one member of a specified set. In Jacaltec in the same slot in which the allotive morpheme occurs we also find a partitive morpheme -uj which is used in such phrases as 'one of the plants', 'one of the gourds', etc. The well-known use of the French preposition de to express partitive can also be cited here.

One of the most un-Indoeuropean systems of number inflection found anywhere is that of Kiowa (Wonderly, Gibson, Kirk 1954). Kiowa has in its notional structure singular, dual, and plural. These are somewhat imperfectly and tortuously marked in the surface structure in that with some noun classes, dual and singular are ambiguous, with others, dual and plural are ambiguous, with others singular and plural, and with still others, all three numbers. Specifically, there are four classes of Kiowa nouns so that class one nouns are ambiguously dual/singular but when occurring with a special morphological element, the number suffix, are marked as plural; class two stems are ambiguously dual/plural and when taking the number suffix are marked as singular; class three nouns (a small group) are unambiguously dual, but when taking the number suffix, are ambiguously, singular or plural; and class four nouns (also a very limited group) are not inflected in any way for number. The various noun classes serve more purposes than simply marking in arbitrary ways the number categories. They also serve as an important agreement and concord feature with cross-reference to surrounding adjectives and demonstratives as well as to verbs which they accompany.

3. CONCRETION

I choose this term to label the notional structure counterpart of the phrase level in the surface structure. However, the relationship between what I here call concretion and surface structure phrases is far from direct. By concretion I mean the natural grouping of certain notional elements which in turn feed as units into surface structure predications. That there are such natural groupings seems hardly to be controversial. We will consider first the evidence for substantive or noun concretions and then continue to consider the evidence for verbal concretions.

The term concretion is primarily applied to 'a solid mass formed by, or as by coalescence or cohesion'. As a geological term it specifically means 'a rounded mass of mineral matter occurring in sandstone, clay, etc.,often in concentric layers around a nucleus'. These dictionary definitions are of value in showing the possible metaphorical use of concretion as a linguistic term.

3.1 Nominal Concretions

It has been admitted for some time (cf. Lakoff 1966; cites Curme 1931.162) that there are certain noun groupings which do not come about by conjunction of predications. Thus while we can say _Tom agreed with Bill_ or _Tom and Bill agreed to do it_ (again, meaning mutual agreement), this cannot be broken down into _Tom agreed to do it_ and _Bill agreed to do it_. The point precisely is _Tom and Bill agreed to do it_. Similarly with _Oil and water don't mix_. This is not a conjunction of _Oil doesn't mix_ and _Water doesn't mix_. The point rather is that _Oil and water do not mix with each other_. Likewise with _Tom, Dick, and Jane inherited ten thousand dollars_. According to the most normal meaning of this sentence, it simply is not true that _Tom inherited ten thousand dollars, Dick inherited ten thousand dollars_, and _Jane inherited ten thousand dollars_, rather the three of them together inherited ten thousand dollars. In all of these cases we have nominal groupings, noun noun conjunctions, which do not come about as a result of conjoined predications. To such groupings as these (and others mentioned below) I apply the term NOMINAL CONCRETION.

With this as a solid clue that nominal concretions exist in the notional structure of language, it is plausible to look about for other nominal concretions of a different sort. I have handled as noun inflection the marking of singular, plural, or dual on a noun stem. Chafe also handles as noun inflection quantifiers such as the English words _all_, _any_, _some_, _certain_, and _a few_. It seems to me that the latter and the nouns which follow them are more plausibly construed as nominal concretions than as nominal inflection. They do not typically encode as noun affixes in the world's languages. If this be true, it may well be that patterns in which a numeral modifies a noun head are essentially of this same sort. Such numerals appear to be more specific quantifiers than the English words just listed. It may also be that nouns plus deictic particles also have the notional structure of nominal concretions. The basic idea in deixis seems to be whether something is relatively near in reference to the speaker/hearer or relatively removed in reference to him. Sometimes a similar category of in sight or out of sight is marked as well. Systems are not uncommon which mark *here* in the sense of the immediate presence of the speaker/hearer versus *here* in the sense of in his general locality versus *there* in the sense of further removal. Deixis in noun concretion is similar in some respects to directional inflection in verbs.

In accordance with the suggestions in the above paragraph the following would be considered to be nominal concretions in their underlying structure:

> *all* *the* *books*
> *a* *certain* *book*
> *five* *books*
> *that* *book*

In the light of the previous discussion of the notional structure status of adjectives, we may well wonder if certain noun adjective combinations are not notional structure concretions as well. As we have seen, adjectives can be construed as predicates. Is it not possible, however, that at least some adjectives would be better construed as participating in underlying concretions which involve nouns and adjectives rather than simply as surface structure noun phrases which have developed from underlying predications? In the discussion on the notional status of adjectives, I cited Dixon's work on the adjective in universal grammar. Dixon believes that in some languages the adjective class may be very small but that even in such languages, it includes such things as age, value, color, and basic dimension terms. To pose the issue very succinctly: in many if not most of the languages of the world is it more natural to analyze such terms as *young*, *good*, *red*, and *big* as features of nominal concretions (the deep structure counterpart of the noun phrase) or are these always better analyzed as predicates in the notional structure?

Body parts and kinship also raise the possibility that they might better be considered to be noun concretions than predications. Thus Tom's arm and Tom's head seem a far more natural way of talking than to say Tom has an arm, Tom has a head, Tom has a leg. If there is something unusual about the body part or about its condition we may, however, have perfectly natural sentences of the following sort: Tom has a wooden leg, Tom has a broken leg, Tom has a long head. Similarly with kinship terms, we speak freely of Tom's mother, Tom's father, Tom's sister, but are not so likely to say Tom has a mother--unless again there is something special or unusual about the individual indicated. Thus we can say Tom has a step-mother or Tom has a good mother and there is no difficulty. It seems therefore plausible to suggest that genitive constructions which involve body parts and kinship might well encode nominal concretions rather than underlying predications. It is probably significant that in many American Indian languages body parts and kinship terms, as obligatorily possessed items, are distinguished from other optionally possessed items.

3.2 Verb Concretions

What I tentatively label verb concretions include constructions of whose analysis I am less certain. Verb concretions, if indeed we are right in calling them that, are obscured by the fact that verbal features above the inflectional level may have associated with them intrusive nominal elements.

In 2.1.2 I presented under verbal inflection the phasal elements inception, termination, and continuation. It was pointed out there that in such sentences as I started doing it, I finished doing it, I kept on doing it the actual verbal event is indicated in the verb do and that the use of verbs start, finish and keep on simply indicates phases of the activity. What, however, about such sentences as He started them talking, or He started the motor running, He kept them going, He stopped them stealing? Here we have intrusive nominal elements them or the motor which in the surface structure seem to be objects of the first verb and subjects of the second verb.

Inflections involving modality may likewise occur with an intrusive nominal element. Thus, we have not only John wants to do it, but John wants Bill to do it. Similarly, while we can also say Bill was able to do it we can say Bill enabled John to do it.

Such examples are clearly indicative of a broader pattern which is parallel to X had/made Y Vb Z or X caused Y to Vb Z as mentioned under Chapter 5, Sec. 2.2 and finally considered to be instances of the underlying structure of efficient cause and result (Chapter 3, Sec. 4.2.1). But a nagging question remains: Why do phasals and modals structure plausibly as verb inflection when there is no intrusive nominal element, and equally plausibly as efficient cause plus result when the nominal element is present?

Perhaps here the notion of verbal concretions could be useful--especially when nominal concretions need to be posited as argued above. Here we have structures which seem to outrun the inflectional level and involve the close partnership of two verbs:

John wanted Tom to do it
Mary helped George butcher the hog
Henry permits Olga to do things that her mother doesn't like
Harry made Phyllis do it
Grandfather started the motor running

Transparently, all the above involve causality with an extra causer. Possibly they are taken care of under the notion of efficient cause (Chapter 3, 4.2.1). On the other hand, since they resemble elements of verbal inflection, possibly they can be considered to fall under the category of verbal concretions.

4. PERFORMATIVES

Defining the UTTERANCE as the stretch between when a speaker begins to talk and when the same speaker ceases talking, we may with confidence couple some performative verbs with the utterance, and other performatives with the various types of monologue discourse. An utterance may be of any size relative to the size-levels of monologue discourse--provided it can be pronounced in isolation. Notice here that we do not equate utterance and discourse, since (1) a conversational discourse is a series of alternating utterances, and (2) a monologue discourse can conceivably be begun by one speaker and finished by another. Nevertheless, a monologue is normally one utterance--although it may report any number of utterances within it. Furthermore, as already explained (Chapter 2), utterances belong to the structure of dialogue discourse in which the units are: utterance, exchange, dialogue paragraph, and dialogue discourse, while the grammatical structure of monologue (Chapter 7) constitutes a separate hierarchy. The two hierarchies intersect in various ways, but are best kept distinct. At any rate, every utterance, whether part of a dialogue, reported in a monologue discourse, or constituted by a monologue discourse, involves a (implicit or explicit) performative, and, in turn every monologue discourse type involves a performative as well.

4.1 Repartee Performatives

Thus, within a dialogue whenever a question is asked, there is an implicit or explicit performative verb such as _question_ or _ask_ involved on the part of the speaker. Similarly, whenever there is a proposal in the notional structure, there is an implicit performative verb of broad meaning _propose_, which can be indicated by more specific verbs such as _request_, _ask_, _suggest_, _command_, _advise_, _invite_, _plead_, etc. When a remark is made in the notional structure of dialogue, there is an implicit performative verb _remark_ which is indicated by more specific verbs such as _tell_, _assert_, _claim_, _contend_, _argue_, _remark_, _say_. For the resolving utterances in the notional structure of repartee we may say that wherever an answer is involved, there is an implicit performative verb _answer_. When a response is involved, there is an implicit performative verb _respond_. When an evaluation is involved, there is an implicit performative verb evaluate, which, however, rarely surfaces as such, but rather as _remark_, _assert_, _claim_, _contend_, _argue_. What is interesting here is that we do not find the surface structure performatives for resolving utterances to be as specific as the performatives for initiating utterances. Thus, e.g., _reply_ functions as a surface structure performative with answer, response, and evaluation. For counter tokens we apparently have complex performatives involving _counter_, i.e. _counter-question_, _counter-propose_, _counter-remark_, etc. What I am in effect proposing here is that the underlying structures of repartee in Chapter 2 be considered to be indicative of corresponding performatives.

We must face here the fact of the very determined effort made on the part of some generative semanticists to abolish question and command (cf. my proposal) as primitives (cf. Calbert 1971.93 and his bibliography). Thus the attempt is made to reduce _I ask you if he went_ (which actually has a fuller structure _I ask you if he went or not_) to _I command that you say that he went_. Sometimes rather than _command_ an abstract verb is suggested here. I want to point out, however, that _I command/desire that you say that he went_ is a far cry from asking a question. You can say _I command you to say he went_ or you can say _I command you to say that he didn't go_ but you cannot at once command a person both to say that he went and to say that he didn't. What is missing in all such formulations is precisely the element of uncertainty which makes a question a question, i.e., the _whether_ element. In brief, I believe that we must continue to consider the question to be a primitive which is therefore not reducible to a combination of predications. At least it is certain that a question is not reducible to volition or some expression of volition plus a verb of speech. A question normally implies that the speaker does not know something, that he thinks that the hearer might have the information that he wants, and that some solicitation is necessary to secure the information.

Similarly, the proposal must be retained as a primitive. Such surface structure verbs as _request_, _suggest_, _command_, _advice_, _invite_ are directed toward some possible future act on the part of the hearer. It is obvious that the speaker wants the hearer to perform an action and that what he says is equivalent to an attempt to get the hearer to perform it. It is obvious also that he believes that the hearer is able to perform the desired action. Nevertheless, the expression of a proposal by means of one of these performative verbs is not reducible to volition as such. An expression such as _I want you to go downtown this afternoon_ is simply a background condition for the expression of a request. It is not the expression of the request itself. The indispensable element in the expression of a request is the solicitation of action, just as the indispensable element in a question is the solicitation of information. I believe that these two must remain as primitives along with remark which is simply a declaration concerning something, possibly concerning the speaker's own feelings. The distinguishing feature of a remark is that it solicits evaluation from the hearer.

The repartee relations and the performatives that necessarily are implied by them also have application to the study of monologue discourse. Thus, a narrative can pattern as an initiating utterance (remark) or as a resolving utterance (usually answer). In the first instance a speaker volunteers a narrative as a remark for someone to evaluate, i.e., he hopes that someone will appreciate the anecdote (or more extensive narrative) or at least express some reaction to it. In this sense a literary work assumes and desires an audience. In the second instance someone is asked a question and answers by giving a spontaneous narrative (Labov and Fanshell 1977). Here the narrative patterns as a resolving utterance in the surface structure.

The foregoing considerations are important for the internal analysis of monologue discourse. For example, many discourses which are tape recorded in the languages of minority cultures around the world are elicited by an initiating utterance that is a question: "What's it like in your home village?" "Where did your ancestors come from?" "How did you chop down trees with stone axes before the Europeans came?" Similarly, the eliciting anthropologist or linguist may employ an initiating utterance that is a proposal: "Tell me about your last hunting trip." "Tell me an animal story." "Tell me how you build a house." Discourses elicited under such conditions typically bear evidence of the elicitation situation. For example, they often lack features of title and aperture that a discourse might have when it patterns as an initiating utterance. The investigator should, therefore, record the dialogue matrix in which a dialogue is elicited if he is to understand--among other things--the relative formality or informality of initiating a discourse.

4.2 Type-Specific Performatives

If an utterance is a monologue discourse it has, however, a further type of performative associated with it as well. Not only does a monologue discourse imply a dialogue relation and a repartee performative, it also calls for a performative which is specific to its discourse type. The use of such a type-specific performative is assumed in every monologue discourse and surfaces as an explicit performative in certain situations. The most frequent situations in which an implicit performative surfaces are those in which a discourse functions as an initiating utterance rather than as a resolving utterance. I will, therefore, in the balance of this chapter consider such situations, i.e., those in which monologue situations are initiating utterances. As already mentioned, this situation is the pragmatic situation of literary authorship, i.e., the author initiates a dialogue of sorts with the reader whom he hopes to be able to please, stimulate, instruct, outrage, or influence in some other way. In literary production the initiating utterance is extended at the expense of the delayed and often rudimentary response. There are areas and cultures, however, where the storyteller, preacher, or other framers of public discourse expect a running response from the hearers and are, in fact, unable to function well without such reassuring response.

The relation of the repartee performative to the type-specific performative is close but the two can not be identified. The first type is coupled to the utterance and the mechanics of dialogue while the second is coupled to the typology of monologue discourse. Furthermore, monologue discourse can have layers of embedding in which--without speaker change--there is shift from one type of discourse to another; this results in a shift of the type-specific performatives as well. Furthermore, compound discourses occur in which there is a shift of monologue type and of type-specific performative midway in the discourse. Thus, the _Epistle to the Ephesians_ is such a compound discourse the first half of which is expository and the second half of which is hortatory. This shift also entails a shift of the type-specific performative, i.e., EXPLAIN gives way to PROMPT. Thus both embedding and compounding of discourse types can give a discourse more than one type-specific performative.

Type-specific performatives are indicated at the onset of a discourse which patterns as an initiating utterance. A storyteller may start his story by saying, _I'm going to tell you a story of_ .... Or a procedural discourse may begin, _I'm going to tell you how to build a house_. Or a descriptive discourse may begin, _I'm going to tell you what New Orleans is like_. Or an explanatory discourse may begin, _I'm going to tell you all about linguistics_. Or a hortatory discourse may begin, _Now I'm going to tell you ten good reasons why you should stop smoking_. I will go over this ground again in more detail suggesting some abstract type-specific verbs for the various discourse types and the type of response which we might expect if each were an initiating utterance and a resolving utterance were to appear.

We may think of narrative discourse as being an initiating utterance (remark) whose abstract type-specific performative verb is RECOUNT: _I recount to you X._ The resolving utterance (evaluation), if one were present, would be something on the order of _That was a good story_, _That was a bad story_, _That was a confused story_, etc. Procedural discourse requires two sorts of abstract type-specific performative verbs depending on whether the giver of the discourse is giving it with a view to the hearer implementing the procedures, or is merely recounting certain customs or activities in which he scarcely expects the hearer to join. For the first type of discourse we can assume an initiating utterance (proposal) whose abstract type-specific verb is PRESCRIBE: _I prescribe for you X_. The resolving utterance (response) here, if one were present, would be something on the order of _Okay, I'll try following these procedures_ or _Nuts, you wouldn't catch me trying that_. On the other hand, procedural discourse which does not seriously invite the hearer to join in the activity has, like narrative, the abstract performative verb RECOUNT: i.e., _I recount to you X_ or _I recount to you how we do X_. Here the resolving utterance (evaluation) would be something on the order of _That was interesting_.

Expository discourse (strictly conceived) is an initiating utterance (remark) with the abstract type-specific verb EXPLAIN: _I explain to you X_. Its resolving utterance (evaluation) is something on the order of _That's clear_ or _I still don't understand_. For the subvariety of explanatory discourse--which may well be a discourse genre in its own right--that we call descriptive discourse, we can conceive of the verb DESCRIBE as figuring as the abstract type-specific performative, i.e., _I describe to you X_. Here the resolving utterance (evaluation) is something on the order of _Yes, I can picture that to myself_ or _I can almost see what it is like_.

For hortatory discourse there are a variety of possible performative verbs such as _urge_, _suggest_, _command_, _advise_; perhaps PROMPT can serve as an abstract type-specific performative verb here. The initiating utterance (proposal) is something on the order of _I prompt you to X_. And the resolving utterance (response) is something on the order of _I'll do it_ or _I won't do it_.

Notice that in every case we have for all our monologue discourse types an initiating utterance that is--from the standpoint of simple dialogue--inordinately and artificially prolonged and a resolving utterance that is reduced or entirely absent. The underlying repartee structures seem in every case to be remark or proposal followed by the matching evaluation or response. The structure question plus answer does not often figure in here in that it is somewhat more difficult to artificially prolong a question with a totally absent or reduced answer. Where a speaker does bombard a hearer with a long sequence of questions he usually is not soliciting information, he is trying to show the hearer's ignorance or to taunt him in some fashion. Thus in the final windup of the book of _Job_ in the Old Testament, chapters 38-41 are one long sequence of questions. The purpose of these questions is not to get information from Job, but rather to overwhelm Job with a sense of all that he doesn't know and the greater wisdom of God compared to his own. Similarly, when Hawthorne in the chapter "Governor Pyncheon" of _The House of the Seven Gables_ plies the governor with a long list of rhetorical questions, he is clearly not soliciting information from the judge. The judge is, in fact, dead and the purpose of the questions is simply to taunt him and to reveal his true position to the reader. It appears, then, that monologue discourses essentially solicit evaluation or a response from the hearer. They profess to give information but do not often solicit information.

Perhaps, here one of the peculiarities of epistolary discourse begins to emerge, i.e., it is possible to write a personal letter which is one long sequence of questions, soliciting information from the person to whom one writes. The answers are necessarily postponed until the correspondent writes in reply. Normally, however, a letter will have a paragraph or two requesting information of various sorts and will have further paragraphs in which information is given--possibly in response to queries in a previous letter. The process of exchanging letters is a sort of delayed dialogue, and the individual letter may have characteristics which reflect a mixture of the monologue types.

The practical value of associating performative verbs with utterances--especially when they are whole monologue discourses--is that some of the presuppositions of individual sentences may be relegated to the entire unit so that the presuppositions need not be assumed to be repeated for every single sentence or for every single clause, but go once and for all with a higher unit (Wise 1972). This is, in fact, one of the underlying motivations for constructing discourse grammars rather than sentence grammars.

NOTE

1 Alternatively, (SOME) water can be handled as two separate surface structures, i.e., water and some water. This results in the following non-one-to-one notional-surface correspondence (suggestion of Huttar):

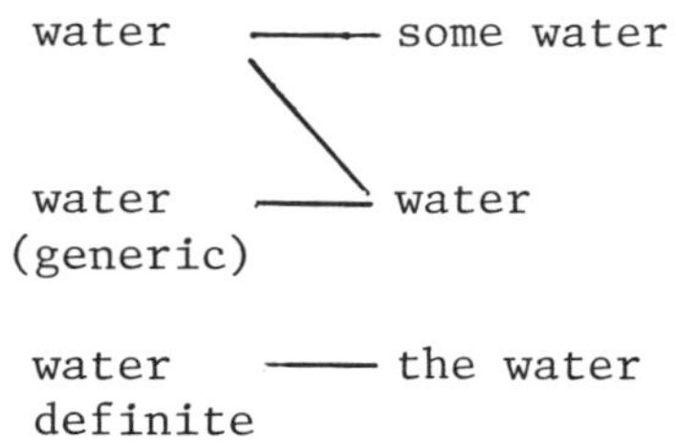

water	——	some water
	╲	
water (generic)	——	water
water definite	——	the water

CHAPTER 7

A FRAMEWORK FOR DISCOURSE ANALYSIS

It is evident that some sort of hierarchical principle is reflected in the organization of this book, which begins with considerations of discourse and dialogue as a whole and ends up with chapters on the internal structure of predications and possible levels of organization lower than that. The purpose of this chapter is two-fold: to make this hierarchical principle explicit and to relate it to the surface structure of discourse; along with this, to expound a contemporary view of tagmemics as a framework for the study of discourse. More about the latter consideration first.

Actually, my over-riding concern is that people interest themselves in the study of discourse. To me this is more important than that they work upon discourse from the particular point of view which I myself find fruitful. Nevertheless, tagmemics--which earlier than some other schools of grammar interested itself in the study of discourse--has, I believe, some insights to offer which should not be lost in the shuffle. This, then, is not meant to be a sectarian chapter as such, but a contribution to the further understanding of discourse. Specifically, I am not claiming here that tagmemics is the best of all frameworks for the study of discourse. I am simply saying that this particular framework has insights which should not be forgotten (cf. Longacre 1977b).

To some degree, however, tagmemics can offer itself to the student of linguistics as an underlying, minimal theory. It has long been observed that tagmemics is looser than some other frameworks of past and present--this indeed, has been one of the persistent criticisms of the theory. It is also, as Algeo observed (Brend 1974:7), somewhat eclectic.

It may be then that as former frameworks of considerable rigidity lose their appeal and as there is now more of an interest in the data than a particular notational device, tagmemics can provide a hang-loose framework which has something to commend it. Before going on to develop in detail hierarchy, tagmeme, syntagmeme and other matters, I want to briefly offer here some explanation of the original foment which led to the development of tagmemics in the late forties and early fifties.

Tagmemics takes its name from the tagmeme concept. In explaining this concept and its importance to discourse, I go back to a certain dilemma in U.S. structuralism in the 1940's and early 1950's. In spite of the brilliance of the Chomskyian revolution and (subsequent work) to some degree this hang up is still with us whenever we consider the matter of constituent structure. How do we, for example, describe the internal structure of the following English noun phrases: a) the hairy green monster, b) the underpaid struggling factory workers. Regarding example a), it is not hard to say in terms of word classes and their distribution--which is as far as we can get in constituent structure--that its internal structure consists of: determiner, adjective, noun. But what about example b)? We could say that it has a structure: determiner, adjective, adjective, adjective, noun. But we do this at the price of treating what are essentially verb (underpaid, struggling) and noun (factory) forms as adjectives. We have to pause here and stipulate that they are used as adjectives in this context. Actually, in resorting to explanations such as this, American structuralism and subsequent systems of constituent structure have been responding to the function of these forms rather than to the word classes that are found there. Tagmemics has attempted to tidy up this area of confusion by insisting on the distinction between function-slot and filler-set, while at the same time, bringing the two together in a functional unit, viz. the tagmeme. According to this concept, function has no reality apart from the filler-set and the set itself has no distinguishing property aside from its occurrence in a function-slot. Since this was a new concept it called for a new term so it appears we are stuck with some such term as tagmeme if we are to use a concept as novel as that indicated.

According to this point of view the second English noun phrase above, and for that matter the first as well, could be subsumed in the following formula:

$$NP = i\ A^{n}\ HEAD$$

where small i, A, and HEAD are function slots whose fillers are determiners (for i, identifier); adjectives, past participles, present participles, (for A, attribute with ^{n} signifying multiple occurrence); and nouns (for HEAD). Thus we no longer have to persuade ourselves that factory is an adjective in the second phrase. It can remain a noun but it is now functioning as an attribute. Similarly, underpaid and struggling can continue to be verbal forms although used in attributive functions. Commonly in tagmemic literature a colon (:) is used to mark the relationship between function-slot and filler-set as in the following:

$$i\text{:}\ \{\text{determiner}\}\quad A\text{:}\ \begin{Bmatrix}\text{adj}\\ \text{part}\\ \text{noun}\end{Bmatrix}\qquad HEAD\text{:}\ \begin{Bmatrix}\text{n}\\ \\ \text{np}\end{Bmatrix}$$

Although tagmemics usually does not use braces to symbolize a set, the concept of fillers as constituting a set is assumed everywhere. In fact, tagmemics is about 9/10ths (implicit) set theory.

If the tagmeme concept is important for even the analysis of a structure as relatively simple as the English noun phrase, it is even more important to the study of the constituents of the discourse and the paragraph. For example, how is it best to describe discourse constituents? It is possible to say that discourses of the simpler sort are composed of paragraphs. But what of a discourse as complex as a novel; what are its constituents? Chapters? Episodes? But chapter often approaches an orthographic convenience, and episode seems to refer more to plot structure than to a size-level chunk which is bigger (e.g., than a paragraph). Do paragraphs build into chapters and chapters into episodes and episodes into the whole? Or should we order differently and say that chapters build into episodes? Or is episode a different sort of unit entirely?

In dealing with questions of this sort, it seems to me that a routine plugging in of certain basic concepts of tagmemics is helpful. First of all, a) positing of such intermediate levels as chapter and sentence cluster (within the paragraph) is only patchwork at best; b)we need only discourse, paragraph and sentence, plus recursion; c) any string of paragraphs that belong together can be shown to have the structure of a discourse of a recognizable type; and d) any string of sentences that belong together can be shown to constitute a paragraph of recognizable type. On these premises there are no loose ends. Thus the constituents of a discourse are discourse level slots which are filled either by a paragraph or an embedded discourse (with the latter ultimately composed of paragraphs as well). Similarly, the constituents of a paragraph are paragraph level slots which are filled by sentences or paragraphs (with the latter ultimately composed of sentences as well).

To recognize the fundamental simplicity of what is going on here, we must realize that the hierarchical analysis of a discourse is different in principle from a constituent outline of it. An outline has as many heads, sub-heads, and sub-heads of sub-heads as are needed; layers of indentation are often multiple. It is assumed that each division and sub-division represents a constituent of the discourse. Furthermore, no distinction is made between the number of such constituents and the nature of the constituents. A hierarchical analysis does not assume, however, that the number of layers of indentation necessarily correspond to distinctions among the discourse constituents; rather, it is assumed that there is recursive use of similar or same units.

In the sub-sections of this chapter which immediately follow, these crucial concepts will be gone over in detail and exemplified. Before going into this in detail, note, however, that tagmemics, by virtue of its concept of syntagmeme as well as tagmeme, is not locked into over-emphasis on constituent structure as such. To be true, a discourse or a paragraph has a constituent structure, and much can be learned by studying it. But it is also necessary to emphasize that the whole is greater than the sum of its parts and that there are features of any syntagmeme, for example, a discourse or a paragraph, which can be studied in non-hierarchical, non-constituent fashion, often with considerable profit. The two approaches which involve use or non-use of constituent structure analysis are complementary to each other and neither should be neglected.

1. HIERARCHY

The abiding importance of the notion of grammatical hierarchy is seen in the fact that hierarchy is the organizing principle of surface structure. By sorting out surface structure constructions according to the hierarchical principle, we are able to compare genuinely comparable constructions. We can compare word types, clause types, sentence types, etc. Within a given level of hierarchy, we can partition constructions. Thus, for example, the phrase level constructions can be partitioned to noun phrases, verb phrases, adjective phrases, pronoun phrases, etc. The constructions thus distinguished and classified are then seen to be related to each other via the same hierarchical principle. Thus the various word types emerge as constituents of phrase types, the phrase types as constituents of clause types, the clause types as constituents of sentences, etc.

Tagmemics does all this with the directness that traditional immediate constituent analysis could never attain. Immediate constituent analysis yielded ad hoc hierarchies, posited new in every separate sentence which was analyzed. It did not yield genuinely comparable constructions because of its binary bias whereby breaks of considerable importance were confused with comparatively trivial layering tendencies. I repeat this point (cf. Longacre 1960) because it is a point which was consistently missed by the first generation of transformationalists (e.g., Postal and Lees) in their critique of "contemporary constituent structures" (as a cover term for all non-TG approaches).

But if hierarchy is the organizing principle of surface structure, does this not in itself make hierarchy trivial? Not at all. In this regard we have to contend with a certain mind set which would like to attach "mere" before "surface structure" in the phrase "mere surface structure." No one who has ever concerned himself with language learning, rhetoric and composition, or translation could ever attach the word "mere" before "surface structure." Everything that one says in a given language must perforce be poured through the mold of the available surface structures of that language. Ideas can be expressed in no other way. Furthermore, I will argue later on in this chapter that surface structure constructions must be considered to have meaning which is imposed over and sometimes at tension with the underlying notional structure. I believe that the attempt to banish all components of semantics from the surface structure is in the end futile. A surface structure that habitually encodes a given underlying notional structure comes to carry some of the meaning of that notional structure itself. Therefore, if we put such a surface structure to a rather unusual use, we may find that the surface structure carries overtones of meaning even at variance with the underlying meaning encoded within it. This makes possible no end of word play and humor as well as misunderstanding. Some ungrammatical constructions will need to be explained as unsuccessful use of a given surface structure to encode a notional structure not usually encoded within it.

Hierarchy is by no means the exclusive discovery of tagmemics. To begin with, hierarchy, like any valid linguistic notion, is a traditional notion. People have talked about words, phrases, clauses, sentences, paragraphs, and discourses for a long time. Early American structuralism in its preoccupation with morphological structure elaborated quite well the distinction between derivation and inflexion, in what I would now call stem versus word structures (cf. Nida 1949). Otherwise, however, neither structuralism nor early TG grammar paid much attention to the traditional hierarchical notions. Among linguists of Neo-Firthian tradition, hierarchy, however, has been long recognized as RANK--although they have usually confined their work (like most schools of linguistics) to the sentence level or lower. Halliday and Hasan's work on cohesion in discourse (1976) expresses a view--similar to that found in stratificational grammar--that constituent structure (of a sort found on lower levels) does not characterize structures above the sentence. Stratificational grammar is not unfriendly to the idea of grammatical hierarchy but has not made the idea very focal.

All this bring us to the question: "Is a systematic theory of hierarchy possible?" Harris dreamed of this in his early and important article "From Morpheme to Utterance" (1946). Here Harris speaks of patterns of progressively larger substitution which enable us to go from morpheme to utterance in a systematic way. Harris too is one of the few linguists of his period to refer overtly any word to such units as phrase, clause, sentence and paragraph (compare Harris 1954).

2. TAGMEME AND SYNTAGMEME

Tagmemics provides a unique foundation for a theory of grammatical hierarchy in its concepts of tagmeme and syntagmeme. This is why I have watched with great concern recent modifications of these two concepts on the part of Pike and his immediate students at the University of Michigan, and in recent field workshops. I want to go back to Pike's original definition of tagmeme as SLOT-CLASS which I have paraphrased as FUNCTION-SET. For this there exists a necessary corollary: the notion of syntagmeme as construction. I will not here retrace all the ground covered some time ago in my (1965) article, "Some Fundamental Insights of Tagmemics", but I have changed little from the point of view reflected in that article. In regard to the syntagmeme, to me part of the aesthetic appeal of tagmemics is that the utterly foggy notion of construction in American structuralism of the 40's and 50's is here replaced by a very concrete and definable notion. Although I do not regard this as an idle claim, I will not repeat the rather lengthy attempt to establish this claim that is found in the article mentioned above. Rather, I content myself with the following quotation:

> Simply conceived, a syntagmeme is a structurally contrastive type on a given level of hierarchical structuring, e.g., a word type (in terms of internal structure), a phrase type, a clause type, a sentence type, a paragraph type, a discourse type. More explicitly: a syntagmeme, as a functionally contrastive string on a given level, has (1) closure and internal coherence; (2) a minimal structure (a nucleus at least part of which is obligatory) and usually an expanded structure (the entire nucleus plus the optional periphery); and (3) contrast, variants, and distribution. It may be characterized by internal layering or grouping and by multiple nesting. Requirement (1) reminds us that any structured string must be bounded (it starts and stops), and must have parts which are in functional relation with each other (hence patterned and restricted as to the choice and structure of each part). Requirement (2) allows for varying degrees of structural elaboration while at the same time it allows us to connect functionally a minimal structure (say a single noun) and its expansion (say the noun with various qualifiers)

so that both manifest the same syntagmeme. The distinction of nucleus versus periphery is furthermore useful in that nuclear tagmemes are especially characteristic of the syntagmemes where they occur. Nuclear tagmemes also tend to be in sharper structural contrast than do peripheral tagmemes. Requirement (3) is basic not only to the syntagmeme but to any linguistic unit. (Longacre 1965:70-1).

Representing tagmeme with the Greek letter T and syntagmeme with the Greek letter Σ, I symbolize below two fundamental interrelationships of tagmeme and syntagmeme.

$$\Sigma = \{T_1 \ . \ . \ . \ T_n\}$$
$$T_f\!: \ \{\Sigma\}$$

The first formulization expresses the law of composition. Here the equal sign may be read as 'composed of', i.e., syntagmeme is composed of tagmemes. Typically the tagmemes occur in linear order. It may approach an unordered set in the clause structure of a language with very free word order. In low level syntagmemes (words and stems) we may find an occasional stacking of tagmemes so that one tagmeme occurs simultaneously with another. This is true when one tagmeme is expounded by a phonological feature such as tone or nasalization which is imposed over the phonological stuff of another tagmeme's manifestation.

The set of tagmemes characteristically partitions into nucleus and periphery. Thus, a clause level syntagmeme, specifically a transitive clause, may have such constituent tagmemes as the following within a given language: predicate, subject, object, manner, location, time. This may be partitioned into the nuclear tagmemes, predicate, subject, object, and the peripheral tagmemes, manner, location, and time (Longacre 1964b). The set of tagmemes may be further partitioned as to obligatory and optional tagmemes, in which case we may find that predicate and subject are obligatory while object, manner, location, and time are optional. Here the two partitions of the set according to nuclear versus peripheral and obligatory versus optional are not isomorphic. While object belongs to the set of nuclear tagmemes, it does not belong to the set of obligatory tagmemes in a language where it need not be mentioned anew in every individual clause, but is understood from context.

The second formulization above tells us that the function of a tagmeme is expounded by a set of syntagmemes. (Exponence, the relation between function and set, is symbolized by a colon.) There are several things to say about this formulization. For one thing it treats morpheme as a syntagmeme with zero internal structure so that the morpheme is the zero level of syntagmemic organization. Secondly, various sorts of sets may expound the function of a tagmeme. The set members may be all from the same level of syntagmemic organization, e.g. a set of noun phrases, a set of verb phrases, or a set of affixes (morphemes) which expound a tense category. More likely, however, a tagmeme is expounded by a set whose members come from various levels of syntactic organization. Thus within a given language the subject tagmeme of a transitive clause may be expounded by noun phrases, morphemes (pronouns), and relative clauses. Here reference to the three levels, phrase, morpheme, and clause, provides a partitioning of the set of syntagmemes which expound subject tagmeme. A tagmeme may, however, be expounded by a unit set. Thus in the English verb phrase the negative tagmeme is expounded by the unit set consisting of the morpheme not.

What is exponence then? Strictly speaking, exponence is the relationship between the function of a tagmeme and its manifesting set. We may shorten this to say the relationship between a tagmeme and its (expounding) syntagmemes. The latter shortening is merely in the interest of facilitating discourse. Whenever we want to stop and ask what we are really doing we'll prefer speaking more lengthily and accurately.

Notice the correlativity of the above two formulizations, whereby tagmemes compose syntagmemes and syntagmemes expound the function of tagmemes. This means that, whenever we are generating actual utterances or portions of utterances from a syntagmemic formulization, we may substitute for the tagmeme symbol the set of expounding syntagmemes. We may then choose to select one of these syntagmemes to be the particular exponent for occurrence within an actual utterance. We work on down substituting syntagmeme for tagmeme until we reach the bottom level of formulizations. This gives us a ready and natural way to generate utterances from syntagmemic formulas (Longacre 1964b:24-32).

3. THE LAW OF PRIMARY EXPONENCE

Harris searched for a way to get from morpheme to utterance and I have claimed here that tagmemics provides a more explicit way to accomplish what he attempted to describe in terms of increasingly larger patterns of substitution. This way of getting from morpheme to utterance--or, from utterance to morpheme--I call the law of PRIMARY EXPONENCE. Primary exponence may be formulized as follows:

$$T_n\text{:} \; \{\Sigma_{n-1} \; V \; \Sigma_o\}$$

(I omit here $_f$ from T in that it is confusing to append two subscripts, both $_f$ and $_n$, to T. Whenever T occurs before a colon in any formulization, however, it is to be considered to have an unwritten $_f$ following it.)

What the above formulization says is that the function of a tagmeme on any given level is expounded by a set of syntagmemes from the next lower level (descending exponence) and/or syntagmemes from level zero (level-skipping to zero). To illustrate the above formulization take, for example, a sentence type, i.e., a sentence-level syntagmeme, in such a language as English. We can expect the constituent tagmemes of a sentence to be expounded by clauses, in that clause is the next descending level below the sentence. We do find, however, that there are bits and pieces of sentences, in fact essential parts of their framework, which are composed of functional morphemes, i.e., syntagmemes of level zero. Thus, in an antithetical sentence in English, the antithetical link is expounded by <u>but</u>: and in the coordinate sentence in English, the coordinate link is expounded by <u>and</u>. Functional morphemes of this sort are found on all levels of structure. They are as fundamental a part of the framework of their constructions, i.e., their syntagmemes, as are tagmemes whose exponents are syntagmemes from the next lower level. What we say in this formulization is that the primary elements of construction are elements from the next lower level of construction and such functional morphemes.

It is very important to add the second bit of formulization above: Σ_o. Without this we get into a ridiculous hassle; we have to defend an indefensible thesis that primary exponence equals descending exponence. We have to say e.g., that the sentence _I went downtown but Mary stayed home_ is composed of three clauses and that the word _but_ in the center must be some sort of minimal clause because it is a constituent part of a sentence. This hassle is far from imaginary; it is precisely the source of an interchange between Halliday (1966) and P. H. Matthews (1966). Halliday's original formulization of RANK (= hierarchy) had not taken account of functional morphemes.

The law of primary exponence covers, of course, any level of structure. We will therefore expect discourse to be composed primarily of paragraphs, paragraphs to be composed primarily of sentences, sentences to be composed primarily of clauses, clauses primarily of phrases, etc. Various corollaries follow. For example, we are able to set up a law of proportion such as the following:

$$\frac{D}{\P} = \frac{\P}{S} = \frac{\mathcal{E}}{C} = \frac{C}{P} \text{ etc.}$$

Here we see that the way in which sentence relates to discourse is via constituency within the paragraph while the way that clause relates to paragraph is via constituency within the sentence, etc. This in turn leads to the recognition of such units as simple paragraph (whose nucleus contains only one sentence) and simple sentence (whose nucleus contains only one clause).

4. GENERAL THEORY OF EXPONENCE

Primary exponence is sufficient to get us from morpheme to utterance, but does not account for all possible forms of exponence. We know, for example, that phrase may occur within phrase, clause within clause, sentence within sentence, paragraph within paragraph, discourse within discourse. Let us call this type of exponence SECONDARY EXPONENCE or RECURSION, and give it the following formulization:

$$T_n\colon\ \{\Sigma_n\}$$

This formulization tells us that the function of a tagmeme on any level may be expounded by a set of syntagmemes on the same level as itself. Recursion gives a type of structure which may be called a nest instead of a string, as in the noun phrase _the proposition of the committee of the senior_ members of the legislature of this state--which is really a nest of thirteen phrases, the outermost of which is the whole which breaks down into the proposition plus all that follows and the second of which is of the committee of the senior members of the legislature of this state and so on down to further embedded phrases and to the ultimate constituents (words and functional morphemes). This phrase may serve to illustrate one important feature of recursion wherever it occurs and on whatever level: Recursion is parasitic on primary exponence in the sense that it must eventually give way to primary exponence. Ultimately the constituents of the lowest level of a nest of phrases such as the one above are words and functional morphemes such as the, committee, senior, members, legislature, etc., in the bottom row of phrases which are the proposition, the committee, the senior members, the legislature, this state. Recursion is no denial of primary exponence but merely a delay in its actualization.

If recursion be considered to be secondary exponence, we may consider that there is tertiary exponence of two varieties: backlooping and levelskipping other than to zero. By backlooping I mean an apparent turning upside down of hierarchy so that, e.g., a clause occurs as a constituent of a noun phrase or a paragraph as a constituent of a sentence. The first is exemplified in the frequent phenomenon of relative clauses, the boy who lives next door. The second is exemplified in the occurrence of a paragraph within the quotation slot of a quotation sentence. Neither of these structures is unusual or bizarre per se, but appears to be a regular device within the structure of the world's languages for accommodating backlooping. Again notice that backlooping does not contradict primary exponence. What goes up must come down. If a relative clause modifies the head noun of a noun phrase, that relative clause itself is composed of phrases which in turn are composed of words and stems right down to the morpheme level.

Backlooping need not, however, be confined to the regular devices of the sort exemplified above. We also have more irregular sorts of backlooping dependent upon tricks of intonation and juncture. The stem formatives -ism and -ish are especially productive in English of such special backlooping devices. Notice the following passage quoted by Pike (1967:107 from Martin Luther King): We are through with tokenism and gradualism and see-how-far-you've-come-ism.

We're through with we've-done-more-for-your-people-than-anyone-else-ism. The above sentences contain the normal uses of -ism in tokenism and gradualism. In see-how-far-you've-come-ism, a clause structure backloops into the structure of a noun stem in that -ism occurs on the end of the whole unit. In we've-done-more-for-your-people-than-anyone-else-ism, a sentence structure backloops into a noun stem. Both of these indicate more than first order backlooping. First order backlooping involves going to the first level above a construction for an exponent of some tagmeme of the construction. Going to a still higher hierarchical level constitutes a higher degree of backlooping. Thus the occurrence of a clause within a noun stem is third degree backlooping (since clause is three levels above stem) while the occurrence of a sentence within a noun stem is fourth degree backlooping (since sentence is four levels above stem). As for the stem formative -ish, notice the following: His now-you-see-me-now-you-don't-ish attitude disturbs me. Here in place of such a noun root as snob in snobbish we have a whole sentence structure run into the stem slot: now-you-see-me-now-you-don't. This is another example of fourth degree backlooping. A similar example (but without -ish) is What about his 'Hello, how are you? Goodby' attitude? Here 'Hello, how are you? Goodby' is a paragraph structure backlooped into a noun phrase as a modifier of the headword attitude. This is another example of third degree backlooping. It is important to note that these more irregular examples of backlooping involve special intonational and junctural features--level run-on intonation and open juncture.

Somewhat more normal for English are such examples as Jack-in-the-pulpit where Jack-in-the-pulpit is a phrase run into the head slot of a word. This is only first degree backlooping, as are also the terms for in-law: brother-in-law, sister-in-law, mother-in-law, etc. Similar to Jack-in-the-pulpit is forget-me-not except that forget-me-not is a clause structure run here into the head slot of a word and therefore involves second degree backlooping.

Backlooping may be formulized as follows:

$$T_n: \{\Sigma_{n+a}\}$$

where a is equal to or greater than one.

Level-skipping other than to zero is abother variety of tertiary exponence. Level-skipping exponence occurs whenever we find a tagmeme expounded, not by a set of syntagmemes from the next lower level, but by a set of syntagmemes from a still lower level. I exclude here level-skipping to zero since I consider the use of functional morphemes (syntagmemes of level zero) to be a variety of primary exponence. Level-skipping other than to zero is illustrated by the occurrence of a noun phrase which expounds sentence topic within the periphery of a sentence structure, such as in the sentence, _As for John, he came home, put his books on the table, made himself a peanut butter sandwich, ate it, and headed for the sandlot_. Here _As for John_ is part of the periphery of a coordinate sentence. It goes not simply with the first clause of that sentence, but with the entire coordinated structure, yet it is itself a noun phrase. Here a sentence level tagmeme is expounded neither by a clause nor by a functional morpheme (as in primary exponence) but by a phrase. This is first order level-skipping. In general, level-skipping to other than zero is not as common as level-skipping to zero (which is classifiable as primary exponence).

Level-skipping may be formulized as follows:

$$T_n\colon \ \{\Sigma_{n-a}\}$$

where a is greater than one. To exclude from this formulization level-skipping to zero we add the proviso:

$$\Sigma_{n-a} \neq \Sigma_o$$

The accompaning diagram (Diagram I) exhaustively summarizes all possible types of exponence in any language anywhere. My excuse in offering this chart again (cf. Longacre 1965 and 1968a) is that previous versions of it have not been as full as the present extensive version. I also want to comment on the chart from a few new angles.

As to the overall characteristics of the chart, note that the vertical parameter represents tagmemes on the various levels from discourse down to stem. Morpheme is not represented in the vertical parameter in that the morpheme is the level of zero internal organization where no constituent tagmemes occur. Types of exponence (level-skipping, descending, recursive, and backlooping) are

	LS_6	LS_5	LS_4	LS_3	LS_2	LS_1	DE	R	BL_1	BL_2	BL_3	BL_4	BL_5	BL_6
T_D	M	St	W	P	C	S	¶	D						
$T_¶$		M	St	W	P	C	S	¶	D					
T_S			M	St	W	P	C	S	¶	D				
T_C				M	St	W	P	C	S	¶	D			
T_P					M	St	W	P	C	S	¶	D		
T_W						M	St	W	P	C	S	? ¶	*D	
T_{St}							M	St	W	P	C	S	? ¶	*D

Diagram I

represented in the horizontal parameter. The cells are filled with symbols for syntagmemes on various levels so that each cell is an intersection of the two parameters. A hierarchically ordered sequence of symbols runs from left to right (M to D) across every row. A partial sequence in this same order runs from bottom to top within each column. Left ascending diagonals contain the same symbol. These are the significant features of the arrangement.

The chart symbolizes exponence as a relation between a tagmeme on a given level (symbolized in the vertical parameter) and a syntagmeme on a given level (symbolized in a particular cell). Thus, the intersection of T_D with the column labeled descending occurs at the cell filled with the symbol for paragraph. This means that in descending exponence a discourse level tagmeme has a paragraph as its exponent (T_D expounded by ¶). The column labeled descending summarizes this type of exponence exhaustively. This column plus the bottom left ascending diagonal containing the symbol M (level-skipping to zero) together symbolize primary exponence (in double lines).

Notice that only the two central columns of the chart, the ones marked descending and recursion, are filled columns, although filled in different ways since the descending column lacks D but has M while the recursion column has D but lacks M. The fact that the two central columns are both central and filled underscores the crucial place of descending and recursive exponence not only to the theory of hierarchy but to the very existence and use of language. While, therefore, our chart provides for all conceivable sorts of exponence, it highlights the position of primary and secondary exponence (recursion). Furthermore, we shall see that as we go out to successive orders of backlooping and level-skipping (proceeding from the central columns toward either the right or the left of the chart), we involve ourselves in constructions that are progressively harder to document, of increasingly marginal grammaticality, and rarer statistically (presumably the particular patterning of statistical frequency will vary from language to language).

Furthermore, it is important to note that although the scheme as thus conceived accomodates a considerable variety of bizarre and off-beat data it is not conceived only to accommodate such data. Rather, descending, recursive, level-skipping, and backlooping exponence (all of which the scheme embraces) are essential to the description of natural language in its most basic aspects. Without descending exponence we could not have constituent structure at all, rather only simple, uncomplicated, linear sequence of elements. No such language exists. Without recursive exponence we could not have the open-endedness which makes all languages to consist of infinite but describable sets of constructions. Without level-skipping to zero (a further variety of primary exponence) we could not have the functional morphemes or particles which characterize all languages. Without backlooping we could not have subordinate clauses that qualify nouns nor quotation. These types of exponence are required to describe basic characteristics of natural language. Once this scheme is posited, however, we find that many other apparently abberrant phenomena may be subsumed and described within it.

The chart is a complete summary for all theoretically possible intersections of types of exponence with levels in a language with the EIGHT LEVELS: morpheme, stem, word, phrase, clause, sentence, paragraph, discourse. In that the morpheme level is level zero in regard to internal tagmemic structure, the vertical parameter of the chart has but seven variables. In that the exponence of a tagmeme may be a morpheme as well as syntagmeme, there are eight symbols in each row of cells. The number of cells is therefore the product of eight times seven, that is 56. To generalize it we may say that the number of cells (representing all conceivable types of exponence intersecting with all levels) is the product of the number of levels times the number of levels minus one, as in the following formulization:

$$(L)\ (L-1) = \text{number of cells}$$

No further types of exponence are possible. Thus, e.g., we might posit level-skipping of the seventh order. This could be symbolized by moving the symbol M up and out of the chart on the diagonal one cell to the left. This would not, however, symbolize anything which could occur in a language with eight levels in that the M in that cell out of the chart would no longer have a tagmeme of which it can be exponent.

But if the chart contains all conceivable types of exponence, may it not also contain some inconceivable ones? Thus, although we make much of the fullness of structure in the columns marked descending and recursion, are there lurking problems in even these columns? What about the fact that word structure in English and many other languages is a string and does not invite recursion? As a matter of fact we have in English one and only one inflectional suffix on a given noun, verb, adjective, or pronoun. We remind ourselves, however, that the chart is framed to summarize and include not only regular but irregular and bizarre uses of language as well. Take then such a sentence as the following: How many had's are there in this paragraph? Had is here a verb word inflected with the past tense suffix, but which occurs nevertheless within the word structure had's, i.e., with the pluralization of a noun following it. This then is an example of recursion on the word level, i.e., word structure within word structure. Call it metalanguage, call it hypostasis, call it what you please, even such bizarre examples as these occur--and are accommodated within the scheme.

Otherwise our two central columns provide no source of difficulty in regard to exemplification. Certainly discourse within discourse is the rule rather than the exception. A story of any length and complexity consists not simply of paragraphs, but of whole sub-stories which expound episodes of that story, i.e., there are discourse level tagmemes expounded by discourses. Paragraph within paragraph is so commonplace that it would be impossible to analyze paragraphs without taking account of this. Otherwise we would have to posit an infinite number of paragraph types in a given language to account for recursive structures of this sort. Sentence within sentence is similarly recursive. While clause tends to be a string, it is also by no means uncommon to find a nominal clause in subject or object slot. Phrase within phrase, stem within stem, are likewise structural commonplaces.

The question therefore remains as to whether there are any cells on this chart which can never be filled in any language anywhere. We would expect to find them in high order backlooping or high order level-skipping. Let's consider the last first. Notice that our highest order of level-skipping, level-skipping six, is really primary exponence since we have defined the use of functional morphemes as primary exponence. Here we have for instance the use of the word amen to close a prayer discourse. We might well doubt if we would ever have level-skipping of order five, i.e., would we ever find a discourse level tagmeme expounded by a stem which is not expandable into a word but is simply a minimal stem? In that, however, the four patterns of English inflection (i.e., of word structure) are nominal, verbal, adjectival, and pronominal, we, as a matter of fact, sometimes do find an internally complex form (i.e., a stem) that nevertheless is not capable of being inflected as a word. A clear possibility here has to do with the title slot in discourses where we may have such a word as Because for a title (of a song). Because is certainly a stem but is hardly an adequate candidate for a word structure. Level-skipping to word structure (T_D:W) is a bit hard to document in English for the simple reason that most words may be considered to be minimal phrases (especially verbs or nouns). The sole possibility is pronouns which may be considered to be inflectable, i.e., he to him, she to her, I to me, etc. , but not all of which are normally expandable into phrases (while poor little me may pass inspection *poor little I is less successful). Notice again the importance of the title slot in discourse. Charles Lindberg's book We has a title which is an unexpandable-to-a-phrase pronoun word. Here a word expounds a discourse level tagmeme--which makes this fourth order level-skipping.

In regard to high degrees of backlooping we do run into some doubtful--if not inconceivable--situations. An English speaker might conceivably say His Hello-How-are-you-Goodby's disturb me. Above I identified Hello. How are you? Goodby in His 'Hello. How are you? Goodby' attitude as a paragraph which expounds a phrase level tagmeme and hence exemplifies third degree backlooping. But the present example presumably offers the same paragraph as a backlooping exponent of paragraph into a (noun) word. I believe that for this to happen (a) a paragraph must be extraordinarily brief and rudimentary in nature, and (b) it must be more unified intonationally (level contour) than is required of the same rudimentary paragraph when serving as backlooping exponent of a phrase-level tagmeme. Somewhat even more extreme and similarly restricted is His 'Hello-How-are-you-Goodby'-ish attitude disturbs me. Here a paragraph presumably backloops into a stem. On the chart I mark these two cells (intersection of T_w with BL_4 and of T_{st} with BL_5) with a question mark to indicate the restricted nature of such constructions.

The preceeding paragraph considered the possibility of paragraph backlooping into word and stem with the verdict: possible but restricted. I now consider the two cells marked with the asterisk, i.e., the intersection of T_w with BL_5 and of T_{st} with BL_6. In brief, can a discourse backloop into word and stem structures? The question turns largely on the definition of discourse. If *Hello, How are you? Goodby* in the above examples be considered a discourse, then the answer is affirmative. Obviously, however, a discourse of any complexity--even a short narrative, oration, essay, or poem--can scarcely be conceived to backloop into word or stem. The above examples of paragraph backlooping into structures on these two levels pushes us to the limit of credibility and grammaticality. For this reason I have marked the two rightmost 'D'-cells on the chart with an asterisk. Backlooping of discourse into phrase and higher levels is somewhat more conceivable. Imagine a sentence: *I never tire of hearing his 'Fourscore and seven years ago...'* [text of Lincoln's Gettysburg Address]--backlooping of discourse into phrase; and *I have memorized 'Fourscore and seven years ago...'*--backlooping of discourse into clause.

We may expect that individual languages will differ as to what portions of the accompanying chart they are able to fill in. We will predict, however, that all will be able to fill in the two central columns, that none will be able to fill in the cells which are marked with asterisk, and that the documentation of higher degrees of backlooping and level-skipping will be spotty for many languages.

It might be objected here that we have failed to mention portmanteau exponence, i.e., the function of a given lexical string as simultaneous manifestation of tagmemes and of syntagmemes on two or more levels . Thus: *come* is a main tagmeme of its verb phrase; predicate tagmeme of an imperative clause; and sentence base tagmeme of a simple sentence. As a phrase, *come* may be expanded to *do come* and *don't come*. As a clause, it may be expanded to such strings as *come here immediately* or *come to dinner without your tuxedo*. As a sentence, it may be expanded still differently: *Come, I need you*; *Come but be quiet*; or *Come if you must*. Portmanteau exponence of this sort may be schematized as follows where L symbolizes a string of lexical items which manifest the same syntagmeme:

$$\begin{Bmatrix} \Sigma_{n+2} \\ T_{n+2} \end{Bmatrix} \qquad \begin{Bmatrix} \Sigma_{n+1} \\ T_{n+1} \end{Bmatrix}$$

$$\Sigma_n \; [\text{where } L(\Sigma_n) = L(\Sigma_{n+1}) = L(\Sigma_{n+2})]$$

Seen in this fashion portmanteau exponence is not a further variety of exponence unsymbolized in the chart. It is really descending hierarchy along a chain of minimal structures functioning simultaneously on various levels.

Before going on to the following section I want to emphasize once more the central importance of primary exponence to the theory of hierarchy. I quote here from an earlier paper a passage which has seemed relevant to some readers:

> Hierarchy is like a river meandering from its source (discourse level) to the sea (morpheme level where no further grammatical distinctions are posited). Often, the course of the river is smooth (descending hierarchy); there may be, however, a cataract here and there (level-skipping) or eddies of various degrees of turbulence (backlooping) or lakes (recursions). The presence of cataracts, eddies, and lakes in no way contradicts the fact that the river is progressing in a general downward direction. Without the downward pull of gravitation, no river would exist. Similarly, without the generally downward thrust of constituent structure, there could not be hierarchy. Descending hierarchy and level-skipping are but different instances here of the same tendency. Furthermore, both recursion and backlooping must, eventually, terminate and give way to the downward thrust (Longacre 1970a:186).

5. CHARACTERISTICS OF THE VARIOUS LEVELS

The view of hierarchy here presented has been criticized for the place it gives to primary exponence. Peter Fries (1973) has suggested that, taking discourse as primary, the theory of hierarchy could be constructed quite well primarily from the standpoint of the role of the various levels in discourse structure. While I have no quarrel with Fries' desire to make discourse a primary consideration of linguistics (quite the contrary), it seems to me that something more is needed to establish hierarchy. I think that Harris had a true instinct in his morpheme to utterance idea. He came very close to saying something of what I am saying in his emphasis on patterns of progressively larger substitution. It seems to me that some sort of law of combination is needed to get from morpheme to discourse, and that without such a law of combination we cannot really have hierarchy. Nevertheless, it is interesting to attempt to state the characteristics of the various hierarchical levels, some of their possible idiosyncrasies, and their placement in discourse--as Fries has suggested.

First a look at the lower hierarchical levels. Stem is the surface level which encodes derivation. It may be a linear string, i.e., a root plus a derivative affix or a compound of several root morphemes. Alternatively, it may be a nest so that we may have, e.g., adjective stem derived to a noun stem derived to another noun stem and in turn derived to a verb stem. The word is the surface level which encodes inflection. A further peculiarity of both word and stem is the large number of functional morphemes that they have within them. Thus while the word is twice removed from the level of zero internal syntagmemic organization, namely, the morpheme, it typically consists of a base and a string of inflectional morphemes. If the stem level intervenes below the word within a given language then every one of these inflectional morphemes is a tagmeme with level-skipping exponence. Inasmuch, however, as this level-skipping is to zero, it is still classifiable as primary exponence.

The phrase level might almost be called the level of constituent structure since phrases are constituents of clauses. The noun phrase is typically a three-layered level. We here distinguish level and layer; between the layers on the same level there is (so to speak) extensive backlooping and level-skipping so it is not plausible to set them up as separate hierarchical levels. For languages in which the noun phrase is such a three-layered level we find: (a) The bottom layer is the attributive noun phrase, i.e., head noun with various sorts of modifiers, quantifiers and determiners . (b) Above that is a further layer of coordination and apposition. (c) Above that still is a further layer in which prepositions or postpositions are attached to any of the above phrase types, thus yielding relator-axis phrases. It is evident, however, that a relator-axis phrase may occur freely within an attributive noun phrase, e.g., as a modifier of the head noun (the house on the corner) and that relator-axis phrases may themselves be coordinated, e.g., on the corner and in front of the delicatessen. We have here nothing as well defined as a set of three levels but we do have a discernible layering. Verb phrases are characteristically very different from noun phrases, just as verb words are typically quite different from noun words. There seems no reason however to believe that they cannot both be considered to be on the same level of hierarchical structuring in that both are simply the constituents of clauses.

Clauses are, broadly speaking, predicational strings, although both PREDICATIONAL and STRINGS must be qualified somewhat. Thus many languages contain non-verbal or nominal clauses. Nominal clauses differ considerably in internal relationship from language to language but one frequently expressed relation is EQUATION, e.g., John [is a] teacher . Such a clause is a statement of set membership, i.e., John ε teachers) rather than a prediction in the narrower definition of the word. Verbs on the order of be verbs are used in equational clauses in some languages. Similar verbs are used to express EXISTENCE in many languages as well (cf. Chapter 5, 2.4). Whether existence is, properly speaking, a predicate, is a question I here gladly refer to philosophers. That clauses tend to be strings is true provided we admit that some nesting--noticeably use of nominalized or relativized clauses as exponents of subject and object--occurs as well.

Verbal clauses typically occur in systems which have transitivity and mood parameters. The first gives us such distinctions as intransitive, transitive, and ditransitive. The latter gives us declarative, interrogative, imperative, conditional, optative, and the like. The intersection of the two parameters gives us such clause types as intransitive declarative, intransitive interrogative, and the like (cf. Liem 1966).

Verbal clauses as well as the nominal clauses mentioned constitute a two-layered level in which independent and dependent clauses are distinguished. The latter either involve a particular type of predicate structure or consist of clauses marked as dependent by the occurrence of a subordinating relator such as when, while, where, or who which substitute for the corresponding clause level tagmemes (i.e., you came yesterday→when you came). The latter sort of clauses may be called RELATOR-AXIS CLAUSES.

Linear order of the nuclear tagmemes of clauses varies greatly from language to language. A few typical normative orderings are especially common. Thus, for Mixtec, Trique and many Otomanguean languages the order PSO (predicate, subject, object) is normative. For Japanese and Korean SOP is normative. English and many other languages have still a third normative order: SPO. In these three normative orderings, the subject precedes the object. This restriction in normative orderings is not, however, universal. In Apurina (data from Wilbur Pickering) and in Hixkaryana (Derbyshire 1979) a normative order involving OS occurs.

The sentence is propositional rather than merely predicational. It typically has more grammatical closure than the clause. Suggestions have been made by Pike (Pike and Pike 1977) and Thomas (1975) that MOOD (or illocutionary force) be reserved for the sentence level. Mood, however, can on the one hand make for many internal changes in the structure of a clause (cf. interrogative transform in English); and on the other hand appears as a component of the paragraph in some languages (e.g., Fore). I hesitate, therefore, to make presence of mood a defining feature of sentence.

Sentence, it seems to me, is preeminently the level of clause combination (i.e. predications combined into propositions). As such we can distinguish among the languages of the world two main models of sentence structure: (1) the CO-RANKING model; and (2) the CHAINING model. The two models may occur side by side in the same language or a given language may exclusively have sentences of one model.

Ignoring elements such as vocative and exclamation (which I relegate to the outer periphery of the sentence), the co-ranking model has sentences of the structure shown in the Diagram II: (a) their nuclei contain one or more independent clauses; and (b) their (inner) peripheries contain subordinate clauses of time (temporal margin), condition (conditional margin), concession (concessive margin), cause (cause margin), purpose (purpose margin), and the like. In many but not all languages which feature this model, certain margins, especially temporal margins, are typically

PERIPHERY	NUCLEUS	PERIPHERY
Temporal M Conditional M Concessive M etc.	of Simple S of Coordinate S of Antithetical S of Reason S etc.	Cause M Purpose M etc.

Diagram II. Sentences in co-ranking languages (M = margin; S = sentence)

prenuclear while others, noticeably cause margin and purpose margin, are post-nuclear. We thus find sentences such as: When I stopped in, Mother was sewing, my younger brothers and sisters were watching TV, and Dad was reading. Here the nucleus of the sentence contains three clauses none of which is subordinated to the other or has a verb of subordinate rank. The entire nucleus is accompanied by a time margin expounded by a subordinate clause: When I stopped in.

The chaining model has sentences which do not permit two independent verbs in the same sentence. A sentence such as that above would single out one verb--typically the last verb (was reading)--for special treatment as a FINAL verb, and make all other verbs in the sentence a different structure which we may call the MEDIAL verb. Final and medial verbs in turn determine final and medial clauses. The first link in such chains, i.e., the first clause, can however be specialized in function somewhat like our TEMPORAL MARGIN in English. The sentence in languages which feature this model (Highland Papua New Guinea, many parts of S. America) conforms to the scheme given in Diagram III in which I distinguish three essential parts: (a) first link; (b) medial link(s); and (c) final link. Thus, the English sentence above would be rendered into such a structure with When I stopped in as the first link, with Dad was reading as the final link, and the other two clauses as medial links. The verb was reading would be rendered by a final verb and all other verbs would be medial. The first link would be distinguished mainly by its discourse function

first link	medial links	final link
Temporal M with medial verb	further clauses with medial verbs	clause with verb of distinctive structure

Diagram III. Sentences in chaining languages

of recapitulating the final verb of the previous chain of clauses.

Either type of sentence structure may be (1) subordinated and embedded within another sentence; (2) reduced to a STRIPPED-DOWN or merged sentence; (3) have a minimal exponent which consists on one clause. Thus, in English, we may subordinate and embed such a complex unit as _I was downtown but Mary was at home_ by adding a subordinator: _While I was downtonwn but Mary was at home_.... The same thing may be done in a chaining structure where by no means are all chains simple units without embedding. Secondly, constructions may be specialized by reducing all but one verb to less than finite verb status and by imposing rather severe phonological and lexical restrictions. Thus English has such units as _I urged Mary to go_, _I made her do it_, and _I started to do it_ where only the first verb is a finite verb, where there are overall phonological units, and where the lexical choice of the first verb is considerably restricted. These units still resemble sentences--as combinations of clauses--but have more specialization of structure than characterizes most sentences. I call such units MERGED SENTENCES. Chaining structures such as are found in Highland Papua New Guinea have chains of stripped-down verbs with few intervening nouns and have a medial or final verb as their last unit. They exhibit phonological and lexical specialization not unlike English MERGED SENTENCES. To call such units in English or Papua New Guinea languages COMPLEX CLAUSES (Lanier 1968; Scott 1973) appears to me to obscure the fact that the clause is essentially a simple predication and the sentence a combination of predications. Finally, SIMPLE SENTENCES occur with either model of structure. But a simple sentence in such a language as English is not necessarily structurally simple. All that is simple about it is its one-clause nucleus. The periphery of a simple sentence may embed very complex structures--whole embedded sentences--as, e.g., temporal margin. Thus: When I came, saw the situation, and realized its hopelessness, I was staggered.

The paragraph is the developmental unit of discourse. It is the typical unit of argumentation or exhortation in hortatory discourse, of explanation and exposition in expository discourse, and of episode in narrative discourse. It's in general a looser and larger package than the sentence. While we do not usually think of paragraphs as having grammatical closure, in certain linguistic areas, noticeably in Highland Papua New Guinea, we find grammatical closure not only for the sentence but for the paragraph as well. Thus, in the Fore language of Papua New Guinea, the final verb occurs at the end of the paragraph. A special type of medial verb (almost = semi-final verb) occurs at the end of the sentence within the paragraph (Longacre 1970b, 1972a).

Discourse is the level of the whole, just as morpheme is the level of the smallest part. I leave out here problems of morpheme segmentation. Obviously if we are going from morpheme to discourse we start with the smallest part which we want to take account of as linguists. It may not be the irreducible minimum of segmentation possible in the text, but it may be that we feel that to dissect any further would be unprofitable. We therefore take this set of morphemes as our starting point.

6. VARIETY IN NATURE

The above scheme of hierarchical levels is very prevalent in the world's languages. Nevertheless, there are a few proven exceptions to it. In some languages we find one level less in the lower hierarchical ranges. Thus, in the Mayan languages we do not seem to need both word and phrase, although we do very definitely have a stem level. In dealing, e.g., with verb morphology in a Mayan language, a typical analyst will posit as affixes the morphemes which occur very close to the verb stem. Morphemes occurring a bit further out are likely to be called enclitics or

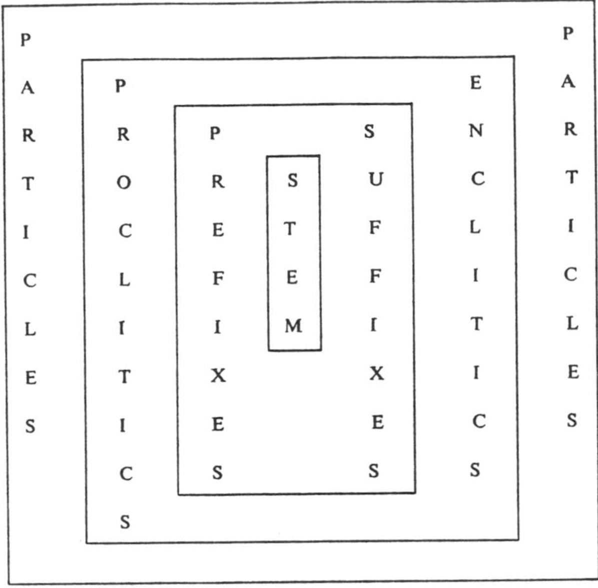

Diagram IV. The common word-phrase level in Mayan

proclitics while those occurring still further out but obviously related to the verb and having a certain freedom of movement are often called particles. There is here an unbroken continuum between morphemes closely associated with the verb base and those further out. There seems no point at which this continuum can consistently be broken into word versus phrase. Indeed this distinction would only introduce a needless complication. The whole constitutes one structure capable of description within the same set of rules. Mixtecan languages (Mixteco, Cuicatec, and Trique) apparently are languages where word and stem cannot profitably be distinguished.

Still other languages apparently have one level less in the upper hierarchical ranges. Three Australian aboriginal languages (Walmatjari, Mantjiltjara, and Wik-Munkan) and one Papua New Guinea language (Bahinemo) seem to have no need of the three levels, paragraph, sentence, and clause, but only

	Marsh & Hudson	Sayers
L_2 =	¶	S
L_1 =	S	Cl

Diagram V. Collapse of Clause, Sentence, Phrase into 2 levels in three Australian languages. Marsh calls the two levels SENTENCE and PARAGRAPH; Sayers terms them CLAUSE and SENTENCE.

two levels. Precisely what nomenclature to use in reference to the two levels is somewhat problematical. Marsh (1970) and Hudson (1970) posit paragraph and sentence. Sayers posits sentence and clause. The lower of the two levels is much like a simple sentence in European languages. Its nucleus has only one clause but subordinate clauses may occur in the periphery of the construction. The higher level takes up all other sentential functions (combinations of predications as described in Chapter 3) and dialogue (cf. Chapter 2) as well. In brief the two levels found in these languages distribute the functional load in a way not parallel in any close manner to paragraph and sentence versus clause or to paragraph versus sentence and clause in a European language (cf. Diagram V.) Muinane (Colombia) handles sentence and clause as one level by heavy use of case-marking particles; coordination of clauses does not occur and every subordinate clause has a case marker which relates it to the verb of the main clause much like the case markers relate noun phrases to the main verb (Walton 1977).

It is noticeable here that we have in the case of Mayan and Mixtecan one level less on the lower range; and in the three Australian languages, Bahinemo (Papua New Guinea), and Muinane (Colombia) referred to, one level less in the upper range. An interesting question is: Would we ever find a language anywhere with a level missing in both the upper range and in the lower range? In brief, can we ever find a language anywhere with less than seven hierarchical levels?

7. SIMILARITIES BETWEEN LEVELS

It is not strange that there should be similarities between certain levels, especially between contiguous levels. Thus, between discourse and paragraph there are some not unexpected similarities. Narrative paragraph and narrative discourse have a common chronological framework as do also procedural paragraph and procedural discourse. When do we have simply a long paragraph and when do we have a short discourse? We can be guided here somewhat by features of beginning, end, and climax of such structures. In general, discourse permits a more elaborate opening, peak, and closure than does the paragraph. Thus, a narrative discourse may have a formulaic aperture (Once upon a time) and finis (that's all, that's the end) as well as stage (following aperture) and closure (preceding finis) slots. By contrast, while we have similar slots on the paragraph level, e.g., paragraph setting and paragraph terminus in narrative paragraphs, they are characteristically briefer and customarily involve only a sentence or two. In addition, a climactic narrative discourse has a surface structure peak marked by some sort of change of pace in the story (in tense, person, vantage point, orientation, relative amount of conjunctions and transition, sheer length of units or other features, cf. Chapter 1, 4.3). While paragraphs also have peaks they are much more simply marked, e.g., by a special conjunction, or by use of back-reference for the first time in a paragraph. When we find peaks at all elaborately marked we presumably have a short narrative discourse rather than a paragraph. Nevertheless, the similarity of narrative paragraph to narrative discourse, of procedural paragraph to procedural discourse, of expository paragraph to expository discourse, of hortatory paragraph to hortatory discourse, and of dialogue paragraph to dramatic discourse cannot be denied.

We may also compare paragraph and sentence. There is an inevitable similarity of the two because both (aside from dialogue paragraphs) are based on the notional structure relations of the statement or propositional calculus. The paragraph is a more diffuse surface structure treatment, the sentence is a more compressed and packaged sort of treatment. There is a certain similarity of a short paragraph to a sentence and of a long sentence to a paragraph. Where surface structural signals are not clear, some ambiguity can result as to the structural status of such a string. Where surface structure signals are clear to distinguish sentence from paragraph, some very interesting comparisons emerge.

Thus, in Highland Papua New Guinea chaining languages, clause chaining is in the domain of the paragraph in some languages and in the domain of the sentence in others. In a language such as Wojokeso (West 1973) where the chain of medial clauses terminating in a final clause is equivalent to a sentence, we have very clear grammatical evidence of sentence closure. It is not difficult in such a language to distinguish a long sentence (a single chain) from a paragraph (which is a sequence of such chains). Wojokeso has a procedural paragraph which normally consists of a series of step tagmemes each of which is expounded by a single sentence. Dorothy West observes, however, that sometimes a procedural paragraph may simply consist of one long run-on sentence, in which case all the steps of the underlying structure are combined in one surface structure sentence package. A striking example of this in the corpus of Wojokeso texts which she has prepared is the procedural discourse "On housebuilding" (Longacre 1972a, text volume). This discourse consists of an aperture, an introduction, three procedures and a closure. Procedure one is expounded by a rather long procedural paragraph with a total of seven steps. The sentences in this paragraph run from two to four lines, except for one sentence which is eight and a half lines long. Procedure two is expounded by another procedural paragraph with a total of six steps. The longest sentence in this paragraph is six lines. On turning to the final procedure we find, however, that it is expounded by a one-sentence procedural paragraph and that this one sentence has no fewer than twenty-one lines (cf. Chapter 1, 4.3.4). Here we see clearly exercised the option of the speaker in choosing to encode basically the same sort of information not as a series of sentences but as one long sentence.

Such a choice is clearly not random, but is dictated by the grammar (over-all shape) of the discourse. To begin with, we note that treatment of a subject as a paragraph involves a certain deliberate, seriatim approach to the matters being discussed, while treatment as a sentence involves a more run-on, connected, and packaged sort of structure. This contrast is, in effect, the surface structure meaning of paragraph as opposed to sentence. In the Wojokeso discourse just mentioned, however, the shift from paragraph structure to run-on sentence structure occurs in the last procedure of the discourse where it marks the notional structure target procedure which is also the surface structure peak. The shift to a one-sentence paragraph helps, therefore, to articulate the overall shape of the discourse. A similar phenomena is noted in Wojokeso narrative text where the single longest sentence in the narrative text "Woodchip" (Longacre 1972a, text volume) is found in the peak of that story as well (cf. Chapter 1, 4.3.4). Seen from this perspective, sentence and paragraph are not size level chunks per se. The sentence may be fully as long as the paragraph. They are different structural units which involve different stylistic options.

Passing on then to sentence versus clause, we perceive fully as much similarity between sentence and clause as we have just perceived between discourse and paragraph and between paragraph and sentence. There are certain features of the periphery of the sentence which are reminiscent of the structure of a clause. Thus the sentence topic (Longacre 1968 2:35-9) in *As for Tom, he gave up and went home* is not unlike the clause level subject. To be true the sentence topic need not correlate with the subject of the following clause. We have examples where the sentence topic correlates with possessor of the subject *As for John, his horse came in last* or where it correlates with the object *As for Henry, a sniper bullet killed him*, or with the locational expression *As for Marietta, I lived there as a boy*. Nevertheless, the sentence topic indicates that about which we are talking in the sentence, just as the clause level subject indicates that about which we are talking on the clause level. Furthermore, sentence peripheries contain margin tagmemes that are similar to certain peripheral tagmemes on the clause level (Longacre 1968.2.30-53). Thus, we not only have a clause level time tagmeme but also a sentence level temporal margin; the former in *I went there yesterday* versus the latter in *when I was down there yesterday, I saw Tom, visited Bill briefly, went to the supermarket, and came home*.

I think it is instructive to pause here and note the intermediate nature of paragraph in relation to discourse on the one hand and to sentence on the other, and the similarly intermediate nature of sentence in respect to paragraph on one hand and to clause on the other. Furthermore, by portmanteau exponence we can have one sentence paragraphs and one clause sentences--so that the simple paragraph (suggestion from Healey) is needed no less than the simple sentence. I do not think we need to feel excessive frustration at the ambiguity which is sometimes encountered at these points. We note to begin with that some languages do have grammatical markers for paragraph and/or sentence and that the potential ambiguity is not necessarily there to the same degree in all languages. We notice secondly that undoubtedly there are differences structurally between discourse, paragraph, and sentence, regardless of their similarities. All we are faced with here is a problem which we must learn to live with as linguists: that our formulas will generate all possible structures but will not unambiguously analyze all examples.

At first blush, clause and phrase do not seem very similar. We need to remind ourselves however that in many languages a verb phrase is a minimal clause, and there are cases where we must treat this simple verb phrase as a complete clause. Here, too, clauses seem in some ways to resemble the sentence on one hand and the verb phrase on the other. Take for example the construction in Spanish _El libro me lo dio a mí_ (he gave me the book) where _me lo dio_ (he gave it to me) is the predicate phrase in the center of the entire clause and where _el libro_ cross references to _lo_ and _a mí_ to _me_ in the predicate phrase. Here we see how tenuous in certain examples is the boundary between clause and phrase.

Similarities between contiguous lower levels exist also. As to the similarity of phrase and word, it is perhaps sufficient to reiterate that in one great family of languages, the Mayan family, which embraces over 30 languages, we find phrase and word collapsed into the same structural level. As to word and stem, when derivational and inflectional structures are not carefully distinguished from each other they merge into the same level. Both are morphological structures in the old sense of the word MORPHOLOGICAL. Even as to stem versus morpheme we find similarity in that we sometimes do not know whether to cut a linguistic form apart into two morphemes or to accept it as one unit. For example, it has been fashionable to cut _who_, _which_, _when_, _where_ into an interrogative stem _wh_ plus other morphemes which are distinctive of the various particular interrogatives to which they belong. Nevertheless, in terms of the canonical forms of English we simply do not have morphemes which pattern as the first consonant of CVC forms. To cut off wh in this fashion as a general interrogative morpheme is, from this point of view, as arbitrary as to cut off the initial sl from slip, slurp, slash, slop, or the initial fl from flicker, flimsy, flight, flame, etc.

On the lower levels there are also some interesting similarities between noncontiguous levels. Thus, it appears that word and clause are typically string structures while phrase and stem are typically nests, (i.e., phrase and stem invite wholesale recursion within them while clause and word do not). (Longacre 1970a.188-90).

Sentence is also recursive and in this respect resembles the noncontiguous phrase and stem levels. But this latter observation is not too helpful in that all the higher levels--sentence, paragraph and discourse are markedly recursive. What do we make however of this similarity of certain noncontiguous levels? Does this indicate that certain levels, (e.g. word and clause), are more basic than others? We have here some of the germinal stimulus for the idea of hierarchy in paired levels--which I explicitly reject in the next section.

8. SOME DEVIANT SCHEMATIZATIONS

Some contemporary approaches to grammar, while partially recognizing the hierarchical principle, do not exploit that principle to the full.

(a) Thus, stratificational grammar of the variety taught specifically by Gleason has DEFECTIVE HIERARCHY. I do not mean defective hierarchy in the sense that grammars have been written in which no structures have been described on certain hierarchical levels; I mean rather there is an explicit denial that structure exists for certain levels (i.e. the higher levels), in the same sense that structure exists for the lower levels. Specifically, Gleason says that tree structure and constituent grammar characterize clause and the levels on down while network structures characterize sentence, paragraph and discourse (Gleason 1968.59, fn. 6; Cromack 1968). As already mentioned Halliday has recently expressed a similar view (Halliday and Hasan

1976.1-2).

(b) Similar to such views as the above, which exemplify defective hierarchy, are LEVEL-COALESCING SYSTEMS. Again I am not referring to occasional treatments which are necessitated by the empirical facts of the world's languages (e.g., the matters dealt with under Section 6) but to approaches to grammar in which the reality of the structural separation between certain levels is denied. Thus within the framework of tagmemics, Blansitt (1970) and Trail (1973) have argued vigorously that sentence and clause should not be distinguished. A similar collapsing of sentence and clause into the same structural unit characterizes Zellig Harris' string analysis of sentence structure (1962). He in effect works with the following levels: word, phrase, and clause-sentence as do (implicitly) many on the current scene.

(c) An opposite tendency is seen in LAYER-PROLIFERATING SYSTEMS. I'm thinking here especially of Robert Allen's approach to grammar which he calls sector analysis (Allen 1966). Sector analysis is in many ways similar to tagmemics but has a much more extensive system of levels. Thus, in the analysis of a sentence by sector analysis, various internal clusterings are distinguished. Not only are clauses posited but clausids, not only the predicate but the predicatid, not only the sentence but the sentence trunk, etc.

(d) Finally we have to contend with a suggestion of Pike and Pike (1977) and Huttar (1973) that hierarchy should be according to PAIRED LEVELS. Specifically Pike and Huttar would group morpheme and stem, word and phrase, clause and sentence, and (in Pike's work) paragraph and monologue discourse. This pairing is coupled with the assumption that morpheme, word, clause and paragraph are more basic, while stem is an elaboration of morpheme, phrase is an elaboration of word, sentence is an elaboration of clause, and monologue discourse is an elaboration of paragraph.

Huttar feels that the development of hierarchy in paired levels is partly due to stimulus from me (Huttar 1973.72 fn. 1 which refers to a reprint of Longacre 1970a). It is also necessary to remember that Huttar's article was written primarily to defend the clause-sentence distinction, not to weaken it.

In objecting to hierarchy in paired levels, I remind the

reader of my contention above that sentence is no more similar to clause than it is to paragraph, while paragraph in turn is no more similar to sentence than it is to discourse. From this point of view, Pike and Huttar's pairing of levels seems to be arbitrary.

I also object to paired hierarchy on the grounds that one of the most significant threshholds in the whole hierarchical lineup is that between clause and sentence. The clause level exists primarily to encode elements of the predicate calculus while the sentence level exists to encode elements of the propositional (or statement) calculus. If we have to pair anything, it would be better to pair sentence with paragraph. But in regard to paragraph we have shown above that paragraph is fully as similar to discourse as it is to sentence.

Further implications of PAIRED HIERARCHY trouble me as well. To be true, Pike's paired hierarchy brings together morpheme and stem--and we often are at loss to know whether something should be cut into two morphemes or not. On the other hand, it separates word from stem while as a matter of fact in some languages derivational and inflectional layers are so intertwined and interdependent that it may be somewhat useless to posit two separate levels. Again, paired hierarchy brings together word and phrase into the same pair, implying that, after all, words compose clauses and phrases are merely grouping of words. Yet the phrase may have a certain wholeness which the individual word does not have, so that, for instance, case endings in classical languages really belong to the noun phrase not to the individual word as such. Furthermore, in some languages, the verb phrase rather than the verb word is a minimal clause.

It therefore seems to me that paired hierarchy does not fit the empirical facts of language. By and large, however, my greatest objection to paired hierarchy is that for me it destroys the linear descent from utterance to morpheme which gives us something approaching a mathematical law of combination to undergird hierarchy.

Actually, Pike's motivation in setting up PAIRED HIERARCHY was a semantic one: to posit the units which are most basic to discourse and to distinguish them from elaborations of those basic units. I will try to demonstrate, in Section 12, that this desire of Pike's can be met in a somewhat different way by setting up notional structure levels (derivation, inflection, predication, proposition, repartee, and plot) and mapping them in a non-one-to-one fashion onto surface levels. At any rate, we do not obtain semantic or notional structure levels by combining surface structure levels!

Having said all this, we must however face the fact that some of the above alternative schematizations may be resorted to operationally in regard to particular problems within particular languages. Thus, it may serve certain purposes to act as if hierarchy did not exist above the clause level and to treat sentence, paragraph and discourse as network relations. Undoubtedly, much insight is gained into the structure of these units by looking at them as networks. I repeat that I do not object to this operationally. I object to it, however, as an ontological hypothesis (i.e., as a dogma that there is a qualitative difference of this sort between the upper and the lower grammatical levels). Again, we may view level-collapsing as an operation--and sometimes a desirable one. That is, it may be desirable under certain conditions to pull the pegs of the hierarchical tent and let the whole structure collapse on the gound so we can walk around and look at it on a flat plane. Thus, by level-collapsing and for particular ends we may treat sentence and clause together, or paragraph and sentence. Again, I do not object to this as an operation; I object to it simply as an ontological hypothesis. Similarly, level-proliferating operations similar to sector analysis may be carried out with profit on the corpus of a given language for given purposes. And again, I have no objection to this as an operation. Nor do I object to an operation (such as Pike suggests) in which we treat certain pairs of hierarchical levels together to see what might come of the pairing. Again, all I object to is the status of any of these as ontological hypotheses. I would claim that on the contrary, hierarchy in the sense of a linear descent from discourse to morpheme is a natural characteristic of all languages.

9. NOTIONAL AND SURFACE STRUCTURE IN A HIERARCHICAL FRAMEWORK

All that I have said so far in this chapter has had to do with surface structure hierarchy, in fact with hierarchy as the organizing principle of the surface structure of discourse. As such it gets us a long way. For example, it secures comparable constructions in the sense that ad hoc immediate constituent analysis never secured. Having analyzed a discourse, we find that it belongs to a certain discourse type, but that as such, it does not stand isolated. Other discourses also belong to the same type. The same holds true of paragraph analysis and paragraph types. Coming on down into the constituent sentences of that paragraph, we find that the various sentence types occurring there occur in other paragraphs as well so that we can compare coordinate sentences across paragraphs, antithetical sentences, conditional sentences, quotation sentences, etc. Going down then into the constituent clauses of the various sentences we find transitive clauses, intransitive clauses, ditransitive clauses, etc. and these may be compared with other clauses of the same sorts occurring in and out of the same paragraph. Likewise we may compare phrase types, word types, stem types, on down to the morpheme.

But what of notional structure (on all levels within a discourse), such as plot structure in narrative, repartee or dialogue, inter-clausal relationships, case (role)? I once wrote with considerable confidence as follows regarding clause structure:

> By function is meant the peculiar office or role of one formally distinguishable part of a construction type in relation to other parts of the same construction. Thus, a predication clause may be considered to pose a drama in miniature. The verb gives the PLOT. Such functional segments as subjects, objects, and indirect objects give the DRAMATIS PERSONAE. Further functional segments indicating manner, time, place, instrument, etc. give us SETTING and STAGE PROPS. (Longacre 1965:65-6.)

I now see that in writing this I went too far too fast. Predication indeed involves relationships of the sort mentioned in the quoted passage. The role structure is better seen, however, in the notional structure of the clause than in its surface structure. Thus, in the notional structure we have such roles as agent, experiencer, patient, range, instrumental, locative, source, path, goal, and possibly a few others (Chapters 4 and 5). These categories give us the true dramatis personae, setting, and stage props to which I refer above. But what of such surface structure categories as subject and object? What is their place? Here we also find meaning, but meaning of a more indirect and vague sort. Subject is what we are talking about. It is often equivalent to old information. The object is that on which the reference of the verb is considered to terminate; it is often new information. Furthermore, part of the meaning of surface structure categories is the sum total of the notional categories that they are able to encode. Thus, subject comes to mean something on the order of 'that which we are talking about' or old information partly because it encodes so many varying and different notional relations (e.g., cf. Becker 1966).

On the other hand, it is a curious, psychological test to ask anybody to give an example of a transitive clause in English. Almost invariably they will give you such a sentence as John hit Bill in which John, the subject, is clearly agent. It seems, therefore, that the primary motivating cause for the existence of a surface structure subject tagmeme is to encode agent. This is brought out by tests with aphasic patients. Thus if aphasics are given the sentences, John opened the door, The door opened, and The key opened the door, it will be much easier for the aphasic to handle the first sentence that to handle the other two. Why? For the simple reason that in the first sentence, subject is used in its primary encoding of agent, while in the second sentence, subject encodes patient and in the third sentence, subject encodes instrument. The latter two uses of surface structure subject are secondary rather than primary. Presumably the aphasic finds it easier to handle structures when surface and notional structures are in phase than when surface and notional structures are out of phase (data from Hanna Ulatowska).

What then? Tagmemic structure is a split level affair. To describe the structure of English clauses, one must not simply describe the surface structure clause types, he must also describe the notional structure case frames, i.e., the verb types which characterize each case frame and the roles which associated nouns play within those case frames (cf. Chapter 5). Then one must map the case frames onto the surface structure clause types. We'll find that some clause types are very elastic, i.e., they may stretch over a variety of notional structures). This is true of the English transitive clause type, which embraces a great variety of underlying case frames. Other clause types such as the descriptive clause the book is red and the equative clause John is a soldier are relatively non-elastic structures (the former, however, is also used to encode ambient state predications such as it's hot or it's cold).

Can the tagmemic framework comfortably assimilate the split level separation of grammar into notional and surface structure? There is a built-in temptation within tagmemic theory to want to shift some or all of the notional categories summarized in this volume into a third hierarchy--formerly called lexical, now called referential hierarchy. This was the turn taken, in fact, by such students of Pike as Mary Ruth Wise (1968) and Tom Klammer (1971)--in the days of lexical hierarchy. The temptation was strong within earlier tagmemics because there was much talk of three hierarchies and the third hierarchy was somewhat shadowy and unexploited. Here then, was a chance to fill in the contents of a third hierarchy by considering that notional structures belonged to it. Pike and Pike's present notion of referential hierarchy (1977) has recognized, however, that most notional categories, e.g., case notions, belong to the grammar, and that referential hierarchy embraces the speaker's sum total of knowledge or, in other words, his encyclopedia. I continue to feel that all the notional categories summarized in this volume, including even such discourse level features as plot structures belong to the grammar of discourse.

I have stated elsewhere (Ballard, Conrad, and Longacre 1971a:74) my reason for not wanting to assign notional grammar to a third lexical, semantic, or referential hierarchy. My reluctance to do this is based on the fact that notional and surface structure seem to be very similar in broad outline so that the roles and case frames which we find in predications are not unlike the tagmemes and clause types of surface structure. The former are simply a more consistent and detailed set of categories than the latter. Similarly, the inter-clausal relations which Ballard, Conrad, and I set up for Ibaloi and which have been elaborated elsewhere (Longacre 1972a, 1976, and Chapter 3 of this book) are not different in kind from the surface structure sentence types. Again, they are simply a more consistent and detailed set of categories than we find in surface structure. I believe that both sets of categories, the grammatical surface structure and the notional structure here described, are much more similar to each other than either is to phonology or to matters of referential-content structure.

But to me an even more pressing reason for keeping what I call notional structure within the grammatical hierarchy is the fact that notional and surface structures are not a dichotomy, but POLES. Here the metaphor of deep and surface structure becomes relevant. We often have to face the fact that a certain structure should not be assigned thoughtlessly either to the deep or to the surface but that we have to evaluate its RELATIVE depth. Take, for example, paraphrase. On the deepest level of structure, on the level of pure semantic structure, probably something is said only once and paraphrase does not exist. Perhaps paraphrase is essentially a surface structure phenomenon. On the other hand, we find that the same type of paraphrase may occur in several distinct surface structures (Longacre 1972a.57-62). Thus, in the sentence, _I want to take this poison up; I don't want to let it lie around_ we have negated antonym paraphrase in that _to take up_ and _to let lie around_ are antonyms. When we negate one member of an antonym we come out with one of the closest approximations to a pure paraphrase obtainable in any language anywhere, so that, e.g., _not black, but white_ is a closer paraphrase than to attempt to use any pair of synonyms. But negated antonym paraphrase occurs in more than one surface structure sentence type. Thus, in the sentence quoted above we have what is probably a surface structure paraphrase sentence, i.e. a juxtaposed sentence type which rejects the use of medial conjunction). If we turn the position of the negative and positive members of the pair around we may encode it in the surface structure antithetical sentence (i.e., _I don't want to let this poison lie around, but on the contrary, I want to take it up_). I have furthermore heard such a sentence as this encoded as a simple sentence with a cause margin: _I want to take this poison up, because I don't want to let it lie around_. Here the second clause is probably an abbreviation of something on the order of _I don't want anybody to be hurt by this poison lying around, I don't want any children to eat it_ or something like that. But in the form in which this sentence is cast it is a pure tautology. Here then it is desirable to set up negated antonym paraphrase as a deep structure for the quite sufficient reason that it occurs in more than one surface structure and we need to map it onto those various surface structures. On the other hand, as we have noted, on the very deepest of all levels, on the level of profound semantic structure, probably paraphrase does not exist at all (see Diagram VI). Now if we once separate off our deep or notional structure and put it into a seperate lexemic, semantic, or what-have-you hierarchy, we are in a bind. We no longer can freely treat surface and deep as poles with various degrees of depth between them, but we now must treat these structures as a dichotomy, (i.e., we must decide at every point whether we are dealing with grammatical structure OR lexemic/semantic structure). We cannot really raise the question of what DEGREE of depth a certain analysis reflects because our deep structure is now in an entirely separate hierarchy. Consequently, we will be engaged in endless squabbles as to the precise separation of lexicon from grammar.

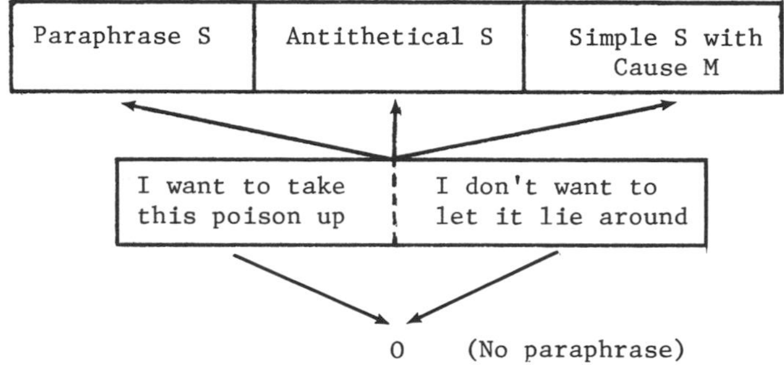

Diagram VI

Paraphrase as a medium-depth notional structure

More positively, however, by associating notional structure and surface structure in the grammar itself, we are able to bring the two into fruitful union and comparison in all sorts of ways. This is precisely what Pike has been doing over a period of years in his multi-celled representations of the tagmeme. Pike's nine-celled tagmeme of 1972 and his present (1977) four-celled tagmeme (Diagram VII) agree in putting surface structure in the top row and notional structure into the second row. Thus, if box one is subject, the box immediately under it is a case category. The same presentation, it seems to me, could be applied to grammatical structure on any hierarchical level. Thus, the surface structure peak of a story could be represented in his cell one and the underlying cell could specify whether it is climax or denouement in the notional structure. My expanded tagmemic apparatuses of the sort illustrated in

Slot	Class(es)
Role	Cohesion

Diagram VII. Pike's four-celled tagmeme (Pike and Pike 1977.35)

the introduction to the Papua New Guinea report (Longacre 1972a.xiv and xxii) do the same thing, in a slightly different way. I separate the old bidimensional array of tagmemics (Longacre 1978.ix-xii) into two halves by drawing a solid line across the center. Under the solid or double line goes the notional structure, above the line goes the surface structure, and at the bottom I have room for any rules or any structural notes that may be needed to guide the mapping process from one to the other (see Diagram VIII).

I have suggested above that we classify surface structures as to elastic and non-elastic structure. Again, I do not mean a dichotomy. I might rather say, we can classify surface structures as to their degree of elasticity, defining elasticity as their versatility in encoding notional structures. In the fourth chapter of my Papua New Guinea report (Longacre 1972a) I have done this in reference to sentence and paragraphstructures in three Papua New Guinea languages. In every case the structures are classified as to their degree of elasticity. We may also classify surface structures as to their degree of TRANSPARENCY. By transparency of surface I mean a surface structure with a minimum of surface structure marking so that the notional structure shows clearly through and must in fact determine to a large degree the analysis. By opaque surface structure, I mean surface structure which is heavily marked and more autonomous of the notional structure.

It is the rule that opaque surface structures invite their being thrown out of phase with the underlying structures. Considerable stylistic effect may be gained by throwing well-marked surface structures out of phase with underlying structures. This can happen especially on the discourse level. Thus (Longacre 1972a. 135-7), I describe a Fore discourse (Scott 1973) in which there are four

+ $Base_1$ ($Action_1$)		+Simultaneous Link	+$Base_2$ ($Action_2$)	±Simultaneous Link	+$Base_3$ ($Action_3$)
Indicative clause Simple sentence		jey	Indicative clause Simple sentence Direct quote sentence	jey	(probably the same as $Base_2$)
Overlap	$\underline{P}$	Δ	$\underline{Q}$		but only
	$\underset{.}{P}$	Δ	$\underline{Q}$		examples
	$\underline{P}$	Δ	$\underset{.}{Q}$		here are:
Succession	$\underset{.}{P}$	$\Delta_{\rightarrow}$	$\underset{.}{Q}$(Cf. Eventuation sentence)		P $\Delta_{\rightarrow}$ $\underset{.}{Q}$ $\Delta_{\rightarrow}$ $\underset{.}{R}$
Coupling	Pa	Λ	Qa(Cf. Coordinate sentence)		
Paraphrase	gPa	≡	sPa(Cf. Paraphrase sentence		
	Pa	≡	$\overline{P}$a"(Cf. Paraphrase sentence		
Rule: Bases may permute.					

Diagram VIII. Simultaneous sentence

notional structure episodes, followed by notional structure climax and notional structure denouement which in turn breaks down hierarchi callyinto an embedded discourse with stage, episode 1, episode 2, all this being followed by closure. In the surface structure, however, episodes 1 and 2 of the underlying structure of the main discourse are grouped into one surface structure paragraph, while episodes 3 and 4 of the underlying structure of the main discourse are similarly grouped into one surface structure paragraph. That we have these four underlying episodes is undeniable. There is a recycling of lexical materials much as we have, for example, in such a fairy tale as "The Three Little Pigs". Nevertheless, in surface structurealthough there is clear transition lexically, i.e., in terms of the lexical items used, between episode 1 and episode 2, they constitute but one surface structure paragraph (the paragraph in Fore being equivalent to a chain with a final verb at the end, while sentences within the paragraph are the domain of the same subject. There is, furthermore, reason to believe that this is done partly to achieve stylistic effect in the Fore tale (i.e., as the story progresses toward its surface structure peak), there is a bringing into phase of the surface structure units and the notional structure episodes which are out of phase in text initial.

This in-phase out-of-phase game of musical chairs also applies to discourse genre and type. To refer again to the newspaper story mentioned in Chapter 1, 1.3, we have here a firsthand account by a reporter of an apartment fire (Davenport 1973). Covertly this is a first person narrative, but in the surface structure it has all the hallmarks of a procedural discourse: "You awake at three o'clock a.m., you smell fire, you run out to the kitchen, etc." (i.e., the choice of pronoun is that of a non-specific person as in procedural discourse and the choice of tense is that of projected time rather than the accomplished time of a narrative). In this case, the newspaper reporter has chosen to cast his narrative into the surface structure of procedural text. He is, of course, fooling nobody. He is giving a first person account of what happened, but he tries to take you there so that you can feel that all this could happen to you and this is what you as an apartment dweller might find yourself doing in a fire. The tension here between the surface structure and the notional structure is stylistically very effective. Similarly, we may ask an informant in an aboriginal culture for a procedural discourse on how to build a house, we get instead a narrative discourse: "How My Father Built His House Exceptionally Well" (cf. for example, two Dibabawon texts in Longacre 1968. 3.269-78). Here we have our desire for a procedural text satisfied not by a step-by-step procedure, but by the story of how a capable master-builder built a house in that culture. The underlying purpose of procedure is answered in a surface structure narrative. Or surface structure narrative and drama may be used to teach moral lessons, where we encode hortatory content in surface structure narrative or dramatic form.

The point to be learned from study of Fore--and the text just mentioned in particular--is that opaqueness of surface structure invites this stylistic throwing of notional and surface structures out of phase. Considerations of relative transparency of surface structures are not limited, however, to the higher levels. It is a valid observation that in clause units the nuclei of the distinctive clause types contain tagmemes that are better marked in the surface structures than are the tagmemes of the peripheries. Thus, while surface structure tagmemic analysis quickly uncovers predicates, subjects and objects of various sorts, there is more slowness and hesitancy regarding analysis of such peripheral tagmemes as location, time, manner, etc. While I, for example, have favored a rather extensive and full labeling of such structures, others (e.g., Franklin 1971) have wanted to lump many such structures together as surface structure ADJUNCTS. Apparently, nuclear tagmemes are less transparent (or even opaque) by comparison with peripheral tagmemes. The notional structure shines through the peripheral tagmemes to the extent that some tagmemicists feel that there is almost no surface structure to be found there. Regarding a syntagmeme as a wave it should be no surprise that waves are thicker and less transparent at their crest than on their onset and decay.

I believe that these two concepts of relative elasticity and transparency of syntagmemes and parts of syntagmemes are capable of being worked up into an insightful theory of surface structure. Note, too, how well such concepts fit into a dynamic WAVE approach to linguistic structure instead of a static one--as does also the emphasis on deep and surface structures as poles rather than as a dichotomy.

10. SURFACE STRUCTURE MEANING

Early in this chapter I affirmed my belief in surface structure meaning and thus took issue with those who consider surface structure to be postsemantic. In one sense, my contention here is simply a reaffirmation of the old belief that any change in wording must perforce lead to a change in meaning (i.e., that no exact paraphrases exist). But the issue in the present context is: should all distinctions in surface structure wording be imputed to notional structure distinctions or is a choice among similar surface structures in itself a meaningful choice in that those very structures carry overtones of meaning.

Put slightly differently the issue is: shall we elaborate ad infinitum our notional structures to accommodate any and all shades of meaning or can we let part of the meaning reside in the surface structures of various languages?

The latter point is so important that it invites reinforcement. Chafe (1970.86-7) objects to Lakoff's suggestion that such sentences as the following have the same underlying structure:

a) Seymour sliced the salami with a knife
b) Seymour used a knife to slice the salami

Chafe objects that there are differences of meaning involved in these two sentences. Since Chafe equates semantic structure with underlying structure, and since surface structure is in his view post-semantic and phonological, he has no choice but to elaborate here whatever notional-semantic-underlying structures are necessary to explain the differences in meaning between the two sentences. My point of view here is that (1) the underlying structure is the same, (i.e. a predication involving a verb of action-process plus nouns in the roles of agent, patient, and instrument); and that (2) the surface structures with their attendant overriding meanings are different. Thus, (a) above has a surface structure which means 'transitive action with object and instrument'. (I posit here a surface structure instrument adjunct consisting of with plus a noun phrase.) The first sentence reflects rather faithfully--and without further semantic overtones--the notions that it encodes. The second sentence (b), however, overlays it own surface structure meaning 'one action performed in order to achieve another action' over the meaning of the underlying case frame-- which it presents as TWO predications. The second sentence has a surface structure (nucleus plus purpose margin) which typically encodes FINAL CAUSE (cf. Chapter 3). The use of this surface structure here in use a knife to slice the salami adds an element of deliberacy and teleology which is not found in the first sentence. We can imagine the following exchange:

A) We didn't have a paring knife so Jim used an obsidian blade to pare the apple.
B) How smart of him! I wouldn't have thought to do that. Isn't that a new use for an obsidian blade?
A) No, it's a rather OLD use.

Notice how well use an x to do y fits into the above exchange where improvisation in tools is featured in this discourse.

In such an analysis as I suggest here surface structure is not post-semantic and largely phonological. It is not a mere end product of the process of transformational derivation. Rather choice of one surface structure against another is a meaningful option on the part of the speaker in accordance with the overall thrust of his discourse or some part of it.

In the remainder of this section I try to marshall examples to further demonstrate--at certain points and in certain languages--a tension (even a conflict of sorts) between the acknowledged notional structure meaning and the imputed surface structure meaning. If we can demonstrate that people react to both sorts of meaning this may be taken as evidential for the existence of meaning correlates in the surface structure. Misunderstanding, humorous uses of language, and intentional distortions of meaning are relevant here for they are based on double meanings which sometimes prove illuminating.

I emphasized above the primacy of agent as the notional structure which most characteristically encodes within the English subject slot (in active clauses). All case frames that can be classified as action or as action process (Chapter 2) have surface structures in which the active subject is agent. Is it any wonder, then, that some overtones of this notional structure meaning become associated with the surface structure active subject slot? Let us call this overtone meaning which is associated with the active subject, the ACTOR. Our task then is to see if the surface structure meaning actor attaches to certain surface structure active clauses which do not encode an underlying agent. Let us begin with the physical action process case frame (E 3) which permits transformation to several special surface structure focus types in which the underlying instrument or patient is encoded as subject. I suggest here that the overtone meaning of actor attaches even to such sentences as the following:

<u>This</u> <u>key</u> <u>opens</u> <u>that</u> <u>door</u>.
<u>The</u> <u>door</u> <u>opened</u> <u>silently</u>.

That we tend to regard <u>key</u> as an actor of sorts in the first example can be seen from such a dialogue as the following:

A) I won't need a doorman anymore.
B) Why?
A) I got a key made. Don't keys open doors?

In the second example we likewise tend to regard the door itself as actor. A dialogue such as the following would not be inappropriate:

A) The door opened silently at exactly 12:00 midnight.
B) It opened by itself?
A) I dunno. But I didn't SEE anybody open it.

In still other examples such as This store opens at 9:00 and closes at 6:00 the store may even be a metonymical reference in which the physical building stands for the business and those who work there--in which case the reference to some sort of actor is not at all farfetched.

In examples of patient as subject in which successful process is implied we still get overtones of actor (i.e., of the subject as something active in the process):

A) This fabric washes well.
B) Good, have you been able to get it to wash itself yet?

On occasion, a surface structure clause type that is intransitive and encodes something other than agent, may be perversely or facetiously misunderstood as an encoding of a case frome which involves an agent. Consider (with apologies to women readers) the following bit of male chauvinism:

The light that lies in woman's eyes, and lies, and lies, and LIES!

Here, the light that lies in woman's eyes is initially understood as a locative state predication with a notional structure similar to The key is in the drawer or The key is lying in the drawer. At all events light is to be understood as patient. It is evident, however, in the second half of the line that lies is to be reinterpreted as a verb of speech and light is to be construed as the agent/source. This pun is based not merely on the presence of homophones ('to recline' versus 'to prevaricate') but on the fact that the subject slot so readily carries overtones of actor.

English intransitive clauses which are derived by suppressing the patient (of the corresponding transitive clause) provide an illustration of surface structure intransitivity imposed over underlying transitivity (in physical action process case frame). Thus we have *Mother washes every Monday and irons every Tuesday*. Here the notional structure patient (probably *clothes*) is suppressed and we have the surface structure of an intransitive clause (Appendix A). What is gained by the transformation in which an essentially transitive predication is expressed as intransitive? Apparently, what is achieved is focus on the predicate itself (as an activity). Thus, in the first dialogue below the question provokes an answer as to what was washed, while in the second dialogue the question centers on what activities are afoot:

I. A. *Your Mother certainly had a long line of clothes this morning. What all did she wash?*
B. *She washed the accumulated dirty clothes of my two older brothers and their families. They had been traveling for four days.*

II. A. *What does your Mother do on Mondays?*
B. *She washes.*

Notice that in (II) above the activity still involves the washing of clothes and the activity is still an action process but the surface structure is intransitive with predicate focus.

Somewhat similar are surface structure intransitive clauses (of the same case frame) that suppress the reflexive object:

He washed and shaved.

Here again, the focus is on the predicate itself.

Note also surface structure passive clauses in English. These are considered at length in Chapter 5, 2.3, where I assign the surface structure meaning FOCUSED UNDERGOER to the construction. I note also at that point a predilection of the passive for general, i.e. gnomic statements.

Surface structure meaning can also be illustrated in reference to sentence structure. The English surface structure antithetical sentence carries the meaning OPPOSITION. The notional structures that it most frequently encodes--and which result in the acquisition of this surface structure meaning--are contrast and expectancy reversal (see Chapter 3). How does it happen, however, that this surface structure also encodes underlying negated antonym paraphrase? Thus, we have sentences like:

It's not black, but on the contrary it's white.

and more briefly:

It's not black but white.

We can imagine a dialogue such as:

Q. *Where's that old blackened pan of yours?*
A. *It's not black but white. I scoured it for two hours this morning.*

Nevertheless, although the fuller structure might be *It's not black--as you say; but white--as I say* (cf. underlying contrast), as stated here we have a surface structure which expresses opposition overlaying notional structure paraphrase. The result is a conflate meaning: emphasis on antonyms.

The English antithetical sentence has a gnomic subvariety often used to express proverbial or quasi-proverbial sayings:

Man proposes; God disposes.
Old men for council; young men for war.

It is therefore somewhat disconcerting to be told the following:

Heads I win; tails you lose.

We here expect opposition but we don't get it; the underlying structure is probably a variety of paraphrase. The meaning that comes through is: 'I've rigged it so that you lose in any and all circumstances.'

The English coordinate sentence exists to encode coupling (cf. Chapter 3) as in:

I'm a salesman, my brother is a university professor, and my sister, a ballet dancer.

Nevertheless temporal succession may be expressed in a coordinate sentence--even without use of then:

I got up and got myself some breakfast.

Here the speaker simply reports two activities. Had he cared to make explicit the time sequence he could have said after I got up I got myself some breakfast. The coordinate sentence, when encoding temporal succession plays down the temporal element.

Likewise a coordinate sentence may encode contrast as in:

My horse is black and your horse is white.

Here the speaker is deemphasizing the contrast. In fuller context he might have said:

Okay, my horse is black and your horse is white--what's so wonderful about that?

Stylistically, then, the coordinate sentence, when used to encode other than coupling plays down and deemphasizes the notion that it encodes--and this must be considered to be a semantic feature of its surface structure.

In many areas of the world (e.g., Philippines and Papua New Guinea), there are contrasting sentence types, the sequence sentence and the simultaneous sentence. In Ibaloi (northern Philippines) distinct conjunctions separate three types of sequence sentences from the simultaneous sentence (Ballard, Conrad, Longacre 1971). Among these asan is a coordinating (sequence) conjunction which means 'and then'; and jey is a coordinating (simultaneous) conjunction which means 'while' or 'at the same time'. An asan sentence may have an indefinite number of bases and has certain restrictions such as the rule that all component clauses must have the same subject. A jey sentence has two or at the most three bases (rare) and does not share the restrictions of an asan sentence. The asan sentence regularly encodes temporal overlap. It is surprising to find, however, some examples of jey sentences which unmistakenly encode temporal succession as in:

> They withdrew to the hills jey the Spaniards arrived.

Here it is evident in context that the withdrawal preceded the arrival of the Spaniards since no one was found in the village on the latter's arrival. Why then is the simultaneous sentence with jey used to express this situation? Evidently, here the sense is 'about as soon as they had withdrawn the Spaniards arrived'. In brief, surface structure simultaneity imposed over notional structure succession yields CLOSE SUCCESSION in Ibaloi. Simultaneous sentences with jey are also found embedded in other Ibaloi sentences; there the use of jey serves to emphasize the logical connection of the coupled clauses as opposed to the embedding matrix sentence--even if simultaneity is not involved.

In the previous section of this chapter examples are given of surface structure procedural discourse which encodes narration, and of surface structure narrative discourse which encodes procedure. Here, again, the simplest way to explain the stylistic effects achieved is to posit that there are meanings attached to the surface structures of both procedural and narrative discourses.

We cannot, then, assign all meaning to the deep, underlying, or notional structure, and only formal characteristics to the surface structure. In the next section I argue that we likewise cannot assign all the formal characteristics to the surface structure and no formal characteristics to the notional structure.

11. NOTIONAL STRUCTURE FORM

It is especially evident on the level of interpredicate relations (cf. Chapter 3) that there are formal characteristics of notional structure. These formal characteristics are configurations in which synonyms, antonyms, repeated predicates, repeated but negated predicates, identical terms, nonidentical terms, or the same item now as first term now as second term all play their parts. Consequently, with an extensive but still limited set of symbols one is able to represent these patterns, and teach them to others who in turn can go out to look for them in various languages. Thus

$Pa \wedge Pb \wedge Pc$ can be only parallel coupling. We need only to teach the student to look for the same predicate repeated with regular change of one term in the successive repetitions (and NO 'or' signal). The same formal structure with an 'or' signal is alternation: $Pa \vee Pb \vee Pc$. $Pa \wedge P''b$ can be only contrast. Here we teach the student to look for antonymical predicates with differing terms. I will not labor this point further. The whole complicated symbolism worked out in Chapter 3 can be invoked here, however.

What then? Surface structure, while primarily the domain of form, has some meaning correlates. Likewise, notional structure, while primarily the domain of meaning, has some formal correlates. Here as elsewhere every linguistic unit is a form-meaning composite.

12. MAPPING OF NOTIONAL LEVELS ONTO SURFACE LEVELS

To begin with, I note that the number of underlying levels eventually arrived at in our survey of notional categories is now the same as the number of surface levels posited for English (and probably for most languages). It was not my original intent to come out with such congruence. I assumed, rather, that notional and surface organizations would differ more radically. That a certain congruence is found indicates notional structure motivation for the surface structure levels.

Roughly speaking, derivation matches the surface structure stem level, inflection matches the word level, concretion the phrase, predication the clause, proposition the sentence, repartee the paragraph, and plot the discourse. But some qualifications are necessary. Concretion makes a somewhat poor match with phrase in that only a very few surface structure noun phrases encode concretions. Repartee makes a poor match with paragraph. While surface structure dialogue paragraphs encode repartee, other surface structure paragraph types encode elements of the propositional (combinational level. Nevertheless, it is significant that we cannot get along in the notional structure with FEWER levels than we find in the full scheme of hierarchical surface structure.

It seems that the purpose for the existence of the surface structure clause is to encode underlying predications. Therefore, the primary encoding of the notional predication is as a surface structure clause. But we know very well that in most if not all languages a notional predication need not necessarily encode as a surface structure clause. It may be nominalized into a phrase or into a word structure, so that John hit Bill may be partially nominalized to John's hitting of Bill and even more thoroughly nominalized as John's blow.

A notional structure predication may also in some languages be expressed as a surface structure sequence of two clauses, usually two clauses in rather close partnership (often in a MERGED SENTENCE, but not necessarily so). Thus in Trique, John said to Mary is expressed as John said Mary heard without any phonological pause between the two clauses, but with as much phonological unity as a single clause. Here a surface structure sentence encodes an underlying predication, with a verb of speech, an agent, and an experiencer. Likewise in Trique there are no verbs bring or take. These are expressed rather by such two-clause combinations as the following: I had the basket I came meaning 'I brought the basket' or I had the basket I went meaning 'I took the basket'. Here again a notional structure predication is expressed as two surface structure clauses.

A common phenomenon in West Africa is the expression of instrument as a two-clause combination in such a sentence as I had the knife cut the meat meaning 'I cut the meat with a knife' (Pike 1966:66-9). It seems to me that this surface structure is just as specialized as any Indo-European structure with a special instrument case. I had the knife cut the meat is just as specialized in structure as I cut the meat with a knife. It does not mean 'First I took the knife and then I cut the meat' for no temporal succession is involved. It cannot even be paraphrased well as 'I used the knife cut the meat' unless we understand that the use of the knife is precisely in the act of cutting the meat; it is not an act separate from the latter. We must get together the cutting of the meat with the use of the knife. I think this is best done by setting up a notional role INSTRUMENT in universal grammar and saying that in West African languages we have an underlying predication expressed as a surface structure merged sentence. All these encodings of a predication as something other than a surface structure clause (whether word, phrase, or sentence) are secondary encodings, in that the primary encoding of a predication is the surface structure clause.

We may say also that the reason for the existence of a surface structure sentence is to package together several predications. As we have seen, paragraph is a looser bundle with more deliberate seriatim treatment of its constituent elements. Nevertheless, both the surface structure of the sentence and of the paragraph are best considered to be primary encodings of the elements of the notional structure (i.e., of the statement or propositional calculus). This unique situation--that one underlying level should have two primary encodings as surface levels--lies behind the fact that in some languages (cf. Section 6) sentence and paragraph are not distinguished. Certain elements of the statement calculus may on occasion, however, be encoded as single clauses. Thus, notional structure contrast of the EXCEPTION variety as in Everybody-minus-John didn't speak up, John spoke up (with the presupposition that John is a member of everybody), typically encodes as a surface structure clause with an adjunct unit in English: Nobody except John spoke up. English here illustrates a secondary encoding of elements from the statement calculus.

Repartee is the notional structure of dialogue. Although repartee primarily and typically encodes as s surface structure dialogue paragraph, we may encounter secondary encoding of repartee as a surface structure sentence. There is a limited use of this in English: When I asked her how she felt, she answered 'Fine'. Here the question is in a sentence margin, i.e., in the time margin , and the answer is in the sentence nucleus. Western Bukidnon Manobo (Elkins 1971) has a question and answer sentence with both question and answer in the sentence nucleus. Such structures are not uncommon. It is somewhat rarer, however, to have full-fledged dialogue of an unrestricted sort reported in a single sentence, yet this happens in certain South American languages (cf. Chapter 2). Here the whole long string which reports a dialogue can be one sentence; subordinate verbs signal same or different subject from that of the main verb. The same dialogue can, however, be reported equally well as a paragraph with each speech verb in its quotation formula a main verb which concludes a separate sentence. Here again we have an interesting option between encoding the same material as a sentence and encoding it as a paragraph. It would appear that again it's a matter of whether we want to present it as a package deal. Moreover, the overall structure of the discourse or some part of it may be the crucial determing factor.

Plot, etc. is the notional structure of discourse. Narrowly speaking, plot is the structure of narrative discourse; the etc. following plot is a reminder that similar structure must exist for other discourse types. I presented in Chapter 1 the rhetorician's scheme of plot structure and showed that it is insightful to consider this to be the notional structure of narrative discourse.

I will make short shrift of the lower notional levels and refer the reader again to Chapter 6 where they are discussed. Derivation as used here refers to the features of nouns and verbs that enable us to classify them, as verbs are classified in Chapter 5. These features are either inherent in morphemes and stems or are added via surface level stem formation. The notional structure status of adjectives is discussed in the same chapter. There is evidence that not merely noun and verb but adjective as well should be posited in the underlying structure.

Inflection covers such verbal increments as space-time coordinates, phasals, aspect, modalities, and inferentials, and such nominal increments as definite, generic, aggregate, plural, dual, unique, random, and allotive. These features are often marked by verbal or nominal affixes on the word level or by elements in the verb phrase or noun phrase. Verbal inflection (phasals and aspect) partially emerges in the surface structure of English as merged sentence, i.e., verb plus complement.

The concretion level must be posited to take care of certain noun phrases that cannot be explained by clause conjoining. How much surface structure this level should be considered to underlie is still problematical. Does the use of quantifiers and deictics with nouns belong here? If adjectives have status in the notional structure, do adjective-noun groupings--or at least some such groupings--have concretion

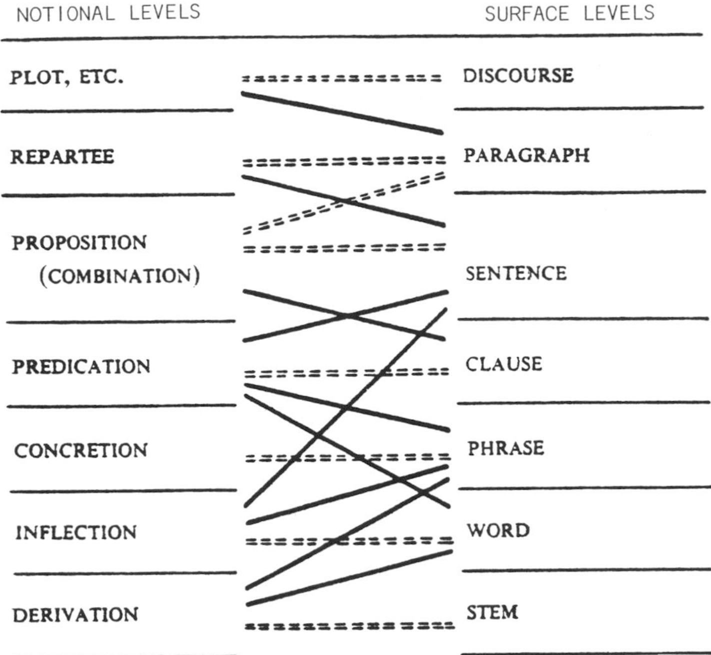

Diagram IX
Spaghetti mappings of notional and surface levels

as their notional structure? What about kinship and body parts, the inalienably possessed items of many languages? Are they more naturally analyzed as noun phrases than as predications? Once we know--as we now know--that SOME noun phrases have notional structure correlates in a level such as is here posited, what is the limit of usefulness of this notion and where does its abuse begin? I have likewise suggested (Chapter 6, Section 3.2) that certain closely-knit causative constructions in English could be considered to be verbal concretions.

A tentative diagram (Diagram IX) of some notional surface mapping among hierarchical levels is appended here (cf. Longacre 1972a. 87). In this diagram double lines indicate primary encodings and single lines secondary encodings.

This diagram is simply a device for indicating in broad outline how the notional levels relate to the surface structure levels. Within the context of a given language such a summary device can (and ultimately should) be accompanied by rules which spell out in detail the mapping process.

Again, we note that once a surface structure is well articulated (opaque) then we can begin to play the game of throwing surface structures out of phase with notional structures. Indeed, successful discourse structure requires this. If, for example, every predication in the underlying structure is a surface structure clause, we find a discourse so diffuse (and confused) that it is impossible to thread our way through it. It is essential that certain predications be nominalized or at least subordinated in some fashion and shoved to the side. They must not be permitted to impede the flow of the discourse. Similarly, in discourse it is often important that a sequence of predications be bundled into the same sentence and disposed of summarily without being given undue attention by development as separate sentences. Again, the flow of discourse would be inpeded were we to do otherwise. Conversely, there are spots in a discourse where great poignancy is achieved by separate clauses and by separate sentences.

13. TAGMEME AND SYNTAGMEME IN THIS SETTING

We might well wonder, once we have such a split level structure, just where all this leaves tagmeme and syntagmeme. Perhaps we need to go back to an early clue in Pike's original formulation of tagmemics, i.e., back to his trimodal structure, with its distinction of the feature mode versus the manifestation mode versus the distribution mode. Let us say that notional structure belongs primarily to the feature mode of the grammar, although

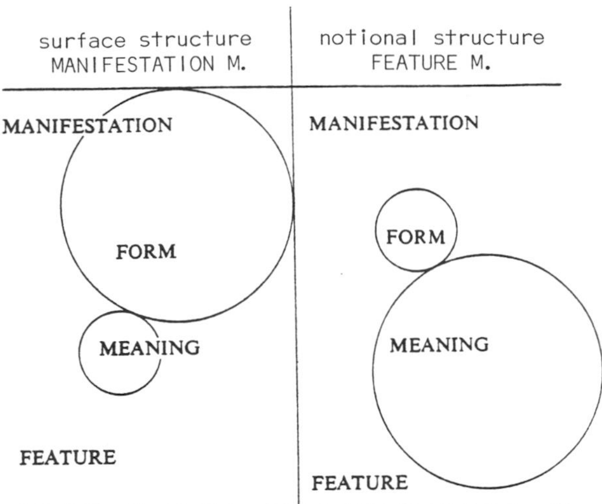

Diagram X
Relative Importance of Form and Meaning
in Notional and Surface Grammar

its units like any units are characterized by all three modes of structure. Let us say also that surface structure belongs primarily to the manifestation mode of the grammar although its units in turn are trimodally structured. Such a view of things enables us to accept meaning in the surface structure and form in the notional structure, while leading us to expect to find most of the formal characteristics in the surface structure and most of the meaning in the notional structure. The explanation is simple. If surface structure is the manifestation mode (of grammar), then its formal characteristics are the manifestation mode of the manifestation mode, i.e., the formal characteristics are doubly reinforced. If notional structure is the feature mode, then the meaning associated with it is the feature mode of the feature mode (of grammar), i.e., meaning is doubly reinforced. This point is aptly made by my late colleague Darlene Bee in her posthumous work.

"...we acknowledge that the really significant part of the feature mode of language is indeed its feature mode...." (1973:10). Note the accompanying Diagram X.

This view of notional and surface structure has further appeal in that it seems to be coming increasingly clear that underlying structure is essentially unordered, i.e., the elements of the underlying structure (aside from occurrence in temporal succession) are an unordered set. As elements of the feature mode, rather than of the manifestation mode, the lack of linear ordering is understandable. In the manifestation mode, however, the structure is linearly ordered. The degree and rigidity of the linear ordering varies, of course, from language to language and from structure to structure within a given language. Nevertheless, linearity is a feature of surface structure, not of notional structure, and this would seem to fit well the assignment of the former to the manifestation mode.

I do not object to presenting tagmeme and syntagmeme in any way a person wants to present them--via Pike's nine boxes, his abbreviated six boxes, or his four boxes--provided this is not permitted to obscure the fact that primarily the tagmeme is a function-set correlation. Indeed there is no reason why any of these notions per se need obscure the concept of the tagmeme. At any rate, function has to be understood in a split-level way with reference to surface structure function and to possible encodings of notional structure function. This of necessity complicates our notation. Syntagmeme must also be understood in a split-level fashion, in terms not only of surface structure construction types, but in terms of such notional units as case frames which encode within those constructions. I have attempted to adjust to these necessities by expanding the tagmemic apparatus for a syntagmeme (cf. Section 9). That these are complications in a once simpler theory is not to be denied. We can choose to view these complications as an embarrassment or an enrichment. I, with Pike, choose the second option. And both of us have to work out new notations to accomodate the enriched theory.

14. MULTIPLE PERSPECTIVE

From early in the development of tagmemics, Pike has argued (1959) that alternative perspectives on linguistic reality are particle, wave, and field. Just as in physics it has been impossible to explain light exclusively as particle or wave, but has been necessary to take insights from both concepts and add to them the idea of light as a field in which energy is distributed, so with language. It is a fact, however, that most work in syntax and in discourse analysis has been particle-oriented. We have assumed that there are discrete non-overlapping parts of the discourse.

Obviously, discourse could be approached with considerable profit from the standpoint that it consists of wave phenomena. Waves have centers and waves may intersect each other, partly cancelling each other out, or creating defraction grids of various sorts. Thus we often have a problem in the analysis of a discourse as to precisely where one paragraph ends and another begins. We can feel very certain that there are two paragraphs involved, but does a given sentence terminate one paragraph or initiate the following? Again, we may feel certain that there are two embedded discourses at a certain point in a matrix discourse, but does a given paragraph terminate one discourse or initiate the following? Again, in a complex discourse we may assume that there is an introductory part at the beginning which introduces the whole discourse, but then when we are faced with the first embedded discourse of the main discourse, we wonder if we should not have made that same section introductory to the embedded discourse. We are faced with the problem, does this given section introduce the main discourse or the embedded discourse? We may have a similar problem regarding closure of a book. Does a certain paragraph, section, or long embedded discourse close the whole book, or does it close simply some part of the book? Some of these problems are reminiscent of problems in phonology. Thus we may be very sure that we have two syllable nuclei, two bursts of energy actualizing as vowels, but with several consonants at the border between the syllable there may be genuine doubt as to whether a given consonant belongs to the coda of one syllable or the initiation of the next syllable.

A beginning at handling of discourse as wave phenomena (cf. also Pike 1970:46-51) was made in Linda Lloyd's analysis of the Epistle to the Hebrews (Lloyd 1976). Thus, e.g., she takes the first four verses of Chapter 1 of that epistle as introductory to the whole epistle, but also introductory to embedded discourses on three layers of embedding. She likewise takes the material in verses 4:11-13 as simultaneously concluding discourses on several layers of embedding.

This, of course, is a wave perspective instead of a particle perspective. Presumably, waves can overlap, but particles do not so conveniently overlap with each other. Nevertheless, it is worth pointing out that tagmemics with its separation of function-slot from filler set facilitates such an approach. We can have two function slots such as closure of one discourse and introduction of the second which are filled by the same portmanteau paragraph. The system is not jarred by absorbing such innovations. Meanwhile we can hang loose regarding whether to use or not use such concepts in a given discourse. There is no reason why two waves cannot be discrete, i.e., why one wave cannot end before the following wave starts. On the other hand, one wave may continue into the onset of the following wave. The question is, to approach the data at this point with an open mind and see where the data lead us. Meanwhile, it is not amiss to point out that if wave insights prove as valuable as this, a more thorough-going wave approach to discourse and to linguistics in general, might well be fruitful if one were to embark on such a course of research and development.

It seems to me that those who emphasize cohesion and network rather than structure in relation to discourse and paragraph, are essentially approaching discourse and paragraph as a field structure rather than as particle or wave. As such, no one can deny the validity of their perspective within the basic assumption of tagmemics, even though they themselves work outside these assumptions.

15. A TRIMODAL MODEL

As seen in section 13 of this chapter, another tenet of tagmemics since its inception has been the belief in trimodal structure. This is not a belief that language has three components: a phonological component, a grammatical component, and a lexical (or what-have-you) component. It is rather a belief that the whole of language may be described by any one component, (i.e., the whole discourse may be handled in terms of its phonology, the whole discourse in terms of its grammar, or the whole discourse in terms of its content or colligational structure).

The history of this notion has been very complex within tagmemics. As originally stated by Pike (1954-60), trimodal structure was something very subtle. The three modes were called the feature mode, the manifestation mode, and the distribution mode. In speaking of the phonology, the grammar, and the content structure of a discourse, we have to take account of the fact that any one of the three is trimodally structured. A phonological unit such as the phoneme has its feature mode, its manifestation mode, and its distribution mode according to Pike's original formulation. But feature mode is especially related to phonology; manifestation mode is especially related to the content or the lexical structure; and distribution mode is especially related to the grammar. So we come out in the end with phonology, grammar, and lexicon as somewhat equivalent to the three original modes which Pike posited. Actually, looking at the current context of things in various schools of grammar besides tagmemics, there is nothing all so revolutionary about positing phonology, grammar, and lexicon (or semantics) as separate concerns. The pie may, however, be cut various ways, especially in regard to what we posit as the third mode. More about that later.

Certainly a discourse has phonology. There is a phonology of large units. It has long been recognized, ever since the old juncture days of Trager and his contemporaries, that what happens at the borders of large phonological units (although ignored as units) seriously affects the phones that are found there. Thus, we may have voicing or devoicing, presence of glottal attack or aspirated release, relative speed-up or slow-down, intonational rise or fall, and the like. The careful observation of such phenomena, especially in the work of Eunice Pike (1977) and Sarah Gudschinsky, was pivotal in the development of discourse phonology (as Mayers, 1976, now calls it). Thus, a discourse has a final intonational wind-down. It indicates large breaks within it by pronounced phonological junctures. Within these units, which we may call phonological paragraphs, there are phonological sentences with a different sort of phonological event happening at their boundaries. In turn, within the phonological sentence there occur phonological clauses, phonological phrases, and phonological feet and syllables, on down to the phoneme itself. This phonological organization is not arbitrary or meaningless. Note for instance, the careful analysis of intonational units as "information units" by Halliday (1967) in his work on English clause structure.

That a discourse has grammar is of course one of the main assumptions of this volume. It is assumed by such people as myself that there are grammatical discourses and grammatical paragraphs, there is a slot-class structure of such units, there is a tree structure of such units, and there are overt signals to mark the surface structure of such units, and there are transformations which may be carried out on the structure of even large units such as discourse and paragraph. There is a notional or deep structure which must be derived into a surface structure, just as with any lower level units such as clause or sentence.

But what else is there to the study of discourse? One thing which must not be forgotten is the sheer content or colligational structure of a discourse. Such work was carried on extensively by Zellig Harris and his students in the 50's and 60's. An attempt is made in Harris style discourse analysis (1952a, 1952b, 1963) to standardize the grammar as much as possible from sentence to sentence throughout a discourse. If a discourse can all be reduced to a standard grammatical format then in a sense the grammatical structure of the discourse can be set aside (like finding the lowest common denominator in an equation and then eliminating the denominators) and we can concentrate on its colligational structure. The questions of importance then become; What lexical items occur? How do they collocate with each other? What equivalence chains are there? How do equivalence chains of lexical items collocate with each other? In this way an abstract representation of the content structure of the discourse is achieved.

Meanwhile, Pike, and more recently, Pike and Pike, have been developing first lexical and now referential hierarchy as the third mode of structure allowed for in tagmemics. I have been for a long time skeptical about the hierarchical structuring of the third mode. It seemed to me that it was more like an encyclopedia than a hierarchical structure. On the other hand, a reference encyclopedia must have its information available in some fashion and it is quite certain that we do not have anything akin to mechanical alphabetization to keep track of information in the human brain. Rather, it appears, that information is kept track of in the human brain by virtue of patterns of similarity and difference in information content. If we grant this, then probably some organizing principle of semantic hierarchy in terms of general and specific is involved as well. It seems to me, therefore, more and more feasible that some sort of hierarchical arrangement is required if we keep track of information as we do in the human brain. The concept of FRAMES that van Dijk (1977.135ff, 159ff) and others have been developing is probably an intermediate level of referential organization (Metzing 1980). It is much similar to the term script as used by other people (Shank 1975, Jones 1977.116ff). It is also certain that within a language there are various universes of discourse which organize extensive areas of the vocabulary of that language. We therefore seem to have at least hierarchical organization and referential structure which involves the levels concept, frame, universe of discourse, and the entire language.

Granting, however, that the linguist can discuss somewhat independently the phonology, the grammar, and the content or referential structure of a discourse, we are confronted with several further questions. One is the problem of relating the three modes of structure to each other. Do they relate as in stratificational grammar? It is important to note here that the modes of structure here sketched do not really correspond well to the three strata of some brands of stratificational theory. The content structure, i.e., the surface structure vocabulary, even when highly abstracted and tabulated (as in Harris's discourse analysis) does not correspond well to the sememic stratum. The sememic stratum of stratificational grammar encodes much of what we have within the notional or deep structure of the grammar proper in our way of looking at things. A more interesting question might be that of trying to correlate the phonology and grammar of a tagmemic approach with the apparently parallel strata in stratificational theory. Stratificational grammar has had considerable success in encoding grammar into phonology, but this has been almost entirely on the lower levels having to do with such relations as that of morpheme to phoneme. It remains to be seen whether, granted a full discourse phonology and a full discourse grammar, stratificational grammar can work out simple and helpful rules regarding how grammar relates to phonology on the higher levels. There is a great deal of skewing and a great deal of failure of coinciding at the boundaries of the two sorts of units.

My personal feeling is that we would do better to relate the three modes in terms of intersection of different structures. To go back to the symbol of wave once more, if we have phonological waves, and grammatical waves, and referential waves, and we think of these as intersecting at various angles, we get a defraction grid of interfering wave patterns. We get an overall pattern of great complexity which is a product of the three waves which hit each other at various angles. Or to take a different figure of speech, we have three grids and looking through the three we get a moiré pattern which is the result of the intersection of the three. At any rate, discourse as we confront it in real life is a whole. We get the impact of it as a whole. We do not stop to analyze out its phonology, its grammar, or its colligational structure. It hits us with all its complex interrelationships. I suggest that using the figures of defraction grids, moiré patterns, interference, or something of this sort, the time is much overdue for us to make a serious attack on the interrelationships of phonology, grammar, and content structure.

Another possible avenue of research would be to use more effectively the concepts of underlying and surface structure in phonology, grammar, and lexicon. Thus, we could say that a given discourse has of necessity a minimal phonology, a minimal grammar (even if we were to reduce it to the standard grammar form that Harris uses in doing his content analysis), and some sort of minimal lexicon (pre-lexical notions?) which is subsequently elaborated into surface structure lexicon of great versatility and flexibility. If we could relate in some fairly straight-forward way the deep (notional) grammar, the deep phonology, and the deep lexicon of a discourse and then show the ways in which these three elaborate out into the highly complex interlocking patterns of the surface structure, this would be another possible attack on the problem of unity and diversity in the structure of discourse.

But what about pragmatic considerations; that is, speaker-hearer relationships and other elements of the communication situation? Here we could with profit go back to an early insight of Pike in his massive work of 1967. In fact, the title itself puts it quite well: _Language in Relation to a Unified Theory of the Structure of Human Behavior_. How do we put language into its proper, pragmatic, non-linguistic context? Probably by simply recognizing that verbal behavioremes are part of still larger, complex patterns of behavior and that understanding the structure of the whole gives us insight as to what is happening within the verbal component contained within it. Possibly when all is said and done, this is the best way to fit pragmatics into the overall picture.

CHAPTER 8

A CONCLUDING ESSAY: TOWARDS MAXIMUM CONTEXT

This volume is based on the conviction that language is language only in context. That such context is two-fold has long been recognized. In any utterance but those of very simple structure, the linguistic constructions which occur are found in linguistic context. It is plain to see that a sentence taken from its matrix in a discourse can ultimately be understood only by reference to the linguistic context from which it comes. But language is in turn part of broader patterns of human behavior; one must, therefore, also refer to the situational or behavioral context of any utterance with which we have to do. So we are driven from the study of linguistic context to broader patterns of non-linguistic or only partially linguistic context.

It is probably misleading to think of language as embedded in simple fashion within the still broader context of human behavior. Verbal activity does not embed in non-verbal activity like an egg in a paper bag. Rather, to a large degree man's verbal activity informs, interprets, and structures his non-verbal activity. Patterns of human activity are very complex and language can not be left out of account at any turn. At any event, however, any given stretch of verbal activity must be considered to be part of broader situational and behavioral patterns which are not exclusively and often not even primarily verbal.

The preceding arguments are part of the basic motivation for discourse grammar or textlinguistics (as it is called in Europe). First of all, apparently, has come the realization that sentences must be studied in context if the study is to be meaningful. This germinal insight soon led to the demand that we inspect not simply the immediate context (e.g., the preceding and following sentence), but the structure of the whole surrounding discourse. It was increasingly realized that the whole determines many structured details of the parts, even as vice versa the former is inferred from the latter. Secondly, however, has come the growing realization that even all this is not enough. Discourses must also be studied in their behavioral/sociological/cultural/psychological--or what-have-you context. At this point, text-linguistics crosses over the frontier from linguistics narrowly conceived and becomes interdisciplinary.

But does the search for context not drive us on to further considerations? What about man and his activities--activities in which language plays so large a part? What about context for the whole human endeavor? In fact, taking language as indexical of the human venture, what sort of questions need we raise relative to this venture? Are there questions which arise from the very consideration of language itself?

Before considering such questions, however, we need to back up and survey in retrospect some of the things which this volume has tried to do. This book is a volume on systematic aspects of discourse. It has been argued that languages not only have a surface grammar but also a less obvious and quasi-universal notional grammar. One of the purposes of this volume has been to muster a catalogue of these notional categories so as to provide a universal reference base for the study of discourses in particular languages. What notions are indispensable to human speech? What categories does anyone speaking any language anywhere inevitably implement and use as soon as he starts talking? Does not the very universality and necessity of such categories tell us something about human nature?

Take, for example, the apparatus of case frames consisting of various sorts of predicates and nouns in associated roles (Chapters 4 and 5). To begin with, we find that ways of expressing observations about the environment in which man lives and our reactions to that environment are symbolized in rows A and Á of the case frame chart. Then, in row B, we find ways of expressing our emotive and psychological states, and ways in which we enter into such states or induce such states in other people. Whether nervous, happy, discouraged, frightened, cheerful, annoyed or what have you, means exist here for expressing in language such states, changes of states, and inducements of states in other people. We also find here verbs of impingement in which one animate being impinges upon another. In C we have verbs which refer to man as a knowing and learning being, who also engages in such further activities as teaching and study. In row D we find cognitive and emotional states directed toward goals, i.e., acquaintance, knowledge, and appreciation of persons as well as verbs of desire and evaluation . In D', the last row of the top half of our case frame chart, we find verbs referring to sensation and speech. Various physical states, processes, instigated processes, and actions figure in row E. By means of such verbs we characterize objects in our environment, speak of changes in such objects and how they are induced--often by means of the use of some instrument--and express various physical activities in which we engage. Measure is expressed in row F. In G and G' expressions of location and motion are found. Here we see man orienting himself spatially to his environment and to things in his environment. In rows H and H' man's bent for acquiring possessions is expressed, as well as various sorts of exchange among human beings, including exchanges in which one person finds himself in transitory possession of objects intended for someone else. All this is indicative of our exhaustive apparatus for talking about everything imaginable in sky, earth and sea--or in planets and universes as yet unvisited.

In spite of the limitations of my representation of this apparatus (and of any such scheme), we find here system and beauty. In the top half of the chart, we find the role experiencer. In the bottom half of the chart, we find the role patient. In the top half of the chart we see man as one whose nervous system registers stimuli from the environment and from other entities within the environment. In the bottom half of the chart we see man as observing physical states, bringing about changes of such states, and carrying out various actions within the physical environment, including motion and locomotion. We also see man as acquirer of possessions which he exchanges with his fellowman. If we look at the two halves of the chart, left and right, we see man as agent--interacting with his fellowman and modifying his environment--emerging on the right half of the chart. The compilation of any such chart is a summary of man and his works.

Looking then at the apparatus described in Chapter three, we are impressed with man as logician. It is an imposing rational apparatus. To begin with, man couples like activities and things. Other activities, things, or qualities he contrasts. Here we see man's incurably taxonomic approach to his universe. In classifying things as like or different we arrive at the fountain head of western philosophy as seen in Platonism. We also find alternation as man is faced with options of varying triviality or importance. Furthermore, man organizes his world temporally by classifying actions as overlapping or as succeeding each other. In addition, man organizes his world logically according to various implicational relationships. Causation in particular is an ineradicable concept in his approach to things, In all these attempts to conceptualize reality man resorts to paraphrase, (i.e., the effort to pin a concept down more adequately by expressing it in different ways). He also resorts to illustration, to comparison, to exemplification. He has various devices of deixis whereby he can predicate existence of something and say something about it or make equational statements about predications. Finally, he reports the speech of himself or of other men, verbalizes his own psychological states, and indulges in beginning metalanguage when he defines terms in going from one universe of discourse or language to another.

It must be insisted that all this is quite related to life. It is not an abstract rational apparatus reserved for man's use as an occasional inhabitor of an ivory tower observation post. Without recognizing samenesses and differences, we could scarcely exist. We could not sort out the universe in any useful way even in terms of survival value. In a symposium on the concept of the hero in modern life (Hutchins and Adler 1973), Sidney Hook (pp. 67-8) contends that we cannot have the daily commerce of human life--much less an adequate theory of cultural and historical change--without such basic notions as causation, contrafactuality, and alternation. Thus he specifically rejects the notion that the web of human affairs is "of such spectacular complexity that isolable causal chains cannot be discerned". Hook also points out the importance of the contrafactual in daily life: "For unless we can discourse validly about the would-have-beens and might-have-beens we cannot rightfully claim to understand the whys or causes of anything that happens in human life. Human behavior on the streets, in the home, in the courts, in the commercial marts, would be completely unintelligible. The logical analysis both of hypotheticals which are contrary to fact, as of their speculative causes, may be difficult; nonetheless, common sense and common practice--indeed human survival--depend upon our awareness of such things. We stake our lives on them every moment of the day. _You might have been (or would have been) hurt if you had not stepped out of the path of the speeding car_ is an expression that no sane man would disregard as meaningless or as not worth his consideration. Hook's emphasis on the importance of alternation is coupled with a belief in the "presence of eventful men in history". Thus he takes issue with "those who contend that the direction of historical and social changes is so completely determined by economic forces that there are no momentous alternatives of development" and thus deny the presence of such men in history. He believes that history cannot really be intelligible without a belief in such "fateful alternatives".

Similar claims could doubtless be made about other parts of man's logical apparatus. A perception of temporal relations is, (e.g., of no small importance both for survival and for cultural progress. Timing can be a matter of life or death. Furthermore, by distinguishing succession and overlap (and subvarieties of them) we are able to carry through complicated procedures and to integrate our activities socially. If western man has become somewhat preoccupied with time, all men everywhere are conscious of temporal relations and employ them.

Finally, frustration (expectancy reversal)--that part of our logical apparatus which intersects many of the other categories--is such a pervasively human thing that we can scarcely discuss it without overtones of humor. This part of man's apparatus testifies to his finiteness as a creature who is often confronted with forces which prevent his realizing normal expectations--so he builds it into the structure of his language and reserves the right to laugh (as long as laughter is still possible).

In brief, in man's use of his rational apparatus he is not isolating himself from life but ever plunging himself more deeply into it. At the same time there is no attempt here to deny that man is an emotive and volitional being as well as a rational one. Rather, we insist that even his emotion and volition take place within the overall framework indicated within language categories of the sort which we have catalogued.

But even more striking than man's conceptual and logical apparatus is his discourse-building capacity as seen in the structure of monologue and dialogue (Chapters 1 and 2). Story telling and the ability to carry on a conversation are uniquely human. Whatever the outcome of the controversial experiments in teaching language to higher primates, the fact remains that there is something severely limited in the accomplishments of even the most "learned" primates. Whatever they learn is apparently limited to signals-in-the-here-and-now. Chimpanzees can't tell stories; they can't even recount their own activities earlier in the same day, much less narrate someone else's activities. By contrast, man's narrative ability is an impressive endowment. He can sit in a room and recount the activities of other individuals who are distant from him in time and space. He not only can arrange this account in order but he uses the particular resources of his language to distinguish varying levels of information relevance. In addition, he can structure the story so as to feature certain motifs (thematic content) and create an atmosphere of suspense and drama (plot structure). Scarcely less striking is the ability of two individuals to sit together in a common setting and converse of people and events far removed from the here and now of that setting. In discourse structure, whether monologue or dialogue, man rises above his limitations of time and space.

What then? Man's conceptual/logical/flying-carpet-of-Bagdad linguistic apparatus, as seen in every phase of language structure and function--from morpheme to discourse--presents us with an impressive panorama of categories and functions. But do language and we its speakers have any metaphysical context which can give the whole venture any meaning? I sketch here a series of concentric questions relative to this main query.

Question 1: Is there rationality (intelligence) out there in the heart of things or is the human psyche (or if one prefers, nervous system) the sole repository of such rationality as we here catalog? If we accept the second view, man is a raft of rationality adrift on a sea of meaninglessness. Whatever rationality he thinks he sees in things is simply ex post facto observation of the sort which we make when we observe any product of random generation and impose a pattern on it. It is like a bunch of stones thrown down at random on the ground or a picture made by tying a painter's brush to a donkey's tail and letting him brush randomly at a canvas. Our intelligence creates a pattern from the random distribution which we find, but the pattern was not there in the mind of any creator; it just happened.

What I want to challenge here is, in effect, the good faith of those who profess to accept this second view. Does anyone really believe it? Or are elements of purpose and meaning inevitably smuggled into the picture while we are not looking? Do we really believe that rationality such as we find exemplified in language and its categories arose randomly from chaos and has nothing to match it in the rest of the universe?

Positing of other intelligences randomly developed in other parts of the universe, doesn't help the picture, it only further compounds the difficulty. It is marvelous enough that rationality could have emerged by pure chance in one corner of the universe; if it has emerged in several corners it makes the odds even less that this rationality came about apart from some cosmic rationality behind it. And, of course, as popular as the view may be, we have no evidence as yet that there are other intelligent creatures out there somewhere in deep space waiting to enter into communication with us. Our persistent belief that such creatures must exist somewhere is based not so much on science as on a neoplatonic hangover from the doctrine of plenitude (Lovejoy 1936). It just doesn't seem right to us that there should be all that WASTE SPACE out there without other intelligent creatures to share it. At any rate, all this is hardly relevant to the question before us. The only intelligent creatures which we know to date in the universe are found on the planet which we inhabit, and we have the immediate problem of accounting for rationality here.

Notice that the above argument is not an argument from design and teleology as such; it arises rather out of a crying need to explain the presence of rationality in human beings in a universe which is increasingly believed to be devoid of meaning and purpose[1]. It is a here and now question not a speculative matter of remote origins. I'm simply raising the question as to whether anybody can or does really live with a belief in the fundamental irrationality of things. Does he not rather state such a belief as his overt creed and then resort implicitly to a different view of things in order to get through the day?

Question 2: Does language as a reflection of our rationality give insight into extra-linguistic reality? At first this question seems to have been: Is there any consistent thing called Language (with a capital L), as opposed to particular languages, that reflects reality and structures it for us? Thus several decades ago, considerable interest was given to Whorf's contention that the categories of particular languages inevitably structure the universe for us in different ways so that in effect the Hopi lives in a different sort of universe from a person speaking English. Or, as Heidegger (1971.5) expressed it, "Some time ago I called language, clumsily enough, the house of Being, . . . If man by virtue of his language dwells within the claim and call of Being, then we Europeans presumably dwell in an entirely different house than Eastasian man . . . and so a dialogue from house to house remains nearly impossible." W. T. Jones has recently expressed the same thought (1973.26) in the metaphor of a fly escaping from one bottle into another bottle. There are only various fly bottles, no evidence of any structure that characterizes all the fly bottles. "Though the fly may escape from this or that bottle, he only lands in another: perhaps there is no common ground, no common world outside all fly bottles."

I believe that this is one issue which is currently being settled by linguistic study. The evidence is coming in that there are language universals which underlie the surface structure categories of particular languages and that languages differ more in their surface structure than in these underlying categories. Or as Jones also suggests in the same article (126), if Heidegger's "many houses" are to be taken seriously, all houses at least may be seen to be built on a common architectural plan. From this point of view the purpose of this book has been to demonstrate some features of the common architectural plan which underlies all the world's languages.

The question, however, goes deeper. All that we prove by positing these various language universals is that there is such a thing as Language underlying the various particular languages. We have not yet solved the question of the possible matching of language and reality or even faced the issue as to whether or not this is an intelligent question to ask. One thing seems obvious: there is no general stance outside language whereby we may view reality and compare it with language; language itself so structures our world for us that we have no clear way to view the world apart from language and its categories. Thus, every fact which we have, even scientific fact, consists essentially of an observation plus discourse. That we are back here on Kantian ground is beyond denial. Our a priori categories undisputably structure reality for us and our very observation and conceptualization of it.

What then if language is a terrible cheat? What if it in some bad way distorts reality for us so that we have to correct for the bias caused by language and its categories in really understanding things? Here again we have no basis for correction because we have no stance outside language itself. We can only correct purported abuses of languages by further doses of the same thing, i.e., by language itself. We can only patch a language tire with other pieces of language tire.

In my review (1956) of Urban's book, Language and Reality, I quoted and summarized an appendix (741-7) in which he refers to three mutually contradictory criticisms of language each of which is based on the claim that language distorts reality. Not only do these criticisms of language to some degree cancel each other out, but not one of them can claim to be based on a view of reality apart from language and its categories. Indeed, philosophers of language who are very anxious to correct it for bias and distortion in our view of reality proceed to correct language by massive doses of further language. It appears that whatever the assumed abuses on the part of language are, they are not so deep but what they can be corrected by more doses of the same thing. I think the moral of the story is that rather than language and its categories veiling reality, they are windows into it. To learn more about reality we further elaborate language and its categories (even in inductive and empirical study); we do not try to get rid of them.

Where have we come then? I suggested in respect to the first question above that the second viewpoint is really unlivable. Is a negative answer to question 2 likewise unlivable? I have emphasized above that language and human life are ultimately inseparable. Man conceptualizes his universe, his works, and his own psyche by various categories of predication (case frames); he organizes things in ways essential to emotional health and brute survival by his ways of combining predications; he is able to be a viable social creature thanks to the apparatus of repartee; and he rises to heights of self-expression and probing of the universe by virtue of his ability to create discourses. Can we really live with the proposition that the whole fabric of language is a great cheat, a veil over the face of things as they really are? I think not. Such a view ultimately stultifies discourse. But man cannot live with a paralysis of language; we cannot survive as intellectual and spiritual aphasics.

But is there any convergence of the above lines of thought? Let us assume that living in the world as viable human beings all but necessitates (in *my* view, *does* necessitate) a belief that there is rationality at the heart of things. Let us further assume that language and its categories, which reflect our rationality as human beings, are insightful into non-linguistic reality. Then we may well ask: can the rationality which is in the heart of things and the rationality which we find in language and which gives insight into things, be unrelated? And if the two rationalities are related, then how do they relate? Ultimately there are but two possible answers here: (a) that the two rationalities are one, so that in a sense man projects his rationality out into the heart of things and finds himself to be part of a greater Whole; or (b) man and his rationality are creatures of God and His rationality. The first answer is that of pantheism; the second that of theism. These considerations in turn bring us to our third main question which has to do with man's exercise of his rationality (and his language) in an attempt to understand the universe.

Question 3: Is the God revealed in the Judeo-Christian Scriptures the missing piece, the key piece, in all man's abortive attempts to understand his universe? While I readily agree here that some systems of thought are more viable than others, can any non-theistic or only weakly theistic theory prove adequate or be even weakly viable?

Much can be learned in regard to this question by a careful consideration of the history of the controversy between idealistic and realistic world views. As good a place as any to study this is in an excellent and beautiful volume, again by Wilbur Marshall Urban, called *Beyond Realism and Idealism* (1949). That Urban himself did not succeed in getting where the title indicates, i.e., did not succeed in elaborating such a position, is a typical failure of the idealist who thinks that he is advancing to neutral ground but stays on typically idealistic ground after all

(Buswell 1960.116-20). That is hardly the point, however. Urban's volume illustrates graphically the many twists, turns, and involutions of the idealism-realism controversy in which A starts out arguing P and B starts out arguing Q only to end up with A arguing Q and B arguing P. Thus, for example, a realist may so qualify his argument that he ends up by assuming in effect a position similar to that of the idealist, and vice versa.

The idealist always has trouble keeping facts from evaporating. He has difficulty in accepting facts that are not experienced and observed. He so emphasizes the correspondence of mind and reality that he cannot conceive of reality apart from structuring by some mind. As the old contention goes, if the tree falls in the forest and there is no one to see it fall, then it is not a fact. That this partly caricatures the idealistic point of view is not to the point. The fact remains that idealism invites caricatures of this sort. Thus Urban, one of the sanest and most moderate of the idealists, himself had to say in the end, "It cannot be shown either empirically or logically that inexperienced entities exist." (Language and Reality, p. 104).

Confronted with the evaporation of reality in the hands of the idealist, the realist screams out, kicks his chair, and insists that the chair is really there. He insists that he may turn his back on the chair and the chair does not disappear, but continues to be. So far so good. But the philosophic realist must face the fact that his facts are ultimately meaningless aside from statement and interpretation by language and its categories. In fact he knows reality only through such a medium. If he insists that facts are there OUT OF ALL RELATION TO MIND, he has to accept brute fact. From the acceptance of brute fact, it is only a step or two down to the acceptance of purposelessness, absurdity, and even chaos. So realism leads to naturalism, and naturalism to loss of meaning. Dewey and instrumentalism (called contextualism below) were only a rear-guard delaying action on the route to alienation and despair. The brute facts of the world are, in fact, very brute. Man himself is, from this point of view, only a brute fact and his rationality is a blob thrown on the wall.

Philosophically, we see this come to full fruition in existentialism in Europe. Philosophy here comes full circle to the denial of philosophy. Man is an alienated creature thrown into an absurd universe. Birth, life, and death are all equally absurd and meaningless. Whatever freedom we have is a "monstrous spontaneity" (Sartre) and man himself is a "useless passion".

This can best be seen, however, not so much in avowedly philosophical writing, as in popular drama, novel, and art. As Joy G. Bayum says in the same symposium referred to above. "Television, film, and radio, processing the cultural materials of the past and present, making palatable for mass consumption great art and great ideas, have informed a self-satisfied homme moyen of what the elite had thought it alone was able to perceive: that the human condition is absurd, that man is alienated and miserable. Popularizing contemporary philosophy and literature, the mass media have made 'hope' and 'meaning' seem naive terms" (Hutchins and Adler 1973.58-9). Chaim Potok observes in the same volume (74): "More than any other art form--with the possible exception of montage--the novel has served to reflect the breakup of the older order of things, ..." On the same page Potok speaks of "the gritty flatness of human existence".

What then? Facts evaporate in the hands of the idealist and facts become a useless ensemble without purpose and meaning in the hands of the realist. Is there any way to have and keep an INTELLIGIBLE world? I suggest that the Judeo-Christian God revealed in the Scriptures of those two religions must be central to a satisfactory world view. In such a world view we have significant facts and we have valid connections between mind and fact and between fact and fact. The facts themselves are not brute. Whether we ever observe them as human beings or not, the facts are there by God's design and are His creation. They are first of all related to His intelligence. They are mind-created and mind-saturated facts whether we ever observe them or not. The topographical features of some far-off planet are known to the intelligence of God and are facts with Him whether we as human beings ever get around to seeing them or not.

Another way of getting at an answer to question 3 above is via the study of the comparative morphology of the great philosophies of the western world. Stephen Pepper has done much of this for us in his admirable volume World Hypotheses (1942). Pepper lists seven possible world views and dismisses quickly certain of them--including the belief in a personal God. This latter view, which he classifies under

ANIMISM, he considers essentially to be man creating God in his own image. He admits, however: "Every child is a natural animist, and so (if the secret be known) is every man, not only primitive man, but civilized man as well. This view of the world is the only one in which a man feels completely at home. It is perhaps as well for us to learn early, therefore that we shall probably never feel completely at home in a world view that is adequate. For the world does not seem to be made after man's own image" (120).

Having disposed of this and other "inadequate hypotheses", Pepper proceeds to treat in detail the four "relatively adequate hypotheses"--all of which are well-known views, although he gives some of them novel labels. For each of these world hypotheses he tries to give the root metaphor, the basic categories, and the theory of truth. He does not believe in eclecticism, which, he says, leaves us, among other things, with no root metaphors and thus emasculates the very theories which it tries to combine (104ff.). Rather, the various world hypotheses are regarded (to use a Pikean term) as MULTIPLE PERSPECTIVES on reality.

Pepper demonstrates, however, that each relatively adequate world hypothesis runs ultimately into frustration. He argues, therefore, that each needs the others as further perspectives. Might we not also argue, however, that each view runs into frustration because it leaves the key piece out of the puzzle?

The first "relatively adequate hypothesis" that Pepper examines is the stream of thought which harks back to Plato and Aristotle and which he calls FORMISM--a point of view in which taxonomic questions of sameness and difference and preoccupation with archetypal patterns are prominent. Pepper criticizes formism for "its looseness of categorial structure and consequent lack of determinism", so that we are bound to feel that "nature is intrinsically more organized than the formistic categories suggest". This, Pepper suggests, hands us over "into the firmer categories of mechanism".

I suggest here that we can accept formism as a <u>partial</u> perspective on the universe if and only if we posit a creator-god who exhaustively knows his universe. Taxonomic indeterminacies, endless hassles of splitters and joiners, beautiful classifications which end up in arbitrary hair-splitting--all this can be tolerated if we believe in an ultimate structure of things given to them by their creator. We can relax with leaky taxonomies that are viable enough for us--as less than omniscient creatures. We can frankly accept the formist view as only a partial perspective, and go on to examine other views.

Pepper likewise admits that mechanism, in spite of his attraction to it, also has certain built-in weaknesses, the greatest of which is the gap between primary and secondary categories, including the mind-body problem (231). How ultimately can secondary sensory qualities such as color and sound be connected with such primary qualities as mass and energy? Obvious answers in terms of correlations of the two and emergence (another word to hide our ignorance) still leaves us dissatisfied (217). As Pepper puts it:..."there is a difficulty here which mechanists have instinctively felt" (218).

Again, however, with a creator, the gap can be bridged between primary and secondary qualities. More of this later when I consider color at the end of this chapter. For the moment, note a rather obvious point: mechanism works best if we have God as creator, operator, and maintenance man. The deus ex machina--that which the theory has striven so hard to banish--is really what it needs to make it work.

Contextualism (pragmatism or instrumentalism) is Pepper's next "relatively adequate hypothesis". Here there is preoccupation with the live event, with its connecting strands, with change, and with novelty. Although Pepper singles out the historic event as the root metaphor, I am inclined to interpret contextualism by a linguistic metaphor: a portion of a discourse and its connections. Pepper finds in the following dilemma the weakness of contextualism: "Either you must confine yourself to believing only the facts of direct verification in which case your theory lacks scope; or if you admit the validity of indirect verification and acquire scope, you must admit that nature has a determinate structure and so fall into the contradiction of both offering and denying the structure of nature" (279). In brief, if you pin a contextualist down, he will retreat into the particular event in the present, but as soon as you cease to press him, he broadens and reasserts his claims without restriction.

Again, the Christian theist can admit contextualism as a partial perspective--which is all that Pepper asks his reader to do--but the theist again has his necessary condition: you must admit God as Ultimate Context. The present event has significance and has adequate context because God exists. Since He is a God of infinite variety, novelty (from OUR point of view) can and does emerge. Since He is GOD, novelty does not destroy the fabric. The emergence of a new design may delight the weaver as it grows in his loom, but he is not taken by surprise by his own art.

Finally, Pepper considers organicism--which is his name for absolute or objective idealism (whose culmination is the philosophy of Hegel). He describes this as the belief that "every actual event in the world is of more or less concealed organic process". Fragments, connections among fragments, and contradictions all take their place in the whole which is implicit in the fragments, transcends the contradictions, and preserves all without loss. This is a monistic view of the universe while contextualism is open and pluralistic. Its weakness? It has no room for time and change (much less the Christian doctrine of sin). The Absolute must include all facts and hence embrace contradiction.

The Christian theist finds common ground with this system (qua system) only to the prejudice of his own viewpoint. God the creator presides over a created world where time, change, and even temporary disorder are found. God is separate from his creation. He runs the show and he writes the book but he is not one with the show or the book. Nevertheless, the Christian finds himself in sympathy with the emphasis on the organic whole within the created world. In fact, we can have a whole creation only if we have a creator--and the Absolute of Hegel doesn't fill the bill (see below).

This brings us to our next question. But before passing on to it, let's review the argument so far: man is not isolated in his rationality, but Rationality is somehow in the heart of things. Man's language expresses rationality akin to that Rationality (and derived from it) and language gives valid insight into reality. Man's exercise of his reason in creating philosophic systems runs into frustration and contradiction because God, the key piece, is left out.

Question 4: What sort of God is satisfactory for such a world view? Notice here that I am not arguing for a vague amorphous theism. I am arguing specifically for the God presented in the Judeo-Christian Scriptures. The God revealed there is an infinite-personal God. He has personality and can love while at the same time He knows exhaustively every fact in the universe. The objection is made that such a being is a contradiction in terms. I do not think that such a being is a contradiction in terms so much as that this phase of His being is something unimaginable for us and beyond our conception. These are not the same thing. There is no necessary contradiction in the infinite and the personal. Man himself has been able to make great systems for information storage and retrieval. Is it inconceivable that there could be a being with infinite storage capacity and instant retrieval who at the same time is personal? At any rate, this is precisely the God which we find presented to us in the Judeo-Christian Scriptures.

This is not the God of Plato and Aristotle (formism) which in effect had two deities: the Unmoved Mover, and the Demiurge. The former sits in cold, uninvolved splendor, while the latter is fecund and creative (Lovejoy 1936). In this splitting of deity, neither half is the God of the Scriptures, who is neither the one nor the other nor both combined. Nor is this God the Absolute of Hegel--which rather resembles the first of Plato's deities. Inadequate views of deity have plagued Western thought through the so-called Christian centuries. Such was the price for Christianity's early marriage to Platonism. Equally unfortunate was religious liberalism's flirtation with Hegelianism, which is seen in retrospect to have been a greased slide down to pantheism, atheism, and the so-called death of God theology. This bring us, however, to our last question.

Question 5: If such a God exists, is language capable of talking about Him? Many would answer this question negatimely. Finite language cannot talk about the Infinite. The language of time and sense cannot be retooled to be God-talk. In brief, if there be a God, we can't talk about Him intelligently. Van Buren, to whom any existential statements regarding God, whether affirmative or negative, are equally beside the point--comments from his point of view on the absurdity of divine revelation: "But, if such an 'other' God were to speak, how could we understand Him and be able to say that He had spoken? If we could not understand a lion who talked how much less could we understand a God who talked?" (1972.73). As for the word God itself, the same author regards it as the ultimate nonsense word which we utter as we fall gasping at the threshhold of mystery (132-50).

All this seems to me quite beside the point. I would rather insist that if there be a God _of the sort revealed in the Scriptures_, then we have good reason to believe that language is fit to talk about Him. There is a certain begging of the question here on the part of critics of God-talk. First of all, they reduce the concept of God to something less than the Infinite-personal God of the Scriptures, then they proceed to say that such a God cannot reveal Himself--which seems to be a valid conclusion. Accepting, however, the opposite premise, i.e., that such a God as described in the Scriptures exists , then His revealing Himself is not a problem of the same quality or size. Ultimately this God lies back of the universe, ourselves, and our language (i.e., back of the encoded, the encoder, and the code). Has He then let the code develop along lines such that He is unable to communicate Himself through it?

Furthermore, the God of the Scriptures is PERSONAL, and it is of the nature of persons to communicate. Much of His being--His infinity, eternity, omnipotence, exhaustive knowledge of the past, and control of the future--ultimately eludes us and outruns our conception and expression. We express much of this by way of negation, i.e., God is not limited in this or that respect . But His personal characteristics, holiness, justice, goodness, and love are more within the resources of language and more understandable to us as human beings.

As we have already observed, language is tooled to express more than the here and now. We can discourse effortlessly of events or persons far removed in time and space. We talk not only of the physical but of the psychical, i.e., of the interior life (Chapter 2). We use verbs of motion and locomotion to express movement not only through physical space but also through logical space. Even in its central and primary usages, language is a flexible tool for expressing many non-physical concerns. Furthermore, as we have tried to show in chapter three, paraphrase and illustration--including simile and exemplification--are an integral part of the structure of language and extend its effectiveness.

Language is set up, therefore, to discuss both the physical and the non-physical and has built-in resources of paraphrase, simile, and exemplification to further facilitate discourse. The literatures of the world are eloquent witness to these resources.

What of God-talk then? It is, as has been observed since Aquinas, basically ANALOGICAL.[2] This is, however, no peculiarity of religious language as such. Predicates used primarily with a given subject and object are often used analogically of other subjects and objects and we take such analogies quite in stride. Thus, while <u>kick</u> is used primarily of a man or of an animal, i.e., of a being possessing a leg capable of delivering a blow, we can also speak of the <u>kick</u> of a discharging rifle or of the <u>kick</u> of a potent alcoholic beverage. The latter two uses are, of course, analogical. But they are not for that reason necessarily inferior, suspect, or equivocal uses of language. Similarly, we can admit that "God loves" is an analogic predication, modeled on the love of husband and wife and of parent and offspring. But this does not reduce the predication to nonsense. In fact the analogies involved--husband's love for his wife and a father's love for his children--are specifically and repeatedly invoked by the documents in which the statement "God is love" is found.

With the God of the Scriptures at the center of our world view, language takes its place in God's creation along with man who speaks it. For the Biblical theist it is instinctive to espouse a high view of language and its categories. Whatever the ultimate nature of the universe, God, in giving us language (or letting us develop it) has not duped us. He has given us a quick and ready means of indexing things, finding our way around, and having practical insight into reality. Whatever there is that is ineffable about matter and spirit, language at least gives us an open-ended way of grappling with it. And just as no one can dogmatize about the limits of the physical accomplishments of man's body (with e.g., new athletic records being set all the time), so no one can intelligently dogmatize on the limits of language.

Language is not simply symbol but PARABLE. To this end, I suggest an analogy with color perception (remember the mechanist's problem of primary and secondary qualities). Color perception is our sensuous response to differing wave lengths per se; we react to them encoded as different colors. We have the whole riotous parable of color instead of dry scientific pointer readings. I must say I like it better this way. But--and this is an important point--my color perception is based on the physical reality of differing wave lengths falling on objects of various composition and texture. Color perception is not only magnificent, it is also indicative of reality. So, I believe, language indexes in its own inimitable way a physical reality of subatomic, atomic, molecular, biological, psychical, and spiritual realities. It is at once a gigantic parable--and indicative of reality as we confront it as human beings. And back of the world of color and the world of language stands the supreme Symbol Maker who in creating intelligent creatures has given them ways to interact in practical poetry with their environment, each other, and Himself.

In calling language practical poetry, analogous to the perception of physical color, we must not lose sight of its truth-revelatory nature. The supreme Symbol Maker has given us the parable of language not to veil reality from us but to reveal it to us. In the Judeo-Christian Scriptures the parable of language emerges in various genres and types: in narrative, law-code, oration, poetry, proverbs, parable (narrowly conceived), letters--and, last but not least, in propositional statements scattered through the above. These propositional statements concern God, man, and the universe. While all, even 'literal' propositional statements involve elements of analogy, I have suggested above that such analogy characterizes language as a whole, not just religious language, and that analogy is not a synonym for inaccuracy.

One thing at least is clear: everywhere in the Judeo-Christian Scripture it is assumed that God is able to tell us about Himself in human language. The validity of language and its categories is assumed everywhere in this literature. In the Old Testament the clearest and most self-conscious affirmations of the validity and value of language are in the wisdom literature. To cite but one passage (Proverbs 1:23), wisdom personified stands and calls out to those who pass by: "I will pour out my spirit unto you: I will make known my words unto you." Everywhere in the wisdom literature <u>words</u> convey insight and give life, so that the <u>spirit of wisdom</u> and the <u>words of wisdom</u> cannot be separated. A similar identification is made in the New Testament in the writings of John--where <u>words</u>, <u>know</u>, <u>life</u>, and <u>light</u> are key lexical items. This time the one who stands and calls out is the central Personage of the Christian revelation

(John 6:63): "The words that I speak unto you, they are spirit and they are life."

The Christian Scriptures carry the identification of spirit and words even further. Without apotheosizing language, Christ--as God communicating to man--gets described in linguistic terms in the first verse of the Gospel according to St. John: "In the beginning was the Word, and the Word was with God, and the Word was God."

NOTES

1 In terms of background and stimulus I am here and at many other places indebted to Francis Schaeffer's writings (1968a, 1968b).

2 Holmes (1973) has suggested that religious language is essentially on three levels: the extensional or referential level (e.g., historical statements concerning Christ in the New Testament), the intensional level where relevance to system or context is of special importance (so that God becomes a key word in a system of ideas), and the personal level of illocutionary acts. He criticizes the positivist and religious existentialist for forgetting this "triune nature of language". Regarding the latter Holmes remarks: "We see him jump in theology from events denuded of theological intension to their existential impact, rather than moving from event to theological intension to personal confrontation, as is the case it seems to me in Scripture" (92).

APPENDIX

THE NOTIONAL AND SURFACE STRUCTURE OF ENGLISH CLAUSES

The purpose of this appendix is to suggest in broad outline a description of English clauses in which both surface features and notional structure features are given adequate weight and balance. The tabulations which follow include only indicative active clauses. Interrogative and imperative clauses, which are not tabulated here, can be systematically described on the basis of the indicative. Passive clauses exist in several varieties and also need to be integrated into the scheme. Nor have I taken account here of the clause-level elements which Halliday (1967) calls resultative attribute, depictive attribute, and condition. The present work is only a beginning.

Nevertheless, in this pilot study I attempt to demonstrate the feasibility of an analysis which (1) takes the five transitivity types (intransitive, transitive, ditransitive, descriptive, and equative) as basic but divides according to subtypes which add further surface structure tagmemes: instrument, locatives of various sorts, complement (expressions of measure), indirect objects of various sorts, and combinations of certain of these; and (2) marshals under each surface structure subtype the case frames which constitute its notional structure. In the apparatus which follows, a double line divides between surface and notional structures within each tagmemic apparatus.

In respect to (1) above, a summary shows that the transitivity dimension in English determines a system of clause types which is somewhat irregular but has certain basic regularities. It turns on a parameter which consists of the five basic transitivity types plus an intersecting parameter consisting of further surface structure features. See the smaller chart which follows and which precedes the detailed tabulation of types, subtypes, and case frames.

Besides the abbreviations used in Chapter 5, I use here:

Pi, intransitive predicate
Pta, transitive active predicate
Pda, ditransitive active predicate
Pic, intransitive copula predicate
R-A Ph, relator-axis phrase
R, relator
intr., intransitive
tr., transitive
ditr., ditransitive
nom., nominative
acc., accusative

TRANSITIVE VALUE \ FEATURES	BASIC PATTERN	±In	+Comp	+IO/ IO'	+Loc	+ [±Loc' ±Loc" ±Loc"]	Combi-nations
Intr	X	X	X	X	X	IO	+ [±Loc ±Comp]
Tr	X	X	X	X	X	IO'	+ [±M/In ±IO' ±Loc']
Ditr	X				X	X	+ [±M ±IO']
Desc	X	X					
Equ	X						

System of Surface Structure Clauses in English

1. INTRANSITIVE

1.1 Basic pattern

+S	$+P_i$	
NP attributive NP possessive NP coordinate NP appositional infinitive clause gerund clause Pronoun (nom.)	Active VP [verbs of intr. class except for 1.1.4 & 1.1.5]	
1.1.1 Ø	{P-AMBIENT} (A 2)	Restricted to it as surface structure subject, or to a noun such as weather or climate (in 1.1.1).
1.1.2 Ø	{A-AMBIENT} (A 4)	
1.1.3 P	{P-PHYSICAL} (E 2)	
1.1.4 P	some: {AP-PHYSICAL MOTION} (G' 3)	Suppresses notional structure Agent, Source, Path, Goal; achieves subject/Patient focus by permuting Patient into the subject slot; manner adverbs common here.
1.1.5 P	some: {AP-PHYSICAL -INSTRUMENT} (E 3)	Suppresses notional structure Agent, Instrument; achieves subject/Patient focus by permuting Patient into subject slot.
1.1.6 P	{S-PHYSICAL MOTION} (G' 1)	In these subtypes of G' 1 and G' 2 no other noun phrase beside subject/Patient occur.
1.1.7 P	{P-PHYSICAL MOTION} (G' 2)	

1.1.1 It's warming up.
It's cooling off.
1.1.2 It's raining.
It's snowing.
1.1.3 The dish broke.
The pig died.
The bolt came loose.
1.1.4 This car drives nicely.
This javelin throws straight.
1.1.5 This store opens at 7:00 a.m. and closes at 9:00 p.m.
1.1.6 The machine is going/running/functioning.
1.1.7 The motor is speeding up/slowing down.

1.2 ±In

+S same	$+P_i$ [verbs of tr. class]	±In R-A Ph whose R: with	
1.2.1 A/P	some: {AP-PHYSICAL (INSTRUMENT) REFLEXIVE} (E 3)	I	These are reflexive transitive verbs that suppress the reflexive pronoun and achieve predicate/process focus.
1.2.2 A	some: {AP-PHYSICAL (INSTRUMENT)} (E 3)	I	These achieve predicate/process focus by suppressing the notional structure Patient; expressions of time are common here.
1.2.3 P	some: {AP-PHYSICAL (INSTRUMENT) (E 3)	I	These achieve subject/Patient focus by permuting the Patient into subject slot; manner adverbs are common here.

1.2.1 John washed and shaved.
He shaves with an electric razor.
I usually wash with a wash cloth.

1.2.2 Mother washes every Monday and irons every Tuesday.
They hunt every day.
Almost everybody fishes here.
Mother washes with an automatic washer.
Theodore hunts with bow and arrow.

1.2.3 This fabric washes well (with Tide).
This meat cuts easily with a really sharp knife.

1.3 +Loc

+S same	$+P_i$ same [intr. verbs]	+Loc R-A Ph in which R: in, at, on, by
1.3.1 P [inanimate]	{S-PHYSICAL LOCATIVE POSTURE} (G 1)	L
1.3.2 A/P	some: {AP-PHYSICAL LOCATIVE POSTURE REFLEXIVE} (G 3)	L
1.3.3 A/P	{A-PHYSICAL LOCATIVE POSTURE} (G 4)	L
1.3.4 P	{P-PHYSICAL MOTION} (G' 2)	L (when L is selected rather than Source, Path, and Goal)
1.3.5 A/P	{A-PHYSICAL MOTION} (G' 4)	L (when L is selected rather than Source, Path, and Goal)

1.3.1 The house stands on the corner.
The key is lying on the rug.
1.3.2 John sat down in the chair.
Mary lay down in bed.
The monk knelt at the altar.
1.3.3 The returning POW stood by his wife.
Governor Smith sat in the chair.
Phyllis is lying on the bench.
1.3.4 The ship sank at sea.
The ship drifted in the calm sea.
David fell down on the ice.
1.3.5 Harriet traveled in Europe.
Gwendolyn swam in the icy waters off New Zealand.

1.4 +[±Loc' ±Loc" ± Loc"']

+S	$+P_i$	+[±Loc'	±Loc"	±Loc"']
same	same [intr. verbs]	R-A Ph in which R: <u>from</u>	R-A Ph in which R: <u>via</u>, <u>across</u>, <u>through</u>, <u>over</u>	R-A Ph in which R: <u>to</u>, <u>towards</u>
A/P	A-PHYSICAL MOTION (G' 4)	(Source)	(Path)	(G)

1.4 Dempsey traveled from Frankfurt to Rome via Milan.
The baby crawled from the kitchen to the front room.
Sam swam through the water towards the raft.
The car crossed over the bridge from Minneapolis to St. Paul.

1.5 +Complement (see chart on top of next page)
1.5.1 The statue weighs 5 tons.
It costs $6.50.
1.5.2 He's grown an inch.
Mary has gained 50 lbs.
My bonds went down 10%.
1.5.3 The squadron advanced a mile.
The Cowboys gained five yards.
The army retreated one hundred miles.

(1.5 +Complement)

+S same	$+P_i$ same [intr. verbs]	+Complement NP which contains numerals or other qualifiers
1.5.1 P	{S-PHYSICAL MEASURABLE} (F 1)	M
1.5.2 P	{P-PHYSICAL MEASURABLE} (F 2)	M
1.5.3 A/P	{A-PHYSICAL MEASURABLE} (F 4)	M

1.6 +[±Loc ± Complement]

+S same	$+P_i$ same [intr. verbs]	+[±Loc same	±Complement] same
P	{S-PHYSICAL MOTION (COMPLETABLE)} (G' 1)	Path	R Time is often obligatory with expression of complement in this frame.

1.6 The earth rotates on its axis.
The earth rotates one full rotation every 24 hours.
The wheel spun around one full turn.
The moon revolves around the earth (once each month).

1.7 +IO (These clauses, although with ditransitive verbs, suppress the Patient and achieve object/Goal focus.)

+S same	$+P_i$ [ditr. verbs]	+IO NP Pronoun (Acc.) or R-A Ph in which R: to [when permuted out beyond the O]
A/S	{AP-PHYSICAL POSSESSION DIRECTED} (H 3)	G

1.7 Please pay the cashier.
Rich men should give to poor men.

2. TRANSITIVE
2.1 Basic Pattern

+S	$+P_{ta}$	+O	
same	Active Vb Ph [tr. verbs]	cf. S Pronoun (acc.)	
2.1.1 E	{S-EXPER COMPLETABLE} (C 1)	R	
2.1.2 E	{P-EXPER COMPLETABLE} (C 2)	R	
2.1.3 A	{AP-EXPER COMPLETABLE} (C 3)	R	[suppresses Experiencer; and achieves object/Range focus]
2.1.4 A/E	{A-EXPER COMPLETABLE} (C 4)	R	

2.1.5 E	{S-EXPER DIRECTED} (D 1)	G	
2.1.6 A	{A-EXPER DIRECTED} (D 4)	G or E/G	
2.1.7 E	{P-EXPER DIRECTED COMPLETABLE} (D' 2)	S or R-S or R	
2.1.8 A/E	{A-EXPER DIRECTED COMPLETABLE} (D' 4)	S or R-S or R	
2.1.9 I	{AP-PHYSICAL INSTRUMENTAL (E 3)}	P	[suppresses Agent; and Instrument is permuted into subject slot; <u>subject</u>/<u>Instrument</u> focus]
2.1.10 A/P	{A- PHYSICAL COMPLETABLE} (E 4)	R	
2.1.11 G	{S-PHYSICAL POSSESSION DIRECTED} (H 1)	P	
2.1.12 G	{P-PHYSICAL POSSESSION DIRECTED} (H 2)	P	

2.1.1 Susan really knows algebra.
Tom understands the matter quite well.

2.1.2 Susan has learned a lot of algebra.
Harry learned his lesson.
Tom forgot the whole matter.

2.1.3 Mr. Smith teaches algebra.

2.1.4 Susan is studying algebra.
Ralph memorized the times table.
The burglar studied the approaches to the house.
2.1.5 Mary wants a cadillac.
Tom desires her.
Mary loves Tom.
2.1.6 John despises Mary.
Mary praises Tom.
The judge condemned the prisoner.
The governor pardoned him.
2.1.7 Tom heard (the sound of) an owl.
George smelled (the odor of) onions.
David saw/caught sight of Bathsheba.
I saw a strange sight on Boston Common this morning.
2.1.8 Tom listened to (the sound of) an owl.
George eagerly sniffed the odor of the onions.
The audience watched the performance.
2.1.9 This key opens that door.
A knife will cut that rope but scissors won't.
2.1.10 Stephen ran a race/the hundred yard dash.
The children played a game/cops-and-robbers.
The carpenter made a table.
2.1.11 Dick has a new book.
Tom owns a lot of real estate.
Tom's acquired a St. Bernard.
2.1.12 Mary obtained her visa (where obtain = 'come to have').
2.2 ±Instrument (see chart on top of next page)
2.2.1 The stranger (inadvertently) scared the baby with his black moustache.
He frightens me with his brusque manner.
2.2.2 He amused me with his funny stories.
I cheered her up.
He scared me with a firecracker.
2.2.3 John hit Bill (with his fist/with a stick).
John kissed his wife (with a greasy mouth).
Harry petted the cat (with both hands).
2.2.4 Raymond cut the rope with a knife.
Edward speared five fish.
The construction company is widening the road with a bulldozer.
2.2.5 Richard kicked the chair (with his foot).
Gregory tapped on the glass (with his finger tips).
2.2.6 They planted the field with rice.
They strewed the property with litter.
2.2.7 The U.S. supplies Israel with armaments.
The housekeeper will supply you with linen and bedding.

(2.2 ±Instrument)

+S same	$+P_{ta}$ same [tr. verbs]	+O same	±In R-A Ph in which R: <u>with</u>
2.2.1 [possessor of body part or characteristic]	{P-EXPER (INSTR)} (B 2)	E	I(=body part or characteristic)
2.2.2 A	{AP-EXPER (INSTRUMENTAL)} (B 3)	E	(I)
2.2.3 A	{A-EXPER (INSTRUMENTAL)} (B 4)	E	(I) [⊂ body parts]
2.2.4 A	{AP-PHYSICAL INSTRUMENTAL} (E 3)	P	I
2.2.5 A/P	{A-PHYSICAL DIRECTED (INSTRUMENTAL)} (E 4)	G	I [⊂ body parts]
2.2.6 A	{some: AP-PHYSICAL LOCATIVE} (G 3)	L	P
2.2.7 A/S	{some: AP-PHYSICAL POSSESSION DIRECTED (MEASURABLE)} (H 3)	G	P

2.3 +Outer Indirect Object (=IO')

+S same	$+P_{ta}$ same [tr. verbs]	+O same	+IO' R-A Ph in which R: for
Path	{S-PHYSICAL POSSESSION MOTION} (H' 1)	P	G

2.3 Dick has a book for you.
Tom has tickets for all of us.

2.4 +Loc (nuclear)

+S same	$+P_{ta}$ same [tr. verbs]	+O same	LOC R-APh in which R: in, on, at, by, against, etc.
A	{AP-PHYSICAL LOCATIVE (POSTURE)} (G 3)	P	L

2.4 Harriet placed the book by the telephone.
Jim stood the rifle against the wall.
They planted rice in the fields.
They strewed litter all over the property.

2.5 +[Loc' ±Loc" ±Loc"'] (see chart on top of next page)

2.5.1 Tom threw the knife across the room into the box.
Tom threw the knife at me.
We pushed the boat out into the current.
Smith tossed a dollar over the counter.

2.5.2 Dick drove the car across the United States from Maine to California.
Jeff threw the horseshoe from the right to the left bank of the river.

(2.5 +[±Loc' ±Loc" ±Loc "'])

+S same	$+P_{ta}$ same [tr. verbs]	+O same	+[±Loc' R-A Ph in which R: from	±Loc" R-A Ph in which R: across, through, over	±Loc"'] R-A Ph in which R: at, into, toward
2.5.1 A/ Source	{AP-PHYSICAL MOTION} (G' 3)	P		Path	Goal
2.5.2	same	P	Source	Path	Goal

2.6 ±M/In ± IO' ± Loc' (see the chart on the next page)
2.6.1 Bill received a book from Tom.
Bill bought the book from Tom for five dollars.
2.6.2 George grabbed the book from Tom
John caught the ball.
Mary picked the coal up with tongs.
2.6.3 Bill bought this book for his wife for five dollars.
He bought this book from Jim Smith.
Shall I receive this shipment for you?
2.6.4 Levi collected taxes for Rome.
Eric grabbed the book from Tom for me.
Give me a napkin, please.
Don't get it for me with your bare hands.

2.7 ±Complement

+S same	$+P_{ta}$ same [tr. verbs]	+O same	±COMPLEMENT NP which contains a numeral or other quantifier R-A Ph in which R: by
A	{AP-PHYSICAL MEASURABLE} (F 3)	P	M

2.7 I shortened it two inches.
I've lightened the cargo 35 lbs.
We'll reduce the cost 10%.

(2.6 ±M/In ± IO' ±Loc')

+S same	$+P_{ta}$ same [tr. verbs]	+O same	±M/ ±In: R-A Ph in which R: for, which	±IO' same	±Loc' same
2.6.1 A/G	{some: AP-PHYSICAL POSESSION DIRECTED MEASURABLE} (H 3)	P	(M)		(Source)
2.6.2 A/G	{A-PHYSICAL POSSESSION DIRECTED (INSTRUMENT)} (H 4)	P	(I)		(Source)
2.6.3 A/ Path	{some: AP-PHYSICAL POSSESSION MOTION MEASURABLE} (H' 3)	P	(M)	(G)	(Source)
2.6.4 A/ Path	{A-PHYSICAL POSSESSION MOTION} (H' 4)	P	(I)	(G)	(Source)

3. DITRANSTIVE
3.1 Basic pattern (see chart next page)
3.1.1 Mr. Smith taught Susan algebra.
He taught algebra to Susan.
3.1.2 Hilary introduced Tony to Nancy.

3.1.3 The mother told her child a story.
Jenny sang me a song.
The artist showed Tom the painting.
The artist showed the painting to Tom

(3.1 Basic pattern)

+S same	$+P_{da}$ same [ditr. verbs]	+IO NP Pronoun (Acc.) or R-A Ph in which R: to [when permuted out beyond the O]	+O same
3.1.1 A	{AP-EXPER COMPLETABLE} (C 3)	E	R
3.1.2 A	{AP-EXPER DIRECTED} (D 3)	E	G
3.1.3 A/ Source	{AP-EXPER DIRECTED COMPLETABLE} (D' 3)	E	R

3.2 ±M

+S same	$+P_{da}$ same	+IO same	+O same	±M: R-A Ph in which R: for
A/ Source	{AP-PHYSICAL POSSESSION DIRECTED MEASURABLE} (H 3)	G	P	(M)

3.2 Tom gave Hepzibah a book.
He gave it to her for a pack of chewing gum.
Mr. Smith sold Irvine a convertible.
He sold him the convertible for $800.
I sold my car to Wiggins.

3.3 +IO' ±M

+S same	$+P_{da}$ same	+IO same	+O same	+IO' same	±M same
A/ Source	{AP-PHYSICAL POSSESSION MOTION MEASURABLE} (H' 3)	Path	P	G	(M)

3.3 Mr. Smith sold Tom a convertible for his wife.
He sold it to Tom for his wife for $800.

4. DESCRIPTIVE CLAUSE (⟶ NP attributive)
4.1 Basic pattern

+S same	$+P_{ic}$ Act Verb Ph [Vb be]	+Attribute Adj	
4.1.1 Ø	[marks stative]	{S-AMBIENT} (A 1)	Restricted to it as subject; or to a noun such as weather or climate
4.1.2 E	[marks stative]	{S-AMBIENT EXPERIENTIAL} (A' 1)	
4.1.3 P	[marks stative]	{S-PHYSICAL} (E 1)	
4.1.4 P	[marks stative]	{S-PHYSICAL LOCATIVE} (G 1)	

4.1.1 It's hot.
It's cold.
It's sunny.
4.1.2 The patient is hot.
The patient is cold.
4.1.3 The dish is broken.
The blanket's wet.
The pig is dead.
4.1.4 The knife is in the box.
The key is on the table.
(These may be transformed to attributive noun phrases such as: the hot weather, the cold patient, the broken dish, and the knife in the box.)
4.2 ±In (as stimulus/depressant)

+S same	P_{ic} Act Verb Ph [Vb be]	±Attribute Adj	±In R-A Ph in which R: at, about
E	[marks stative]	{S-EXPERIENTIAL (INSTRUMENT)} (B 1)	I

4.2 The cat's nervous.
John is discouraged about his work.
Mary is happy at the prospect.

5. EQUATIVE CL (⟶ NP appositional)

+S same	$+P_{ic}$ Act Verb Ph [Vb be]	+Classifier NP
member		set

5. John is a soldier.
She's my aunt.
Mona Lisa is a masterpiece.
(These may be transformed to appositional noun phrases: John, a soldier; and Mona Lisa, a masterpiece; not *She, my aunt.)

BIBLIOGRAPHY

Abrams, Norm
1968 Koronadal Bilaan sentences. Unpublished ms. Nasuli (Bukidnon Province, Philippines): Summer Institute of Linguistics.

Allen, Robert L.
1966 The verb system of present-day American English. Janua Linguarum series practica, 24. The Hague: Mouton.

Anderson, John M.
1971 The grammar of case: Towards a localistic theory. Cambridge: The University Press.

Ashley, Seymour and Lois
1971 Outline of sentence types of Tausug. Philippine Journal of Linguistics. Manila (Philippines).

Bach, Emmon, and Robert Harms
1968 Universals in linguistic theory. New York: Holt, Rinehart, and Winston.

Ballard, D. Lee, Robert J. Conrad, and R. E. Longacre
1971a The deep and surface grammar of interclausal relations. Foundations of Language 7.70-118.

1971b More on the deep and surface grammar of interclausal relations. Language Data, Asian-Pacific Series, No. 1. Ukarumpa (Papua New Guinea): Summer Institute of Linguistics.

Barnard, Myra Lou
1968 Dibabawon text in Longacre 1968.3.

Barnard, Myra Lou, and Jannette Forster
1959 Introduction to Dibabawon sentence structure. Preliminary studies on some Philippine languages, Howard McKaughan and others. Journal of East Asiatic studies 3.2.205-43. Manila: University of Manila.

Baron, Stephen P.
1971 Some cases for case in Mandarin syntax. Fillmore 1971.35-52.

Bayum, Joy G.
1973 Heroes in black and white. Hutchins and Adler 1973.57-62.

Beavon, Keith H.
1979 Studies in the discourse structure of Konzime--a Bantu language of Cameroun. Arlington: University of Texas at Arlington thesis.

Becker, Alton
1967 A generative description of the English subject tagmemes. Ann Arbor: University of Michigan dissertation.

Bee, Darlene L.
1973 Neo-tagmemics, an integrated approach to linguistic analysis and description. Posthumous publication edited by Alan Healey and Doreen Marks. Ukarumpa (Papua New Guinea): Summer Institute of Linguistics.

Beekman, John
1970 Propositions and their relations within a discourse. Notes on Translation 37.6-27. Ixmiquilpan, Hidalgo (Mexico): Instituto Lingüístico de Verano.

Beekman, John, and John Callow
1974 Translating the Word of God. Grand Rapids: Zondervan.

Bennett, Charles
1945 New Latin grammar. Boston: Allen & Bacon.

Bishop, Ruth
1979 Tense-aspect in Totonac narrative discourse. Jones 1979.31-68.

Blansitt, Edward J., Jr.
1970 Sentence and clause in universal grammar. Anthropological Linguistics 12.4.112-21.

1973 Cognitive tagmemics. Linguistics 104.5-14.

Bolinger, Dwight
1973 Transitividad semántica en el ingles. Paper read at 18th annual congress of the International Linguistic Association, Arequipa, Peru.

Brend, Ruth M., ed.
1972 Kenneth L. Pike, Selected writings. The Hague: Mouton.

Bridgeman, Loraine
1966 Oral paragraphs in Kaiwa (Guarani). Bloomington: Indiana University dissertation.

Brown, Colin
1969 Philosophy and the Christian faith. London: Tyndale Press.

Buck, Pearl S.
1965 A field of rice. Ten American short stories, ed. by David A. Sohn, 111-23. New York: Bantam Pathfinders Editions.

Buswell, James O.
1960 A Christian view of being and knowing. Grand Rapids: Zondervan.

Calbert, Joseph P.
1971 Modality and case grammar. Working Papers in Linguistics of the Ohio State University 10.85-132.

Carcelen, Maria Cecilia
1974 The coordinate, antithetical, and alternative sentence in Spanish. Arlington: University of Texas at Arlington thesis.

Chafe, Wallace
1970 Meaning and the structure of language. Chicago: The University of Chicago Press.

Chomsky, Noam
1965 Aspects of the theory of syntax. Cambridge, Mass.: M.I.T. Press.

Church, Clarence and Katherine
1961 The Jacaltec noun phrase. Mayan studies 1, ed. by Benjamin Elson, 158-70. Norman (Oklahoma): Summer Institute of Linguistics.

Cook, Walter A.
1970 Case grammar: From rules to roles. Languages and Linguistics Working Papers (Georgetown University) 1.14-29.

1971a Case grammar as deep structure in tagmemic analysis. Languages and Linguistics Working Papers 1.1-9.

1971b Improvements in case grammar, 1970. Languages and Linguistics Working Papers 2.10-22.

1972a A set of postulates for case grammar analysis. Languages and Linguistics Working Papers 4.35-49.

1972b A case grammar matrix. Languages and Linguistics Working Papers 6.15-47.

1973 Covert case roles. Languages and Linguistics Working Papers 7.52-81.

1979 Case grammar: Development of the matrix model (1970-8). Washington: Georgetown University Press.

Cox, Doris
1957 Candoshi verb inflection. IJAL 23.129-40.

Crane, Stephen
1957 The open boat. Great American short stories, ed. by Wallace and Mary Stegner, 257-86. New York: Dell Publishing Co.

Crim, Keith R.
1973 Hebrew direct discourse as a translation problem. The Bible Translator 24.3.

Cromack, Robert E.
1968 Language systems and discourse structure in Cashinahua. Hartford: Hartford Seminary Foundation dissertation.

Curme, G.
1931 A grammar of English: Syntax. Boston: D.C. Heath & Co.

Davenport, John
1973 Apartment fire tragedy. Dallas Morning News, April 20.

Deibler, Ellis
1971 Uses of the verb 'to say' in Gahuku. Kivung 4:101-10.

Dewar, Dorothy
1970 Duidui sentences. Unpublished ms. Ukarumpa (Papua New Guinea): Summer Institute of Linguistics.

van Dijk, Teun A.
1972 Some aspects of text grammars. The Hague: Mouton. See extensive bibliography of further work, 347-8.

1977 Text and context: Explanations in the semantics and pragmatics of discourse. London: Longman.

van Dijk, Teun A., and Janos S. Petöfi, eds.
1977 Grammars and descriptions. Research in Text Theory 1. Berlin: Walter de Gruyter.

Dixon, Robert M. W.
1971 A method of semantic description. Semantics, ed. by Danny D. Steinberg and Leon A. Jakobovits, 436-71. Cambridge: University Press.

1977 Where have all the adjectives gone? Studies in Language 1:1.19-80.

Dye, Wayne and Sally
1970 Verb, sentence, and paragraph in Bahinemo. Unpublished ms. Ukarumpa (Papua New Guinea): Summer Institute of Linguistics.

Eckerd, Stephen
1979 Of men, machines, and planets. Papers on case grammar (Eckerd, Martens, and Palmer). Research Papers of the Texas SIL at Dallas 6.1-20.

Elkins, Richard
1971 Western Bukidnon Manobo sentence structure. Lingua 27:216-62.

Fillmore, Charles J.
1966a Towards a modern theory of case. The Ohio State University project on linguistic analysis, Report 13.1-24.

1966b A proposal concerning English prepositions. Report of the 17th Round Table, Georgetown monograph series 19.19-33. Washington, D.C.: Georgetown University Press.

1968 The case for case. Bach and Harms 1968.1-88.

1977 The case for case reopened. Grammatical relations, Peter Cole and Jerold Sadock, eds., 59-82. Syntax and Semantics 8. New York: Academic Press.

Fillmore, Charles J., ed.
1971 Working papers in languages and linguistics No. 10. Ohio State University.

Forster, Jannette
1964 Dual structure of Dibabawon verbal clauses. Oceanic Linguistics 3.1.26-48.

Forster, Jannette, and Myra Lou Barnard
1968 A classification of Dibabawon active verbs. Lingua 20.265-8.

Forster, Keith
1977 The narrative folklore discourse in Border Cuna. Longacre and Woods 1976-7, Part 2.1-23.

Fowles, John
1969 The French lieutenant's woman. Boston: Little, Brown, & Co.

Franklin, Karl
1971 A grammar of Kewa, New Guinea. Pacific Linguistics, Series C, No. 16. Canberra: The Australian National University.

Freyre, Ricardo Jaime
1962 Indian justice. Classic tales from Spanish America, William C. Colford, ed. and trans. New York: Barron's Educational Series.

Fries, Peter H.
1974 Some fundamental insights of tagmemics revisited. Advances in tagmemics, ed. by Ruth M. Brend. Amsterdam: North Holland Linguistic Series, No. 9.

Fuller, Daniel P.
1959 The inductive method of Bible study. 3rd edition. Mimeo. Pasadena: Fuller Theological Seminary.

Gerdel, Florence L., and Mariana Slocum
1976 Paez discourse, paragraph, and sentence structure. Longacre and Woods 1976-7, Part 1.259-443.

Givón, Talmy, ed.
1979 Discourse and syntax. Syntax and Semantics 12. New York: Academic Press.

Gleason, H. A., Jr.
1968 Contrastive analysis in discourse structure. Report of the 19th Round Table, Georgetown monograph series 21.39-63. Washington, D.C.: Georgetown University Press.

Grimes, Joseph E.
1976 The thread of discourse. The Hague: Mouton.

Grimes, Joseph E., ed.
1978 Papers on discourse. Summer Institute of Linguistics Publications in Linguistics 51. Dallas: Summer Institute of Linguistics and University of Texas at Arlington.

Hale, Austin
1973 Towards the systematization of display grammar. Clause, sentence, and discourse patterns in selected languages of Nepal, Vol. 1: General approach 1-38. Summer Institute of Linguistics Publications in Linguistics 40. Norman (Oklahoma): Summer Institute of Linguistics of the University of Oklahoma. Also printed in: Trail 1973. Vol. 2.3-36.

Hale, Austin, ed.
1973 Clause , sentence, and discourse patterns in selected languages of Nepal, Vol. 1: General approach; Vol. 2: Clause (co ed. by D. Watters); Vol. 3: Texts; Vol. 4: Word lists. Summer Institute of Linguistics Publications in Linguistics 40. Norman (Oklahoma): Summer Institute of Linguistics of the University of Oklahoma.

Hall, William C.
1969 A classification of Siocon Subanon verbs. Anthropological Linguistics 11.7.209-15.

Halliday, M. A. K.
1961 Categories of the theory of grammar. Word 17.3.241-93.

1966 The concept of rank: A reply. Journal of Linguistics 2.110-18.

1967-8 Notes on transitivity and theme in English (in 3 parts). Journal of Linguistics 3.1.37-81; 3.2.199-244; 4.2.179-215.

Halliday, M. A. K., and Ruqaiya Hasan
1976 Cohesion in English. English Language Series 9. London: Longman.

Harris, Thomas A.
1967 I'm OK - You're OK. New York: Harper & Row.

Harris, Zellig
1946 From morpheme to utterance. Lg. 22.161-83.

1952 Discourse analysis. Lg. 28.1-30.

1954 Transfer grammar. IJAL 20.259-70.

1962 String analysis of sentence structure. The Hague: Mouton.

Haugen, Einar
1956 The syllable in linguistic description. For Roman Jakobson 213-21. The Hague: Mouton.

Healey, Phyllis
1964 Teleéfoól quotative clauses. Linguistic Circle of Canberra Publications, Series A, No. 3. Canberra.

1966 Levels and chaining in Telefol sentences. Canberra: Australian National University.

Heidegger, Martin
1971 A dialogue on language. On the way to language. Translated by P.D. Hertz. New York: Harper & Row.

Hemingway, Ernest
1938 The short stories of Ernest Hemingway, 126-27. New York: The Modern Library.

Hockett, Charles F.
1955 A manual of phonology. Memoir 11 of IJAL.

Hoenigswald, Henry
1960 Language change and linguistic reconstruction. Chicago: University of Chicago Press.

Hollenbach, Barbara
1973 A preliminary semantic classification of temporal concepts. Notes on Translation 47 (March 1973). Dallas: Summer Institute of Linguistics.

Hollenbach, Bruce
1974 Discourse structure, interpropositional relations, and translation. Unpublished ms. Mexico City: Instituto Lingüístico de Verano.

Holmes, Arthur F.
1973 Three levels of meaning in God-language. Journal of the Evangelical Theological Society 16.83-94.

Hook, Sidney
1973 The hero as a world figure. Hutchins and Adler, 1973.63-9.

Hopper, Paul J.
1979 Aspect and foregrounding in discourse. Givón 1979. 213-42.

Hudson, Joyce
1970 Walmatjari paragraph types. Unpublished ms. Ukarumpa (Papua New Guinea): Summer Institute of Linguistics.

Hutchins, R. M., and Mortimer J. Adler, eds.
1973 The great ideas today, 1973. Chicago: Encyclopedia Britannica.

Huttar, George L.
1973 On distinguishing clause and sentence. Linguistics 105.69-82.

Hwang, Shin Ja Joo
1975 Korean clause structure. Summer Institute of Linguistics Publications in Linguistics 50. Norman (Oklahoma): Summer Institute of Linguistics of the University of Oklahoma.

Jacobs, Kenneth, and R. E. Longacre
1967 Patterns and rules in Tzotzil grammar. Foundations of Language 3.325-89.

Jones, Larry, and Linda K. Jones
1979 Multiple levels of information relevance in discourse. Jones 1979.3-28.

Jones, Linda K.
1977 Theme in English expository discourse. Lake Bluff (Illinois): Jupiter Press.

Jones, Linda K., ed.
1979 Discourse studies in Mesoamerican languages. Vol. 1: Discussion; Vol. 2: Texts. Summer Institute of Linguistics Publications in Linguistics 58. Dallas: Summer Institute of Linguistics and University of Texas at Arlington.

Jones, W. T.
1973 The widening gyre: Philosophy in the twentieth century. Hutchins and Adler 1973.78-129.

Katz, J. J., and J. A. Fodor
1964 The structure of a semantic theory. Lg. 39.170-210.

Kilham, Christine A.
1974 Thematic organization of Wik-Munkan discourse. Canberra: Australian National University dissertation.

Klammer, Thomas P.
1971 The structure of dialogue paragraphs in written dramatic and narrative discourse. Ann Arbor: University of Michigan dissertation.

Labov, William, and David Fanshel
1977 Therapeutic discourse: Psychotherapy as conversation. New York: Academic Press.

Lakoff, George, and Stanley Peters
1966 Phrasal conjunction and symmetric predicates. Mathematical linguistics and automatic translation (Harvard Computation Laboratory, Report No. NSF-17. VI-1 to VI-49). Reprinted in Reibel and Schane 1969.113-42.

Langendoen, D. Terrence
1970 Essentials of English grammar. New York: Holt, Rinehart & Winston.

Larson, Mildred L.
1978 The functions of reported speech in discourse. Summer Institute of Linguistics Publications in Linguistics 59. Dallas: Summer Institute of Linguistics and University of Texas at Arlington.

Lawrence, Helen
1972 Viewpoint and location in Oksapmin. Anthropological Linguistics 14.8.311-16.

Lawrence, Marshall
1970 Oksapmin discourse and paragraph structure. Unpublished ms. Ukarumpa (Papua New Guinea): Summer Institute of Linguistics.

Liem, Nguyen Dang
1966 English grammar: A combined tagmemic and transformational approach (A contrastive analysis of English and Vietnamese, Vol. 1). Linguistic Circle of Canberra Publications, Series C, No. 3. Canberra: The Australian National University.

Lloyd, Linda
1976 A discourse analysis of Hebrews. Arlington: University of Texas at Arlington thesis.

Lockwood, David G.
1972 Introduction to stratificational linguistics. New York: Harcourt, Brace, and Jovanovich.

Longacre, Robert E.
1956 Review of language and reality by Wilbur M. Urban and Four articles on metalinguistics by Benjamin Lee Whorf. Lg. 1956.298-308.

1958 Items in context: Their bearing on translation theory. Lg. 34.482-91.

1960 String constituent analysis. Lg. 36.63-88.

1963 Review of string analysis of sentence structure by Zellig Harris. Lg. 39.473-8.

1964a Grammar discovery procedures. The Hague: Mouton.

1964b Prolegomena to lexical structure. Linguistics 5.5-24.

1965 Some fundamental insights of tagmemics. Lg. 41.65-76.

1966 Trique clause and sentence: A study in contrast, variation, and distribution. IJAL 32.242-52.

1967 The notion of sentence. Report of the 18th Round Table, Georgetown monograph series 20.15-25. Washington, D.C.: Georgetown University Press.

1968 Discourse, paragraph, and sentence structure in selected Philippine languages, 3 volumes. (Final Report, Contract No. OE-0-8-062838-0391, Dept. of HEW). First two volumes published as Summer Institute of Linguistics Publications in Linguistics 11. Santa Ana: Summer Institute of Linguistics.

1970a Hierarchy in language. Method and theory in linguistics, ed. by Paul Garvin, 173-95. The Hague: Mouton.

1970b Paragraph and sentence structure in New Guinea highlands languages. Kivung 3.150-63.

1970c Sentence structure as a statement calculus. Lg. 46.783-815.

1972a Hierarchy and universality of discourse constituents in New Guinea languages. (Final Report, Contract No. OE-0-9-097756-4409(014), Dept. of HEW). Two volumes: Discussion, Texts. Washington, D.C.: Georgetown University Press.

1972b Narrative versus other discourse genre. From sound-stream to discourse, Papers from the 1971 Mid-America Linguistics Conference, ed. by Daniel G. Hays and Donald M. Lance, 167-85.

1972c Taxonomy in deep and surface grammar. Proceedings of the 11th Congress of Linguists, Bologna.

1976a An anatomy of speech notions. Lisse: Peter de Ridder Press.

1976b Discourse. Tagmemics I: Aspects of the field, Ruth M. Brend and Kenneth L. Pike, eds. Trends in Linguistics, Studies and Monographs 1. The Hague: Mouton.

1976c "Mystery" particles and affixes. Papers from the 12th regional meeting of the Chicago Linguistic Society 468-75. Chicago: Chicago Linguistic Society.

1977a Generating a discourse from its abstract. The third LACUS forum (1976).355-67. Columbia (S.C.): Hornbeam Press.

1977b Tagmemics as a framework for discourse analysis. Second Annual Linguistic Metatheory Conference (1977 Conference Proceedings). Lansing: Michigan State University.

1979a The discourse structure of the Flood Narrative. Journal of the American Academy of Religion 47.1 Supplement (March 1979) B 89-133.

1979c Texts and text linguistics. Text vs. sentence. Janos S. Petöfi, ed. Papers in Textlinguistics 20. Part 1.258-71. Hamburg: Buske.

1979d Towards a better understanding of Old Testament Hebrew narrative. Paper read at the meeting of the Evangelical Theological Society in St. Paul, Minnesota, December 1979.

1979e Why we need a vertical revolution in linguistics. The Fifth LACUS Forum (1978).247-70. Columbia (S.C.): Hornbeam Press.

Longacre, Robert E., ed.
1971 Philippine discourse and paragraph studies in memory of Betty McLachlin. Pacific Linguistic Series C, No. 22. Canberra: The Australian National University.

Longacre, Robert E., and Fran Woods
1976-7 Discourse grammar: Studies in indigenous languages of Columbia, Panama, and Ecuador, Parts 1-3. Summer Institute of Linguistics Publications in Linguistics 52. Dallas: Summer Institute of Linguistics and University of Texas at Arlington.

Loriot, James, and Barbara Hollenbach
1970 Shipibo paragraph structure. Foundations of Language 6.43-66. (Circulated by J. Loriot as unpublished ms. from 1958 on).

Lovejoy, Arthur O.
1936 The great chain of being. Cambridge, Mass.: Harvard University Press. [Reprinted 1960 by Harper and Row, New York.]

Lyons, John
1968 Introduction to theoretical linguistics. Cambridge: University Press.

Mansen, Richard and Karis
1976 The structure of sentence and paragraph in Guajiro narrative discourse. Longacre and Woods 1976-7, Part 1.147-258.

Marsh, James
1970 Paragraph structure of Mantjiltjara. Unpublished ms. Ukarumpa (Papua New Guinea): Summer Institute of Linguistics.

Matthews, P. H.
1966 The concept of rank in 'Neo-Firthian' grammar. Journal of Linguistics 2.101-10.

Mayfield, Roy
1972 Agta sentence structure. Linguistics 85.21-66.

McArthur, Harry S.
1979 The role of aspect in distinguishing Aguacatec discourse types. Jones 1979.1.105-21.

McKaughan, Howard
1958 The inflection and syntax of Maranao verbs. Publication of the Institute of National Language, Manila.

McLachlin, Betty, and Barbara Blackburn
1971 An outline of Sarangani Bilaan discourse and paragraph structure. Philippine discourse and paragraph studies in memory of Betty McLachlin, ed. by R. E. Longacre, 1-84. Pacific Linguistics Series C, No. 22. Canberra: The Australian National University.

Metzing, Dieter, ed.
1980 Frame, conceptions, and text understanding. Research in Text Theory 5. Berlin: Walter de Gruyter.

Miller, Jeanne
1964 The role of verb stems in Mamanwa kernel verbal clauses. Oceanic Linguistics 3.1.87-100.

Murane, Elizabeth
1974 Daga grammar: From morpheme to discourse. Summer Institute of Linguistics Publications in Linguistics 43. Norman (Oklahoma): Summer Institute of Linguistics of the University of Oklahoma.

Nida, Eugene A.
1949 Morphology. Ann Arbor: The University of Michigan Press.

1964 Toward a science of translating. Leiden: Brill.

Palmer, T. R.
1965 A linguistic study of the English verb. London: Longman.

Pepper, Stephen C.
1970 World hypotheses: A study in evidence. Berkeley: University of California Press.

Petöfi, Janos S.
1969 On the problems of co-textual analysis of texts. Paper delivered at the International Conference on Computational Linguistics, Songa-Säby (Sweden).

1971 On the comparative structural analysis of different types of 'works of art?'. Semiotica 3.4.365-78.

1972a The syntactico-semantic organization of text-structures. Poetics 3.56-99.

1972b Towards a grammatical theory of verbal texts. Zeitschrift für Literaturwissenschaft und Linguistik.

Pickett, Velma B.
1960 The grammatical hierarchy of Isthmus Zapotec. Supplement to Language 36.1 (Part 2). Language Dissertation No. 56.

Pike, Eunice V. and Kenneth L.
1947 Immediate constituents of Mazateco syllables. IJAL 13.78-91.

Pike, Kenneth L.
1958 On tagmemes, nee grammemes. IJAL 24.273-78.

1964 Discourse analysis and tagmeme matrices. Oceanic Linguistics 3.1.5-25.

1966 Tagmemic and matrix linguistics applied to selected African languages. (Final Report, Contract No. OE-5-14-065). Ann Arbor: University of Michigan Center for Research on Language and Language Behavior. [Republished 1970 as Summer Institute of Linguistics Publications in Linguistics 23. Santa Ana.]

1967 Language in relation to a unified theory of the structure of human behavior. The Hague: Mouton. [Earlier published seriatim in 3 parts, 1954-1960, Summer Institute of Linguistics.]

1972 Agreement types dispersed into a nine-cell spectrum. Paper read at Linguistic Society of America meeting, Atlanta, 1972.

Pike, Kenneth L. and Evelyn G.
1977 Grammatical analysis. Summer Institute of Linguistics Publications in Linguistics 53. Dallas: Summer Institute of Linguistics and University of Texas at Arlington.

Pike, Kenneth L., and Ivan Lowe
1969 Pronominal reference in English conversation and discourse: A group theoretical treatment. Folia Linguistica 3.68-106. [Reprinted in Brend 1972. 263-97.]

Platt, John T.
1971 Grammatical form and grammatical meaning: A tagmemic view of Fillmore's deep structure concepts. Amsterdam: North Holland Linguistic Series.

Porter, Doris
1968 Tagabili paragraph and discourse analysis. Nasuli (Bukidnon Province, Philippines): Summer Institute of Linguistics.

Potok, Chaim
1973 Heros for an ordinary world. Hutchins and Adler 1973.70-6.

Price, Reynolds
1965 Michael Egerton. Ten American short stories, ed. by William A. Sohn. New York: Bantam Pathfinders.

Propp, V.
1958 Morphology of the folktale. Translated by Lawrence Scott from 1928 original. Indiana University Publications in Anthropology, Folklore, and Linguistics, No. 10.

Rand, Ayn
1943 Atlas shrugged. New York: The New American Library.

1957 Fountainhead. New York: The New American Library.

Reibel, David A., and Sanford A. Schane
1969 Modern studies in English. Englewood Cliffs, N.J.: Prentice-Hall.

Reid, Aileen, Ruth G. Bishop, Ella M. Button, and R. E. Longacre
1968 Totonac: From clause to discourse. Summer Institute of Linguistics Publications in Linguistics 17. Santa Ana: Summer Institute of Linguistics.

Reid, Lawrence A.
1970 Central Bontoc: Sentence, paragraph, and discourse. Summer Institute of Linguistics Publications in Linguistics 27. Santa Ana: Summer Institute of Linguistics.

1971 Tense sequence in procedural discourse. The Archive 2.2.15-42.

Robins, Robert H.
1972 The case theories of Maximus Planudes. Paper read at the 11th Congress of Linguists, Bologna.

Sacks, Harvey, Emanuel A. Schegloff, and Gail Jefferson
1974 A simplest systematics for the organization of turn-taking for conversation. Lg. 50.696-735.

Sandburg, Carl
1939 Abraham Lincoln, Vol. 1: The war years, 1861-64. New York: Harcourt, Brace, and Co.

Sartre, J. P.
1956 Being and nothingness. Translated by H. Barnes. New York: Philosophical Library.

Sayers, Barbara J.
1976 The sentence in Wik-Munkan: A description of propositional relationships. Pacific Linguistics, Series B, No. 44. Canberra: Australian National University.

Schaeffer, Francis
1968a Escape from reason. Chicago: Inter-Varsity Press.

1968b The God who is there. Chicago: Inter-Varsity Press.

Schane, Sanford A.
1971 The phoneme revisited. Lg. 47.503-21.

Schegloff, Emanuel
1979 The relevance of repair to syntax-for-conversation. Givón 1979.261-86.

Scott, Graham
1973 Higher levels of Fore grammar. Pacific Linguistics,

Series B, No. 23. Canberra: Australian National University.

Searle, John R.
1970 Speech acts: An essay in the philosophy of language. Cambridge: University Press.

Shand, Jean
1968 Ilianen Manobo sentences. Unpublished ms. Nasuli (Bukidnon Province, Philippines): Summer Institute of Linguistics.

Shank, Roger C., and colleagues of the Yale Artificial Intelligence Project
1975 SAM (Script Applier Mechanism)--a story understander. Research Report 43 (Yale University).

Silverstein, Michael
1976 Hierarchy of features and ergativity. Grammatical categories in Australian languages, R. M. Dixon, ed. Canberra: Australian Institute of Aboriginal Studies, Linguistics Series 22.

Stoll, Robert E.
1961 Sets, logic, and axiomatic theories. San Francisco: W. H. Freeman & Co.

Stucky, Alfred and Dellene
1970 Ek Nii sentences and paragraph types. Unpublished ms. Ukarumpa (Papua New Guinea): Summer Institute of Linguistics.

Thomas, David D.
1975 Notes and queries on language analysis (Language Data, Asian-Pacific Series 10). Huntington Beach (California): Summer Institute of Linguistics.

Thrall, William F., Addison Hibbard, and C. Hugh Holman
1961 A handbook to literature. New York: The Odyssey Press.

Tolkien, J. R. R.
1966 The lord of the rings, Vol. 1: The fellowship of the ring; Vol. 2: The two towers; Vol. 3: The return of the king. New York: Ballantine Books.

1966 The hobbit. New York: Ballantine Books.

Trail, Ronald L., ed.
1973 Patterns in clause, sentence and discourse in selected languages of India and Nepal, Vol. 1: Sentence and discourse; Vol. 2: Clause; Vol. 3: Texts; Vol. 4: Word lists. Summer Institute of Linguistics Publications in Linguistics 41. Norman (Oklahoma): Summer Institute of Linguistics of the University of Oklahoma.

Twain, Mark
1964 A Connecticut Yankee in King Arthur's court. An Airmont classic. New York: Airmont Publishing Co.

Urban, Wilbur Marshall
1939 Language and reality. New York: Macmillan.

1949 Beyond realism and idealism. London: George Allen and Unwin.

Van Buren, Paul M.
1972 The edges of language: A study in the logic of a religion. New York: Macmillan.

Van Haitsma, Julia and Willard
1976 A hierarchical sketch of Mixe as spoken in San José el Paradíso. Summer Institute of Linguistics Publications in Linguistics 44. Norman (Oklahoma): Summer Institute of Linguistics of the University of Oklahoma.

Venneman, Theo
1971 The syllable. Paper read at the summer meeting of the Linguistic Society of America. Buffalo, New York.

Wallace, Stephen
1978 Adversative passives. Paper read at the Linguistic Society of America meeting, Boston.

Walrod, Michael R.
1979 Discourse grammar in Ga'dang. Summer Institute of Linguistics Publications in Linguistics 63. Dallas: Summer Institute of Linguistics and University of Texas at Arlington.

Walton, James
1977 Participant reference and introducers in Muinane clause and paragraph. Longacre and Woods 1976-7, Part 3.45-65.

Waltz, Carolyn
1977 Some observations on Guanano dialogue. Longacre and Woods 1976-7, Part 3.67-110.

Waltz, Nathan E.
1976 Discourse functions of Guanano sentence and paragraph. Longacre and Woods 1976-7, Part 1.21-146.

West, Dorothy
1973 Wojokeso sentence, paragraph, and discourse analysis. Pacific Linguistics, Series B, No. 28. Canberra: Australian National University.

Whittle, Claudia
1971 Atta discourse and paragraph structure. Longacre 1971.194-282.

Wise, Mary Ruth
1968 Identification of participants in discourse: A study of form and meaning in Nomatsiguenga. Ann Arbor: University of Michigan dissertation. [Published 1971 as Summer Institute of Linguistics Publications in Linguistics 28. Santa Ana: Summer Institute of Linguistics.

1972 Lexemic structures in discourse. Paper read at the 11th Congress of Linguists, Bologna.

Wonderly, William L.
1951 Zoque III: Morphological classes, affix list, and verbs. IJAL17.137-162.

Wonderly, William L., Lorna Gibson, and Paul Kirk
1954 Number in Kiowa: Nouns, demonstratives and adjectives. IJAL 20.1-7.

Woods, Fran
1970 Dialogue in Halbi. Unpublished ms. Ukarumpa (Papua New Guinea): Summer Institute of Linguistics.

Wrigglesworth, Hazel
1971 Discourse and paragraph structure of Ilianen Manobo. Longacre 1971.85-194.

INDEX